THE CLASSICS
OF **WESTERN**
SPIRITUALITY

THE CLASSICS OF WESTERN SPIRITUALITY
A Library of the Great Spiritual Masters

President and Publisher
Lawrence Boadt, CSP

EDITORIAL BOARD

Farid ad-Din 'Attār's Memorial of God's Friends

LIVES AND SAYINGS OF SUFIS

TRANSLATED AND INTRODUCED BY
PAUL LOSENSKY

PREFACE BY
TH. EMIL HOMERIN

PAULIST PRESS
NEW YORK • MAHWAH

Cover and caseside design by Cynthia Dunne
Book design by Lynn Else

Library of Congress Cataloging-in-Publication Data

'Attār, Farid al-Din, d. ca. 1230.
    [Ta ẓkirat al-awliya'. English]
    Farid ad-din 'Attār's Memorial of God's friends : lives and sayings of sufis / trans-
lated with an introduction by Paul Losensky.
        p. cm.
    Includes bibliographical references and index.
    ISBN 978-0-8091-4573-7 (alk. paper)—ISBN 978-0-8091-0518-2 (alk. paper)
    1. Muslim saints—Biography. 2. Sufis—Biography. I. Losensky, Paul E. (Paul
Edward), 1956- II. Title.
    BP189.4.A813 2009
    297.4092'2—dc22
    [B]

                                                            2008041126

Published by Paulist Press
997 Macarthur Boulevard
Mahwah, New Jersey 07430

www.paulistpress.com

Printed and bound in the
United States of America

CONTENTS

CONTENTS

Contributors to This Volume

Translator of This Volume

PAUL LOSENSKY (PhD, University of Chicago, 1993) currently serves as associate professor in the Department of Central Eurasian Studies and the Department of Comparative Literature at Indiana University, Bloomington, where he teaches courses on Persian language and literature and translation studies. His publications include *Welcoming Fighāni: Imitation and Poetic Individuality in the Safavid-Mughal Ghazal* (1998), numerous journal articles on Persian poetry and literary history, and frequent contributions to the *Encyclopaedia of Islam* and the *Encyclopaedia Iranica*. His research focuses on Persian literary historiography and biographical writing, intertextuality, and the poetry of the Persiphone world of the sixteenth and seventeenth centuries. He is currently working on a study of the literary description of architecture and the poetic use of architectural images and metaphors in Iran, India, and Central Asia during this period.

Author of the Preface

TH. EMIL HOMERIN is professor of religion in the Department of Religion and Classics at the University of Rochester, where he teaches courses on Islam, classical Arabic literature, and mysticism. Among his publications are *From Arab Poet to Muslim Saint: Ibn al-Fārid, His Verse and His Shrine* (rev. ed., Cairo: American University in Cairo Press, 2001); *ʿUmar Ibn al-Fārid: Sufi Verse, Saintly Life,* Classics of Western Spirituality (New York: Paulist Press, 2001); and *The Wine of Love and Life: Ibn al-Fārid's al-Khamrīyah and al-Qaysrī's Quest for Meaning* (Chicago: Middle East Documentation Center at the University of Chicago, 2005).

PREFACE

The recounting of saintly lives has been a prominent feature of Western spirituality. The saints display heroic virtue, profess sound religious doctrine, and perform miracles attesting to their devotion and surrender to the divine will. They undertake ascetic practices and dedicate themselves to prayer and selfless service to others, and yet, though they may be graced by God, their lives are never easy. There are many struggles—against the body, against worldliness, against Satan, against pride—and sometimes the saints are martyred for their faith. Later, their pious lives become lessons and models for leading an honest life and for being true to oneself and, most of all, to God.

But even more, perhaps, the saints become another means of salvation as visits to their graves and petitions for their aide offer hope for intercession and immortal life for lesser mortals. Many readers of the Classics of Western Spirituality are undoubtedly familiar with the genre of hagiography, particularly in the Catholic tradition, as represented by Bonaventure's *Life of St. Francis.* Now, readers have the opportunity to explore the world of Muslim saints, brought to life by Paul Losensky in his deft translation of the *Tazkerat al-owliyā, the Memorial of God's Friends,* by the thirteenth-century Persian mystic Farid ad-Din 'Attār.

As Losensky notes in his introduction, 'Attār was a gifted poet, most famous for his beautiful, mystical allegory the *Conference of the Birds.* In his *Memorial* he presents another side of Islamic spirituality, one concerned less with doctrine and more with behavior and practice. Within Islam, the *owliyā* are God's special friends who are protected by him, and they include, first and foremost, the family and companions of the prophet Muhammad. Martyrs and mad people, too, have been reckoned among God's friends, as well as Muslim mystics, especially the early masters of Sufism, who are 'Attār's focus in the *Memorial.* 'Attār was not the first Muslim scholar to compile stories of these pious Sufis, but his *Memorial* is certainly one of the most eloquent works of

FARID AD-DIN 'ATTĀR'S MEMORIAL OF GOD'S FRIENDS

Muslim hagiography as he combined his extensive knowledge of
Islamic mysticism with his elegant Persian prose.

Like other hagiographers, 'Attār venerates his subjects, while
offering them to his readers for inspiration and imitation, as did
medieval Christian writers. Similar, too, are the many "shapes and
sizes" of sanctity, as 'Attār compiles his accounts in such a way as to
portray particular aspects of Muslim spirituality. His brief introductions to each life set both the scene and the issues to be addressed: from
faith to fear, asceticism to altruism, selfishness to love, and finally,
martyrdom. Moreover, an austere attitude prevails throughout the
Memorial, as one saint after another eschews riches, fame, and power:

Anyone who pursues his lust for this world saves demons
the trouble of pursuing him. (Malek)

If a dervish hovers around the wealthy, know that he is a
hypocrite. If he hovers around the sultan, know that he is a
thief. (Sofyān)

As with saints in other religious traditions, these Muslim mystics
may go to extremes in their denial of the world; 'Attār remarks in one
account, "He was so far from the normal way of things." This is particularly the case with human interactions, nearly all of which are fraught
with temptation:

For Sufis, disaster lies in talking to children, socializing with
opponents, and being friends with women. (Yusof)

Stay away from the pretty young boys and women who are
not of your family, especially today when there are women
and children here on the pilgrimage. Don't let your eyes
wander. (Ebrāhim)

Within the Christian tradition, sanctity is usually tied to celibacy,
if not always virginity, but within Islam, Muslims are encouraged to
marry and procreate. In the *Memorial*, then, we hear of loyal wives and
loving children, but sometimes with a sense of ambivalence and reticence:

PREFACE

Nothing comes of any disciple who takes a wife and writes learnedly. (Joneyd)

The dervish who marries boards a ship, and when a child is born, it sinks. (Ebrāhim)

As 'Attār clarifies, taking a wife entails physical, emotional, and financial obligations that will distract a man from his religious devotions and that may lead him to divided loyalties, as he will love his wife and children along with God. Indeed, in several stories, a saint despairs when he realizes that love for his child has made him forgetful of God, and he is relieved when the child suddenly dies. 'Attār likens these incidents to the prophet Abraham, who was willing to sacrifice his son at God's command. Muslim readers would also know that, according to the Qur'ān, dead children are brought to paradise, where they will greet their parents on judgment day, as another of 'Attār's saints inform us.

Though the vast majority of saints in the *Memorial* are men, holy women also appear as spiritually insightful and wise, particularly in the case of Fātema, the wife of Ahmad-e Khezruya, and of Rābe'a-ye 'Adaviya. 'Attār gives a long account of Rābe'a, highlighting her ascetic practices and love of God, noting that "when a woman is a man on the path of the Lord most high, she cannot be called a woman." Still, perhaps with a touch of humor, 'Attār relates that one day a group of men chided Rābe'a by asserting that all the virtues had been given to men, and that there had never been a woman prophet, to which she replied: "Everything you said was true....[a]nd no woman has ever been a pederast."

'Attār also recounts many miracles at the hands of Rābe'a, including bringing a dead donkey back to life, and these are among the many fantastic events that occur throughout the *Memorial*. Saints travel from Iran to Mecca in the blink of an eye, converse with angels, and foretell the future of others; these abilities underscore the saint's spiritual advancement. Nevertheless, in one story, 'Attār tells of a master's one-thousand disciples, all of whom could walk on water, although all but one of them was still unworthy to meet the great Bāyazid. The reason was, as always, spiritual pride, the "self" of egoism and selfishness that is the mystic's greatest foe:

The most difficult of veils is the vision of the self. (Zu'n-Nun)

xiii

The difference between the urgings of the self and the temptations of the devil is that when the self begs for something
and you forbid it, it will keep after you until it gets what it
wants, even if it takes a while. When the devil calls you and
you oppose him, he'll give up. (Joneyd)

Opposing selfishness is a lifelong struggle; alone, a profession of faith
is not enough. Perhaps taking a swipe at more worldly Muslims, 'Attār
tells the following story:

It is related that a Zoroastrian was told to convert to Islam.
He said, "If Islam is what Bāyazid does, I don't have the
strength for it and I can't do it. If it's what you do, I don't
have any need of it.

Thus, fearing egoism and hypocrisy, the saints practice their austerities, ever-mindful of God, and may spend days in seclusion and deny
themselves food and sleep. Their emaciated physical condition comes to
embody their denial of selfish pride, and with God's grace, they ultimately succeed is suppressing selfishness, thus performing the greatest
of miracles. Though this is a personal struggle, most of these saints were
not alone but in community with their spiritual masters and, subse-
quently, disciples of their own. One of the most engaging aspects of the
Memorial is the many stories involving teachers leading their students
to moments of realization. Even the great Joneyd had moments of doubt
when he was a young man learning the Sufi way from his sheikh and
uncle, Sari-ye Saqati. Sari felt that his nephew had accomplished much
and that it was now Joneyd's turn to preach in public:

Joneyd vacillated. He was not fond of the idea and said, "It's
not polite to preach in the presence of the sheikh." Then one
night, he saw the Prophet (peace and blessing be upon him)
in a dream. "Preach!" he told Joneyd.
    At dawn Joneyd got up to talk to Sari. He saw Sari stand-
ing at the door. Sari said, "Were you waiting for others to
tell you to preach? Now you must—your words have been
made the salvation of the world's people. You did not preach
at the urging of your disciples. You did not preach at the

pleading of Baghdad's religious leaders. You did not preach
when I told you to. Now that the Prophet (peace and blessing be upon him) has commanded it, you must preach.

Joneyd consented and, apologizing, he asked Sari, "How
did you know that I saw the Prophet (peace be upon him) in
a dream?"

"I saw the mighty and glorious Lord in a dream," Sari
replied. "He said, 'I sent my Messenger to Joneyd to tell him
to speak from the pulpit.'"

The *Memorial* is filled with such stories of the early Sufi masters,
their misgivings, realizations, and eventual success with the grace of
God. Significantly, 'Attār concludes nearly every saint's story with an
account of how the deceased mystic was seen in a dream as having
earned God's favor and a place in paradise. Thus, their saintly status is
assured, and we may trust their words and advice, which form a large
portion of each saintly life:

Hold no one in contempt, even if he is a polytheist. (Zu'n-Nun)

If you want to see how this world will be after your death,
see how it is after the death of others. (Hasan)

The most powerful person is one who overcomes his anger.
(Sari)

Open the closed purse, and close the open mouth. (Ebrāhim)

Rapture is a tongue of flame that the innermost self cannot
contain and it emerges from yearning, so the limbs of the
body move, whether with joy or sorrow. (Nuri)

'Attār cites many such proverbs in the *Memorial,* so that his readers might pause and examine their own lives. To remain spiritually
sound, 'Attār notes, "Read eight pages of their sayings everyday." With
this fine translation of the *Memorial* by Paul Losensky, many more
have the opportunity to read, reflect, and remember.

Th. Emil Homerin

ON THIS TRANSLATION

Memorial of God's Friends (Tazkerat al-owliyā') is the sole extant prose work of the great Persian Sufi poet Farid ad-Din 'Attār (d. ca. 1230). Integrating the writings of generations of Sufi scholars and historians, it relates the saga of Islamic spirituality through the lives and sayings of some its most prominent exemplars, from the time of the Prophet to the death of Hallāj in 922. With the same literary skill found in poetic works such as *Conference of the Birds,* 'Attār combines popular legend, historical anecdote, ethical maxim, and speculative meditation in lively and thought-provoking biographies. Sufism is presented not as a doctrinal system but as a lived experience, and 'Attār's lucid and economical style encourages readers to participate fully in the efforts of these pioneers of the sacred to live out and express their unfolding encounter with the divine. Scholars, shopkeepers, princes, and outcasts—God's friends come from all classes of medieval society and embody the full range of religious attitudes, from piety and awe to love and ecstatic union. *Memorial of God's Friends* merges the miraculous and the everyday in one of the most engaging and comprehensive portrayals of spiritual experience in the Islamic tradition. This translation makes the major biographies of *Memorial of God's Friends* available in their entirety for the first time to a general audience in a contemporary American idiom. The lives translated here include such formative figures as Hasan of Basra, Rābe'a-ye 'Adaviya, Zu'n-Nun of Egypt, Bāyazid of Bestām, and Joneyd of Baghdad, as well as a sampling of shorter biographies.

As desirable as an unabridged translation might be in purely academic terms, it would defeat the fundamental purpose of all translation—opening the work to a new readership. In the original Persian the text of the *Tazkerat* runs to almost six hundred pages, and a full translation without annotations weighs in at over eight hundred. The cost of a book of this length would limit its distribution to specialists, and size alone would discourage many students and readers with an interest in the

Islamic faith traditions. 'Attār himself was well aware of such practical considerations. In his introduction he appeals to a hadith, or saying of the Prophet, to defend "taking the path of brevity and abridgment." This path was also taken by an earlier English translation. A.J. Arberry's *Muslim Saints and Mystics* presents only extracted narrative "episodes."[1] This approach, however, seriously distorts the basic structures of 'Attār's biographies. Throughout the *Memorial* the words of God's friends feature as prominently as their deeds. Teaching and experience go hand in hand, and the dicta give intellectual and spiritual substance to the stories. By omitting the aphorisms as well as the preface to each biography, Arberry's version deprives the *Memorial* of its conceptual depth, leaving behind a collection of mystical exotica that is of limited usefulness for most serious purposes. By presenting the major biographies in their entirety (constituting almost two-thirds of the entire text), I aim to preserve the integrity of 'Attār's complex portraits of these vital representatives of the principles of Islamic spirituality.

Memorial of God's Friends is itself an example of the translator's art. As 'Attār claims in his introduction, the sayings of the friends of God are a commentary on the Qur'an and hadith and thus lie near the heart of the Islamic revelation. But since these sayings are in Arabic, they have remained closed to those who cannot devote time to the formidable task of mastering this language. 'Attār undertakes the task of rendering them into Persian "so everyone," from the common people to the elite, "can be included." This inclusivity implies an approach to translation that stresses the naturalization of the source text for a broad target audience. In rendering the Persian into English, I have tried to make 'Attār's principles my guide. This decision has a number of implications for usage and style. Whenever possible, I have avoided importing Arabic and Persian words directly into English. There are, however, a few culture-specific terms that have resisted my efforts to find appropriate English equivalents and have been incorporated into my translation without italics. Some of these are likely to be known to most readers. The Qur'an is God's revelation to Mohammad and the scriptural foundation of Islam; the Ka'ba is the main shrine at Mecca and the goal of the Muslim pilgrimage or hajj. Less widely known perhaps is "hadith," the body of reports of the sayings and actions of the Prophet, that provides an essential guide for the behavior and beliefs of all pious Muslims, Sufi or otherwise. "Rak'at" is the sequence of physical movements made by the Muslim worshiper during prayer, such as bowing, kneeling, and touching the forehead to the ground, accompanied by prayers and recitations from the Qur'an. "Dinar" and "dirham" are the names of gold and silver coins respectively.

In the same spirit I have used a simplified, pronunciation-based Persian transliteration for proper names. Most of the diacritical markings in scholarly transliterations are based on Arabic sounds and letters that have no effect on Persian pronunciation and would serve little purpose in the present context. Simplified Persian spellings should help bring the names more easily to the mind and tongue of the general reader, while those familiar with the original Arabo-Persian spellings should have little trouble recognizing the names in this form. Persian consonants are pronounced like their English equivalents with three exceptions: "kh" is sounded like the "ch" in Bach; "gh" is the same consonant voiced, that is, sounded with vocal cords vibrating; and "q" is pronounced like a "k" pushed to the very back of the mouth (the uvula). The vowels also have near equivalents in English: "a" is pronounced as in "cat"; "e," as in "pet"; and "o" as a short version of the vowel in "coat." The Persian "i" is like the long vowel in "meet," and the "u," like "lute." The long "ā" indicates an open sound similar to the vowel in "call." Where there is a possibility of confusion with other standard transliterations of these names into Latin characters, I have included full consonantal diacritics in the notes and bibliography based on the Library of Congress Persian transliteration system. In the interest of guiding pronunciation, I have also indicated the assimilation of the Arabic definite article where appropriate: "al-Hoseyn," but "as-Sādeq."

I have purposely kept annotations to a minimum. 'Attār remarks that if he had provided a commentary on all the sayings of God's friends, "it would have required a thousand sheets of paper." The same might be said of extensive explanatory notes to this translation. Passages from the Qur'an are identified by chapter and verse in brackets following the quotation. I have included a glossary of proper names that appear more than once in the text and notes on the sole occurrence of others. In identifying historical figures, I have relied on the annotation provided by Mohammad Este'lāmi in his edition of the *Tazkerat*, as well as standard reference works, such as Dehkhodā's encyclopedic Persian dictionary *Loghatnāma*, the *Encyclopaedia Iranica* (abbreviated *EIr*), and the second edition of *Encyclopedia of Islam* (*EI²*). Entries in these latter two works will provide the interested reader with additional historical information on the major figures included in the *Memorial* and some suggestions for further reading. Dates in the notes and glossary are given in current era reckoning. The spelling of geographical names follows the third edition of *Merriam-Webster's Geographical Dictionary*. I have annotated only those place-names that do not appear in this standard reference work.

A few other points of usage should be mentioned here. Although 'Attār was rigorous in his efforts to render his Arabic sources into Persian, he did let certain passages stand in their original language. For the most part, these are fundamental religious texts, such as hadith and quotations from the Qur'an (with which most of his audience would have been familiar), but they also include the occasional proverb or line of poetry. I have used italics to indicate passages that are translated directly from Arabic into English. 'Attār sometimes follows an Arabic passage with a Persian translation; in these cases, I render the Persian into English and note only those passages where 'Attār's Persian translation differs markedly from the literal sense of the Arabic.

Many everyday words gradually acquired specialized meanings in the Sufi lexicon. The expressions "this clan" and "this folk," for example, usually refer to the Sufis and other friends of God. I have generally adhered to a single English equivalent throughout the text when such words are used in a technical sense; *zohd,* for example, is rendered as "renunciation," and *morāqabat* as "watchfulness." In rendering this technical lexicon, I have tried to find equivalents with a broad semantic range in English. God's friends themselves offer repeated and varied definitions of such terms, and too narrow an English translation would cramp this exploration of meaning. I have also felt free to deviate from these equivalencies when such words are used as part of the common vocabulary of the language. In one case, however, I felt that it was crucial to preserve the play between the technical and the common lexical meanings. In Arabic (though more rarely in Persian), the word *nafs* serves as a reflexive pronoun, "self"; in mystical writing the word further denotes the part of the human personality that is bound up with status, material values, and individuation. Modifiers such as *carnal* or *lower* are not only verbally clunky, but also overemphasize the physicality of *nafs,* a concept that encompasses bodily desire, egoistic

ON THIS TRANSLATION

identity, and public standing. I have attempted to signal this complexity by playing the English reflexive—"He said to himself"—against an apparently ungrammatical possessive—"He said to his self."

Note should also be made of one especially problematic term. Many members of the spiritual elite cultivated an intuitive and experiential knowledge of God called *ma'refat* in Arabic and Persian; those especially noted for this type of knowledge are called *'ārefān*. These terms are often translated as "gnosis" and "gnostic" respectively. For the English reader, however, these words are probably too closely associated with the Gnostic movements of early Christian and late Hellenistic philosophy to ever return to their original lexical meanings. Although diverse forms of Gnosticism were among the threads woven into the fabric of Islamic spirituality, "mystical intuition" took on senses in the lives and sayings of God's friends that have little kinship with the dualism often associated with Gnosticism. I have therefore opted for the term "realization"; one who has undergone the immediate experience of "realization" enters the ranks of "the realized."

My translation maintains the distinctions among the three terms 'Attar uses to refer to the deity. "God" renders the Arabic *Allāh*, and "Lord," the Persian *Khodā*. Following Michael Sells,[2] I have translated *Haqq* as "the Real" to convey the sense that God is the only absolute, ontological reality—as 'Attār writes, *"If we ponder existence, nothing exists but him."* Although the coalescence of the terms *realization* and *the Real* creates a pun that does not exist in the Persian original, it is one that is appropriate to both the beliefs and the word play of the Sufis. I have chosen not to capitalize adjectives and pronouns referring to the deity. This decision is based in part on the usage of the original; the Persian alphabet lacks the distinction between uppercase and lowercase letters, and imposing it except in the case of grammatical necessities like the beginning of sentences and proper nouns seemed an unnecessary intervention. More important, in *Memorial of God's Friends*, as in other mystical texts, there is a constant interplay between the transcendent and the immanent aspects of the divinity, and capitalization would threaten to put a typographic foreclosure on this dynamic.[3] In this regard, the Persian pronoun system has one other virtue that I have been unable to bring over into English—it is gender neutral. English grammar insists on an overt marking of gender in the pronouns, and following convention, I use "he" and "him" to indicate a reality that is ultimately beyond all demarcations of gender or typography.

The basis of my translation is the text of *Tazkerat al-owliyā'* edited by Mohammad Este'lāmi, which is based on two early manuscripts copied within a century of 'Attār's death.[4] Though less philologically reliable and containing some obvious scribal interpolations, the earlier edition of Reynold A. Nicholson proved useful for correcting the occasional misprints in Este'lāmi and shedding light on a few especially obscure passages.[5] It was reassuring to find that some of the sentences that most puzzled me were also the bane of medieval scribes. As is common practice in modern critical editions, Este'lāmi has punctuated the Persian text fully. However useful, this punctuation does not have manuscript authority, and I have deviated from Este'lāmi's division of sentences when it seemed necessary to maintain the pacing and rhythm of 'Attār's prose.

Decisions about parsing sentences are only one small aspect of the daunting challenge of doing justice to the prose style of *Memorial of God's Friends* in English. At the time 'Attār was writing, Persian prose was well on its way to developing a rhetorically ornate and syntactically complex "high" or "artificial" prose style. Though signs of this emerging style can be found in the rhymed epithets that open each biography, 'Attār for the most part employs a much simpler and more straightforward diction. The *Memorial* is often regarded as the last great masterpiece in the so-called plain style (*nasr-e sāda*) in Persian prose. A recent Iranian critic identifies word choice, resonant phrasing, and inimitable brevity as the factors that most contribute to the power and grace of 'Attār's artfully artless style.[6] Arberry's translation pays little regard to these qualities. At his best, Arberry demonstrates a keen accuracy in selecting English equivalents for Persian words and a knack for turning a phrase. All too often, however, the laconic and almost colloquial vigor of 'Attār's Persian is replaced by an English that is stilted, archaizing, and unidiomatic in its over-literal rendering of Persian idiom. Readers are seldom allowed to forget that they are reading a translation of an "oriental" text. In attempting to re-create 'Attār's style in English, I take his poised restraint as my model. I have tried to resist temptations to spice up 'Attār's lexicon with unnecessary synonyms, to smooth out his short prose periods by subordinating and fusing sentences, and to create a more obviously "polished" flow by adding or deleting transitional phrases. My goals have been well-defined syntax, elevated natural diction, and rhythmically crisp phrasing. Though I cannot pretend to rival 'Attār's mastery, I do hope to have conveyed accurately the stylistic register and inflection of the original as well as my ear permits.

While I remain as close as possible to the style and phrasing of the text, certain changes were inevitable if the naturalness of the Persian was to be brought over to English. Whenever too literal an adherence to syntax or wording resulted in awkward "translator-ese," I did not hesitate to modify it in keeping with contemporary American usage. I have adapted Persian phrase order to the usages of native English syntax and consistently altered a few sentence structures that are natural to Persian but invariably sound forced when brought directly into English, such as long, non-specific relative clauses ("the one who"). Persian pronoun reference is much looser than its English counterpart, and I have sometimes substituted the appropriate noun where the reference in Persian is clear but would be vague in English. Finally, in the long section of sayings and aphorisms that are an essential component of every biography, I have used line spacing and quotation marks in place of the repeated citation verb "s/he said" *(goft)* that demarcates the sayings in Persian.

This translation of *Memorial of God's Friends* has taken shape over the course of several years. It was too often set aside for other projects, for unexpected professional convulsions, and for an extended period of medical convalescence. During all this time, however, the *Memorial* was never far from my thoughts or my pen and was a valued companion through all these vicissitudes, as 'Attār would have wanted it to be. This extended gestation tried the patience of more friends and colleagues than I can name here and has earned them my deepest gratitude. This project began when Michael Sells first asked me to undertake the translation of the biography of Rābe'a-ye 'Adaviya for his book *Early Islamic Mysticism;*[7] it is a testament to both the power of 'Attār's words and Michael's encouragement that what first seemed to be the diversion of a few weeks became an obsession of many years. Over this time I received great moral and intellectual support from colleagues that I first met at the University of Chicago, Th. Emil Homerin, Franklin Lewis, and Sunil Sharma. Devin DeWeese, Jacques Merceron, Kemal Silay,

and Suzanne P. Stetkevych were among the many who offered counsel
and friendship during the ups and downs of the work-a-day world at
Indiana University. The enthusiastic response of my colleagues at
Indiana's Medieval Studies Institute and of the students in my courses
on Persian mystical literature assured me that 'Attār's world could
indeed be translated across language, culture, and time. In the final
stages of the project the editor of the Persian text of the *Tazkerat,*
Mohammad Este'lāmi, kindly sent me the introduction for the forthcom-
ing revised edition. Leonard Lewisohn shared many an illuminating
word of strength and insight during some very dark days. I can only
hope that my efforts here begin to requite them all for their enduring
generosity. Despite this collective wisdom and good will, I have no
doubt often gone astray of my own volition and ignorance. In the words
of the great translator of Plotinus, Stephen MacKenna, "The present
writer must have made mistakes, some perhaps that to himself will one
day appear inexcusable: his one consolation is that the thing he will that
day welcome from other hands has most certainly passed through his
own, and been deliberately rejected. Where he appears most surely to
have sinned against the light, it is most sure that he has passed through
an agony of hesitation."[8] My wife, Arzetta Hults Losensky, shared in
all these agonies and hesitations and in the joys and delights as well;
she read through every draft, painstakingly compiled lists of names
and quotations, and still woke up with a smile in the morning—to her
I dedicate this book.

TRANSLATOR'S INTRODUCTION

> Society's praise can be cheaply secured, and almost all men
> are content with these easy merits; but the instant effect of
> conversing with God will be to put them away. There are per-
> sons who are not actors, not speakers, but influences; persons
> too great for fame, for display; who disdain eloquence; to
> whom all we call art and artist, seems too nearly allied to
> show and by-ends, to the exaggeration of the finite and self-
> ish, and loss of the universal.
> —Emerson, "The Divinity School Address"

Like all good titles, *Tazkerat al-owliyā'—Memorial of God's
Friends*—can tell us much about the purpose and topic of the book. The
Persian word *tazkerat,* like the English word *memorial,* is related in form
and meaning to ideas of memory and remembrance. Etymologically, the
causative verbal noun *tazkerat* comes from the Arabic root *dh-k-r* and
means "to make remember" or "to remind." In later centuries *tazkerat*
would become common in the titles of collective biographies (especially
of poets), but 'Attār was apparently the first writer to employ the word in
this way.[1] Earlier biographical compendiums had commonly been called
tabaqāt; roughly meaning "rank" or "layers," this word indicates a
method of classification according to social and professional classes or
generational succession. Like these earlier works, 'Attār's *Memorial* follows a broadly chronological sequence. The choice of title, however,
speaks less to the organization of the work than to its intended effect and
purpose.

This purpose has its foundations in scripture and devotional practice. Remembrance, as Michael Sells observes, "is one of the core concepts of the Qur'an and of Islamic civilization."[2] In explaining his
reasons for composing the *Memorial,* 'Attār quotes the opening sentence of Qur'an 11:120, activating the memory of the reader to recall
the conclusion of the verse:

1

FARID AD-DIN 'ATTĀR'S MEMORIAL OF GOD'S FRIENDS

*We make your heart firm with all the stories of the prophets
that we relate to you. In them there has come to you the truth
and an exhortation and a remembrance to those who believe.*

"Remembrance," *dhikrá,* in turn, evokes its echo in *tazkerat.* The
Memorial thus partakes in the work of the Qur'an itself—to exhort
believers to follow the path of mindful awareness and to remind them
of God's constant omnipresence. It does so by recalling the words and
lives of those who believe with a special intensity, the men and women
who best exemplify humankind's continuing relationship with the
divine in a post-prophetic age. Following etymological memory to its
source, we arrive at *zekr* (*dhikr*). Remembrance here manifests itself in
a broad range of Sufi devotional practices. These typically involve the
ritualistic repetition of God's names and attributes but may extend to
regulated breathing, prescribed movements, or dance. In this wider
sense *zekr* is closely bound up with all varieties of contemplation and
meditation.³ Whatever form it may take, the purpose of *zekr* is always
the same: to purify oneself in order to draw closer to God.⁴

The rich linguistic and cultural resonance of the title word *tazkerat* suggests how 'Attār approaches his task as biographer. Although he
has a remarkable command of the sources available to him, his purpose
is not primarily to give an accurate, well-documented historical record.
Rather, like architectural monuments built to commemorate deceased
national heroes, *Memorial of God's Friends* serves to assure the continuing significance of certain ideals in the present. It provides a locus of
veneration and emulation. At the end of his introduction, 'Attār summarizes the reasons that motivated him to collect and transmit the words
of God's friends, emphasizing the devotional aims of his work:

> First, [these words] make people's hearts cold to this world.
> Second, they make the mind dwell continually on the after-
> world. Third, they bring out the love of the Real in people's
> hearts. Fourth, when people hear this sort of discourse, they
> begin to prepare provisions for the endless road.

In memorializing the spiritual heroes of the past, 'Attār hopes to free
his readers of the material and worldly attachments of the self, to focus
their attention on the true reality of the sacred realm, to rekindle their

primordial bond with God, and to prepare them for the endless journey toward divine union. 'Aṭṭār boasts that his book is the best of all books in creation because it constitutes a commentary on the Qur'an and the prophetic traditions. 'Aṭṭār's statement of purpose recalls similar passages in the Qur'an itself:

> *True believers are those whose hearts fill with fear when God is remembered and whose faith increases when his verses are recited and who put their trust in their Lord.* [8:2]

Memorial of God's Friends is not primarily a historical recreation of a lost past, but rather an act of sacred remembrance and devotion that intends to enable its readers to transcend the limitations of the self and reconnect with ultimate values and realities.

So, who are these friends of God? This brings us to the second word in 'Aṭṭār's title, *owliyā'*, the plural form of *vali*. The word derives from the Arabic root *w-l-y* meaning "to be near or close." In its basic sense, then, the *vali Allāh* is someone who enjoys an especially close relationship with God.[5] The nature of this relationship can vary. In some regards, as one scholar has recently suggested, the affinity between God and the *vali* can best be described in terms of patronage and alliance. The *owliyā'* are those who "aid God's cause on earth,"[6] his allies and helpers rather than his friends. For some *owliyā'*, such as Hasan of Basra and Dāvud-e Ṭā'i, the relationship with God is shaped largely by fear of divine wrath and seems to fall outside our usual notion of friendship. In the Qur'an, God characterizes himself as *vali* on several occasions, but even false idols can be identified as *owliyā'*. In such contexts the word is usually rendered as "protector" or "patron":

> *God is the protector of those who have faith. He will lead them out of the darkness into light. The patrons of those who reject the faith are idols, and they lead them out of the light into darkness.* [2:257]

An essential element of the bond between God and his closest followers, then, is guidance, alliance, and mutual support.

FARID AD-DIN 'ATTĀR'S MEMORIAL OF GOD'S FRIENDS

'Attār recognizes the various affiliations embraced by the term *owliyā'*. In his introduction he sketches the diversity of God's friends:

> Some are adherents of mystical realization and some of proper conduct; some are adherents of love and some of unity; and some are all of these. Some are self-possessed, and some are ecstatics.

The attributes here include not only the intuitive apprehension of God and ecstatic participation in the unity of being that we associate with the Sufi way, but also the moral rectitude, self-restraint, and pietistic conduct of those whose devotion falls within more normative ideals of ritualistic law and faith. Nevertheless, when 'Attār renders the Arabic-derived *owliyā'* in words of strictly Persian origin, he uses the expression *dustān-e khodā*—"friends of the Lord." 'Attār is less concerned with the precise nature of the relationship than with its ardent closeness, an intimacy that embraces deferential respect, painful yearning, brash forwardness, awestruck trepidation, and loving union.

To better understand 'Attār's concept of *owliyā'*, let us turn to one of his lyric poems. In a *ghazal* that can aptly serve as a verse introduction to *Memorial of God's Friends*, 'Attār describes many of the typical features and paradoxes of these spiritual heroes. As the poem opens, 'Attār alludes to two hadith. The first, a *hadith-e qodsi,* relates the words of God as spoken by Mohammad and employs an architectural image to express the secluded and privileged converse between God and his friends: *My friends are under my domes, and no one knows them but me.* The effect of such communion, in Emerson's words, is to put away society's praise. As so often in Sufi literature, this detachment from the world is represented by poverty. According to 'Attār's interpretation of the Prophet's saying *Poverty is on the verge of unbelief,* God's friends fall outside the pale of social respectability and religiosity not simply because of the material impoverishment that characterizes many of their lives, but because of their estrangement from the mundane and their disregard for conventional societal mores. Living in the world of time and space, but existing with God beyond both, they suffer from the very yearning that brings them into the proximity of the divine.

4

TRANSLATOR'S INTRODUCTION

On your path, there are people hidden
from themselves, without form or direction,
nameless, leaving not a trace.
Beneath a secret dome,
"where no one knows them but me,"
beloved from eternity,
they are veiled from the world.
They have pitched a tent, woven of poverty
"so close to unbelief." They remain hidden
from people behind the grimy faces of the poor.

They are a folk neither good nor evil,
not self-less, not self-possessed,
neither existent, nor nonexistent,
absent in plain sight.
In the world of me and we,
they are neither me nor we.
With you in time and space,
they remain timeless and placeless.
Their souls universal in the truth,
their bodies are one with the law:
They are both all soul and all body,
but neither this nor that.

Turning like a circle, fixed at its center,
a hundred circles climbing to the empyrean
without leaving the point of the soul—
seeing the essence of subsistence,
they pass away from themselves.
Drowned in the sea of certainty,
they are lost in the deserts of doubt.
From the tip of every hair,
they speak in myriad tongues,
but muteness leaves them
speechless and dumb.

All flying quickly with weighty reason
and suddenly burdened by light spirit.

Endless worlds beyond hope and fear—
under a writ of protection,
they are emaciated by dread.
The backs of the warriors were broken
by riding too quickly. The mount vanished,
the hands are left holding the reins.
With high aspiration, they happily sold
both worlds for a loaf of bread,
but they remain dependent on two loaves
from the unhappiness of the world.
A person never of mother born:
all of them just so,
yet still with you through poverty.

When 'Attār explained the path of such folk,
his heart palpitated,
and he nearly breathed his last.[7]

Memorial of God's Friends presents "the path of such folk" in all its glory and pain. Like the title of the work, this poem encapsulates the subject and the purpose of 'Attār's compendium of the words and deeds of these broken yet victorious warriors. In remembering those who seem "never of mother born," 'Attār finds himself on the verge of slipping his mortal bonds and entering a realm of pure spirit, a state of being not unlike that of God's friends themselves.

Earthly Remains: 'Attār's Life and Works

'Attār marks the end of this *ghazal* by inscribing his name in the final verse. Though this closing act of self-naming is conventional in the Persian lyric, it does remind us of how few traces 'Attār left of his material existence. We know virtually nothing of his personal life, and like the mystical quest for knowledge of the divine, the painstaking research of modern scholars has been more successful in defining who 'Attār was not than in revealing the attributes of who he was. Legend, for example, gave 'Attār a lifespan of 114 years, the same number as the chapters in the Qur'an, and credited him with 114 works to match.

TRANSLATOR'S INTRODUCTION

This coincidence cannot withstand even the most mildly skeptical examination, but it indicates the sort of pious legends that accumulated to fill the historical vacuum. When 'Abd ar-Rahmān Jāmi (d. 1492), the great Sufi and poet of fifteenth-century Herat, tells the tale of 'Attār's conversion to the mystical path, he displays a greater command of hagiographic narrative than of positivistic accuracy:

> They say that the reason for his conversion was that one day he working away happily in his apothecary shop. A dervish happened in and several times asked, "Something for God?" 'Attār paid no attention to him. "Sir," the dervish asked, "how will you die?"
> 'Attār said, "Just as you will."
> "Can you die like me?"
> "Certainly."
> The dervish placed the wooden bowl he was holding beneath his head, uttered "God," and surrendered his soul. 'Attār was transformed, closed up his shop, and embarked on this path.[8]

Jāmi's story echoes the anecdotes of the conversions and deaths of God's friends that are basic, recurring elements of the biographies in *Memorial of God's Friends*. Like Sari-ye Saqati (p. 278, below), 'Attār in this story repents of his mercantile concerns to take up a life of Sufi devotion. Like 'Ali-ye Sahl of Isfahan (pp. 385–86, below), the dervish in this story wills his own death; both mystics demonstrate the power of the will over biology in the presence of a representative of the medical profession, an apothecary (pharmacist) in this tale and a phlebotomist (surgeon) in the case of 'Ali-ye Sahl. Though such precedents contribute to the literary force of Jāmi's story of 'Attār's spiritual awakening, they also call into question its validity as an account of a historically unique event. Like 'Attār's accounts of the pioneers of Islamic spirituality, Jāmi's biography of 'Attār tends more to the devotional than to the reportorial.

Another oft-repeated legend of 'Attār's life began to circulate at about the same time that Jāmi was writing. In *Tazkerat ash-sho'arā (Memorial of the Poets)* completed in 1487, Dowlatshāh of Samarqand tells of the meeting of two giants of Persian mystical poetry. Fleeing the

7

city of Balkh in Central Asia, the young Jalāl ad-Din Rumi passes through the city of Nishapur in the company of his father, Bahā' ad-Din:

Sheikh Farid ad-Din 'Attār came to see Bahā' ad-Din. At that time, Jalāl ad-Din was a child. 'Attār gave his book *Asrār-nāma* to Jalāl ad-Din as a gift and said to his father, "It won't be long before this son of yours sets fire to all in the world who are consumed by love and suffering."[9]

As Franklin Lewis has shown, though such a meeting was "theoretically possible," it cannot be supported by another "shred of credible evidence" beyond this late source.[10] Despite its lack of factual substance, however, the story does embody historical reality of another sort: Rumi held 'Attār's poetry in the highest esteem and was profoundly influenced by his work. Their poetic and spiritual encounter was, in fact, more powerful than any actual, face-to-face meeting could have been. The stories in *Memorial of God's Friends* will often put far more strain on the modern reader's credulity than this imagined meeting of 'Attār and Rumi. But in such cases, as here, we must be on the lookout for other realities that the story is meant to convey.

Once late, legendary accretions such as these have been chipped away from 'Attār's life story, the remaining certainties are few.[11] Although 'Attār's exact date of birth is unknown, we can be confident that his life spanned the second half of the twelfth and the first quarter of the thirteenth centuries (1150–1225). His grandfather was named Eshāq, and his father, Ebrāhim. As the penname 'Attār suggests, the family was probably connected to the medical arts in some way, though there is scant direct evidence that the poet himself was active as a professional apothecary. His personal name was Mohammad, and he bore the honorific Farid ad-Din, "Unique in the Faith." He lived and died in the city or district of Nishapur, located in what is today northeastern Iran. The most widely accepted date for 'Attār's death is April 1221, when the Mongols sacked the city of Nishapur and put its inhabitants to the sword. Persuasive arguments, however, can be made for dates as late as 1229 or 1230.[12] Recent research has put forward new suggestions regarding 'Attār's spiritual and literary training, but these findings remain tentative.

8

TRANSLATOR'S INTRODUCTION

The most important traces of 'Attār's earthly existence are, of course, his literary works, and here we are on somewhat firmer ground. As many as twenty-five works have been reasonably attributed to poets with the pen name 'Attār, but philological research has shown that most of these do not belong to our Farid ad-Din. Some appear to come from the pen of another poet who shared the same *nom de plume* and lived in the same area of Iran but was active more than two centuries later— 'Attār of Tun. Others can perhaps be most generously characterized as pious fabrications by otherwise anonymous writers who wished to bask in 'Attār's spiritual aura. Scholars were still sifting through these works as late as the 1990s, and their research has now resulted in what seems to be a general consensus on the authenticity of six poetic works in addition to the one prose work translated here.[13]

Two of these works are, properly speaking, collections. 'Attār's *Divān*, or collected shorter works, contains his lyric poems, an example of which we read above. These include songs of spiritual longing and despair, meditations on mystical themes and symbols, and even short narratives. They are organized alphabetically according to rhyme, a formal scheme of arrangement typical of the collected works of medieval Persian poets. Like the *Divān*, *Mokhtār-nāma* (*The Choice Book*) consists of shorter poems, specifically *robā'i* or quatrains, a genre familiar to English readers through Edward Fitzgerald's translation of Omar Khayyám. The method of arrangement in *Mokhtār-nāma*, however, is thematic rather than formal. Over two thousand quatrains are grouped into fifty chapters according to topic. The first half of the work is devoted to mystical and ethical matters, such as the extinction of the self, bewilderment, union with the spirit, and God's unity; the second half turns to various attributes of the beloved and the phases of amatory and spiritual love. *Mokhtār-nāma* indicates not only the range of 'Attār's poetic vision but also his insistent concern for the coherent disposition of literary material.

The other four poetic works are didactic poems of several thousand verses written in rhymed couplets, a form known in Persian as the *masnavi*. Each of these works is made up of a series of short narratives— drawn from folk tales, history, and religious lore—that serves to illustrate ethical, moral, or mystical themes. This basic structure appears in its simplest form in *Asrār-nāma* (*The Book of Secrets*). This work consists of twenty-two discourses: a basic concept of Sufi teach-

9

ing is first presented in general terms and then elaborated with a number of exemplary tales. In the other three *masnavis* this repeated pattern of theme and illustration is unified by an overarching frame story. The most famous of these is the allegory now known as *Manteq at-teyr* or *The Conference of the Birds*.[14] In it, birds of every species set off in search of the mythical bird Simorgh under the guidance of the hoopoe. As each bird voices its excuses and doubts, the hoopoe takes the opportunity to explain the values and doctrines of the mystical quest with pertinent exemplum. In *Mosibat-nāma* (*The Book of Hardship*), a Sufi pilgrim (*sālek*) in a state of spiritual bewilderment is advised by his elder to appeal to forty celestial and terrestrial entities for relief and enlightenment. Each entity, from the angels and the heavenly throne to the four elements and heaven and hell, comments on its own spiritual state with a series of tales, showing the pilgrim that they are no better off than he is. Only when the pilgrim encounters Spirit does he discover that the answer to his confusion and despair lies within himself. It has been recently demonstrated that the poem we now know as the *Elāhi-nāma* (*The Book of the Divine*) was originally entitled *Khosrownāma* (*The King's Book*).[15] It tells the story of a king who discovers that his six sons have all fixed their aspirations on worldly desires; mixing his counsel with exemplary anecdotes, he tries to persuade them that their goal, if properly understood, can be achieved by drawing on their own spiritual resources.[16]

These frame stories and the pattern of theme and illustration give structure to a wildly heterogeneous mass of anecdotal material. 'Attār's seemingly boundless store of narrative draws on history, legend, folklore, everyday life, and the religious tradition, including some of the same tales of God's friends that are found in the *Memorial*. To show how 'Attār integrated such tales into his longer poems, let us turn to a passage from *Elāhi-nāma*. The king's fifth son expresses his desire to possess the signet ring of Solomon, which would give him power over the entire world of animate creation from humans and genies to insects and birds. His father replies that such political dominion is no more than a transitory pleasure that will cost his son his immortal soul. To drive his point home, the king tells stories of some of the most powerful monarchs in Iranian history, such as Alexander the Great, Mahmud of Ghazna, and Sultan Sanjar, who are reminded of their responsibilities and limitations by sages and commoners alike. Among these tales

we read the story of the conversion of Ebrāhim ebn Adham at the hands
of the immortal spiritual guide Khezr:

Ebrāhim son of Adham sat enthroned;
slaves, arms folded, stood before and behind.
A jewel-encrusted crown upon his head,
he wore a robe embroidered with silver.
Unannounced, Khezr barged into the hall,
dressed in the garb of a camel driver.
Fearful of him, slaves all caught their breath.
Everyone who saw him was overwhelmed.
When Ebrāhim caught sight of him, off guard
he demanded, "Beggar, who let you in?"
"Isn't there a room for me here?" Khezr replied.
"This is an inn. I'll rest here a while."
Ebrāhim son of Adham shouted back,
"This is the castle of a mighty sultan!
Why, you fool, why do you call it an inn?
You seem to be bright enough—are you mad?"
Khezr then loosed his tongue and said, "O King,
who was the first that this country possessed?"
Ebrāhim told him that so-and-so first
conquered the place and then stayed on as king.
After him came so-and-so, after him
one more: "Now I rule here, king of the world!"
Khezr said, "Although the king is unaware,
this palace is an inn and nothing more.
People come and go continuously.
Can one take up residence in an inn?
As many a king has come before you,
passing on whether they were good or bad,
so they will come for you seeking your life
and steal you away from this ancient inn.
Why do you lounge in this caravanserai?
You don't belong here. Why is it you stay?"
When Ebrāhim heard this, he was transformed.
These words set his head spinning like a ball.
When Khezr departed, he ran after him.

11

(How can anyone escape from Khezr's snare?)
He swore him many an oath and begged him,
"Young man, knight, accept me now if you can.
Since you have secretly planted a seed
in my heart, give it water. Give it life!"
Ebrāhim said this and followed Khezr's path
till he became a man of truest faith.
He rejected the old inn of this world.
He gave up sovereignty for poverty.
The great recognized poverty's secret
and purchased it with transitory wealth.
They fled the form and image of kingship,
escaping beggary to find meaning.
Though the realm of this world is sovereignty,
when you look close, at root it's beggary.[17]

The basic story line of Ebrāhim's encounter with Khezr as 'Attār tells it here is virtually identical to the prose version in *Memorial of God's Friends* (pp. 128–29, below). But two differences in plotting are indicative of 'Attār's attention to context. In *Elāhi-nāma*, 'Attār presents the story as part of the king's instruction to his son and points up the thematic message of the story by adding a moralizing coda that contrasts the liberating poverty of the spiritually enlightened with the abject dependency of those blinded by material power and riches. In the *Memorial,* on the other hand, this story is only one element in a longer, compound story of Ebrāhim's conversion. To build narrative suspense 'Attār withholds the identity of the intruder until the end of the tale. Khezr's revelation of his name and subsequent disappearance launch the reader into the second part of the story, in which Ebrāhim wanders dazed through the desert and attains enlightenment through the miraculous speech of a gazelle and a saddle pommel. Such suspense would only muddle the thematic point that the king wants to make in the *Elāhi-nāma* but is appropriate to building tension when the focus falls directly on the story of Ebrāhim himself.[18]

Intellectual Background and Sources of
Memorial of God's Friends

The stories and aphorisms that 'Attār utilized in his poetic works and in *Memorial of God's Friends* are the product of a rich intellectual and poetic tradition. Nishapur, where 'Attār lived and died, was one of the major cities in the broad geographical area known as greater Khorasan. The region is today divided among the countries of Iran, Turkmenistan, Uzbekistan, and Afghanistan. Medieval geographers roughly defined Khorasan as a quadrangle with four cities at its corners: Merv (now Mary), Balkh, Herat, and Nishapur. Located at the boundary of Central Asia and the Iranian plateau, Nishapur was one of the principal trading cities on the network of caravan routes known as the Silk Road. In the ninth century the city also became an important political center. As the centralized rule of the 'Abbasid dynasty in Baghdad lost its influence over more distant reaches of the empire, a succession of local dynasties rose to power in Khorasan, with Nishapur as a key administrative capital. In spite of a series of manmade and natural catastrophes, Nishapur would remain one of the most influential and prosperous cities in the Islamic world for the next four centuries, until its heyday came to a violent end with the Mongol sack of the city in 1221.

Economic prosperity and political independence helped to bring about a florescence in cultural life. Tenth-century Khorasan witnessed the reemergence of Persian as a written language, soon to be on a par with Arabic as a medium of poetry, history, and scholarship. Ferdowsi (d. ca. 1021), the author of the Persian national epic or *Shāhnāma*, came from the village of Tus, located in the district of Nishapur, and the tomb of the famous mathematician and poet 'Omar Khayyām (d. 1122) lies on the outskirts of the city, only a few miles from that of 'Attār. Literary life flourished amid a rich material culture. Excavations have revealed elaborately constructed homes adorned with murals, and local potters created striking painted ceramics with calligraphic, figural, and abstract designs, among the finest ever produced in the Islamic world. So prominent was Nishapur that local historians documented the life of the urban elite in extensive biographical compendiums.[19]

The province of Khorasan was a crucial area for the development of Sufism. *Memorial of God's Friends* includes the biographies of several formative figures active in the region, such as Ebrāhim ebn Adham, Abu Torāb of Nakhshab, and Bāyazid of Bestām, whose teachings informed Sufism for centuries. Modern scholars have speculated at length on the identity of 'Aṭṭār's teachers in poetry and Sufism but with limited success. The most likely candidates are either well-known figures with no established links to the poet or obscure names that add little to our understanding of 'Aṭṭār.[20] In broader terms, however, the identity of his personal mentors is of secondary importance: his intellectual and spiritual life was shaped by over two centuries of poetic achievement and Sufi activity in Khorasan. 'Aṭṭār felt a particularly close kinship to the great Sufi sheikh Abu Sa'id ebn Abi'l-Kheyr (d. 1049).[21] His hospice was a center of religious activity in Nishapur for several decades, and his life is the subject of one of great masterpieces of biographical writing in Persian.[22] Although he probably wrote no poetry himself, Abu Sa'id frequently used secular, popular verse in his sermons and was instrumental in establishing Persian poetry as a vehicle for Sufi teaching and preaching. 'Abdollāh Ansāri (d. 1089) was active further east in Herat but spent some years as a student in Nishapur and left behind a substantial body of writing in both Arabic and Persian. His theoretical treatise *Manāzel as-sā'erān* (*The Stations of the Wayfarers*) systematically lays out the stages of the mystic path. In a series of moving prayers and meditations, *Monājāt*, Ansāri transforms the flexible rhythms and rhymes of the early, hymn-like revelations of the Qur'an into a mesmerizing, incantory Persian prose.[23] Out of this milieu appeared the first great Persian Sufi poet, Majd ad-Din Sanā'i (d. ca. 1138).[24] Though he began his career as a poet of the court, Sanā'i earned his place in literary history through his mystically colored *ghazals* and his *Hadiqat al-haqiqat* (*The Walled Garden of Truth*), the first substantial *masnavi* in Persian devoted to ethical and mystical teaching that survives intact today. Sanā'i's work opened the door for later poets such as 'Aṭṭār and Rumi and had an abiding influence on the subsequent tradition of Sufi poetry.

Of more immediate concern for our present purpose are the authors and works that contributed directly to the making of *Memorial of God's Friends*. 'Aṭṭār, as researchers have often noted, does not list his sources by name, and his reference in the introduction to three works has raised more questions than it has answered. *Sharh al-qalb* (*The Commentary of the Heart*) is apparently one of 'Aṭṭār's early poetic works that he himself destroyed.[25] The other two—*Kashf al-asrār* (*The Unveiling of Secrets*) and *Ma'refat an-nafs* (*Knowledge of the Self*)—have yet to be satisfactorily identified, but it is generally thought that they, too, are lost works by the poet himself. In any case, 'Attār does not refer to these books as sources for the *Memorial* but as commentaries on the mystical aphorisms. Despite his silence on the subject, however, it is clear that 'Attār did his research well, drawing on as many as a dozen sources for information on the words and deeds of God's friends. Though these sources have yet to be thoroughly studied,[26] the Sufi circles of Nishapur and Khorasan produced the three works that contributed most to the *Memorial*. The first of these is one of the earliest accounts of the lives and sayings of the Sufis, *Tabaqāt as-sufiya* (*The Sufi Ranks*) by Abu 'Abd ar-Rahmān as-Solami. Solami was born in Nishapur in 937 and died there in 1021,[27] and his biographical compendium provided 'Attār not only with much of the material, but also with the chronological sequence of *Memorial of God's Friends.* Two other works to which 'Attār was deeply indebted are expository manuals on the Sufi path. Perhaps no book was more important in consolidating and propagating the teachings and ideas of Sufism than the *Resāla* of Abu'l-Qāsem al-Qosheyri.[28] A student of Solami, Qosheyri (986–1072), was another of the great Sufi masters of Nishapur. Originally written in Arabic, his "Treatise" was translated into Persian by a student under Qosheyri's direction shortly after it was written and was no doubt among 'Attār's earliest introductions to the mystical path. A similar work was also composed in Persian at about the same time further east in Khorasan—*Kashf al-mahjub* by 'Ali ebn 'Osmān Hojviri (d. ca. 1072–77).[29] Like Qosheyri's *Resāla, Kashf al-mahjub* sets out to present Sufism as a coherent system of thought in line with mainstream Islamic doctrines and to introduce its fundamental concepts to a learned audience. The two works have a similar structure. A general introduction is followed by brief biographies of the major figures of Sufism; these lay the foundation for the main component of the work: a systematic exposition of the major terms, ideas, and stages of the Sufi path based on the saying of the great sheikhs.

Identifying 'Attār sources, however, is only a first step in understanding how he utilizes this disparate material and organizes it into coherent biographies. 'Attār employs the full resources of what the late André Lefevere defined as "rewriting"—quotation, paraphrase, word-for-word and free translation, the integration of independent sources, and imitation.[30] In its simplest form this process is perhaps most familiar to us today through the anthology or encyclopedia entry, types of rewriting that are essential to education and the formation of a canonical body of knowledge. 'Attār selects key passages from texts that were well over a century old at the time when he was writing and makes them accessible and attractive to a contemporary audience in a single volume. Like modern translators, editors, biographers, and compilers, 'Attār popularizes, propagates, and interprets the written tradition in ways that will ensure its ongoing relevance and significance. In so doing, he creates a new image of his sources that often reaches a larger audience and exercises a greater influence than the source itself.

We can roughly divide the complex processes of rewriting into three stages: assimilation, recasting, and disposition. Assimilation operates most obviously at the level of language and style. Having gathered material from diverse sources in two different languages, 'Attār faced the task of forging it into a consistent and uniform prose. This was most easily done with passages that were already available in Persian. Even a cursory comparison reveals that 'Attār frequently incorporates passages from *Kashf al-mahjub* and the Persian translation of Qosheyri's *Resāla* into the *Memorial* word for word or with minor stylistic revisions. For the most part these revisions modify word choice to reflect current usage or edit syntax to create more concise and elegant sentences. Translating from Solami (and other Arabic sources) presented greater challenges. 'Attār's translation techniques range from an almost word-for-word calque to free interpretation. In the Arabic text of Solami's *Tabaqāt,* for example, 'Attār found this saying attributed to 'Ali-ye Sahl of Isfahan:

> 'Ali was asked about the reality of unity. He said, "It is close
> to speculations, distant in realities," and he recited this verse
> to some of them:
>> I said to my companions, "It is the sun.
>> Its light is near, but grasping it, a remote possibility."[31]

'Attār's Persian translation of the first part of this saying follows the Arabic word for word, adding only a particle or two for clarity:

16

They asked about the reality of unity. He said, "It is near to where there are speculations, but it is distant in realities."

'Attār treats the verse that rounds out the saying in Solami very differently, making it into an independent aphorism that at first glance has little resemblance to its source:

They asked 'Ali-ye Sahl, "Say a few words about the idea of perception."
"Whoever fancies that he is closer is in reality further away. When the sunlight falls through the window, children want to grab a hold of the dust motes. They close their hands. They fancy they have something in their grasp. When they open their hands, they see nothing."

'Attār here exploits the metaphorical link between physical and mental apprehension, between grasping and perception. He then gives the notion of grasping the sun, a patent impossibility, a greater immediacy by introducing what one critic calls "one of the most prevalent motifs for the idea of the unity of being in 'Attār's poetry"—the dust mote.[32] The attempt to take hold of the transcendent through its myriad material manifestations is no longer an absurdly unthinkable gesture but an act of innocent, childlike naivete. 'Attār here translates as a poet, exercising an independent creativity in re-creating his source in a new language and context. Through paraphrase, skillful editing, and translation, 'Attār transforms the disparate idioms of his sources into one of the recognized masterpieces of Persian prose style.

Recasting, or recontextualization, is the way in which an author creates a new compositional setting for earlier material in accordance with a new design and purpose. In the tradition of early Arabic historical writing and hadith scholarship, Solami typically authenticated anecdotes and aphorisms by using a device known as *esnād*. A chain of transmission cites a series of reporters, leading back from the author to a contemporary of the original speaker: "So-and-so told me that So-and-so told him...that So-and-so said." 'Attār announces his decision to omit these *esnāds* in his introduction, and he replaces them with simple formulas like "It is related" or "he said." Unlike Solami, 'Attār does not set out to provide a substantiated and well-documented historical record, but rather to bring the words and deeds of God's friends into the spiritual consciousness of his readers. His work is a reminder (*tazkerat*), not a "classification" (*tabaqāt*). Without the constant interruption of documentary *esnāds*, the biographies gather pace and cohesion. The characters are more sharply delineated as emphasis falls squarely on the anecdotes or aphorisms as expressions of personality and beliefs. 'Attār also recasts the material that he derived from expository treatises like those of Qosheyri and Hojviri. In these sources the sayings of the Sufis are organized topically; under the heading of renunciation, for example, we find pertinent utterances from many different teachers, normally linked together by the author's commentary. 'Attār, on the other hand, places the aphorisms together with the biographical anecdotes with little explanatory elaboration. Interest shifts from abstract principles of behavior or doctrine to the nuances and particulars of the individual encounter with the divine. *Memorial of God's Friends* thus not only epitomizes the rich spiritual heritage of Nishapur, Khorasan, and the wider Islamic world, but it refashions it with a new devotional relevance and experiential immediacy.

Dispositions of Character and Form

Once source material is assimilated to a consistent style and cast to fit a new design and purpose, there remains the problem of how to arrange this vast collection of stories and sayings into a coherent and self-contained whole. It is in the disposition or organization of material that 'Attār's creativity as a rewriter and literary artist is most evident. In the medieval Arabic and Persian tradition, biographical data was handed down in short, independent units that were easily memorized and transmitted orally. Anecdotes typically involve no more than two characters with well-defined roles in a simple story consisting of one major action or discovery. Dicta similarly are seldom longer than a sentence and usually exhibit a straightforward and often formulaic syntax. Even in a sustained discourse, these units tend to remain semi-independent. Flexible, yet clearly recognizable patterns of arrangement were essential if 'Attār was to succeed in integrating these detachable components into complex, cohesive portraits worthy of a reader's devotion and remembrance. In his narrative poems 'Attār achieves structural clarity and cohesion through the use of frame stories. But the greater demand for verisimilitude in biographical writing militates against such carefully crafted allegories. There is no equivalent in *Memorial of God's Friends* to the avian pilgrimage in *Conference of the Birds* or the celestial progress in the *The Book of Hardship*. We can nevertheless observe a conscientious shaping of historical material both in the *Memorial* as a whole and within each biography. Understanding how 'Attār uses disposition to create meaning and character is essential if we are to enter fully into the spiritual, intellectual, and experiential world of God's friends.

The original Persian version of the *Memorial* contains seventy-two biographies.[33] There is nothing in the historical record or in earlier biographical compendiums to dictate this number. Solami's *Tabaqāt* consists of one hundred and five lives, while the biographical portions of Qosheyri's *Resāla* and Hojviri's *Kashf al-mahjub* include eighty-three and sixty-four entries, respectively. The proliferation of three- and four-page biographies toward the end of *Memorial of God's Friends*, however, suggests that 'Attār took pains to reach precisely seventy-two. This number is common in medieval Islamic writings and does not have an exact quantitative value.[34] Seventy-two is used to indicate a general abundance and multiplicity, similar to the English *dozens*. The lack of quantitative specificity, however, only enhances the symbolic potential of the number. Most famously, seventy-two figures in a well-known saying of the Prophet: *"The Jews were split into seventy-one or -two sects; and the Christians were split into seventy-one or -two sects; and my community will be split into seventy-three sects."*[35] This resonance of sacred history seems crucial to 'Attār's calculations. Each of his biographical subjects constitutes, as it were, a sect of one, and together represent the full range of Islamic spirituality, from the uncompromising moral scrupulousness of Dāvud-e Tā'i to the visionary realization of Nuri. Following the mathematics of the hadith further, each reader completes the count at seventy-three, traveling his or her own unique path to the divine. Whether the number of chapters has a specific allusive meaning or a more general symbolic association, it is a first indication of 'Attār's attention to significant structure in *Memorial of God's Friends*.

As we noted earlier, the arrangement of biographies in the *Memorial* follows a roughly chronological (as opposed to geographical or alphabetical) order, based on the sequence established in Solami's *Tabaqāt.* Though chronology is resistant to rhetorical shaping, the beginning and ending of the work show that historical sequence was only one of the factors that entered into 'Attār's arrangements. In strictly chronological terms, the semi-legendary Oveys of Qaran, a contemporary of the prophet Mohammad, is the earliest figure included in the *Memorial.* His biography, however, is postponed, and the first chapter is devoted instead to Ja'far as-Sādeq, the sixth imam (or descendant of the Prophet), who died in 765. The placement of this biography runs counter to two of 'Attār's basic organizational principles. In the introduction he disclaims any intention of writing about the Prophet's family or companions, and in the chronological sequence of biographies, Ja'far's should come ninth or tenth. 'Attār goes out his way to explain this inconsistency:

> We had said that if we were to memorialize the prophets, Mohammad's companions, and his family, it would require a separate book. This book will consist of the biographies of the masters of this clan, who lived after them. But as a blessing, let us begin with Sādeq (may God be pleased with him) for he too lived after them. Since he among the Prophet's descendants said the most about the path and many traditions have come down from him, I shall say a few words about this esteemed man, for they are all as one. When he is remembered, it is the remembrance of them all.

Given the importance of devotion and remembrance in the overall design the *Memorial,* it is only appropriate that 'Attār invoke them again here. But the inclusion and placement of Ja'far's biography is significant in other ways as well. Establishing heirship to the Prophet was a guiding principle in Islamic biographical writing,[36] and with a single stroke 'Attār integrates the family of Mohammad into the Sufi tradition, implying that its later exponents, too, are legitimate heirs of the prophetic lineage. As the *Memorial* progresses, Ja'far takes his place in other networks of association. Dāvud-e Tā'i, for example, makes his first appearance here as one Ja'far's interlocutors, and Ja'far himself will reemerge in an important subsidiary role later as the teacher Bāyazid of Bestām. 'Attār, however, also links biographies without the characters interacting directly. The placement of Ja'far's biography becomes more meaningful when 'Attār initiates the chronological sequence in Chapter 2. Ja'far and Oveys are complementary opposites. The former is of noble lineage, learned, and socially prominent; the latter is an outcast from his own tribe, unlettered, and an impoverished camel herder. Although neither met Mohammad face to face, Ja'far partakes in the prophetic heritage through genealogical descent, while Oveys sees the Prophet with spiritual sight and knows his teachings through divine inspiration. At the very beginning of the work 'Attār thus encompasses the full sweep of spiritual affinity and initiation: familial descent is set alongside devotional affiliation, and genealogical inheritance is balanced against spiritual attraction.

Patterns of interaction and opposition run throughout the course of *Memorial of God's Friends* and open up an expanding series of perspectives on each character. The most important of these oppositions is between two figures who never met—Bāyazid of Bestām and Joneyd of Baghdad. In the two longest biographies in the *Memorial,* 'Attār establishes the famous distinction between the "intoxicated" and the "sober" schools of Sufism, between Bāyazid's cultivation of rapture and self-effacement and Joneyd's struggle for self-control and subsistence in God. The contrast between the private mentor of rural Khorasan and the public preacher of metropolitan Baghdad extends even to their modes of dress. The opposition between these two masters is foreshadowed in the early chapters of the *Memorial*. Hasan of Basra and Rābe'a-ye 'Adaviya lived at the same time in Basra, and 'Attār gives them key roles in each other's biographies, embodying in dramatic form the contrast between Hasan's path of grief and Rābe'a's way of love. Joneyd's repeated appearances create another network of interaction. He plays an important part as a narrative foil in the biographies of more ecstatic mystics. In the account of Abu'l-Hoseyn Nuri, for example, Joneyd acts as a mentor who allows the reader to follow Nuri's spiritual development. In the tragedy of Hallāj, on the other hand, Joneyd represents the religious establishment and is instrumental in Hallāj's condemnation and martyrdom. By interweaving characters through the course of the work, 'Attār creates a sense of a coherent spiritual evolution across the historical sequence of discrete biographies.

'Attār manipulates chronology more subtly at the end of the *Memorial*. Composed at the beginning of the thirteenth century, the work looks back on the lives it recounts from a distance of almost three centuries. From this distance 'Attār could choose his end point as he saw fit. His decision to end with the martyrdom of Hallāj in 922 is so artistically satisfying that it is seldom questioned, but it is not as obvious as it seems. None of 'Attār's sources gives Hallāj this pride of place. If 'Attār's goal were simply to define the end of the classical period of Sufism, Shebli's death in 946 would appear a far more appropriate date. He is mentioned far more frequently than Hallāj in the *Memorial,* but because he died after Hallāj, he is denied his own independent biography. From a purely historical point of view, Shebli is the last of the formative figures to live before the period of consolidation represented by Solami and Qosheyri. Historical precision, however, is not 'Attār's foremost concern. Hallāj's tragic fate, his gruesome execution, and his postmortem miracles give the closure of *Memorial of God's Friends* a resounding power that goes beyond questions of proper periodization.

'Attār's attention to significant form is also evident when we examine the internal structure of the biographies. A common structure provides a basis for comparison and interpretive judgment as we move through the book. Each biography is composed of three basic components. First comes an introduction—prefaced by a series of rhymed, laudatory epithets[37]—that briefly summarizes the subject's beliefs and accomplishments and lists teachers and associates. This is typically followed by a set of brief anecdotes or stories. Aphorisms and sayings are grouped together after the stories. (Each section of sayings in my translation is clearly demarcated.) We can further isolate two recurrent types of anecdote: stories of repentance and conversion to the spiritual life come immediately after the introduction, and stories of death and after-death miracles follow the sayings at the end of the biography. A basic five-part sequence—introduction, conversion, stories, sayings, and death—serves to organize even the longest biographies, such as those of Bāyazid and Joneyd. Variations of this pattern are possible and significant. For example, in the biographies of both Hasan of Basra and Joneyd a short selection of sayings and dicta is placed in the midst of the narrative anecdotes, foregrounding the role of public preaching in their lives. The loving intimacy of Rābe'a's relationship with God is emphasized by the substitution of a section devoted to her private devotions for the more typical maxims and aphorisms. Bāyazid's say-

22

ings culminate in a first-person recital of his visionary ascension into the divine presence. In shorter biographies the narrative content may be reduced to no more than a couple of brief anecdotes, and stories of conversion and death may be absent altogether. In spite of the priority often given to the stories in the *Memorial,* it is the introduction and sayings that constitute the essential core of every biography.

'Attār's introductions to the biographies announce the basic principles exemplified by each of his "sects of one" and guide our reading of the stories and sayings that follow. The opening phrases in the biography of Rābe'a, for example, place before the reader a set of terms and issues, such as sincerity, love, and proximity, that will figure throughout 'Attār's account of her life. The word *veil* alone sets in motion problematic questions of gender and secrecy that take on narrative form in the stories of Rābe'a's upbringing, her confrontations with the eminent men of the day, and even the manipulation of the narrator's point of view.[38] A very different thematic is established in the opening of the account of Dāvud-e Tā'i: "He was the utmost perfection in scrupulousness." His single-minded pursuit of moral probity and purity leads him to withdraw ever further from the compromises and corruptions of human society, until he is "rewarded" with a paralysis that leaves him unable even to attend prayers in the mosque. 'Attār's biographies sometimes develop around multiple themes, exploring the conflicts and connections between apparently disparate ideals. The account of Abu'l-Hoseyn Nuri, for example, takes as its themes altruism and rapture and uses narrative and dictum to show how both are grounded in the sincere sacrifice of the self, whether to others or to God.[39] Even a biography as brief as that of 'Ali-ye Sahl unfolds as a meditation on the conflict between an often-deceptive outward appearance and its transcendent, inward significance, which is broached in the opening rhymed phrases that present 'Ali as both "the seer of human foible" and "the knower of realms invisible."[40]

In his introduction 'Attār places the responsibility for interpretation in his readers' hands. Disavowing any intention to provide commentaries, 'Attār instructs the reader "who happens to need a commentary" to renew the encounter with the text itself, "to look closely at the words of God's friends and interpret them again." This statement is not only a challenge to the reader's attentiveness and intelligence, but also an invitation to join in the creation of meaning and to engage fully in the spiritual universe of each of the "sects of one." In each biography the reader must continually weigh anecdotes and aphorisms against one another: To what extent are they consistent with one another? What are the advantages and the limitations of the character's spiritual experience? How is it reflected, or not, in his words? The give-and-take between anecdotes, between aphorisms, and between action and teaching gives the characters a depth and complexity that prevents them from being reduced to mere typological embodiments of a particular school of thought. For his part, 'Attār organizes his biographies in ways that facilitate the task of reading, creating networks of interrelated images and themes held together at key points by recurring words and motifs.

To get a better idea of how we can enter into these networks of meaning and interpretation, let us look in some detail at the biography of Zu'n-Nun of Egypt (Chapter 10). The introductory paragraph presents a set of key terms. Following the accounts of such masters of asceticism and proper conduct as Hasan of Basra and 'Abdollāh ebn Mobārak, the term *realization* stands out. For the first time in the *Memorial,* the idea of an intuitive, immediate knowledge of God takes prominence, establishing Zu'n-Nun's place in the history of Islamic spirituality and sounding a major theme of his biography. 'Attār uses a closely related concept to suggest a first definition of *realization:* "a precise insight into the secrets of unity." But realization and unity are only half of the picture. They are balanced syntactically and conceptually with complementary themes: affliction, detachment, and blame. The life and thought of Zu'n-Nun unfold as an exploration of the implications and interrelations of these aspects of spiritual experience.

Their interplay is first seen immediately following the introduction in the story of Zu'n-Nun's conversion. Zu'n-Nun has apparently already embarked on his spiritual journey when he comes upon "a devout recluse" hanging from a tree. This seeming model of ascetic discipline deprecates his own deeds and directs Zu'n-Nun to climb further up the mountain. Here he is met by a shocking and gruesome sight: a young man who has amputated his own foot, which now lies before him in a state of advanced decomposition. Such is the punishment that this ascetic has meted out to himself in response to the temptations of carnal flesh. But he, too, finds his sacrifice inadequate and instructs Zu'n-Nun to climb higher still. To this point the story exhibits many of the features of the legendary quest. The mountain provides an arche-typal setting for the struggle to ascend to a higher reality, and in the progression of self-mutilation, we apparently have the first two stages in a typically three-step pattern of cumulative narrative repetition. Here, however, Zu'n-Nun's journey takes an unexpected detour. He does not make the final ascent. Instead, he relies on a secondhand account of the third recluse. Zu'n-Nun's path to enlightenment mirrors that of the reader, who also participates in a spiritual conversion through the medium of story. Further deflecting our expectations, the recluse on the mountaintop, instead of exhibiting a yet more extreme form of self-inflicted mutilation, surrenders himself body and soul to divine sustenance and tastes the sweetness of honey. The summit of self-imposed asceticism is found in trusting submission to God's will. However, even this recluse has taken an oath, a purposive act of per-sonal intention. The final stage of Zu'n-Nun's awakening comes after his ascent up the mountain has ended. The blind bird that miraculously feeds from bowls of silver and gold has no ego to master, no self to dis-cipline, and no reward to gain from doing so. Nevertheless, it too par-takes of divine benevolence and provides an object lesson in unity and immanence.

The story of Zu'n-Nun's conversion creates a first nexus of the themes of affliction, detachment, and unity, condensing into a single narrative the progress from self-willed striving to a complete, intuitive trust in God. As Zu'n-Nun grows into the knowledge and practice inti-mated in this opening encounter with the ways of God's friends, these themes are further inflected, elaborated, and intertwined. Here we can trace only a few of the patterns of association and contrast that extend from this nexus. The first is a pattern of narration. The conversion story is presented to us in Zu'n-Nun's own words as first-person narrative. The following anecdote—Zu'n-Nun and the pot of gold—is told in the third person by a narrator so omniscient that he is able to record the content of Zu'n-Nun's dreams. These points of view are the opposite of what we might expect; the fable-like conversion is presented as autobi-ography, and the private dream vision as public event. This manipula-tion of point of view provides an "objective" verification of Zu'n-Nun's burgeoning spiritual maturity. In rejecting the material riches of the pot of gold, Zu'n-Nun applies the lesson that he learned from the blind bird and is rewarded with the opening of the doors of divine knowledge, a

25

first hint of the theme of realization. The alternation of narrative perspective continues for the next four anecdotes, as other aspects of the conversion story receive a fuller airing. Zu'n-Nun undergoes his own temptation of the flesh in his conversation with the young maiden on the palace roof. His deferred meeting with the mountain-dwelling spiritual master is fulfilled in the person of the recluse who emerges from his cell once a year to cure the sick but who refers Zu'n-Nun to God for the cure of his inner illness. The sequence of tales culminates in a second dream vision—Zu'n-Nun's membership in the spiritual elite is projected back to the choices God gave humankind at the moment of creation in pre-eternity. *Seen* from various points of view, the implications and promise of the conversion tale extend into an increasingly complex network of meaning and association.

The story of Zu'n-Nun's spiritual education, with its surprising turn from the ascetic masters to the blind bird, finds its counterpoint in stories of his career as spiritual educator, teacher, and exemplar. His first student is his sister, who attains such spiritual realization under his influence that she brings down manna from heaven and disappears into the desert. Other disciples are more socially prominent, including a wealthy, young heir and an honored prince, who are both made to recognize the insignificance of material wealth and natural law in the face of the power of divine unity. Zu'n-Nun's most pious disciple, however, has undertaken every manner of devotional exercise without gaining God's favor. When Zu'n-Nun advises him to skip his prayers, the "poison cure" reduces both master and disciple to tears. But the divine rebuke that Zu'n-Nun receives for his unorthodox teachings is followed up in two tales in which roles are reversed and Zu'n-Nun unexpectedly finds himself the student. He is rightly castigated as a "worthless fool" by a nomadic Arab and a woman, two figures from the fringes of the social hierarchy who frequently serve as foils to the renowned saints in the *Memorial*. These stories are all the more powerful for their brevity and the fact that they are narrated by the chastised master himself in the first person.

Patterns of association based on a narrative motif like teaching are complemented by those based on imagery. The blind bird belongs to a cluster of images illustrating the often miraculous "secrets of unity." The jewel-bearing fish, the walking bench, the pills transformed into rubies—all show how divine power permeates material reality and how it can be channeled through God's friends. Another group of related images that gets its start in the story of Zu'n-Nun's conversion concerns physical and spiritual nourishment. The divine honey that sustains the fasting recluse on the mountaintop is echoed in a number of other tales in which food plays a prominent role. Zu'n-Nun's sister, for example, quotes the Qur'an concerning God's gift to the Israelites of manna and quails. Zu'n-Nun himself faces one of his greatest temptations in the humble form of vinegar beef stew. A baker even serves as an ignorant dupe when he misappraises a valuable ring and helps bring about the repentance of a skeptic. Zu'n-Nun's fast during his imprisonment brings him into contact with the sister of another pious exemplar, Beshr the Barefoot.

Zu'n-Nun is imprisoned under charges of heresy and is brought from Egypt to Baghdad to defend himself before the caliph. This story exemplifies another theme broached in the biography's introduction—the skepticism that Zu'n-Nun had to face throughout his life. Here we can also briefly note how patterns of theme and variation like those established within one biography are interwoven throughout the work. From Ja'far to Hallāj, God's friends repeatedly confront worldly power in the person of the caliph. This basic plot motif, however, is open to wide variation. The dragon that materializes before the eyes of the caliph Mansur is a visual manifestation of Ja'far's prophetic charisma. His display of power is almost casually arrogant yet surprisingly private. The onlookers are unaware of the dragon's presence until it is confessed by Mansur, a fact that confirms Ja'far's indifference to public, political dominion. By contrast, Zu'n-Nun's face-to-face meeting with the caliph Motavakkel is understated and almost anticlimactic. Emphasis falls instead on his meetings with common folk on his way to the prison. As we saw in the teaching stories, Zu'n-Nun learns from social outsiders (here an old woman and a water carrier) and teaches the power brokers. In realist fiction, characters are often individuated by idiosyncratic details of behavior and appearance. Though 'Attār is more interested in the exemplary than the particular, these varied and interlinked patterns of theme, image, and motif have a similar effect: they provide his literary portraits with a many-faceted and distinctive wholeness.

A crucial turning point in each biography in *Memorial of God's Friends* comes at the transition between the stories and the sayings and can be especially revealing of 'Attār method of disposition. In the case of Zu'n-Nun this transition begins subtly: "It is related that Zu'n-Nun fell sick." This sickness foreshadows Zu'n-Nun's final illness and death and aptly initiates the closure of the section. When Zu'n-Nun snaps back at his well-intentioned visitor, he condemns the comforting platitudes that mock a truly intimate relationship with God. But even for Zu'n-Nun, this intimacy can only go so far. In the brief snippet from one of his letters that follows, Zu'n-Nun asks to be protected behind "a veil of ignorance." From an aspirant to intuitive realization this is a startling request and a stark recognition of frightening and debilitating possibilities that are best left beyond mortal ken. These rather cryptic intimations are spelled out more fully in the closing anecdote. Zu'n-Nun's encounter with the Zoroastrian pulls together many of the strands that we have traced in earlier tales. Scattering millet for hungry birds gives a more plausible version of the miraculous feeding of the blind bird. As physical food is transformed into spiritual nourishment, it is Zu'n-Nun who offers up a platitude. He is once again instructed by an outsider, a non-Muslim this time, and as we saw in similar tales above, the story is related in the first person. The episode concludes with a moment of divine intuition: an "unseen voice" asserts the inability of human reason and logic to predict "the action of *the one who acts as he chooses.*" This moment of insight into the incomprehensible sets the stage for Zu'n-Nun's private devotions: the veil takes on a more typical meaning as a symbol of the intimacy of direct communion with the divine and the disgrace of public acclaim. This image is given yet another reading in the first entry in the extensive collection of Zu'n-Nun's aphorisms: "The most difficult of veils is the vision of the self."

For modern Western readers, whose literary expectations are based more on narrative forms like the novel and short story than on the gnomic and vatic pronouncements associated with poetry, it is easy to underestimate the crucial role sayings and aphorisms play in *Memorial of God's Friends*. 'Attār, however, leaves no doubt about his priorities:

Leaving aside the Qur'an and the traditions of the Prophet, there are no words loftier than those of the masters of the path—God have mercy upon them. Their words are the outcome of experience and inspiration, not the fruit of memorization and quotation. They come from contemplation, not commentary; from innermost self, not imitation; and from divine knowledge, not acquired learning. They come from ardor, not effort and from the universe of *my Lord instructed me,* not the world of *my father taught me,* for these masters are the heirs of the prophets—the blessings of the Compassionate be upon them all. I saw that a group of my friends took great delight in the words of this folk, and I too had a strong inclination to study their lives and sayings.

'Attār alludes to the narrative lives only as a passing afterthought, lavishing his praise instead on the words of "the masters of the path." From this perspective the stories are not an end in themselves but are valuable primarily because they serve to substantiate and explicate the sayings.

Like the anecdotes, the aphorisms are presented as discrete units within a carefully arranged sequence, organized in thematic clusters. (Such a paratactic arrangement of dicta is not unusual in world literature and can be found in works as diverse as *The Analects* of Confucius and the Gnostic *Gospel of Thomas.*) After beginning with the image of the veil of the self, 'Attār presents Zu'n-Nun's instructions on how it can be removed, placing together some twenty sayings on the actions that a seeker can take of his own volition. These include eating sparingly, asking forgiveness, following the example of the Prophet, and seclusion. The aphorisms, in other words, start where the story of Zu'n-Nun's conversion did, with affliction and self-denial, recalling the figure of the recluse and the motif of nourishment in the stories. The first turning point in the sequence of sayings comes with Zu'n-Nun's utterance "You must attain what you seek with the first step." 'Attār marks its importance by adding one of his rare commentaries and alluding to it again at the end of the section. The placement of this utterance casts a new light on the preceding teachings: even the most diligent asceticism leads nowhere unless it leads to a leap of awareness, to the loss of the self. This saying gives conceptual substance to the pivotal story of Zu'n-Nun's teaching career. The exercises and devotions of his disciple had become ends in themselves and required an unconventional "poison cure." Following this quantum step, the second cluster of aphorisms turns to revelation, loving unity, and realization. These themes

29

culminate in a set of three long utterances beginning with the caution "Beware, do not presume to realization." The reader pauses over another of 'Attār's commentaries, a verse of poetry, and Zu'n-Nun's quotation of one of the most famous of the mystical hadith of the Prophet. All three aphorisms point to the paradoxes of intuitive realization of the divine: it is a wisdom that cannot be claimed, awareness in bewilderment, a knowing that eludes self-consciousness. The disposition of aphorisms thus follows a thematic arc from detachment to unity first voiced in the introductory paragraph.

This pattern expands to incorporate an ever-widening network of concepts and themes in the following utterances. The next cluster begins with renunciation and devotion, self-discipline seen in the light of an ongoing relationship with God. To round out and summarize these ideas, 'Attār includes another long commentary on Zu'n-Nun's definition of watchfulness as a merger of the will of the believer with the will of God. Following the now well-established thematic progression, the fourth group of sayings takes up terms associated with a partaking in the intuitive knowledge of the sacred: ecstasy, trust, intimacy, acceptance, and certainty. The end of this thematic unit is signaled by an unusually long utterance. Zu'n-Nun opens with a startling metaphor— God is more obedient than any disciple. He goes on to explain that the Lord invariably responds to the efforts of anyone who turns to him. In the end, the piety inspired by fear yields to the realization of love and wisdom: "The heart of anyone who fears the mighty and glorious Lord melts away, and the Lord's love becomes firmly fixed in it, and his reason becomes perfect."

The progress from dread through repudiation of the world to unity and realization is recapitulated for a third time in a series of brief dialogues. A question-and-answer session marks the conclusion of the section of aphorisms in many of the biographies. The effect of introducing the dialogical form is twofold. First, the reader seems to become an active interlocutor in a final review of the principal themes of the biography. Second, in the course of a long series of aphorisms, the speaker's voice tends to become abstracted from biographical circumstances and individual identity; this detachment, indeed, gives the aphorisms much of their gnomic authority. However, as we return to the narrative, the speaker again becomes a character in the text interacting with other characters. Like the first-person narratives, Zu'n-Nun's exchanges with his anonymous questioners blur the line between story and saying. In the dispositions of text and character, words emerge as a form of action, and actions become as articulate as words.

The final part of the five-part structure of Zu'n-Nun's biography consists of the narrative of his death and burial. 'Attār again handles the transition with superb and unobtrusive artistry. The closing aphorism combines two distinct utterances. The first again takes up the intimate secrecy of the relationship between the Sufi and God: "The person furthest from the mighty and glorious Lord is the one who outwardly alludes to him the most." This saying recalls previous key points in the biography, such as Zu'n-Nun's rebuke of the well-meaning visitor to his sickbed or his dictum warning against the presumption of realization. Zu'n-Nun's own lack of presumption is evident in the confession of uncertainty in the second, concluding utterance: "For seventy years, I walked in unity, seclusion, detachment, and affirmation, and out of all of this I laid hold of nothing but a conjecture." The reappearance of the first-person pronoun completes the turn from gnomic utterance to biographical narrative. We have heard this note of bewilderment before, and it informs Zu'n-Nun's dying wish—to "know him, if only for a moment." As Zu'n-Nun goes behind the final veil, this moment of knowledge is withheld, as it must be, from onlookers and readers alike. We learn only of Zu'n-Nun's astonishment at "his benevolence." The end of the biography returns to its beginning. The key image of the blind bird that launched Zu'n-Nun on the mystical path now seems to take flight in the birds that spread their wings above his bier.

Memorial of God's Friends draws together a long and diverse tradition of Sufi history and biography into a comprehensive account of the development of Islamic spirituality. As the large number of surviving manuscripts suggests, the *Memorial* shaped how generations of readers understood Sufism and the lives of its formative exponents, and the work continues to exercise its influence today. Assessing 'Attār's literary achievement as a whole, Benedikt Reinert has written, "The thought-world depicted in 'Attār's works reflects the whole evolution of the Sufi movement in its experiential, speculative, practical, and educational-initiatory ramifications."[41] The same can be said of *Memorial of God's Friends* in particular. But it is not simply the scope and inclusiveness of this work that make the *Memorial* a classic of spiritual biography. 'Attār shapes his sources in a way that allows the reader to enter fully into his thought-world. In a prose that is a marvel of laconic eloquence and profundity, 'Attār creates a flexible literary form capable of embracing a wide range of religious experience from the most rigorous asceticism to the most visionary ecstasy. The patterns of repetition, variation, and placement, such as we see in the biography of Zu'n-Nun, give significant structure to the entire work and "set up a necessarily interpretative and critical chain of association in the reader's mind."[42] Principle, expression, and experience are united in literary portraits of these sects of one that are exemplary without being one-dimensional. The friends of God, in Emerson's words, converse with God and are spiritual influences "too great for fame." Perhaps the greatest accomplishment of *Memorial of God's Friends* is that it allows those "who disdain eloquence" to speak eloquently and crafts such artful and memorable biographies without "the exaggeration of the finite and selfish and the loss of the universal." It is 'Attār's artless artistry that distinguishes the *Memorial,* as the product of a poet's pen and makes it a monument of the Islamic spiritual tradition.

NOTES

On This Translation

1. Farid ad-Din 'Attār, *Muslim Saints and Mystics: Episodes from the Tadhkirat al-Auliya'* (*"Memorial of the Saints"*), trans. A.J. Arberry (Chicago: University of Chicago Press, 1966). There are numerous translations of the *Memorial* into various Turkish languages: see Hellmut Ritter, "Philologika XIV: Farīduddīn 'Aṭṭār II," in *Oriens* 11 (1958): 62–76. The Uighur version was published in Paris in 1889 with an accompanying French translation, which was later published separately as *Le Mémorial des Saints,* trans. A. Paret de Courteille (Paris: Editions du Seuil, 1976). I have not been able to examine what is, to the best of my knowledge, the only complete translation in any European language, the Swedish translation of E. Hermelin published in Stockholm in 1931–32.

2. Michael A. Sells, *Early Islamic Mysticism: Sufi, Qur'an, Mi'raj, Poetic and Theological Writings* (New York: Paulist Press, 1996), 7.

3. This usage is becoming increasingly widespread: see, for example, recent translations of the writings of the Christian mystic Meister Eckhart by Oliver Davies (New York: Penguin Books, 1994) and by Edmund Colledge and Bernard McGinn (Mahwah, NJ: Paulist Press, 1981).

4. Farid ad-Din 'Attār, *Tazkerat al-owliyā'*, ed. Mohammad Este'lāmi (Tehran: Zavvār, 1967). The bases of this edition are manuscripts dated 1292 (692 AH) and 1302 (701 AH). For a listing of the large number of surviving manuscripts, see Ritter, "Philologika XIV," 63–68, and C.A. Storey, *Persian Literature: A Bio-bibliographic Survey* (London: Luzac, 1927-): 1, pt. 2, 930–33.

5. Farid ad-Din 'Attār, *Tazkerat al-owliyā'*, ed. Reynold A. Nicholson, 2 vols. (London: Luzac, 1905–07). This text was extensively revised and its spelling modernized by Mohammad Khān Qazvini (Tehran: Kitābkhāna-ye Markazi, 1957).

6. Bābak Ahmadi, *Chahār gozāresh az Tazkerat al-owliyā'-e 'Attār* (Tehran: Nashr-e Markaz, 1997), 118.

7. Sells, *Early Islamic Mysticism,* 151–70.

8. Plotinus, *The Enneads,* trans. Stephen MacKenna, abridged with an introduction by John Dillon (London: Penguin Books, 1991), xxviii.

Translator's Introduction

1. *EI²*, "Taḏhkira. 2. In Persian literature" (J.T.P. de Bruijn).

2. Michael Sells, *Approaching the Qur'ān: The Early Revelations* (Ashland, OR: White Cloud Press, 1999), 40.

3. Muhammad Isa Waley, "Contemplative Disciplines in Early Persian Sufism," in *The Heritage of Sufism*, vol. 1, *Classical Persian Sufism from Its Origins to Rumi* (700–1300), ed. Leonard Lewisohn (Oxford: Oneworld, 1999), 497–548.

4. See *'Umar ibn al-Fāriḍ: Sufi Verse and Saintly Life*, trans. Th. Emil Homerin (New York: Paulist Press, 2001), 30–34.

5. For a more detailed analysis of the scope of the term *valilowliyā'*, see Bernd Radtke, "The Concept of *Wilāya* in Early Sufism," in *Heritage of Sufism*, vol. 1: 483–496, and his entry in *EI²*, "Walī. 1. General Survey."

6. Michael Cooperson, *Classical Arabic Biography: The Heirs of the Prophets in the Age of al-Ma'mūn* (Cambridge: Cambridge University Press, 2000), 141 n147.

7. Farid ad-Din 'Aṭṭār, *Divān*, ed. Taqi Tafazzoli, 4th ed. (Tehran: 'Elmi va Farhangi, 1987), 592–94.

8. Nur ad-Din 'Abd ar-Rahmān Jāmi, *Nafahat al-ons men hazarāt al-qods*, ed. Mahmud 'Ābadi (Tehran: Ettelā'āt, 1991), 597.

9. Dowlatshāh Samarqandi, *Tazkerat ash-sho'arā*, ed. Mohammad Ramazāni (Tehran: Khāvar, 1959), 145.

10. Franklin D. Lewis, *Rumi—Past and Present, East and West: The Life, Teaching and Poetry of Jalāl al-Din Rumi* (Oxford: Oneworld, 2000), 64–65.

11. The foundations of the modern critical investigation of 'Aṭṭār were established by Sa'id Nafisi, *Jostoju dar ahvāl va āsār-e Farid ad-Din 'Aṭṭār* (Tehran: Eqbāl, 1941), and Badi' az-Zamān Foruzānfar, *Sharh-e ahvāl va naqd va tahlil-e āsār-e Sheykh Farid ad-Din Mohammad 'Aṭṭār-e Nishāpuri* (Tehran: Anjoman-e Āsār-e Melli, 1961). The results of these investigations form the basis of the article in *EIr*, "'Aṭṭār, Shaikh Farīd al-Dīn" by Benedikt Reinert, the single best source in English on the poet's life. More recently, Mohammad-Rezā Shafi'i Kadkani's *Zabur-e Pārsi: negāhi be-zendagi va ghazalhā-ye 'Aṭṭār* (Tehran: Āgāh, 1999) has further refined the findings of these scholars and opened up several new avenues of investigation.

12. Shafi'i Kadkani, *Zabur-e Pārsi*, 62–69.

13. The fullest study of 'Aṭṭār's poetic works remains Hellmut Ritter, *Das Meer der Seele* (Leiden: E.J. Brill, 1978). This book has now been translated into English as *The Ocean of the Soul: Man, the World and God in the Stories of Farīd al-Dīn 'Aṭṭār*, trans. John O'Kane with editorial assistance of Bernd Radtke (Leiden: E. J. Brill, 2003).

14. Also known as *Maqāmāt-e toyur*, this work has been frequently translated into English and other European languages. The best translation available is Farid al-Din 'Attār, *The Conference of the Birds*, trans. Afkham Darbandi and Dick Davis (New York: Penguin Books, 1984).

15. Shafi'i Kadkani argues on philological and stylistic grounds that the courtly romance usually known as *Khosrow-nāma* was originally entitled *Gol va Hormoz* and is not a product of 'Attār's pen. The *Khosrow-nāma* properly attributed to 'Attār is, in fact, the poem now called *Elāhi-nāma*. *See* Farid ad-Din 'Attār, *Mokhtār-nāma*, ed. Mohammad-Rezā Shafi'i Kadkani, 2nd ed. (Tehran: Sokhan, 1996), 34–59.

16. For a lineated prose translation of this work in English, see Farid ad-Din 'Attār, *The Ilāhī-nāma or Book of God*, trans. John Andrew Boyle (Manchester, UK: Manchester University Press, 1976).

17. Farid ad-Din 'Attār, *Elāhi-nāma*, ed. Hellmut Ritter (reprint edition, Tehran: Tus, 1989; Istanbul, 1940), 253–54. This passage is also translated in 'Attār, The *Ilāhī-nāma*, trans. Boyle, 235–36.

18. For other stories from *Memorial of God's Friends* included in the *Elāhi-nāma*, see 'Attār, *Ilāhi-nāma*, trans. Boyle, 58, 298–99 (Ebrāhim ebn Adham), 110–11, 272–73, 300–31, 346–47 (Bāyazid), 115–16, 153 (Rābe'a), 165, 173–75 (Hasan of Basra), and 168–69 (Ebn al-Mobārak). Stories from the *Memorial* are also incorporated into *Manteq at-Teyr;* see 'Attār, *Conference of the Birds*, trans. Davis, 76, 145, 151 (Bāyazid), 86–87 (Rābe'a), 99–100 (Mālek-e Dinār), 114 (Hallāj); 135–36 (Beshr the Barefoot), and 137–38 (Ebn al-Mobārak).

19. On Nishapur, see *EI²*, s.v. "Nīshāpūr" (E. Honigmann-[C. E. Bosworth]), and W. Barthold, *An Historical Geography of Iran*, trans. Svat Soucek (Princeton, NJ: Princeton University Press, 1984), 95–102.

20. As Shafi'i Kadkani has noted, there was little mystical poetry of note written during the decades immediately before 'Attār began writing. One early source identifies the little-known poet Shekar as 'Attār's literary mentor (*Zabur-e Pārsi*, 48–53).

21. On Abu Sa'id, see *EIr*, s.v. "Abū Sa'īd ebn Abī'l-Keyr" (G. Böwering). Shafi'i Kadkani has recently proposed a possible spiritual lineage that would link 'Attār directly with Abu Sa'id (*Zabur-e Pārsi*, 70–83).

22. For a complete translation of Abu Sa'id's biography, *Asrār al-towhid*, in English, see Mohammad Ebn-e Monavvar, *The Secrets of God's Mystical Oneness*, trans. John O'Kane (Costa Mesa, CA: Mazda, 1992).

23. On Ansāri, see *EIr*, s.v. "'Abdullāh al-Ansārī" (S. de Laugier de Beaureceuil). For a translation of Ansāri's *Monājāt* in English, see: Kwaja Abdullah Ansari, *Intimate Conversations*, trans. Wheeler M. Thackston, with

Ibn 'Ata'llah, *The Book of Wisdom*, trans. Victor Danner (New York: Paulist Press, 1978).

24. On the development of Persian mystical poetry in general, see J. T. P. de Bruijn, *Persian Sufi Poetry: An Introduction to the Mystical Use of Classical Poems* (Surrey: Curzon, 1997), which contains discussions of all of 'Aṭṭār's poetic works. Sanā'i is the subject of two superb, recent scholarly studies: J. T. P. de Bruijn, *Of Piety and Poetry: The Interaction of Religion and Literature in the Life and Works of Ḥakīm Sanā'ī of Ghazna* (Leiden: E.J. Brill, 1983); and Franklin D. Lewis, "Reading, Writing and Recitation: Sanā'i and the Origins of the Persian Ghazal" (PhD dissertation, University of Chicago, 1995).

25. *See* 'Aṭṭār, *Mokhtār-nāma*, 3.

26. For the beginnings of such a study, see the list and evaluation of 'Aṭṭār's possible sources, in 'Aṭṭār, *Tazkerat*, ed. Este'lāmi, *davāzdah-bist va yak*. To Este'lāmi's list we should probably add Ghazzāli's *Kimiyā as-sa'ādat* and Sahlaji's *Kitāb an-nur men kalemāt Abi Tayfur*.

27. On al-Solami, see *EI²*, s.v. "al-Sulamī" (G. Böwering).

28. On Qosheyri, see *EI²*, s.v. "al-Ḳushayrī" (H. Halm). Substantial portions of Qosheyri's *Resāla* have been translated into English. *See* Sells, *Early Islamic Mysticism*, 97–150 (chapter 3 of the treatise on mystical expressions), and al-Qushayri, *Principles of Sufism*, trans. B. R. von Schlegell (Berkeley, CA: Mizan Press, 1990), which covers chapter 4 to the end of the work. The biographical portion of the *Resāla* has not yet been translated into English.

29. On Hojviri, see *EI²*, s.v. "Hudjwīrī." For an English translation, see 'Alī ibn 'Uṯmān Hujwiri, *The Kashf al-maḥjūb: the Oldest Persian Treatise on Ṣūfism*, trans. Reynold A. Nicholson (Leyden: Luzac, 1911).

30. André Lefevere, *Translation, Rewriting, and the Manipulation of Literary Fame* (New York: Routledge, 1992), 1–10. I have examined some of the issues in 'Aṭṭār's rewriting of earlier sources in more technical detail in Paul Losensky, "The Creative Compiler: The Art of Rewriting in 'Aṭṭār's *Tazkirat al-Awliyā'*," in *The Necklace of the Pleiades: Studies in Persian Literature Presented to Heshmat Moayyad on his 80th Birthday*, ed. Franklin Lewis and Sunil Sharma (Amsterdam and West Lafayette, IN: Rozenberg Publishers and Purdue University Press, 2007): 107–19.

31. Abu 'Abd ar-Raḥmān as-Sulami, *Kitāb Ṭabaqāt aṣ-ṣūfiya*, ed. Johannes Pedersen (Leiden: E.J. Brill, 1960), 229–30.

32. Shafi'i Kadani, *Zabur-e Pārsi*, 263.

33. The twenty-five additional biographies found in some later manuscripts (and as an appendix in the print editions) are the work of another hand. For arguments concerning their authenticity, see 'Aṭṭār, *Tazkerat*, ed. Este'lāmi, *bist va panj-bist va hasht*.

NOTES

34. Ahmad Mahdavi Dāmghāni, "Nazari be-'adad-e 73 dar hadis-e 'tafriqa,'" in *Hāsel-e awqāt: majmu'a'i az maqālāt,* ed. Sayyed 'Ali Mohammad Sajjādi (Tehran: Sorush, 2002): 615–622.

35. Abū Dawud as-Sijistānī, *Sunan Abī Dāwud,* ed. Mohammad Mohyi ad-Dīn 'Abd al-Ḥamīd ([s.l.], Dār Iḥyā' as-Sunna an-Nabawīya, 1970), 4: 197–98 (no. 4596).

36. Cooperson, *Classical Arabic Biography,* 13–16.

37. I have attempted to mimic these rhymes in my translation when possible without distorting the meaning of the text; see, for example, the beginning of the biographies of Mālek-e Dinār, Habib-e 'Ajami, and Ebrāhim ebn Adham.

38. *See* Michael Sells's introduction to my translation of Rābe'a's biography in Sells, *Early Islamic Mysticism,* 151–54.

39. For a detailed analysis of the biographies of Dāvud-e Tā'i and Abu'l-Hoseyn Nuri, see Paul Losensky, "Words and Deeds: Message and Structure in 'Aṭṭār's *Tadhkirat al-awliyā',*" in *Farid al-Din Attar and the Persian Sufi Tradition,* ed. Leonard Lewisohn and Charles Shackle, 75–92 (London: I.B. Tauris, 2006).

40. The biography of 'Ali-ye Sahl is discussed at greater length in Losensky, "The Creative Compiler."

41. *EIr,* s.v. "'Aṭṭār, Farīd al-Dīn" (B. Reinert).

42. Cooperson, *Classical Arabic Biography,* 192.

MEMORIAL OF GOD'S FRIENDS

Author's Introduction

Praise be to God—generous with the finest of favors, benefactor of the greatest of gifts, praised at the loftiest summits of honor and grandeur, adored with the most beautiful of adorations from the depths of the earth to the heights of the heavens, possessor of majesty, might, and magnificence, of glory, sovereign right, and resplendence, the one on high who is veiled from the eyes of onlookers and from the vision of the discerning by the lights of splendor, sanctity, and praise, the one here below who lures the gaze of those who are consumed in the fire of distress.

He joins the final vision of those who plunge into the depths of the sea of his unity to the extinction of the self. He blends the noble extinction of those who are immersed in the profundity of his radiant proximity with genuine subsistence in him. In the glory of poverty in him, he enriches them beyond the humiliating reliance on things. He grants them success in offering praise for what they have received from the treasure house of blessings. Through passing away, he frees them to abide, and through abiding, to pass away. Then they plunge into the light of the extinction of extinction and are purified of the whim of craving. They dismount with intimacy in the courtyard of sanctity, bidding farewell to the extinction of extinction. Eminent among the masses, towering over creation, they withdraw from the delusions of error and the wavering shadows into the true and perfect light.

We praise him for protecting us from the deceit of anyone who opposes us concerning him and for defending us from the evil of anyone who is hostile toward us in his heart or who injures us with his tongue and for distracting from us everything that distracts us from him and for uniting us with everything that unites us with him and for making us his devoted servants and for honoring us with his sublime words and his noble book and for making us followers of his beloved Mohammad and then counting us too among his lovers.

FARID AD-DIN 'AT̲T̲ĀR'S MEMORIAL OF GOD'S FRIENDS

We bear witness that there is no god but God, the One—he has no partner who is his equal and he has no peer who is his like. If we look to the attributes of divinity, there is no God but him, and if we ponder existence, nothing exists but him.

We bear witness that Mohammad is his servant, his messenger, his Prophet, and his true friend. He sent him in truth to all creation. From his lofty position, he untied the knots that bind those who deviate in error. With his divine ordinance, he reduced the ranks of disgrace and humiliation. With his light, he extinguished the fire of sin. He settled his companions in the abode of guidance. He illuminated the hearts of the rightly guided with the glistening pearls of faith. He made them fit to acquire the glorious treasures of certainty. He made them understand the obscure secrets of the prophets. He singled out the elect and the pious among their followers—those who have wiped the dust of the two worlds from their hands, those who have dismissed from their hearts any concern for the comforts of this world or the next—by means of the hidden and unseen evidence of that which the eye's gaze does not perceive and to which the sun of intellect and the stars of speculation do not ascend. He allowed their hearts to attain that which was revealed by their furthest quests and utmost ambitions. He dispelled the clouds of sorrow from their innermost selves by that which shone upon them from their utmost goals. He purified their spirits of blemished lights and murky darknesses by the lights of the holy revelations that he possesses. May God bless him and his family and his companions.

After him, no sun of favor will rise in the East of divine grace, and no distant evening star will set below the horizons of banishment. No lover will be afflicted with remoteness. No guiding bolt of lightning will flash from a solicitous cloud. No truthful speaker will utter a word of love. No passionate step will stir in the desert wastes of ecstasy. May God grant him peace.

Leaving aside the Qur'an and the traditions of the Prophet, there are no words loftier than those of the masters of the path—God have mercy upon them. Their words are the outcome of experience and inspiration, not the fruit of memorization and quotation. They come from contemplation, not commentary; from the innermost self, not imitation; and from divine knowledge, not acquired learning. They come from ardor, not effort, and from the universe of *my Lord instructed me,* not the world of *my father taught me,*[1] for these masters are the heirs of the prophets—the blessings of the Compassionate be upon them all. I saw that a group of my friends took great delight in the words of this folk, and I too had a strong inclination to study their lives and sayings. If I had collected everything, it would have gotten too long. I gathered some for my friends and family—and for you too, if you are among this intimate company.

If anyone wants more than this, many of these sayings will be found in books by early and recent members of this clan. Let him look for them there. If a seeker is seeking a full commentary on the sayings of this folk, tell him to study these books: *Commentary of the Heart, Unveiling of the Secrets,* and *Knowledge of the Self.*[2] It is our opinion that none of the sayings of this clan will remain obscure to him, except what God wills. If I had given a commentary on them here, it would have required a thousand sheets of paper. Taking the path of brevity and abridgment, however, is sound tradition: as the Messenger of God (may God bless him and give him peace) boasted, *"I was given all the words, and the word was abbreviated for me."*[3] I have also omitted the chains of transmission. There were sayings that were related by one sheikh in one book and by one sheikh in another. There were also additions to the stories and differing anecdotes. I exercised caution to the best of my ability.

Another reason for not giving commentaries is that I did not consider it proper to put my words in among theirs and did not find it to my taste. Nevertheless, in a few places remarks have been made to ward off the fancies of the vulgar and the uninitiated. Another reason is that the most suitable thing for anyone who happens to need a commentary is for him to look closely at the words of God's friends and interpret them again.

Another reason is that the friends of God are different: some are adherents of mystical realization and some of proper conduct; some are adherents of love and some of unity; and some are all of these. Some are self-possessed, and some are ecstatics. If I had given a commentary on them one by one, the book would have gone beyond the limits of brevity. And if I had given notices on the prophets and Mohammad's companions and his family, it would have required another, separate book. What capacity does the tongue have to describe a people who are mentioned by God and the Prophet and praised by the Qur'an and the traditions? That realm is another universe, another world. The prophets and Mohammad's companions and his family are three groups. God willing, a book will be collected memorializing them, so a perfume compounded of these three will remain as a memento of the apothecary 'Attār.

I had several motives for collecting this book. The first motive was to please the brethren of the faith who implored me for it. Another was to leave some memento of myself behind, so that whoever reads this book will find some comfort in it and will remember me well in his prayers: perhaps I will be comforted in the grave for having comforted him. So it was that when Yahyā ebn 'Emād[4]—the imam of Herat and teacher of Sheikh 'Abdollāh Ansāri— passed away, someone saw him in a dream and asked, "What did the mighty and glorious Lord do with you?"

He answered, "God spoke to me: 'Yahyā, I had some harsh things to say to you, but one day you were praising us at a prayer meeting, and one of our friends was passing by. He heard what you were saying and had a moment of rapture. I forgave you to gratify him. Had it not been for that, you would have seen what I would have done with you.'"

Another motive is that they asked Sheikh Abu 'Ali Daqqāq[5] (God have mercy upon him), "Are there any advantages to listening to the words of true believers when we cannot act on them?"

"Yes," he answered, "there are two advantages. The first is that if the person is a seeker, his aspiration will be strengthened, and he will seek further. The second is that if he perceives any pride in himself, it will be broken. He will expel pretense from his mind. His good will seem bad, and if he is not blind, he will contemplate himself."

As Sheikh Mahfuz[6] (God have mercy upon him) said, "Do not weigh people according to your own standards, but weigh yourself according to the standards of the men of the path, so you will know their credit and your own bankruptcy."

Another motive is that they asked Joneyd (God's mercy be upon him), "What advantage does the disciple gain from these stories and anecdotes?"

"The words of God's friends," Joneyd said, "are one of the armies of the mighty and glorious Lord. If the disciple's heart is broken, he will be strengthened and aided by that army." The proof of these words is that the Real most high states, *"We make your heart firm with all the stories of the prophets that we relate to you."* [11:120][7]

Another motive is that the Master of the Prophets (peace and blessing and salutations be upon him) states, *"Mercy descends when one recalls the pious."* If someone sets a table that mercy rains down upon, perhaps he will not be turned away from it empty-handed. Another motive is that perhaps the succor of their holy spirits will come to this destitute man and cast a propitious shadow over him before his final day.

Another motive is that I considered the words of God's friends to be the finest words after the Qur'an and the hadith and considered all their words to be a commentary upon the Qur'an and the hadith. I threw myself into this task so that if I am not one of God's friends, at least I might make myself resemble them: *"Whoever imitates a people is one of them."*[8] So it was that Joneyd (God's mercy be upon him) said, "Regard pretenders kindly, for they are seeking certainty. Kiss their feet, for if they had not had high aspiration, they would have pretended to something else."

Another motive is that it is necessary to master Arabic vocabulary, grammar, and syntax to understand the Qur'an and the traditions. Most people were unable to grasp a portion of their meaning. These sayings are a commentary on them, and both the common people and the elite can share in them. Although most of them were in Arabic, I translated them into Persian, so everyone could be included.

Another motive is that I see plainly that when anyone says anything against you, you seek revenge and hold a grudge against him for years on account of that one word. When an idle word has such an effect on your soul, a true word can have an effect a thousand times greater, even if you are unaware of it. So it was that they asked Imam 'Abd ar-Rahmān Akkāf[9] (God's mercy be upon him), "Does the Qur'an have any effect on someone who reads it without knowing what he is reading?"

He replied, "Medicine has an effect on someone who takes it without knowing what he is taking. How can the Qur'an fail to have an effect? Yes, it has a powerful effect." And how much more so when someone knows what he is reading!

Another motive is that my heart would not allow me to speak or listen to anything but these words, except reluctantly and by necessity or compulsion. As a result, I took on the responsibility of relating the words of God's friends to the people of the age, so that I might perhaps drink a cup with them from this table. So it is that Sheikh Abu 'Ali Seyāh[10] (God's mercy be upon him) says, "I have two desires. One is to hear one of God's words. The other is to meet one of his people." He added, "I am an illiterate man. I can't write or read anything. I need someone to speak his words, and I will listen. Or I will speak, and he will listen. If he will not converse in paradise, then Abu 'Ali is through with paradise."

Another motive is that they asked Imam Yusof of Hamadan (God have mercy upon him), "When this age passes, and this clan withdraws behind the veil of concealment, what will we do to remain spiritually sound?"

"Read eight pages of their sayings everyday," he said. Thus I considered it my utmost obligation to compose some daily prayers for the negligent.

Another motive is that from childhood on, for no apparent reason, love for this clan has welled up in my soul, and their words have always brought joy to my heart. In the hope that *"a man will be with the one he loves,"*[11] I have set forth their words to the best of my ability. This is an era when this way of speaking has disappeared entirely. Pretenders have emerged in the guise of spiritual folk, and people of the heart have become as rare as the philosopher's stone. As Joneyd said to Shebli (God have mercy on them both), "If you find anyone in all the world who agrees with one word you say, stick close to him."

Another motive is that when I saw that an age has come when *good is evil* and when evildoers have forgotten the righteous, I prepared a collection of the biographies of the friends of God and named it *Memorial of God's Friends,* so that the wretched of this age will not forget this fortunate folk and will seek out recluses and hermits and take delight in them so that by the gentle breeze of their good fortune, they might be united with eternal happiness.

Another motive is that these are the best of words in several regards. First, they make people's hearts cold to this world. Second, they make the mind dwell continually on the afterworld. Third, they bring out the love of the Real in people's hearts. Fourth, when people hear this sort of discourse, they begin to prepare provisions for the endless road. So, in accordance with these principles, collecting such words is one of our obligations. It can be truly said that there is nothing better than this book in creation, for the words of God's friends are a commentary on the Qur'an and the traditions, which are the finest of all words.

It may be said that this is a book that will turn weaklings into men and turn men into lions and turn lions into paragons and turn paragons into pain itself. How can it fail to turn them into pain itself? Whoever reads this book and reflects on it as he should will become aware of what pain there was in the souls of God's friends to bring forth such deeds and words like this from their hearts.

One day I came to visit Imam Majd ad-Din Mohammad of Khwārazm[12] (God's mercy be upon him). I saw him weeping. "I hope it's for the best," I said.

He replied, "Here's to the commanders who have lived among this people! They are like the prophets (peace and blessing be upon them). As Mohammad said, *'The learned among my people are like the prophets among the Israelites.'*" Majd ad-Din continued, "I am weeping because last night I prayed, 'Lord, your actions are inexplicable. Make me one of this folk or one of their onlookers, for I cannot tolerate any other group.' I am weeping—perhaps my prayer has been answered."

Another motive is that on the morrow of the resurrection they might look on the work of this weak man and intercede on his behalf and will not turn me away in despair, even if I am all skin and bone, like the dog with the companions at the cave.[13]

It is related that Jamāl of Mosul[14] (God's mercy be upon him) suffered and agonized and squandered his property and reputation so he could obtain a place for his grave opposite the area of the cemetery of the Master of the Prophets (peace and blessing be upon him). Then he gave this final testament: "Write on my tombstone: *Their dog stretches his front paws across the threshold.*" [18:18]

O Lord, a dog took a few steps following after your friends, and you made it part of their affair. I too claim the friendship of your friends and tie myself to their stirrups and occupy myself with their words and utter them again. O Lord! O King! Although I am unworthy of these words and know that I am among the least of the travelers on this path, still I love their sayings and stories, their mysterious and allusive teachings. By your unchanging oneness, by the souls of your prophets, messengers, and archangels, by your majesty's friends, elders, and scholars, do not veil this weak stranger from this company. Let this book be the reason that you bring him near your presence and not the reason you cast him into the far abyss. *Truly you have the power to answer this prayer.*

∽ 1 ∽

Ja'far as-Sādeq

The sultan of the people of Mohammad, the proof of prophetic argument, the trustworthy scholar, the world of verity, the lifeblood of God's friends, the heartbeat of the prophets, transmitter of 'Ali's teachings, heir of the Prophet, the knowing lover, Ebn Mohammad Ja'far as-Sādeq—may God be pleased with him.

We had said that if we were to memorialize the prophets, Mohammad's companions, and his family, it would require a separate book. This book will consist of the biographies of the masters of this clan, who lived after them. But as a blessing, let us begin with Sādeq (may God be pleased with him) for he too lived after them. Since he among the Prophet's descendants said the most about the path and many traditions have come down from him, I shall say a few words about this esteemed man, for they are all as one. When he is remembered, it is the remembrance of them all. Do you not see that the people who follow his school follow the school of the Twelve Imams? In other words, the one is twelve, and the twelve are one.

If I try to describe even his attributes, my words will not come out right, for without exaggeration, his expressions and allusions in all branches of knowledge were perfect. He was the exemplar for all the masters, and everyone relied on him. He was the perfect model, the sheikh of all the men of God, and the imam of all the followers of Mohammad. He was both the leader of the adherents of intuition and the guide of the adherents of love. He took precedence among the believers and was honored by the ascetics as well. He was outstanding in recording the inner truths and without peer in the fine points of the inner mysteries of revelation and exegesis. He handed down many great sayings from Bāqer (may God be pleased with him).[1]

I am amazed by those people who have the idea that there is some difference between the followers of the tradition and consensus and the followers of the Prophet's family, for in reality the Sunnis are followers of the Prophet's family. I cannot believe that anyone is caught up in this vain fancy. I believe that anyone who has faith in Mohammad (peace and blessing be upon him and his family), but has no faith in his offspring and family really has no faith in Mohammad (peace and blessing be upon him). It reached the point that the great Imam Shāfe'i (God's mercy be upon him) loved the family of the Prophet so much that they accused him of heresy and imprisoned him. He composed a poem on this topic, and here is one verse from it:

If love of the Prophet's family is heresy,
then let all men and jinn bear witness—I am a heretic!

If acknowledging the Prophet's family and companions is not one of the fundamentals of the faith, you will accept a great deal of useless and unnecessary foolishness. If you acknowledge even this, there is no harm in it; indeed, it is only just that when you acknowledge Mohammad as the king of this world and the next, you must acknowledge the position of his viziers and of his companions and of his descendants in order to be a Sunni of pure faith. Do not take sides against anyone close to the king, except for just cause.

So it was that they asked Abu Hanifa (God's mercy be upon him), "Who was the noblest of the Prophet's followers (peace and blessing be upon him)?"

"Among the elders," he replied, "Abu Bakr and 'Omar; among the young men, 'Osmān and 'Ali; among his daughters, Fātema; and among his wives, 'Ā'esha (may God be pleased with them all)."[2]

47

It is related that one night the Caliph Mansur[3] said to his vizier, "Go, bring Sādeq, so we can put him to death."

The vizier said, "He lives in an out-of-the-way place and has retired from the world. He occupies himself by serving God and has renounced all interest in worldly power. He causes no trouble for the Commander of the Faithful. What use is there in harming him?"

Whatever the vizier said, it did no good. He left. Mansur told his guards, "When Sādeq comes and I take off my hat, kill him."

The vizier brought Sādeq in. Mansur immediately jumped up, ran toward Sādeq, set him on his throne, and knelt down before him on both knees. The guards were shocked. Mansur then asked, "What can I do for you?"

Sādeq said, "You can stop summoning me before you and let me go back to serving the mighty and glorious Lord."

Mansur then gave an order and sent Sādeq on his way with all due honor. At that moment, Mansur began to tremble. He lowered his head and fainted. He was unconscious for three days, or according to one account, until the time for three daily prayers had elapsed. When he came to, the vizier asked, "What happened to you?"

"When Sādeq came through the door," Mansur said, "I saw a dragon—it put one lip under the throne and the other above. The dragon said, 'If you harm him, I will swallow you up along with this throne.' I was so afraid of the dragon that I didn't know what I was saying. I apologized to Sādeq and fainted."

It is related that Dāvud-e Tā'i once came to see Sādeq and said, "Descendant of the Prophet, give me counsel, for my heart has grown dark."

"Dāvud," said Sādeq, "you are the ascetic of the age. What need do you have of my advice?"

"Offspring of the Prophet," said Dāvud, "you are superior to all creatures, and it is your duty to give counsel to all."

Sādeq said, "Dāvud, I fear that at the resurrection, my forefather will lay hold of me and ask, 'Why didn't you live up to your duties in following me?' This affair has nothing to do with sound lineage or powerful ancestors. This affair has to do with conducting oneself in a way that is worthy of the presence of the Real."

Dāvud wept and said, "O Lord, when one whose clay is kneaded with the water of prophecy, one whose forefather is the Messenger and whose foremother is the chaste Fātema, when one like this is so bewildered, how can Dāvud be pleased with his own conduct?"

It is related that Sādeq was seated with his associates one day. "Come," he said, "let us make a pact and take an oath that whoever among us is saved on the resurrection will intercede for all."

"Descendant of the Prophet," they said, "what need do you have of our intercession? Your forefather is the intercessor for all creatures."

Sādeq replied, "Because of my deeds, I will be ashamed to look my forefather in the face at the resurrection."

It is related that Sādeq secluded himself for a time and did not appear in public. Sofyān-e Sowri came to the door of his house and said, "The people are deprived of the benefits of your inspirations. Why have you withdrawn from the world?"

Sādeq replied, "The present looks like this: *The age has decayed, and brothers have changed.*" And he recited these verses:

> *Faithfulness has fled, as flee the fleeting yesterdays,*
> *and people are torn between their fancies and desires.*
> *They make displays of love and faithfulness,*
> *but their hearts are dens of scorpions.*

It is related that Sādeq was seen wearing an expensive fur coat. Someone said, "Descendant of the Prophet, this is not the sort of clothing your family wears."

Sādeq took the man's hand and put it inside the sleeve of his coat. He was wearing sack cloth that chafed the man's hand. "The one is for the people," Sādeq said, "and the other is for the Real."

It is related that they said to Sādeq, "You have all the virtues, asceticism, and inner generosity. You're the apple of your family's eye. But you're very highhanded."

"I'm not highhanded," Sādeq said. "Rather it's the loftiness of the One on high. When I rose above my haughtiness, his loftiness came and took its place. One should not be high-handed because of haughtiness, but should be high-reaching because of his highness."

It is related that Sādeq asked Abu Hanifa, "Who is wise?"

"One who distinguishes between good and evil," Abu Hanifa said.

"Even a beast can distinguish between those who beat it and those who feed it," Sādeq answered.

Abu Hanifa asked, "In your opinion, who is wise?"

"One who distinguishes between two goods and two evils so he can choose the better of two goods and pick out of the lesser of two evils."

It is related that a purse of gold had been stolen from someone. The man grabbed a hold of Sādeq and said, "You stole it!" even though he did not recognize him.

"How much was it?" Sādeq asked.

"A thousand dinars."

Sādeq brought the man home with him and gave him a thousand dinars. The man later recovered his gold and brought a thousand dinars back to Sādeq. "I made a mistake," he said.

"We do not take back anything we have given," Sādeq replied.

Later the man asked someone, "Who is he?"

"Ja'far as-Sādeq."

He turned away ashamed.

It is related that one day Sādeq was going down the road alone, saying, "God, God."

Down on his luck, a man walked along behind him, saying, "God, God."

"God," Sādeq said, "I have no cloak. God, I have no shirt."

A suit of clothes appeared on the spot, and Sādeq put them on.

The hapless man went up and said, "Mister, I was saying God along with you. Give your old ones to me."

This pleased Sādeq, and he gave the man his old clothes.

It is related that someone came to see Sādeq and said, "Show me God."

Sādeq said, "Come on, haven't you heard that Moses was told, '*You shall not see me?*'" [7:143].

"Yes, but this is the community of Mohammad. One calls out, '*My heart sees my Lord,*' and another exclaims, '*I do not worship a lord I do not see.*'"

"Tie him up and throw him in the Tigris," Sādeq said.

They tied him up and threw him in the Tigris. The water pulled him under and tossed him back up again.

"O Son of the Messenger! Help! Help!"

"Water, pull him under!" said Sādeq.

The water pulled him under and tossed him back up.

"O Son of the Messenger of God! Help! Help!"

Once again Sādeq said, "Water, pull him under!"

It pulled him under and tossed him back up like this several times. Having completely given up hope in creatures, this time the man said, *"O God! Help! Help!"*

"Pull him out," Sādeq said. They pulled him out and made him sit for a while until he recovered. Then they asked him, "Did you see the Lord?"

"As long as I appealed to another," the man said, "I was veiled. When I despaired and sought refuge in him completely, a window was opened within my heart. I looked into it. I saw what I was searching for. Until there was despair, it was not there. *Who answers the despairing when they call on him?"* [27: 61].

Sādeq said, "As long as you kept saying 'Sādeq,' you were lying. Now take good care of that window through which the world of the mighty and glorious Lord descended. Whoever says that the mighty and powerful Lord is over something or in something or from something is an unbeliever."

ᘒ ᘒ ᘒ

"Every sin that begins in fear and ends in repentance brings God's servant to him. Every devotion that begins in faith and ends in conceit drives God's servant away from him. To be devout with conceit is to sin, and to sin with repentance is to be devout."

They asked Sādeq, "Who are nobler, the patient poor or the thankful rich?"

"The patient poor, for the hearts of the rich are in their purses and those of the poor are with the Lord."

"Worship does not come out right except through repentance, for the Real most high gave repentance precedence over worship, for as he said, '*The penitents, the worshipers*'" [9:112].

"To recollect repentance while recollecting the Real most high is to remain oblivious of recollection. To remember the Real most high truly is to forget all things beside the Lord, so that the Lord most high takes the place of all things."

"Concerning the meaning of the verse *He reserves his mercy for whomever he pleases* [2:105 and 3:74]—He has removed the means, the reasons, and the causes, so that you may know that his mercy is a pure gift."

"One who believes stands by his self. One who realizes stands by his Lord."

"Whoever struggles against his self for the sake of his self attains wonders. Whoever struggles against his self for the sake of the Lord attains the Lord."

"Divine inspiration is one of the attributes of the blessed. Rationalizing without inspiration is one of the marks of the cursed."

"The ways that the mighty and glorious Lord deceives his servant are more hidden than the motion of an ant going across a black stone on a dark night."

"Love is divine madness. It is to be neither condemned nor praised."

"My innermost divine vision was confirmed when they stigmatized me for madness."

"It is a man's good fortune when his enemy is wise."

"Beware of associating with five kinds of people: first, liars, for you will always feel overconfident around them. Second, fools, for when they want to do something good for you, they will do something harmful and not realize it. Third, misers, for they will cut you off from the best of times. Fourth, cowards, for they will leave you in the lurch in your hour of need. Fifth, the corrupt, for they will sell you out for a piece of bread and they hunger after the smallest pieces."

"The Real most high has a paradise and a hell here in this world. Paradise is sound health, and hell is hardship. Sound health is referring your own works back to the mighty and glorious Lord, and hell is performing the Lord's works for your self."

"Someone who does not have any secrets is dangerous."

"If the company of God's enemies were harmful to his friends, Āsiyeh would have been harmed by her husband, the pharaoh. If the company of God's friends were beneficial to his enemies, Lot's and Noah's wives would have benefited. But there was nothing more than a contraction and an expansion."

Sādeq has many sayings. We speak a few words as a foundation and conclude.

∽ 2 ∽
Oveys of Qaran[1]

The compass for the second generation of Muslims, the exemplar for the Forty Substitutes,[2] the hidden sun, the friend of the Merciful, the Canopus of Yemen, Oveys of Qaran—God's mercy be upon him. The Prophet (God bless him and his family and grant them peace) said, *"The most virtuous of my followers is Oveys of Qaran."* How can my tongue properly describe and praise one whom the Prophet himself praises? Sometimes the Master of the World (peace and blessing be upon him) would turn toward Yemen and say, *"I find that the breath of the Compassionate comes from Yemen."*[3] The Master of the Prophets also said, "On the morrow of the resurrection, the Real most high will create seventy thousand angels in the likeness of Oveys, so that Oveys may rise up among them on the plain of judgment and go to heaven, and no creature will know which among them is Oveys, except as God wills. In the abode of this world, he worshiped the Real under the dome of secrecy and kept his distance from people; so, too, in the afterworld he will be protected from the eyes of strangers, for *my friends are under my domes; no one else knows them.*[4]

In a rarely attested tradition, it is related that on the morrow in paradise, the Master of the Prophets (peace and blessing be upon him) will come out from his palace as though he is looking for someone. A voice will ask, "For whom are you looking?"

Mohammad will answer, "Oveys."

The voice will call out, "Don't bother. Just as you did not see him in the world below, so you will not see him here."

"My God, where is he?"

"In an assembly of truth" [54:55].

"Does he see me?"

The edict will come down: "Why should anyone who sees us see you?"

The Master of the Prophets (peace and blessing be upon him) also said, "There is a man in my community who will intercede on the resurrection for as many people as there are hairs on the sheep of the tribes of Rabi'a and Mozar." And they say that among the Arabs, no tribe has as many sheep as these two tribes.

"Who is this?" Mohammad's companions asked.

"One of the Lord's servants."

"We are all servants of the Lord most High. What's his name?"

"Oveys."

"Where is he?"

"In the tribe of Qaran."

"Has he seen you?"

"With his outer eyes, no."

"Strange that a lover like this has not hastened to serve you."

"There are two reasons. First, overwhelming rapture. Second, reverence for my law—he has a blind and devout mother whose hands and feet have grown weak. By day, Oveys works tending camels and spends his wages to support his mother and himself."

"Will we see him?"

To Abu Bakr, Mohammad said, "You will not see him, but 'Omar and 'Ali will. He is a hairy man, and there are white marks the size of a dirham on his left side and on the palms of his hands. But he is not leprous. When you find him, give him my regards and tell him to pray for my people."

The Master of the Prophets (peace and blessing be upon him) also said, *"The most loving of God's friends are those who are pious in secret."* God's Messenger speaks the truth.

Some people said, "Messenger of God, we don't find him among us."

Mohammad (peace be upon him) said, "He is a camel herder in Yemen. They call him Oveys. Walk in his footsteps."

It is related that when the Messenger (peace and blessing be upon him) was about to die, he was asked, "Messenger of God, to whom shall we give your cloak?"

"Oveys of Qaran."

After the death of the Messenger (peace and blessing be upon him), when 'Omar and 'Ali (may God be pleased with them both) came to Kufa, 'Omar turned to the people of Nejd during his sermon and said, "People of Nejd, stand up." They stood up. 'Omar asked, "Is there anyone from the Qaran among you?"

They said yes and sent some people forward. 'Omar asked about Oveys. They said, "We don't know him."

'Omar said, "The Founder of the Law (peace and blessing be upon him) told me about him, and he doesn't speak empty words. You really don't know of him?"

Someone said, "He's too contemptible to be sought after by the Commander of the Faithful. He's a foolish madman, a wild creature."

"Where is he?" 'Omar said. "We are looking for him."

"He is in the valley of 'Urana, grazing camels so he can get food at night. He doesn't come into the settlements or associate with anyone. He doesn't eat what people eat and knows neither sorrow nor happiness. When people laugh, he cries, and when they cry, he laughs."

'Omar and 'Ali then went to the valley and found him praying. The Real most high had appointed an angel to graze the camels. When Oveys sensed humans, he cut short his prayer. After Oveys said amen, 'Omar stood up and said hello. Oveys returned his greeting. 'Omar asked, "What is your name?"

"The servant of God, 'Abdollāh."

"We are all servants of the Lord. I'm asking about your personal name."

"Oveys."

"Show me your right hand," 'Omar said. Oveys showed it to him. 'Omar saw the sign indicated by the Messenger (peace and blessing be upon him). 'Omar kissed it at once and said, "The Lord's Messenger has sent you his greetings and said, 'Pray for my peoples.'"

Oveys said, "You are more worthy to pray for them. There is no one on the face of the earth more honored than you."

"I do pray for them," 'Omar said, "but you should carry out the Messenger's final will and testament."

"'Omar, take a closer look," Oveys said. "Mustn't it be someone else?"

"The Messenger has indicated you."

"Then give me the Prophet's robe, so I may pray and ask for what is needed." Oveys went to a secluded place further away from them. He set the robe aside, put his face to the ground, and said, "My God, I will not put on this robe until you give me all of Mohammad's people. Your Messenger has turned them over to me here. The Prophet, 'Omar, and 'Ali have finished their tasks. Now only your task is left."

A hidden voice called out, "We give you some of them. Now put on the robe."

"I want them all," Oveys said.

He went on talking and listening, until 'Omar and 'Ali said, "Let's get up close so we can see what Oveys is doing."

When Oveys saw that they had come, he said, "Ah, why have you come? If it weren't for your coming, I wouldn't have put on the robe until he gave me all of Mohammad's people."

When 'Omar saw Oveys with his bare head and bare feet, dressed in a camel-hair blanket, and under that blanket the power of the eighteen thousand worlds, he despaired of himself and the caliphate. He said, "Who will buy this caliphate from me for a loaf of bread?"

"Someone who has no sense," Oveys replied. "What are you selling? Throw it away, so anyone who wants it can pick it up. What do buying and selling have to do with it?"

The Muslim elders cried out, "You have accepted something from Abu Bakr. The work of so many Muslims cannot be squandered. One day of your justice is superior to a thousand years of devotion."

Oveys then put on the robe and said, "By the blessings of this robe, as many of Mohammad's people have been forgiven as there are hairs on the sheep of Rabi'a and Mozar."

Here someone might suppose that Oveys was more advanced than 'Omar, but this is not the case. However, Oveys's special characteristic was detachment. 'Omar had everything, but he also wanted detachment, just as the Prophet (peace and blessing be upon him) used to knock on the old woman's door, saying, "Remember Mohammad in your prayers."

Then 'Ali sat down in silence. 'Omar asked, "Oveys, why didn't you come to see the Prophet?"

"Have you seen him?" Oveys asked.

"Yes," they answered.

"Maybe you have seen his coat. If you have seen him, tell me, were his eyebrows joined or separated?"

Strangely, neither one could say, so imposing was Oveys's presence. Then Oveys asked, "Do you love Mohammad?"

"Yes," they said.

"If you really loved him, why didn't break your own tooth to conform on the day his tooth was broken? Conformance is the condition of friendship." Then Oveys showed them his mouth. There wasn't a single tooth in it. "Without having seen him face to face, I broke off my own teeth to conform with his, for conformance comes from faith."

They were overcome with tenderness. They realized that the dignity of conformance and proper behavior was other than what they supposed and that they had to learn proper behavior from Oveys, though he had not seen the Prophet (peace and blessing be upon him).

'Omar then said, "Oveys, pray for me."

"Let there be no bias in the faith. I have made my prayers. In every prayer, I testify, *'O God, forgive the believers, man and woman.'* If you carry your faith sound to the grave, this prayer will find you on its own. If not, I'm not going to waste any prayers."

'Omar then said, "Give me a parting piece of advice."

"'Omar, do you know the Lord?"

"Yes."

"If you don't know anyone else, it will be better for you."

"Say more."

"'Omar, does the mighty and glorious Lord know you?"

"He does."

"If no one else knows you, it will be best."

"Wait," 'Omar said, "let me get something for you."

Oveys reached into his pocket and pulled out two dirhams and said, "I have earned this from herding camels. If you can guarantee that I will live long enough to spend this, then I will take something else." He continued, "You are troubled. Go back, for the resurrection is near. There will be a meeting there that has no return. I am busy now preparing provisions for the road to the resurrection."

When the people of Qaran returned from Kufa, Oveys was shown great respect among the people. Oveys did not care for this. He fled there and came to Kufa. After that, no one saw him except Harem ebn Hayyān,[5] who reported:

When I heard of the extent of Oveys's intercession, I was overwhelmed by yearning for him. I went to Kufa and sought him out. Unexpectedly, I found him on the banks of the Euphrates, making ablutions and washing his clothes. I recognized him from the description I had heard of him and greeted him. He replied and looked me over. I was about to take his hand, but he would not give it to me. I said, "*May God have mercy on you, Oveys, and forgive you. How are you?"* I began to weep because of my love for him, the compassion that I felt for him, and his poor health.

Oveys wept and said, "*God give you long life,* Harem ebn Hayyān. How are you and who has guided you to me?"

"How did you know my name and my father's? How did you recognize me? You've never seen me."

"The One whose knowledge nothing escapes informed me. My spirit recognized your spirit—the spirits of the believers are familiar with one another."

"Relate to me some story about the Messenger (peace and blessing be upon him)."

"I never saw him, but I heard stories about him from others. I don't want to be a reciter of traditions or a religious scholar or a storyteller. I have my own affairs to keep me from doing these things."

"Recite a verse of the Qur'an, so I may hear it from you."

"I seek refuge with God from the accursed Satan." And he sobbed. Then he recited, *"I have only created jinn and men so they might serve me"* [54:56], and *"We did not create the heaven and the earth and everything between for sport"* [21:16], and from *"We did not create them except for just ends, but most of them do not know it"* up to *"He is the mighty and compassionate"* [44:39-42]. Then he let out such a cry that I thought he had fainted. Then he said, "Son of Hayyān, what has brought you to this place?"

"I wanted to get to know you and to comfort you."

"I never realized that someone who knew the mighty and glorious Lord could get to know any other than him or comfort any other than him."

"Give me counsel."

"Keep death under your pillow when you sleep and keep it before your eyes when you get up. Don't look at how petty a sin is. Look at how great it is, for it led you to rebel against him. If you deem a sin petty, you have deemed the Lord petty."

Harem continued:

I asked, "Where would you say I should settle down?"

"In Syria."

"Can one make a good living there?"

"Ugh, hearts like these! They've been overwhelmed by polytheism and will not take advice."

"Counsel me further."

"Son of Hayyān, your father died. Adam and Eve have died, and Noah and Abraham and Moses and David and Mohammad (peace be upon them). Abu Bakr, his successor, also died. My brother 'Omar died. Alas 'Omar!"

"God have mercy on you! 'Omar hasn't died!"

"The Real most high informed me of 'Omar's death." He added, "You and I are both among the dead." Then he called down blessings on the Prophet and his family and said a prayer. "My counsel," he continued, "is that you take up the book of the mighty and glorious Lord and follow the path of the righteous. Don't let the thought of death slip your mind for an instant. When you reach your people, counsel them. Do not withhold advice from the Lord's creatures. And do not take one step that is not in conformity with the consensus of the community, lest all of a sudden you be left without faith and not know it and tumble into hell." He then said several prayers and said, "You are about to go, son of Hayyān. You will not see me again, nor I you. Remember me in your prayers, for I will remember you in mine. You go this way, and I'll go that."

I wanted to walk with him for a while. He would not allow it and wept. He brought tears to my eyes as well. Most of the things he said to me were about 'Omar and 'Ali (may God be pleased with them both). I watched him walk away until he disappeared, and I heard no news of him after that.

Rabi' ebn Kheysam[6] (God's mercy be upon him) reported:
I went to see Oveys. He was performing the morning prayer. When he finished, he began to count his prayer beads. I waited until he was done. As soon as he got up, he started performing the noon prayer. In short, for three days and nights he did not stop praying and did not eat anything and did not sleep. On the fourth night I was listening to him. His eyes drooped a little from sleepiness. At once, he began to speak intimately with the Real most high and said, "O Lord, I seek refuge with you from my eyes, which sleep too much, and from my stomach, which eats too much."

I said to myself, "This is enough for me." I did not disturb him and turned away.

They say that during his lifetime he never slept at night. One night he would say, *"This is the night for prostration,"* and he would spend that night prostrate. One night he would spend standing up and say, *"This is the night for standing."* One night he would kneel down until daybreak and say, *"This is the night for kneeling."*

They asked him, "Oveys, how do you have the strength to spend such a long night in one position?"

"By the time the day breaks, I have not once yet said, *'Praise to my Lord most high.'* The Prophet's practice was to say it three times. I do this because I want to worship like those who dwell in heaven."

ॐ ॐ ॐ

They asked him, "What is submissiveness in prayer?"

"It is this: If they shoot an arrow into the side of someone while he is praying, he is unaware of it."

They asked him, "How are you?"

"How is someone who gets up in the morning and doesn't know whether he will live until nightfall?"

They asked him, "How goes your affair?"

"Alas for the lack of provisions and the length of the road!"

"If you worship the Lord with all the devotion of the creatures of heaven and earth, he will not accept it from you until you believe in him."

They asked, "How can we believe in him?"

"Have faith that he has accepted you. You will find yourself at ease in worship and will not be distracted by anything else."

"Hell is closer than the jugular vein to anyone who loves three things: first, eating fine food; second, wearing fine clothes; and third, lounging with the wealthy."

༺༻ ༺༻ ༺༻

They told Oveys, "Near here, there is a man who dug a grave thirty years ago and spread out his shroud in it. He has been sitting on the edge of the grave ever since, weeping without rest day and night."

Oveys went there and saw him, thin and pale with his eyes fixed on the pit. "For thirty years," Oveys said to him, "your grave and shroud have held you back from the Lord most high and you have been left behind because of them. These two are the idols of your path."

Through Oveys's light, the man saw that wretchedness within himself. Rapture was revealed to him. He shouted and died and fell into the grave and onto the shroud. If the grave and the shroud can be veils, consider what the veils of others are.

It is related that once Oveys did not eat anything for three full days. The fourth day, he saw a dinar on the road. He did not pick it up. "Someone must have dropped it," he thought.

He went to pluck some grass and eat it. He saw a sheep holding a loaf of warm bread in its mouth. The sheep came up and set the loaf in front of him. Oveys thought, "Maybe the sheep has stolen it from someone." He turned away.

The sheep began to speak and said, "I am the servant of the One whose servant you are. Take the sustenance of the Lord from the servant of the Lord."

"I stretched out my hand to take the bread," Oveys said. "I saw the bread in my hand, and the sheep disappeared."

His good qualities are many and his virtues countless. In the beginning, Sheikh Abu'l-Qāsem of Korakān used to chant, "Oveys! Oveys!" They know their worth.

Oveys's saying is "Nothing remains hidden from one who knows the mighty and glorious Lord." In other words, one can know the Lord by the Lord. Whoever knows the Lord by the Lord knows all things.

Oveys said, "Safety is in solitude." The solitary man is one who is alone in oneness, and oneness is where no thought of the other intervenes, so there is safety. If you adopt solitude in appearance, it will not come out right, for the hadith says, *"Satan is with the solitary man, and he is the more distant of the two."*

He said, "Keep your heart." In other words, it is incumbent upon you to tend to your heart at all times, so the other may not find its way in.

He said, *"I sought grandeur and I found it in humility. I sought command and I found it in wishing people well. I sought chivalry and I found it in truthfulness. I sought glory and I found it in poverty. I sought fame and I found it in piety. I sought nobility and I found it in contentment. I sought comfort and I found it in austerity."*

It is related that his neighbors said, "We figured him for a madman. Finally we asked him if we could build a room for him at the front of our house. A year went by when he didn't have the wherewithal to break his fast. He used to get his meals by gathering date pits from time to time and selling them at night and spending the money on food. If he found some dates, he would sell the pits and give the money away as alms. His clothes were old rags that he picked up from the garbage and washed off and sewed together. He made do with this—the Lord's people derive comfort from such things. He would go out at the dawn prayer and return after the night prayer. In every neighborhood he entered, the children would throw stones at him. He would say, 'My calves are thin. Throw smaller stones, so my feet won't be stained with blood and I won't be prevented from praying. I am worried about my prayers, not about my feet.'"

At the end of his life, so they say, he came to visit the Commander of the Faithful 'Ali (may God be pleased with him). They fought together at the battle of Seffin[7] until Oveys was martyred. *He lived commendably and died happily.*

Know that there is a group of people whom they call the Oveysians. They have no need for a spiritual guide, for prophecy nurtures them in its shelter without the mediation of another, just as it nurtured Oveys. Although outwardly he did not see the Master of the Prophets (peace and blessing be upon him), Oveys was nevertheless nurtured by him. He was fostered by prophecy and was in harmony with the truth. This is a great and lofty station. Who will be made to attain this station and to whom will this good fortune show its face? *That is the grace of God, which he will bestow on whomever he pleases* [5:57].

∽ 3 ∽
Hasan of Basra

Nourished by prophecy, accustomed to victory, the Ka'ba of works and learning, the compass of scrupulousness and restraint, foremost in the seat of honor, at the forefront of religious practice, Hasan of Basra—God's mercy be upon him. His virtues are many and his laudable qualities countless. He was the master of learning and proper conduct, and the fear and the grief of the Real enveloped him constantly.

His mother was one of the retainers of Omm Salama[1] (God be pleased with her). When his mother was busy at some task, Hasan would begin to cry. Omm Salama would place her nipple in his mouth for him to suckle. A few drops of milk would appear. The many thousands of blessings that the Real most high manifested were all the result of that.

It is related that during his childhood at Omm Salama's house (God be pleased with her), Hasan drank water one day from the Prophet's jug (peace and blessing be upon him). He asked, "Who drank this water?"

"Hasan," they said.

The Prophet said, "As much as he drank of this water, so much shall my knowledge permeate him."

It is related that one day the Prophet (peace be upon him) went to Omm Salama's house, and Hasan was set down next to him. The Prophet prayed for him. Whatever Hasan attained was from the blessing of that prayer.

It is related that when he was born, they brought him to 'Omar ebn al-Khattāb (God be pleased with him). He said, "Name him Hasan," meaning handsome, "for he has a pretty face."

Omm Salama (God be pleased with her) raised him and cared for him. Because of the tenderness she felt for him, she began to lactate. She always used to say, "O Lord, make him an example for your creatures!" He chanced to meet one hundred and thirty of the Prophet's companions and saw seventy of those who fought at the battle of Badr.[2] He was the disciple of 'Ali ebn Abi Ṭāleb (God be pleased with him) and received his robe from him.

The beginning of his conversion happened this way: He was a jewel merchant, and they called him Pearly. Once he went to Byzantium and approached the vizier. The vizier said, "We're going somewhere today. Will you come along?"

"I will," Hasan said, and they went into the desert.

Hasan related:

I saw a tent made of brocade with silken ropes and golden pegs and I saw a mighty army, fully equipped for war. It circled the tent for an hour, said something, and departed. Then scholars and scribes came, about four hundred men, and they too circled the tent, said something, and departed.

After that I saw honored elders who did just the same and departed. Then gorgeous serving girls, nearly four hundred of them and each with a platter of gold and jewels upon her head, did the same and departed. Then the emperor and the vizier went into the tent, came out, and departed. I was astonished and thought, "What's going on?"

I questioned the vizier. He said, "The emperor had a beautiful son. He was perfectly accomplished in the various sciences and without peer on the field of battle. His father loved him. Suddenly he took ill. Skilled physicians were unable to cure him, until in the end he perished. They buried him inside that tent.

"Once each year they come to pay their respects to him. First, the mighty army that you saw comes, and the soldiers say, 'O prince, if the condition that befell you could have been warded off with arms and war, we would have all sacrificed our lives to rescue you. But war can never be waged against the one responsible for your condition.' They say this and turn back.

"Then the scholars and scribes come and say, 'O prince, if our learning and philosophy or our science and subtlety could have warded this off, we would have done so.' They say this and turn back.

"Then the honored elders come and say, 'O prince, if it had been possible to ward off this condition with compassion and sympathy or with learning and subtlety, we would have done so. But the one responsible for it will not be bought off with compassion or sympathy.'

"Then the gorgeous serving girls come with their golden platters and say, 'If we could have ransomed you with wealth or pomp or beauty, we would have sacrificed ourselves, but wealth and beauty carry no weight here.'

"Then the emperor and the vizier enter the tent and say, 'O soul of your father! What could your father do? He brought a mighty army, scholars and scribes, elders, intercessors, and counselors, beautiful girls, wealth, and riches of all sorts for you. I myself came too. If anything within my power would have helped, I would have done it. But your condition resides with one before whom your father, with all his grandeur, is helpless. Peace be upon you for another year.' They say this and turn back."

These words moved Hasan deeply, and at once he turned back and went to Basra. He swore that in this world he would never smile until the outcome of his affairs became clear. He tormented himself with such austerities and devotions that no one else in his time could exceed that discipline. For seventy years, his purity was violated only in the privy.

His seclusion was such that he gave up hope in all creation until inevitably he surpassed it all. Thus it was that one day someone got up and said, "Why is Hasan our superior and so much better than we?"

An eminent person was present and said, "Because all creatures are in need of his knowledge, and he needs nothing but the Real. In religion, all creation requires him, but he is free of everything in this world. His superiority and excellence come from that."

He would speak at prayer meetings once a week. Whenever he climbed up to the pulpit, he would come back down if Rābe'a was not present. Once he was asked, "So many important and honored people are present. What does it matter if an old woman's not here?"

"The drink we have prepared for elephants cannot be served to mice," Hasan replied.

Whenever the meeting warmed up, whenever hearts were afire and eyes were swimming in tears, he would turn to Rābe'a and say, *"O noble lady, this is from the embers of your heart."* In other words, "All this warmth comes from one sigh from the depths of your being."

౸ఞ ౸ఞ ౸ఞ

They said, "We know you must be happy when such a huge crowd comes to your meeting."

Hasan said, "Quantity does not make us happy. We are happy if two dervishes are present."

"What is Islam, and who is a Muslim?"

"Islam is in the books, and Muslims are under the earth."

"What is the source of religion?"

"Scrupulousness."

"What destroys it?"

"Appetite."

They asked, "What is the Garden of Eden?"

Hasan said, "It is a palace made of gold. No one reaches it but a prophet or an honest man, a martyr or a just sultan."

Someone said, "How can a sick doctor cure others? 'First cure yourself, then others,' they say."

"When you listen to my words," Hasan answered, "you profit from my knowledge and lose nothing from my ignorance."

"Sheikh, our hearts have fallen asleep, so your words have no effect on them. What should we do?"

"Would that they were asleep! When you jostle a sleeper, he wakes up. Your hearts are dead. They won't wake up, however much you shake them."

They said, "There are some folk who frighten us so much with their words that our hearts shatter from dread. Is this right?"

Hasan said, "It's better than talking with folk who make you feel safe today and leave you stricken with dread on the morrow."

"Some folks come to your meetings and memorize your words just so they can criticize and find fault with them," they said.

"I have seen dark-eyed women who desire the highest paradise and the proximity of the Real most high," Hasan replied. "They never crave men's greetings, for even their Creator will never accept the greetings of such tongues."

They said, "Someone says, 'Do not call the people until you have purified yourself.'"

"The devil desires nothing more than these words," Hasan replied. "He wants these words to adorn our hearts, so we will hold back from commanding good and forbidding evil."

"Does the believer envy?" they asked.

Hasan said, "Have you forgotten Joseph's brothers? But it costs you nothing when you cast a torment from your breast."

∽ ∽ ∽

Hasan had a disciple who would throw himself on the ground and cry out whenever he heard a verse from the Qur'an. Hasan said to him, "If you can stop what you're doing, then you've burned up all your fine conduct in the fire of nothingness. If you can't stop, then you've left me ten stages behind."

"*Thunder comes from the devil,*" he added—when anyone shouts, it is no one but the devil shouting. He laid this down as a general rule that does not apply everywhere. And Hasan himself interpreted it: if one can refrain from crying out and the thunder crashes, then it is the devil's doing.

One day Hasan was speaking at a meeting. Hajjāj entered with many soldiers brandishing their swords. An eminent person was present: "Today I'll test Hasan," he said. "This will be the moment of truth." Hajjāj sat down. Hasan did not so much as glance at him, nor did he interrupt what he was saying until the meeting was completed.

"Hasan means 'beautiful,'" the eminent one said.

When the meeting ended, Hajjāj forced his way up to Hasan, grabbed his arm, and said, "*Look at this man!* If you want to see a man, look at Hasan."

Hajjāj was seen in a dream, fallen prostrate on the plain of the resurrection. "What do you seek?" they asked him.

He said, "I seek what the people of unity seek." He said this because in his death throes, he had said, "O Lord, show these narrow minds the truth of your words: 'I am the most forgiving and the most generous of the generous.' They are in unanimous agreement that you will send me down and not forgive me. Forgive me to spite them and show them: *He does as he wills*" [11:127].

Hasan was told about this and said, "It seems that this wicked man will win over the afterworld with some trick, too."

It is related that 'Ali (peace be upon him) came to Basra. With the camel's lead ropes tied around his waist, he did not linger more than three days. He ordered that the pulpits be torn down, and he banned the preachers. He went to Hasan's meeting and asked him, "Are you a scholar or a student?"

"Neither," Hasan said. "I repeat a few words that reached me from the Prophet."

'Ali did not ban him and said, "This youth deserves to speak." Then he departed. Hasan had recognized 'Ali intuitively. He came down from the pulpit and ran after him until he caught up. "For the Lord's sake," he said, "teach me to purify myself." There is a place called Gate of the Basin. They brought the basin, and 'Ali taught Hasan to perform ablutions and departed.

Once there was a year of drought in Basra. Two hundred thousand people came out to pray for rain. They set up a pulpit and sent Hasan there to pray. "If you wish for rain," Hasan said, "expel me from Basra."

Dread had such dominion over him that when he was seated, you would have said that he was seated before the executioner. No one ever saw a smile cross his lips. He possessed a mighty pain.

It is related that one day Hasan saw someone weeping. "Why are you weeping?" he asked.

The man replied, "I was at a prayer meeting held by Mohammad ebn Ka'b of Qaraz, and he related that for the misfortune of his sins, the truest of believers will remain in hell for many years."

Hasan said, "I can only hope that Hasan will be one of those who is brought out of hell after a thousand years."

It is related that one day Hasan was reading the prophetic tradition: *The last person to come out of hell from among my people will be a man called Honād*. Hasan said, "If only I were Honād!"

It is related that one night Hasan was moaning and sobbing in his house. "Why do you lament," he was asked, "with the life that you lead?"

"It is for fear," Hasan said, "that without my knowledge or intention, something has come over me or I have taken a step in error somewhere that was not pleasing in the court of the Real. Then they will say to Hasan, 'Go, for you have no standing in our court, and none of your service is acceptable.'"

It is related that one day Hasan had wept so much on the roof of his meditation cell that water had run out from the rain spouts and dripped on someone who asked, "Is this water pure or not?"

"No, go wash," Hasan said. "These are the tears of a disobedient sinner."

It is related that Hasan once went up to a funeral bier. When the corpse was interred, Hasan sat on the grave and wept so much that he turned the earth to mud. Then he said, "People! The beginning and the end is the tomb. Behold the end of this world—it is the grave. Behold the beginning of the afterworld—it is the grave: *The first way station on the road of the afterlife is the tomb.* How can you take pride in a world whose end is this? And why don't you fear a world whose beginning is this? Since this is your beginning and your end, you heedless people, arrange your affairs, first and last." The crowd that was present wept so much that all of the people were reduced to the same state.

It is related that one day he passed by a graveyard with a group of people. He said, "In this graveyard there are men, the summit of whose aspirations did not fall short of the seven heavens. But so much regret is mingled with their dust that if one mote of it were displayed to the inhabitants of heaven and earth, they would all collapse in a heap."

It is related that as a child he had been disobedient. Whenever he sewed a new shirt, he embroidered that sin on the collar and then wept so much that he fainted.

Once 'Omar ebn 'Abd al-'Aziz (God be pleased with him) wrote a letter to Hasan, saying, "Give me a bit of counsel in a few words, so I can memorize them and make them my guide." Hasan (God have mercy upon him) wrote this: "When the mighty and glorious Lord is with you, whom do you have to fear?"

Another time Hasan wrote a letter, saying, "Assume that the day has come when the last person is to die. Farewell." 'Omar wrote in response, "Assume that the day has come when this world and the afterworld have never existed." But the afterworld has always existed.

Once Sābet-e Bonāni (God have mercy upon him) wrote a letter to Hasan: "I hear you are going on the pilgrimage. I wish to accompany you." Hasan wrote back: "Let us live in the shelter of the Lord. Being together will reveal our faults to one another, and we will regard one another as enemies."

It is related that he advised Sa'id-e Jobeyr,[3] "Do not do three things. First, do not set foot in the presence of sultans, even if it is entirely out of compassion for God's creatures. Second, do not keep company with any woman, even if she is Rābe'a, and you are teaching her God's book. Third, never pay heed to the emir, even if you have the rank of the truest of believers, for this always involves hardship and in the end will be a self-inflicted wound."

Mālek-e Dinār said, "I asked Hasan, 'What is a scholar's punishment?'
    "'The death of the heart,' he said.
    "'What is the death of the heart?'
    "'Love of this world.'"

An eminent person said, "At dawn one day I went to the door of Hasan's mosque to pray. I saw that the door was closed. Hasan was praying inside the mosque, and some people were answering amen. I waited until it grew light. I set my hand on the door. It swung open. I went inside and saw Hasan all alone. I was amazed. When we had performed the prayer, I told Hasan the story and said, 'For God's sake, let me in on what was happening.'
    "'Don't tell anyone,' Hasan said. 'On Friday mornings before dawn, fairies approach me, and I teach them and pray with them, and they answer amen.'"

It is related that when Hasan would pray, Habib-e 'Ajami would tuck up his robe and say, "I will see it answered."

It is related that an eminent person said, "We were traveling in a group on the pilgrimage. We got thirsty in the desert. We arrived at a well but saw no rope or bucket. 'When I go to pray,' Hasan said, 'you will have water to drink.'

"Then he began to pray, and we went to the water. Water had come to the top of the well. We drank our fill. One of our companions took a canteen of water. The water receded back into the well. When Hasan finished his prayers, he said, 'You did not hold firmly to the Lord, so the water receded back into the well.'

"Afterward we left. On the way, Hasan found a date and gave it to us. We ate the date bit by bit—it had a golden pit. We took it to Medina, sold it for food, and gave that away as alms."

The master of Qur'an reading Abu 'Amr[4] was teaching. Unannounced, a beautiful child came in to learn the Qur'an. Abu 'Amr looked him over with treachery in his eyes and forgot the whole Qur'an from its first letter to its last. A fire blazed up within him, and he came completely undone. He approached Hasan of Basra and told him what had happened. He wept bitterly and said, "This occurred, sir, and I forgot the whole Qur'an."

Hasan was saddened by this affair and said, "It's now time for the pilgrimage. Go and perform the hajj. When you have done so, go to the Kheyf mosque, where an old man will be sitting in the prayer niche. Don't break in on his moment. Wait until he is alone. Then go speak to him, so he will pray for you."

Abu 'Amr did just that and sat down in a corner of the mosque. He saw a dignified old man with some people seated around him. When some time had passed, a man entered wearing a pure white robe. The old man and the people turned toward him and greeted him, and they spoke together. When it was time for prayer, that man departed, and the people went with him. The old man was left alone.

Abu 'Amr related, "I went up to him and greeted him, saying 'God, God, help me!' I told him what had happened to me. The old man was grief-stricken and looked at heaven from the corner of his eye. He had no sooner lowered his head than the entire Qur'an opened up before me."

Abu 'Amr continued, "I collapsed out of sheer happiness. Then the old man asked, 'Who directed you to me?'

"'Hasan of Basra,' I said.

"'When someone has an imam like Hasan, what does he need from anyone else?' 'Hasan has disgraced us,' he added. 'Let us rend his veil too. That old man whom you saw wearing the white robe, who came after the noon prayer and went over to everyone and whom they all honored—that was Hasan. Everyday he performs the noon prayer in Basra, then comes here, speaks to us, and is back in Basra to perform the afternoon prayer.'

"'When someone has an imam like Hasan,' he repeated, 'why ask us for a prayer?'"

It is related that in Hasan's time a man's horse was injured. He was at a loss over what to do and told Hasan what had happened to him. Hasan bought the horse from him for four hundred dirhams and gave him the silver. That night in a dream, the man saw a meadow in paradise. In that meadow there was a horse with four hundred frolicking, frisky colts. "Whose horses are these?" the man asked.

"They were in your name, but now the title has been made over to Hasan."

When he awoke, he went to Hasan and said, "Imam, cancel the sale. I've come to regret it."

"Go on!" Hasan said. "The dream that you had I had before you." The man turned back in sorrow. The following night, Hasan dreamed of palaces and broad vistas. He asked,

"Whose are these?"

"They belong to the one who cancels the sale."

Hasan sought the man out in the morning and canceled the sale.

It is related that Hasan had a Zoroastrian neighbor, a certain Sham'un. He took ill and was on the verge of death. They said to Hasan, "Go help our neighbor."

Hasan came to his neighbor's bedside and saw him all blackened with smoke and fire. "Fear the Lord," Hasan said. "You've spent your whole life in the midst of smoke and fire. Turn to Islam, so that the Lord most high might have mercy upon you."

"Three things keep me from Islam," Sham'un said. "First is that you curse the world, and night and day you go seeking it. Second is that you say, 'Death is the reality,' but you do nothing to prepare for it. Third is that you say, 'The vision of the Real shall be seen' but do everything today that is contrary to his pleasure."

"This is the mark of the enlightened," Hasan said. "Well, if believers talk this way, what do you have to say for yourself? They confess his oneness, and you've spent your life worshiping fire. You've worshiped fire for seventy years, and I have not, and yet fire burns us both and shows no special regard for you. But if my Lord wills, fire will not have the gall to singe even a hair on my body, because fire is created by the Lord, created and under his command. Now come, let's both put our hands in the fire, so you may witness the weakness of the fire and the power of the Real most high."

He said this and placed his hand in the fire and held it there—it was not burned and not one atom of its substance was altered. When Sham'un saw this, he was stunned, and the morning of awareness began to dawn. He said to Hasan, "For seventy years, I have worshiped fire. Now that only a few breaths remain, how can I set my affairs in order?"

"Become a Muslim," Hasan said.

"If you give me a document," Sham'un said, "that the Real most high will not punish me, I will adopt the faith. Until you give me the document, I will not." Hasan wrote out a document. Sham'un said, "Order just men of Basra to witness it." They endorsed the document. Then Sham'un wept profusely and adopted the faith. He gave Hasan his last testament: "When I die, order them to wash me and commit me to the earth with your own hands. Put this document in my hands to serve as my proof."

Hasan said, "I accept." Sham'un recited the testimony of faith and died. They washed his body and performed prayers over it, and they put the document in his hand and buried him. That night Hasan could not sleep for worry, thinking, "What is this I have done? I myself am drowning. How can I help another drowning man? I have no control over my own property—why did I write out a deed for the property of the mighty and glorious Lord?"

Lost in thought, he fell asleep. He saw Sham'un shining like a torch. He was wearing silk with a crown upon his head, smiling and walking gracefully through the fields of paradise. Hasan said, "Sham'un, how are you?"

He said, "Why do you ask? I'm just as you see me. In his bounty, the Real most high brought me near to him and, in his generosity, revealed his face. What he graciously commanded for my sake is beyond description or expression. Now you have fulfilled your obligation to act as my guarantor. Take this document of yours. I don't need it."

When Hasan awoke, he saw the paper in his hand. He said, "Lord, it is clear to me that your actions have no cause but pure grace. Who will suffer loss at your door? You allow a seventy-year-old Zoroastrian into your presence with a single word. How will you exclude a seventy-year-old believer?"

It is related that Hasan was so broken and humbled that he considered anyone he looked at to be better than he was. One day he was passing along the banks of the Tigris. He saw a black man drinking from a large flagon with a woman seated in front of him. It occurred to Hasan that this man was better than he was himself. He fought off this thought: "How could this man be better than I am anyway?"

Just then a heavily laden ship arrived with seven men aboard. Without warning, the ship foundered and sank. The black man entered the water and rescued five of the men. Then he turned to Hasan and said, "Get up, if you're better than I am. I've rescued five of them—you save the other two, Imam of the Muslims! There's water in this flagon, and this woman is my mother. I wanted to test whether you see with the outer eye or the inner one. Now it is clear that you are blind—you saw with the outer eye."

Hasan fell down at the man's feet, asked for forgiveness, and knew that he was one appointed by the Real. Then he said, "O black man! Just as you rescued them from the sea, deliver me from the sea of speculation."

The black man said, "May your eye be illuminated!" And so it was that after that Hasan certainly did not consider himself to be better than anyone else again.

It reached the point that once Hasan saw a dog and said, "God, accept me with this dog!"

Someone asked him, "Are you better or the dog?"

"If I escape the punishment of the Lord, I am better than it. Otherwise, by the glory of the Lord, it is better than a hundred like me."

It is related that Hasan said, "I was astonished by the words of four people: a child, a pederast, a drunk, and a woman."

"How is that?" they asked.

He said, "One day, as I was passing by a pederast, I was gathering up my robe to avoid touching him. 'Sir,' he said, 'our true condition is not yet apparent. Don't pull your robe away from me, for only the Lord knows how things will turn out in the future.'

"And I saw a drunk who was staggering through the mud and I said to him, 'You wretched man, steady your steps, so you won't fall.' 'So presumptuous!' he replied to me. 'Have you steadied your steps? If I fall, I am a drunk soiled by the mud. I'll get up and wash off. It's a simple thing. Fear your own fall!' These words made a profound impression on me.

"And once a child was carrying a lantern. I asked, 'Where did you get this light from?' He blew out the lantern and said, 'Tell me, where did this light go? Then I'll tell you where I got it from.'

"And I saw a woman, a great beauty, with her face and both hands exposed. She was complaining angrily to me about her husband. I said, 'First cover your face.' She said, 'Because of my love for a creature, I've lost my reason. If you had not told me, I would have gone down to the market just like this. With all your presumption of love for God, how is it that you did not fail to notice that my face was uncovered?' This too astonished me."

It is related that when he would come down from the pulpit, he would take aside several members of this clan. He would say, "Come, let us spread the light." One day someone who was not among the people of this tradition went with them. "Go back," Hasan told him.

It is related that Hasan said to his friends one day, "You resemble the companions of the Prophet (peace and blessing be upon him)." They seemed happy. Hasan added, "I'm talking about your faces and beards, not about anything else. If you had laid eyes on that folk, they would have all seemed crazy in your eyes. If they had been informed of you, they would not have called one of you a Muslim. They were in the vanguard, riding on horses, like the wind or a bird in flight. We are stuck on asses, hiding behind our beards."

It is related that a Bedouin came to Hasan and asked about patience. "There are two sorts of patience," Hasan said. "One is patience with affliction and misfortune, and one is patience with those things that the

Real most high has forbidden to us." He explained patience to the Bedouin as it ought to be.

The Bedouin said, "I have never seen anyone more ascetic than you, or heard of anyone as patient."

"Bedouin," Hasan said, "my asceticism is entirely motivated by desire, and my patience is motivated by anxiety."

"Tell me what these words mean," the Bedouin said. "You've shaken my confidence."

"My patience in affliction and service to God tells of my fear of hellfire, and this is the essence of anxiety. My asceticism in this world is desire for the other world, and this is the essence of self-interest." Hasan continued, "Strong is the patience of one who eliminates self-interest, whose patience is for the sake of the Real, not for the sake of saving his body from hell, and whose asceticism is for the sake of the Real, not for the sake of attaining paradise. This is the mark of sincerity."

∽ ∽ ∽

"A man must have useful learning and accomplished works; sincerity is with him. He must have complete contentment, and patience is with him. When these three things are achieved, I don't know what can be done to him."

"Sheep are more aware than humankind, because the shepherd's call keeps them from grazing, while the word of the mighty and glorious Lord does not keep humankind from its desires."

"Associating with the wicked makes people suspicious of the good."

"If someone accuses me of drinking wine, I consider this more amiable than if he accuses me of pursuing this world."

"Realization is not finding a mote of enmity in oneself."

"Eternal, unending paradise is not in a few days' good works. It is in right intention."

"When the people of paradise first look upon paradise, they will faint away for seven hundred years, so the Real most high can reveal himself to them. If they look upon his grandeur, they will be drunk with his awesomeness. If they look upon his beauty, they will be drowned in unity."

"Thought is a mirror that shows you the good and evil within you."

"Words not born of wisdom are the essence of misfortune. Silence not born of thought is lust and negligence. Gazes not born of prudence are idle play and error."

"The Torah says that whoever has been content is without want. Whoever has retired from the created world has found peace. Whoever has crushed lust under foot has been liberated. When anyone refrained from envy, true humanity appeared, and when he was patient for a few days, he found eternal satisfaction."

"People of the heart continually return to silence, so that when their hearts have something to say, it will pervade their tongues."

"Scrupulousness has three stages. First is that God's servant speaks only the truth, whether in anger or pleasure. Second is that he keeps his limbs from whatever will anger the mighty and glorious Lord. Third is that his goal be something of which the Real most high will approve."

"A tiny bit of scrupulousness is better than a thousand years of prayer and fasting."

"The noblest of good deeds are thought and scrupulousness."

"If I knew that there were no hypocrisy in me, I would hold that more dear than anything on the face of the earth."

"Disagreement of inner and outer, of heart and tongue, is part of hypocrisy."

"There were no believers in the past, nor will there be any in the future, who have not quaked with fear, thinking, 'I must not be a hypocrite!'"

"Most surely, whoever says, 'I am a believer,' truly is not." In other words, *do not justify yourselves. He knows best who is mindful* [53:32].

"The believer is one who is deliberate and calm and is not like one who gathers firewood at night. In other words, he is not like one who does something just because he can or who says whatever comes to mind."

"It is not backbiting to point out the faults of three kinds of people: the lustful, the libertine, and the tyrannical imam."

"In atonement for backbiting, it is enough to ask for forgiveness, although you do not seek pardon."

"Adam's poor children! They are pleased with an abode where they are held accountable for what is lawful and tormented for what is forbidden."

"The souls of Adam's offspring will take leave of this world with only three regrets. The first is that they have not had their fill of hoarding. The second is that they have not obtained what they hoped for. And the third is that they have not made provision for a road like the one ahead of them."

Someone said, "So-and-so is giving up the ghost." Hasan replied, "Don't say that—he's been giving up the ghost for seventy years. When he gives up giving up the ghost, where will he go?"

"The lightly burdened are saved, and the heavily laden perish."

"The Lord most high will forgive a folk to whom this world was given as a trust and who returned the trust and departed lightly burdened."

"In my opinion, the clever and knowing are those who destroy this world and erect the afterworld on its ruins, not those who destroy the afterworld and erect this world on its ruins."

"Whoever knows the mighty and glorious Lord loves him. Whoever knows this world despises it."

"In this world, no beast of burden deserves firm reins more than the self."

"If you want to see how this world will be after your death, see how it is after the death of others."

"By God, they did not worship idols, except out of their love for this world."

"Those who came before you considered the Qur'an a letter that had reached them from the Real. They would meditate on it by night and put it into action by day. You studied it and gave up acting on it. You correct its spelling and grammar and make it into bill of lading for this world."

"By God, no one loves silver and gold and holds them dear whom the mighty and glorious Lord does not humiliate."

"It is a fool who sees a people coming up behind him and whose heart does not hold steady whatever happens."

"Before you order someone else to do something, you must first be willing to carry out orders."

"Whoever reports what people say to you will report what you say to them."

"The brethren are dearer to us than family or children, for they are the friends of faith, while family and children are the friends of the world and the enemies of faith."

"God's servant will be held accountable for whatever kindness he shows himself or his mother and father, but not for the food that he sets before his friends and guests."

"Every prayer in which the heart is not present verges on chastisement."

They asked, "What is humility?"
     He said, "A fear that has stopped in the heart and to which it clings."

✑ ✑ ✑

They said, "There is a man who has not come to congregational prayers for twenty years. He has associated with no one and has retired to a secluded place."

Hasan went to him and said, "Why don't you come to prayer or associate with anyone?"

"Excuse me," he said. "I'm busy."

"What are you doing?"

"I do not take a breath without some favor reaching me from the Real or without some disobedience reaching him from me. I am busy giving thanks for that favor and asking forgiveness for that disobedience."

"Remain just as you are," Hasan said. "You are better than I am."

"Have you ever been happy?"

"One day I was up on the roof," Hasan said. "The neighbor woman was saying to her husband, 'For nearly fifty years, I've stayed in your house. Whatever the circumstances, I endured both heat and cold. I looked for nothing extra and I preserved your good name and reputation. I never complained to anyone about you. But there is one thing I will not put up with: You will not choose another to put above me. I did all of this so I would see everyone in you, not so you would see someone else. Today you're showing interest in somebody else. I will appeal to the imam of the Muslims in reproach.'"

Hasan continued, "I was overjoyed, and tears flowed from my eyes. I sought out a parallel for it in the Qur'an and found this verse: *God does not forgive that partners should be set up beside him. He forgives everything else to those whom he pleases*"[5] [4:48].

It is related that someone asked him, "How are you?"

He said, "How are those folk who are at sea, whose ship has broken up, each one clinging to a plank?"

"That's a hard situation."

"That's just how I am."

It is related that one day at the end of the month of fasting, he passed by a crowd that was laughing and playing. He said, "I consider it strange that they laugh when they are unaware of the reality of their situation."

It is related that he saw someone eating bread in the graveyard. "He is a hypocrite," Hasan said.

"Why?" they asked.

He said, "Someone who is moved by his appetite in the presence of the dead would seem to have no belief in death and the afterworld. This is the mark of hypocrites."

It is related that in his intimate prayers he would say: "My God, you have given me favor, and I have not thanked you for it. You have sent misfortune, and I have not borne it patiently. You did not withdraw your favor from me because I did not thank you for it. You did not make misfortune into a continual bane because I did not bear it patiently. My God, does anything but generosity come from you?"

When the moment of death neared, he smiled—no one had ever seen him smiling—and kept saying, "Which sin?" and died.

An elder saw him in a dream and said, "In the course of your life, you never smiled. What happened in your death throes?"

He said, "I heard a voice saying, 'O Angel of Death! Grab hold of him firmly, for one sin still remains.' I smiled with happiness at the thought. I said, 'Which sin?' and died."

A great person saw him in a dream on the night he died: the doors of heaven were flung open, and they proclaimed, "Hasan of Basra has reached the Lord, and the Lord is happy with him."

ॐ 4 ॐ
Mālek-e Dinār

Possessing true leadership, trusting in God's friendship, the righteous paragon, the exemplar on the path of religion, the sultan of those who fly far, Mālek-e Dinār. He was a companion of Hasan of Basra and one of the great members of this clan. He was born while his father was enslaved, and although he was born of a slave, he was free of both worlds. His miracles are famous, and his austerities renowned.

Dinār was the name of his father. But some say that Mālek was once in a boat. When it reached the middle of the sea, they demanded fare for passage on the boat. Mālek said, "I don't have it." They beat him so much that he fell unconscious. When he came to, they demanded the fare. "I don't have it," he said. They beat him again.

"Let's grab you by the feet and throw you into the sea," they said. The fish of the sea came to the surface, each one with a dinar in its mouth. Mālek stretched out his hand and took a dinar from one of the fish and gave it to them. When they saw this, they fell at his feet. He stepped out of the boat, walked over the water, and disappeared. For this reason, his name became Mālek-e Dinār.[1]

This was the reason for his repentance: He was very handsome and wealthy and resided in Damascus. He often went to pray at the Friday Mosque in Damascus, the one that Mo'āviya[2] built and generously endowed. Mālek yearned to be appointed trustee of the mosque; this is the reason why he frequented the mosque. For one year, he worshiped there constantly, so that whenever anyone saw him, he was praying. He used to tell himself, "*You're a hypocrite.*"

After a year, one night he went out for some entertainment and was thoroughly enjoying himself. His friends fell asleep. A voice called out from a lute the musicians were playing, "O Mālek, Mālek, why is it that you do not repent?" When he heard this, he went back to the mosque in dismay.

He said to himself, "For a year, I've been worshiping the mighty and glorious Lord fraudulently and hypocritically. Wouldn't it be better to have some shame and worship him sincerely?" That night he worshiped with a pure heart.

The next day the people came into the mosque and said, "We see some cracks in the mosque. We need a trustee to take responsibility for it." They all agreed that there was no one more suitable than Mālek. They came to see him. He was praying. They waited until he was finished. "We have come," they said, "to implore you to accept the trusteeship."

"My God," Mālek said, "for a year I worshiped you fraudulently. No one looked at me. Now that I have given my heart to you and have firmly decided that I don't want the job, you send twenty people to put it on my shoulders. By your might, I don't want it." Then he left the mosque and set to work and took up the holy struggle.

They say that there was a rich man in Basra. He died and left great wealth behind. He had a gorgeous daughter. She went to see Sābet-e Bonāni and said, "I want to be the wife of Mālek-e Dinār so he can help me serve God." Sābet talked with Mālek. Mālek said, "I have finalized my divorce from this world. Women are part of this world. One cannot have intercourse with a person one has divorced."

It is related that Mālek was sleeping in the shade of a wall. A snake had taken a stalk of narcissus in its mouth and was fanning him.

It is related that Mālek said, "For several years, I longed to fight in the struggle against unbelief. When the chance came for me to go, I caught a fever on the day of battle, so I couldn't. I lay down and said to myself, 'Body, if you had any standing before the Real, you wouldn't have caught this fever.' I fell asleep. A voice called out, 'If you had gone to war today, you would have been taken prisoner. They would have given you pork. You would have become an unbeliever when you ate it. This fever is a great gift to you.'
    "I woke up," Mālek continued, "and gave thanks to the Lord."

It is related that Mālek happened into a debate with a materialist. Their debate stretched on and on. Each one kept saying, "I'm right," until they agreed that the two of them would tie their hands together and put them in a fire. The one who was burned would be proven wrong. When they did this, neither was burned, and the fire went out. They said, "Perhaps we are both right!"
    Mālek came home depressed. He put his face to the earth and prayed privately, "Have I walked in the faith for seventy years only to turn out equal to a materialist?"
    A hidden voice called out, "Didn't you realize that your hand was protecting the hand of the materialist? If the materialist had placed his hand in the fire alone, you would have seen how it would have been."

It is related that Mālek said, "Once I got very sick, so sick that I despaired of my life. When I got better, I happened to need something.

Using all my ingenuity, I managed to get to the market. Without warning, the commander of the city garrison arrived. His bailiffs were shouting, 'Clear the way!' I had no strength, and I was moving slowly. One of the bailiffs came up and struck me with his whip. *'May God amputate his hand,'* I said. The next day I saw that man with his hand cut off."

It is related that there was a depraved young man in Mālek's neighborhood. Mālek was constantly annoyed by him, but he waited patiently for someone else to say something. Finally one day a group went to see Mālek to complain about the young man. Mālek got up and went to see him. The young man was extremely arrogant. He said to Mālek, "I have connections with the sultan. No one has the gall to stand in my way."

"We will speak with the sultan," Mālek said.

"The sultan," the young man answered, "will not stop me from doing what I please. He is pleased with whatever I do or say."

"If one can't talk to the sultan, one can talk to the Compassionate."

"He is too generous to take me to task."

Mālek related:

I was at a loss and left him. Several days passed. His depravity went beyond all bounds. Once again the people rose up to complain and came to see me. I made up my mind to teach him a lesson. On the way, I heard a voice say, "Keep your hands off my friend." I was stunned and went to see the young man. "You're here again!?" he said.

I said, "This time I've come to inform you that I heard this voice."

"Since that's the way it is," he said, "let me give away everything I own for his sake. Let me seek out what pleases the friend. I know that obeying him pleases him. I repent lest I should ever disobey him again." Then he gave away everything he owned, both money and property, and set off. No one there ever saw him again.

But Mālek added, "After some time, I saw him in Mecca. Thin as a toothpick and on the verge of death, he kept saying, 'He has said that he is our friend. I go to the friend's embrace.' He said this and died."

It is related that Mālek once rented a house and had a Jewish neighbor. The prayer niche in Mālek's house faced toward the Jew's house. The

Jew had built an outhouse and relieved himself there. He used to throw the waste toward Mālek's house and pollute his prayer niche.

One day the Jew came to see Mālek and asked, "Doesn't my outhouse cause you a lot of trouble?"

"It does," Mālek said, "but I clean it up and wash off."

"Why do you put up with all this trouble? For whose sake do you swallow your anger?"

"This is the commandment of the Real most high: *Those who hold back their anger and forgive people*" [3:134].

"Ah, what an admirable religion," the Jew said, "when a friend of the Lord endures so much trouble from an enemy of the Lord and never cries out and stays so patient and says nothing to anyone!" He became a Muslim on the spot.

It is related that years went by without Mālek eating either sweet or spicy food. Every night he would go to the baker's shop, buy a loaf of bread, eat the warm bread, and break his fast. Once he fell sick. He felt a craving for meat in his heart. He bore it patiently, but when it got to be too much to bear, he went to the butcher's shop, bought three trotters, slipped them into his sleeve, and left. The butcher had an apprentice. He sent him after Mālek to see what he would do.

The apprentice said, "When Mālek arrived at a deserted place, he took the trotters out of his sleeve, kissed them three times, and said, 'Self, you'll get nothing more than this!' He gave the bread and trotters to the poor and said, 'My weak body, when I inflict all this torment on you, it isn't out of hostility. Just wait a few days; perhaps this hardship will come to an end, and you will experience a bliss that never wanes.'"

Mālek said, "I don't know what this saying means: 'If someone doesn't eat meat for forty days, his mind will grow weak.' I haven't eaten meat for twenty years, and my mind is expanding every day."

It is related that Mālek lived in Basra for forty years without eating dates. When the dates would ripen, Mālek used to say, "People of Basra! My stomach hasn't shrunk, and your stomachs haven't expanded, even though you eat dates every day." After forty years passed, he felt a craving for dates within his self. He checked it until one night a hidden voice called out, "Eat dates, and release your self from its fetters."

To his self Mālek said, "If you fast for forty days, eating neither day nor night, then I will surrender you to this craving."

So, his self relented and fasted. Mālek bought some dates and went to a mosque to eat them. A child cried out, "A Jew has come to the mosque, and he's eating dates!"

The child's father said, "What's a Jew doing in the mosque?" He picked up a stick and came over to beat Mālek. When he saw that it was Mālek, the man fell at his feet and apologized. "Forgive me, sir," he said. "In our district no one eats anything during the daytime except the Jews. When you came here to eat something, the child imagined that it was a Jew. Forgive him—the child didn't recognize you."

"Set your mind at ease," Mālek said. "That was the tongue of the Unknown." Then he said, "My God, you called me a Jew even before I ate the dates. If I eat them, you'll make my name synonymous with unbelief. By your might, I will never eat dates."

It is related that a fire burned through Basra. Mālek picked up his walking stick and shoes and went to high ground. He gazed on the scene. The people were beset by pain and fatigue. Some were burning, some were fleeing, and some were lugging their belongings away. Mālek said, *"The lightly burdened are saved and heavily laden perish."*[3]

One day Mālek went to pay a visit on a sick man. He related, "I saw that the hour of his death was near. I recited the testimony of faith over him, but he did not repeat it, no matter how I tried. He kept saying, 'Ten, eleven.' Then he said, 'Sheikh, there is a mountain of fire in front of me. Whenever I try to utter the testimony of faith, the fire pursues me.'"

Mālek continued, "I asked about his profession. I was told, 'He used to lend out money for interest and profit from it and give short measure.'"

Ja'far ebn Soleymān[4] related, "I was with Mālek in Mecca. When he began to say, *'I am at your service, O God, I am at your service,'* he fainted and fell down. When he came to, I asked him about it. He said, 'I was afraid the answer would be, *'I am not at your service; I am not at your beck and call.'"*[5]

It is related that when Mālek recited, *"We worship you and seek your aid"* [1:5], he would sob. Then he would say, "If this verse were not part of the book of the mighty and glorious Lord, if it were not a commandment, I would never recite it." In other words, we say, "We worship you," but certainly we worship ourselves. We say, "I seek your aid," but we go around appealing to this one and that and thanking them and complaining about everybody.

It is related that Mālek used to stay awake all night. He had a daughter. One night she said, "O father, rest a moment."

"Child," he said, "your father fears the night raids of wrath. I am also afraid that some good fortune might turn toward me and find me asleep."

♫ ♫ ♫

They asked him, "How are you?"

Mālek said, "I feed off the blessings of the mighty and glorious Lord, but I follow Satan's orders."

"At the door of a mosque, if someone calls out, 'Who is the worst of you? Let him come out,' no one will come out but me." When 'Abdollāh ebn Mobārak (may God be pleased with him) heard these words, he said, "Mālek's greatness comes from this." Confirming these words, they have reported that a woman once called out to Mālek, "Hey, hypocrite!" Mālek replied, "It's been twenty years since anyone's called me by name. You know exactly who I am."

"Now that I know people, I don't care whether they praise me or condemn me, since I have not seen anyone praise or condemn without excess." In other words, if someone exaggerates, you cannot put any stock in it, take it for what you will. If a companion does not profit your faith, put him behind you.

"I have found the friendship of the people of the age to be like the food in the market. Its color is nice, but its taste is unpleasant."

"Beware of this sorceress"—meaning this world—"for she makes the hearts of the learned her captives."

"If anyone likes recounting hadith to the people more than he likes sitting alone and speaking intimately with the Lord most high, then his learning is scant, his heart blind, and his life a waste."

"In my opinion, sincerity is the dearest of pious deeds."

"The Lord most high gave this revelation to Moses (peace be upon him): 'Make a pair of shoes and a walking stick from iron. Go over the face of the earth, search for the signs and warnings, and gaze upon blessings and lessons, until those shoes are worn out and that walking stick is broken to pieces.' In other words, one must be patient, for *Truly this faith is firm. Enter into it with gentleness.* In the Torah, it is related that the Real most high says, 'We made you our beloved, but you did not love. We made music, but you did not dance.'"[6]

"I have read in some of the revealed books that the Real most high has given two things to the community of Mohammad (peace and blessing be upon him) that he gave to neither the angel Gabriel nor the angel Michael. One is *Remember me; I will remember you* [2:154] and the second is *Call me; I will answer you*" [40:60].

"In the Torah I have read that the Real most high says, 'Honest men! Enjoy the blessings of this world in remembrance of me, for remembering me in this world is a great blessing. You will receive a boundless treasure in the next world for having remembered me in this.'"

"In some of the revealed books, the Real most high says, 'The least thing that I will do to any learned person who loves this world is take from his heart the sweetness of remembrance and private devotion.'"

"Anyone who pursues his lust for this world saves demons the trouble of pursuing him."

⁂ ⁂ ⁂

At the end of his life, someone asked Mālek for a final testament. Mālek said, "Be content at all times with the Arranger who arranges your affairs, so you will be saved."

When the moment of Mālek's death arrived, an eminent person saw him in a dream. He asked, "What has the mighty and glorious Lord done with you?"

Mālek replied, "I saw the mighty and glorious Lord in spite of all my sins, but because of the good opinion that I have of him and the high expectations that I bring before him, he wiped them all away."

Another eminent person dreamt of the resurrection, when they were bringing Mālek-e Dinār and Mohammad ebn Vāse'[7] into heaven. He said, "I watched to see who would go into heaven first. Mālek went first. 'Strange,' I thought, 'Mohammad ebn Vāse' was more learned and complete than Mālek.'

"'Yes,' they said, 'but Mohammad ebn Vāse' owned two shirts in the lower world, while Mālek owned only one. The difference comes from that.' In other words, Mohammad has to wait until he is quit of the obligation for that shirt.'"

◈ 5 ◈
Habib-e 'Ajami

The friend beneath the dome of loving jealousy, the chosen one within the veil of unity, master of honesty and aspiration, lord of certainty without hesitation, recluse without identity, the pauper of nonentity, Habib-e 'Ajami—may God's mercy be upon him. He was honest and performed all-encompassing wonders and austerities.

In the beginning, Habib was a property owner and usurer in Basra. Every day he went out to exact payment from a debtor. If the debtor handed over the silver, fine; and if not, he would take a fee for making the visit and make that do for his food for the day. So it was until one day he went out to exact payment on a loan. The person was not at home. His wife said, "I don't have anything to give to you, but there's some meat from the neck bones left over. If you want it, I'll give it to you."

Habib took it and brought it home. He told his wife to put on the pot. "There's no firewood or bread," she said.

Habib said, "I'll go and use the same trick to get some bread and firewood." He went and got them and brought them home. His wife prepared the meal. A beggar called out. Habib yelled at him, "You won't get rich off the amount we give you, and we'll be the poorer." The beggar turned away despondent.

When Habib's wife went to the pot to get the food, the food in the pot had turned to blood. She was frightened. She called out to Habib, "Come and look at what happened! Yelling at the beggar was a bad omen."

When Habib observed what had happened, a fire began to burn in his heart, and he regretted what he had done. The next day he went out to search for his debtors and recover the silver, never again to lend it out for interest. It was Friday. He set off for Hasan of Basra's prayer meeting. Children were playing in the street. When Habib came up, they said to each other, "Let's get out of here, so dust from the footsteps of Habib the Usurer won't get on us and make us unlucky like him."

This was hard for Habib to take. He went and repented at Hasan of Basra's prayer meeting. Hasan's sermon had a great effect on Habib, and he fainted. When Habib left the meeting, one of his debtors saw him. He was about to run away. "Don't run away," Habib said. "Up until now you have had to run away from me. Now I have to run away from you."

As he returned home, the children were out on the street again. "Let's get out of here," they said to each other, "so our dust won't get on Habib the Penitent and really make us sinners."

"My God," Habib said, "within the hour that I made my peace with you, you made my name seem goodness itself and made the hearts' drums announce my arrival." He then proclaimed, "Let everyone who is supposed to give something to Habib come and take back their IOUs." They gathered around, and Habib spent all the wealth he had saved up and returned their contracts, until nothing was left. Someone came up and made his claim. There was nothing—Habib gave the man his wife's chador. Another made his claim—Habib gave him the shirt that he was wearing and was left without any clothes on his back.

Habib built a meditation cell on the banks of the Euphrates and there busied himself with his devotions. He studied with Hasan of Basra by day
and worshiped all night long. They called him 'Ajami—the foreigner—
because he could not read the Qur'an.

After some time passed, his wife became an invalid. "We need some
money for household expenses," she said. Habib would go to his meditation cell, devote himself to worship, and return home at night. His
wife asked, "Didn't you bring anything?"

"The person I worked for is generous," Habib said. "Because of
his generosity, I was too ashamed to ask for anything. He will give it
himself when the time comes. He says that he will pay me once every
ten days."

Habib worshiped until the ten days were up. On the tenth day, he
worried, "What will I take home tonight?" He sank into thought. The
Real most high sent a porter to the door of his house with a mule's load
of flour, another porter with a skinned sheep, another porter with honey
and cooking oil, and a beautiful youth with a purse of three hundred
dirhams. He told Habib's wife, "The lord has sent this, and he says to
tell Habib, 'The more he works, the more I will pay.'" He said this and
left.

When night fell, Habib came home pensive and sad. He caught
the scent of food. His wife came out to greet him and said, "For whom
do you work? Keep working—he's a good boss, generous and kind.
Today he sent all these things and said, 'Tell Habib, "The more he
works, the more I will pay."'"

"Amazing!" said Habib, "I worked for ten days, and he showed
me this sort of kindness. If I work more, you know what he will do."
After this, Habib completely shunned this world and turned to the
Real, until he became one of the eminent people whose prayers are
answered.

One day a woman came and cried and cried. "I have a son who is
absent," she said, "and I can no longer stand to be separated from him.
For God's sake, say a prayer so that by the blessings of that prayer, my
son will return."

"Do you have any silver?" Habib asked.

"Two dirhams."

Habib took them and gave them to the poor and prayed. "Go," Habib said. "He is about to arrive." No sooner had she reached the house than her son came home.

"My son," she said, "how have you been?"

"I was in Kerman," he replied. "My teacher sent me to the market to look for some meat. I was buying the meat, when a wind came up and stole me away. I heard a voice saying, 'Wind, as a blessing for Habib's prayer and those two dirhams he gave as alms, take this boy back home.'"

If someone asks, "How can the wind carry him?" say, "Just as it used to carry the blessed Solomon (peace be upon him) on a month's journey in a single day and just as it took the throne of the Queen of Sheba back to Solomon (peace be upon him) in the twinkling of an eye."

It is related that Habib was seen in Basra on the eighth day of the month of the pilgrimage and at 'Arafāt on the ninth.

Once there was a great famine in Basra, and Habib bought a lot of food on credit and gave it all to the poor. He sewed a purse and put it under his pillow. When people came to demand payment, he would pull out the purse, full of dirhams, and pay the debt.

Habib had a house in Basra on the market square, and he had a fur cloak that he always used to wear. Once he went to perform his ablutions and left the fur cloak behind in the market square. Hasan of Basra came by. He saw the cloak and said, "Habib-e 'Ajami left it there. I can't let anyone steal it." He stood there until Habib came back.

"Imam of the Muslims," Habib asked, "why are you standing here?"

"Habib, don't you know you shouldn't leave your cloak out in the market square so someone can steal it? In whose care did you leave it?"

"In the care of the One who kept you here to watch it."

It is related that Hasan came to visit Habib. Habib had a loaf of barley bread and a bit of salt and he set them before Hasan. Hasan was eating when a beggar called out. Habib picked up the food from in front of Hasan and gave it to the beggar. "Habib," Hasan said, "you are a wor-

93

thy man, but it would be better if you had a bit of learning. Don't you even know that one should not pick up food from in front of one's guest? One should give part to the beggar and leave part for the guest."

Habib said nothing. An hour passed. A slave boy came, a tray on his head with roast lamb and fine sweets, and a slave boy with five hundred dirhams. They placed them in front of Habib. Habib gave the money to the poor, and he and Hasan ate the food. "Teacher," Habib said, "you are a good man, but it would be better if you had a bit of certainty. Then you would have both learning and certainty, for learning must come with certainty."

It is related that Hasan of Basra arrived at Habib's meditation cell in the time for the evening prayer. Habib continued praying. He pronounced "praise" as "phrase." Hasan thought to himself, "It's not right to pray behind him," and he performed his prayers by himself.

That night Hasan saw the most glorious Lord in a dream. "My God, what is your pleasure?" he asked.

"You had found what pleases me, but you did not recognize its worth."

"O Lord, what was that?"

"Praying behind Habib. That prayer was to be the seal on your lifetime of prayers, but correct expression held you back from sound intention."

There is a big difference between making the tongue right and making the heart right.

It is related that Hasan fled from Hajjāj's henchmen and went to Habib's meditation cell. The soldiers asked Habib, "Where is Hasan?"

"In my meditation cell," Habib replied.

The soldiers went in, but they did not find Hasan. They came out and told Habib, "You deserve whatever Hajjāj does to you because everything you say is a lie."

"Hasan is in there," Habib said. "If you did not see him, what am I supposed to do?"

They went in again and looked around carefully. They did not see Hasan and went away. Hasan came out of the cell and said, "Habib, do you claim to do your duty to your teacher when you point me out to them?"

"Teacher," Habib said, "you escaped because I told the truth. If I had lied, we would have both been destroyed."

"What did you recite so they wouldn't see me?"

"I recited the Throne Verse [2:255] ten times and *The Messenger believes* [2:285] ten times and *Say: He is the one God* [112:1] ten times. And I said, 'My God, I entrust Hasan to you. Protect him.'"

It is related that one day Hasan was going down a road. He reached the banks of the Tigris. He stopped. Habib asked, "Imam, why have you stopped?"

"To wait for a boat to come."

"Teacher, I have acquired learning from you. Expel men's envy from your heart, make your heart cold to this world, and count hardships a blessing. *See* your actions as coming from the Lord—step on the water and cross." Habib said this, stepped on the water, and walked across.

Hasan fainted. When he came to, they asked him, "What happened to you?"

"Habib acquired learning from me. This very hour he rebuked me and walked on water. If on the morrow a voice calls out, 'Cross over the Narrow Bridge,'[1] what will I be able to do if I am left helpless like this?"

Then he saw Habib and asked, "How did you attain this rank?"

"Because I make my heart white, while you make paper black."

"Others profit from my knowledge," Hasan said, "but I do not."

It is possible that someone might suppose that Habib's rank was higher that Hasan's, but this is not so, for there is no rank on the path of the Lord most high beyond the rank of knowledge. Thus it was that the command came to Mohammad (peace be upon him)—*Say: my Lord increase my knowledge* [20:114]. It is stated in the sayings of the sheikhs that miracles are the fourteenth rank on the path and knowledge of the secrets is the eighteenth, because miracles arise from great devotion and knowledge of the secrets from great meditation. Parallel to this is the situation of Solomon (peace be upon him) who achieved things that no one else in the world could. The demons and the fairies, the clouds and the wind, the wild beasts and the birds were all under his command. Water and fire obeyed him. He set a carpet flying through the air for forty miles and understood the language of the birds and the words of the ants. But God gave Moses the book containing the world of secrets, and for all his grandeur, Solomon was a follower of Moses (peace be upon them both).

It is related that Ahmad ebn Hanbal and Shāfe'i were sitting together when Habib appeared (God have mercy on them). Ahmad said, "Let's ask him a question."

"Don't do it," Imam Shāfe'i said. "They are a strange folk."

When Habib came up to them, Ahmad asked, "What do you say about someone who misses one of the five prayers and doesn't know which one it was? What should he do?"

Habib said, "This is the heart of a person who is negligent of the mighty and glorious Lord. He must punish it and make up all five prayers."

Ahmad was stunned by his answer. Imam Shāfe'i said, "Didn't I tell you one mustn't ask them questions?"

It is related that Habib dropped a needle in a dark room. The room began to shine with light. Habib put his hands over his eyes. "No, no!" he said. "We can only search for the needle with a lamp."

It is related that for thirty years Habib had a serving girl in his house whose face he had never fully seen. One day he said to the serving girl, "My honest woman, call my serving girl."

"I am your serving girl," she said.

"For these thirty years," Habib said, "I have not had the nerve to look at anyone other than him. I didn't give that up even for you."

It is related that Habib was sitting in a secluded place. He kept saying, "May anyone who is not happy with you never be happy. May any eye that is not illuminated by you never be illuminated. May anyone who is not intimate with you never be intimate with anyone."

It is related that they asked Habib, "In what does satisfaction lie?"

He said, "In the heart in which the dust of hypocrisy does not."

Whenever the Qur'an was read before him, Habib would weep. They said, "You're a foreigner and don't know the language. The Qur'an is in Arabic, and you don't know what it means. Why this weeping?"

"My tongue is foreign, but my heart speaks Arabic."

A dervish said, "I saw Habib held a high rank. I thought, 'But he's a foreigner after all. How did he attain this rank?' A voice came: 'Yes, he's 'Ajami—the foreigner—but he is also Habib—the beloved.'"

It is related that they were stringing a murderer up on the gallows. That very night the murderer was seen in people's dreams strutting through the meadows of paradise wearing precious silk. "Weren't you a murderer?" they asked. "How did you attain this rank?"

"At the moment they were hanging me from the gallows, Habib-e 'Ajami passed by and looked at me from the corner of his eye and said a prayer. All of this is from the blessings of that."

∽ 6 ∽
Rābe'a-ye 'Adaviya

Veiled with a special veil, hidden by the curtain of sincerity, burned up in love and longing, enamored of proximity and immolation, deputy of the virgin Mary, accepted among men, Rābe'a-ye 'Adaviya—God most high have mercy upon her. If anyone asks why we placed her memorial among the ranks of men, we reply that the Master of the Prophets (peace and blessing be upon him) declares: *God does not regard your forms*. It is not a matter of form but of right intention. If it is right to derive two-thirds of religion from 'Ā'esha-ye Sādeqa (God be pleased with her), then it is also right to derive benefit from one of his maidservants. When a woman is a man on the path of the Lord most high, she cannot be called woman.

Thus it is that 'Abbāsa of Tus said, "When on the morrow on the plain of resurrection they call out, 'O men,' the first person to step into the ranks of men will be Mary." When Hasan of Basra would not hold a prayer meeting unless a certain person were present, then certainly that person's memorial can be entered in the ranks of men. Indeed, to tell the truth, where this folk are, all are the nothingness of unity. In unity, how can the existence of "me" and "you" remain, much less "man" and "woman"? As Abu 'Ali of Fārmad (God's mercy upon him) says, "Prophecy is the essence of might and sublimity. Noble or common do not enter into it." Being God's friend is thus also exactly like this. This is especially so for Rābe'a, who in her age had no like in proper conduct or realization. She was esteemed by the eminent people of the age and was a decisive proof for those who lived in her time.

It is related that on the night she was born, there was no lamp in her father's house, nor a drop of oil to anoint her navel, nor so much as a piece of cloth to swaddle her in. Her father had three daughters, and Rābe'a was the fourth. And so they called her Rābe'a, meaning "the fourth one."

His wife said to him, "Go to the neighbors and ask for a lamp's worth of oil."

Rābe'a's father had sworn not to ask any creature for anything. He got up, went to the neighbor's door, and returned. "They were asleep," he said.

He fell asleep sore at heart. He saw the Prophet (peace and blessing be upon him) in a dream. The Prophet said, "Don't be sad. This girl is a noble lady who will intercede for seventy thousand of my community." He went on to say, "Go to see 'Isā Rādān,[1] the emir of Basra, and say, 'This last Friday, you forgot how you send your blessings to me a hundred times each night and four hundred times on Friday. Give me four hundred gold dinars in atonement.'"

When he awoke in tears in the morning, Rābe'a's father wrote this dream down on a piece of paper and took it to the door of the palace of 'Isā Rādān. He gave it to someone to deliver. When the emir examined it, he commanded that ten thousand dirhams be given in alms, in gratitude that the Prophet (peace and blessing be upon him) had remembered him. And he ordered that four hundred dinars be given to Rābe'a's father and said, "Tell him, 'I want you to come in, so I may pay my respects to you. But I do not consider it right that one like you, delivering the message of the Prophet (peace and blessing be upon him) should come to visit me. I myself will come and sweep the dust on your doorstep with my beard. By God, whenever you happen to need anything, let me know.'"

Rābe'a's father took the gold and spent it.

When Rābe'a grew older, her mother and father died. A great famine occurred in Basra. The sisters were separated, and Rābe'a fell into the hands of a wicked man who sold her for a few dirhams. Her master ordered her to work long and hard.

One day on the street, she fled from a stranger. She fell and broke her hand. She put her face on the ground and said, "My God, I am homeless without mother or father. I am a captive, and my hand is broken. None of this saddens me. All I need is for you to be pleased with me, to know whether you are pleased with me or not."

She heard a voice say, "Do not be sad. Tomorrow a grandeur will be yours such that the closest of the heavenly company will take pride in you."

So, Rābe'a went to the house. She fasted continuously and prayed all night, remaining on her feet until daybreak. One night, her master started from sleep. He heard a voice. He looked and saw Rābe'a prostrate in prayer, saying, "My God, you know that the desire of my heart is in accord with your command and that the light of my eye is in service to your court. If the matter were in my hands, I would not rest a moment from serving you. But you have put me in the hands of this creature. Because of this, I came late to serve you."

Her master looked and saw a lantern hanging suspended over Rābe'a's head without a chain and the whole room filled with light. He arose and said to himself, "She cannot be kept in servitude." He then said to Rābe'a, "I free you. If you wish to stay here, we are entirely at your service. If not, go wherever you have a mind to." Rābe'a asked leave to go, departed, and immersed herself in devotions.

They say she used to perform one thousand rak'ats of prayer a day. From time to time, she went to Hasan of Basra's prayer meetings. One group says that she lapsed into being a singer, repented again, and dwelled in a ruin. Afterward, she retired to a meditation cell and worshiped there a while.

Later, she resolved to make the hajj and went into the desert. She had a donkey upon which she loaded her belongings. In the middle of the desert, it died. The people in the caravan said, "We'll carry your things." She said, "I have not come this far by putting my trust in you. Go on ahead."

The caravan departed. Rābe'a said, "My God, is this the way kings treat a helpless woman? You summoned me to your house, then killed my donkey half way along the road and left me alone in the desert."

At once, the donkey got up. Rābe'a loaded it and went on. The narrator of this report said that sometime later he saw that little donkey being sold.

While Rābe'a was on her way to Mecca, she was stranded in the desert for several days. She said, "My God, I am sore at heart. Where am I going? I am a clod of earth, and that house is a rock. I must have you."

The Real most high addressed her heart without intermediary: "Oh, Rābe'a, you wash in the blood of eighteen thousand worlds. Don't you see that when Moses (peace be upon him) desired a vision, we cast a few motes of epiphany upon the mountain, and it shattered into forty pieces!"[2]

It is related that she was going to Mecca another time. In the middle of the desert she saw that the Ka'ba had come out to welcome her. Rābe'a said, "I need the lord of the house. What am I to do with the house? Its power means nothing to me. What delight is there in the Ka'ba's beauty? What I need to welcome me is the One who said, *'Whoever approaches me by a hand's span, I will approach by an arm's span.'*[3] Why should I look at the Ka'ba?"

It is related that Ebrāhim ebn Adham (God's mercy upon him) traveled fourteen years to reach the Ka'ba. He said, "Others have crossed this desert with their feet. I will cross it with my eyes!" He performed two rak'ats of prayer for every step he took. When he reached Mecca, he did not see God's house. He said, "What's happened? Could there be something wrong with my eyes?"

A voice said, "There's nothing wrong with your eyes! The Ka'ba has gone to welcome a weak woman who is on her way here." Ebrāhim roared with jealousy, "Who could this be?" As soon as he saw Rābe'a coming, walking with a cane, the Ka'ba was back in place.

"Rābe'a," Ebrāhim asked, "what is this fuss and frenzy that you've caused in the world?"

She said, "It's you who've caused this frenzy in the world, tarrying for fourteen years before you reached God's house!"

"Yes, for fourteen years I traversed the desert in supplication!" Ebrāhim said.

Rābe'a said, "You traversed it in supplication, I in destitution."

She then performed the hajj and wept bitterly and said, "My God, you promised good things both for performing the hajj and for enduring misfortune. Now, if my hajj is not acceptable, this is a great misfortune. Where is the reward for my misfortune?"

Then she came to Basra, staying until the following year. She said, "If last year the Ka'ba came to welcome me, this year I will go to welcome the Ka'ba." When the time came, so Sheikh Abu 'Ali of Fārmad relates, she set out into the desert and crawled for seven years until she arrived at 'Arafāt. A voice called out, "O claimant, what quest has drawn you here? If you want me to manifest myself just once, you will melt on the spot!"

She said, "O Lord of might, Rābe'a does not have the means to attain that rank. I wish only for a drop of poverty."

The voice called out, "Rābe'a, poverty is the drought year of our wrath, which we have placed in people's path. When no more than a hair's width remains before they arrive in the presence of union with us, then things turn around, and union turns into separation. You are still within the seventy veils of your life. Until you come out from under all of these and take a step on our path and pass these seventy stations, you cannot speak of our poverty. Otherwise, behold!"

Rābe'a looked and saw a sea of blood suspended in the air. A voice called out, "This is the blood of our lovers who came seeking union with us. They alighted at the first way station, so no trace or sign of them appears anywhere in the two worlds."

Rābe'a said, "O Lord of might, show me one characteristic of their estate."

Immediately they appeared before her, making excuses. A voice spoke, "Their first station is to crawl for seven years on our path to pay homage to a clod of earth. When they near that clod, they themselves cause the road to be closed before them."

Rābe'a writhed with affliction and said, "O Lord, you do not allow me into your house. Nor will you let me stay in my house in Basra. Either leave me in my house in Basra or bring me to your house in Mecca. At first, I did not bow to the house—I wanted you. Now I am not even worthy of your house."

She said this and returned. She came back to Basra and retired to a place of meditation.

It is related that two sheikhs came to pay their respects to her. They were hungry and said to one another, "We'll consume any food that she brings—it will be ritually pure." Rābe'a had two loaves of bread and set them before her guests. Just then, a beggar cried out. Rābe'a picked up the bread from in front of them and gave it to the beggar.

They were astonished, but at that moment a serving girl came, carrying an armful of warm bread. She said, "The lady of the house has sent these." Rābe'a counted; there were eighteen loaves. "Take them back," she said. "You've made a mistake."

"There's no mistake," the girl said.

"You've made a mistake. Take them back."

She took them back and told the story to her mistress. She added two more loaves and sent them back. Rābe'a counted; there were twenty. She took them and set them before her guests. They ate them and marveled. Later they asked her, "What's the secret behind this?"

She said, "When you came, I realized that you were hungry. I thought, 'How can I put two loaves before two eminent men?' When the beggar came, I gave them to him and prayed, 'My God, you have said, "For each thing given, I will return tenfold." Certain of this, I just gave away two loaves to please you, so that you would give back ten for each one.' When she brought eighteen, I knew that there had been some filching or that they had not been meant for me. I sent them back so she could bring me all twenty."

It is related that one night she was praying in her cell. She fell asleep. A reed pierced her eye, but in such a way that in her total passion and absorption, her utter devotion, she was unaware of it. And one night a thief entered and picked up her chador. As he was trying to carry it off, he could not see the way. He put it back and recognized the way out. He picked the chador back up but again could not see the way. Seven times this happened. A voice came from the corner of the cell: "Man, don't trouble yourself! Several years ago now, she entrusted herself to us. Satan himself doesn't have the gall to come around her. How could

102

a thief have the gall to come around her chador? Don't bother, you petty crook. If one friend is sleeping, the other is awake."

It is related that one day, after Rābe'a had not eaten for many days, her serving girl was preparing a soup from lard. She needed onions and said, "I'll get some from the neighbors."

"For forty years," Rābe'a said, "I have had a covenant with the mighty and glorious Lord not to ask for anything from anyone other than him. Say, 'Onions we'll do without.'"

All of a sudden a bird swooped down from the sky and tossed several onions, already peeled, into her pot. Rābe'a said, "I'm not safe from being tricked." She gave up the soup and ate plain bread.

It is related that one day Rābe'a had gone up on a mountain. Wild goats and gazelles gathered around and gazed upon her. Just then, Hasan of Basra showed up. All the animals shied away. When Hasan saw this, he was perplexed and asked, "Rābe'a, why do they shy away from me when they were so familiar with you?"

Rābe'a asked, "What did you eat today?"

"Soup."

"You ate their lard. Why wouldn't they shy away from you?"

It is related that one time Rābe'a happened to pass by Hasan's house. He was sitting on the roof of his meditation cell, weeping so much that water was dripping from the rainspouts. Several drops landed on Rābe'a. She investigated to find out where this water was coming from. When she realized what was happening, she said, "Hasan, if this weeping is from the foolish whims of the self, hold back your tears, so a sea will well up within you, such a sea that when you seek your heart there, you will not find it *except before a most powerful king*" [54:55].

These words were hard for Hasan to take, but he said nothing. One day he saw Rābe'a on the banks of the Euphrates. Hasan threw his prayer rug on the water and said, "Rābe'a, come here! Let's perform two rak'ats of prayer."

Rābe'a said, "Teacher, are you going to display the goods of the afterworld in the market of this world? You must do what others of your species are incapable of doing." So, Rābe'a threw her prayer rug into the air and said, "Hasan, come here, where you'll be hidden from the people's gaze." She then wished to win Hasan's heart over again. She said, "Teacher, what you did, a fish can do, and what I do, a fly can do. The real business is beyond both."

It is related that Hasan of Basra said, "I was with Rābe'a for one full day and night. I was talking about the path and the truth in such a way that the thought 'I am a man' never crossed my mind, nor did 'I am a woman' ever cross hers. In the end when I got up, I considered myself a pauper and her a devotee."

It is related that one evening Hasan went with some friends to visit Rābe'a. Rābe'a had no lamp, and they needed one. Rābe'a blew on her fingertips—they blazed like a lamp until daybreak.

If someone asks, "What was this like?" we answer, "Just like the hand of Moses (peace and blessing be upon him)."[4] If they say, "He was a prophet," we respond, "Whoever follows a prophet has a portion of those wonders. If the prophet performs miracles, the friend of God performs wonders by the blessings of following the prophet. As the Prophet (peace and blessing be upon him) declares, '*Whoever returns a farthing of what is forbidden has attained a degree of prophecy*'; that is, anyone one who gives back to the enemy Satan a penny of what is forbidden achieves a degree of prophecy."

He also said, "The true dream is a quarter share of prophecy."

It is related that Rābe'a once sent Hasan three things: a piece of wax, a needle, and a hair. She said, "Like the wax, give light to the world as you yourself burn. Like the needle, be naked and work continually. When you have acquired both these traits, be like the hair, so your work will not be in vain."

It is related that Hasan said to Rābe'a, "Do you long for a husband?"

She said, "The marriage knot can only tie one who exists. Where is existence here? I am not my own—I am his and under the shadow of his command. You must ask permission from him."

"Rābe'a," he asked, "how did you attain this rank?"

"By losing in him everything I'd attained."

"How do you know him?"

"You know the how. We know the no-how."

It is related that one day Hasan came to her meditation cell and said, "Say a word to me about the knowledge that, untaught and unheard, came down to your heart without the mediation of any creature."

She said, "I had spun some skeins of yarn to sell and earn a bit of food. I sold them for two silver dirhams. I took one in one hand and one in the other. I was afraid that if I took both in one hand, they would join forces and lead me from the path. My victory today was from this."

They said to Rābe'a, "Hasan says that if he is deprived of the vision of the Real for one moment in paradise, he will weep and moan so much that all the people of paradise will take pity on him."

She said, "This is a fine thing to say. However, if he fails to remember the Real for one moment in this world and it leads to the same anguish and weeping and moaning, then it is a sign that the same thing will happen in the afterworld. Otherwise, it will not be so."

"Why don't you take a husband?"

"I am dismayed by three concerns," Rābe'a said. "If you relieve me of them, I'll take a husband. First, at the moment of death, will my faith be sound or not? Second, will they put the book of my deeds in my right hand or not? Third, which group will I be in on that hour when they lead a group on the right to paradise and a group on the left to hell?"

"We don't know."

"With such anguish before me, how can I worry about taking a husband?"

"Where do you come from?" they asked.

"From that world," she said.

"Where will you go?"

"To that world."

"What are you doing in this world?"

"Grieving."

"How so?"

"I eat the bread of this world and do the work of that."

"Such a sweet tongue! You are fit to be an abbess."

"I am abbess of myself. I do not bring out what is within me. I do not let in what is outside me. If anyone enters and leaves, it has nothing to do with me. I watch over my heart, not mud and clay."

They said, "Do you love the presence of majesty?"

She said, "I do."

They said, "Do you hate Satan?"

She said, "Out of love of the Compassionate, I do not engage in hatred toward Satan. I saw the Prophet (peace and blessing be upon him) in a dream. He said, 'Rābe'a, do you love me?' I said, 'O Messenger of God, is there anyone who doesn't love you? But love of the Real has so enveloped me that there is no place in my heart for love or hatred of another.'"

They asked her about love. She said, "Love came down from eternity without beginning and passed over to eternity without end. It found no one in eighteen thousand worlds to take a single drink of it. It arrived at last to the Real, and of him this expression remains: *He loves them and they love him*" [5:54].

They said, "Do you see the one you worship?"

She said, "If I did not see, I would not worship."

It is related that Rābe'a was always weeping. "Why do you weep so much?" they asked.

She said, "I'm afraid of being cut off, for I've grown accustomed to him. No voice must cry out at the moment of death, 'You are not worthy of us!'"

"When are God's servants contented?" they asked.

"When they are as thankful for tribulation as they are for bliss," she said.

"If sinners repent, does he accept them or not?"

"How can they repent, unless the Lord gives them repentance and accepts them? Until he gives them repentance, they cannot repent."

∽ ∽ ∽

"O children of Adam, from the eye, there is no way station to the Real. From the tongue, there is no path to him. Hearing is the highway of complainers. Hand and foot dwell in perplexity. The matter falls to the heart. Strive to acquire a wakeful heart. When the heart is awake, it has no need for a friend." In other words, the wakeful heart is one that has been lost in the Real. When someone is lost, what is he to do with a friend? Extinction in God is here.

"Asking for mercy with the tongue is the business of liars."

"When we repent ourselves, we need the repentance of another."

"If patience were a man, he would be generous."

"The fruit of realization is turning to the mighty and glorious Lord."

"The fully realized are those who ask the Real for a heart. When he gives them a heart, they immediately give it back to the mighty and glorious Lord, so it will be protected in his grasp and hidden from creatures within his veil."

ॐ ॐ ॐ

Sāleh-e Morri[5] (God's mercy upon him) often used to say, "If you knock on a door, it will open in the end."
　　Once Rābe‘a was present. She said, "How long will you say, 'He will open it again'? When did he close it that he will open it again?"
　　Sāleh said, "Amazing! An ignorant man and a wise weak woman."

One day Rābe‘a saw a man saying, "Oh, sorrows!"
　　She said, "Say it this way: Oh, without sorrows! For if you *were* sorrowful, you wouldn't have the gall to breathe."

It is related that once someone had tied a bandage around his head. She asked, "Why have you tied the bandage on your head?"
　　"My head hurts."
　　"How old are you?"
　　"Thirty."
　　"In these thirty years, have you been mostly healthy or sick?"
　　"Healthy."
　　"Have you ever, in these thirty years, tied on the bandage of gratitude? And now because you have a single headache, you tie on the bandage of complaint?"

It is related that she gave someone four dirhams, saying, "Get a blanket for me."

"Black or white?"

She immediately took back the dirhams, threw them in the Tigris, and said, "Because of an unpurchased blanket, division appeared; must it be black or white?"

It is related that in the springtime she went into a house and did not come out. Her serving girl said, "O mistress, come outside and see the effects of the creation!"

Rābe'a said, "You come in for once and see the Creator! *Witnessing the Creator has kept me from gazing on the creation.*"

Once a group went to see Rābe'a. They saw her tearing apart a piece of meat with her teeth. They said, "Don't you have a knife?"

She said, "I've never owned a knife for fear of being cut off."

It is related that once she did not break her fast for seven days and went without sleep. On the eighth night, hunger overwhelmed her. Her self cried out, "How long will you torment me?" Just then, someone knocked at the door, bringing a bowl of food. She took it and set it down to get a lamp. The cat came and spilled the food.

She said, "I will go and get a jug of water and break my fast." When she left, the lamp went out. As she tried to drink the water, the jug fell from her hand and broke. Rābe'a heaved a sigh that might have burned down the house. She said, "My God, I am so helpless—what are you doing to me?"

She heard a voice say, "Beware, Rābe'a! If you wish, I will bestow the bliss of the world upon you, but I will remove the grief for me from your heart, for the bliss of the world and grief for me cannot be joined in one heart. Rābe'a, you desire one thing, and we another. Our desire and yours cannot be joined in one heart."

She said, "When I heard this speech, I so detached my heart from the world and cut short my hopes that for thirty years now I have performed each prayer as though it would be my last—*I pray the prayer of farewell.* I made myself so independent of creatures, so cut off, that when day broke, for fear that the created world would distract me, I prayed, 'O Lord, so distract me that no one will distract me from you.'"

It is related that she lamented continually. People said, "There's no apparent reason for it. What's the cause of her lament?"

She said, "I have a sickness within my breast that physicians have proved unable to cure. The salve for our wound is union with him. I procrastinate until the morrow when perhaps I will attain my goal. Although I am not among those racked with pain, still I liken myself to them. Anything less than this is impossible."

It is related that a group of great people went to see Rābe'a. Rābe'a asked one of them, "Why do you worship the Lord?"

He said, "The seven levels of hell have a majestic power, and everyone must pass through them, disheartened by the fear and dread of him."

Another said, "The stages of paradise contain an excellent way station, wherein much repose is promised."

"It is an evil servant," Rābe'a said, "who worships his Lord out of fear or reveres him desiring a reward."

So, they asked, "Why do you worship the Lord? Have you no desire?"

She replied, "'The neighbor, then the house,' as they say. Isn't it everything to us that we have been commanded to worship him? If there were no heaven or hell, then it wouldn't be necessary to worship him!? Wouldn't he deserve to be worshiped without intermediary?"

It is related that a great man came to visit her. He saw her clothes in tatters. He said, "There are many people who would look after you if you would just give the word."

Rābe'a said, "I am ashamed to ask for things of this world from someone who has them on loan."

That great man said, "Behold the lofty aspiration of this weak woman! He has brought her to such a height that she refuses to spend her time making requests."

It is related that a group went to see Rābe'a to put her to the test. They said, "All the virtues have been dispersed among men. The crown of nobility has been placed upon the heads of men, and the belt of magnanimity has been tied around their waists. Prophecy has never descended upon any woman. What do you have to boast of?"

Rābe'a said, "Everything you said is true. But egoism, egotism, self-worship, and *I am your highest lord*[6] have not welled up in any woman. And no woman has ever been a pederast."

It is related that one day Rābe'a fell ill. She was asked about the cause of her illness. She said, "In the morning, an inclination for paradise appeared in my heart, and the friend punished me. This illness is because of that."

Hasan of Basra visited her in her sickness. He said, "I saw a rich gentleman of Basra with a pouch of gold sitting and weeping on the doorstep of her cell. I said, 'Why are you weeping?' He said, 'Because of this devoted ascetic, dear to our age. Without her blessing, humankind will perish. I've brought something to take care of her, but I'm afraid she won't accept it. Intercede for me, and perhaps she will.'"

Hasan said, "I entered and delivered the message. Rābe'a looked at me from the corner of her eye and said, 'He does not withhold the daily bread from someone who insults him: will he withhold it from someone whose soul seethes with love for him? Since I've come to know him, I've turned my back on created things. How can I accept someone's money, not knowing whether it's lawful or not? Once I sewed up my torn shirt by the light of the sultan's lantern. A turn of fate had sealed my heart. Until I tore the shirt up again, my heart was not opened. Beg my pardon from the gentleman, so he won't put my heart in bondage.'"

'Abd al-Vāhed ebn 'Āmer[7] relates:

With Sofyān-e Sowri, we paid a sick call on Rābe'a. We couldn't speak for awe of her. They said to Sofyān, "Say something."

He said, "Rābe'a, pray, so the Real most high will ease this pain of yours."

Rābe'a said, "Sofyān, don't you know that the Real most high has willed my pain?"

"Yes."

"You know this and still you tell me to request what is at odds with his will. It is not proper to be at odds with the friend."

Then Sofyān said, "Rābe'a, what do you desire?"

She said, "Sofyān, you are a man of learning. How can you talk this way? By the Lord's might, for twelve years I have desired fresh dates, and you know there's no shortage of fresh dates in Basra. I still haven't eaten any. I am God's servant, and what business does a servant have with desire? If I wish for something and my Lord does not, this is infidelity."

Then Sofyān said, "I can say nothing with regard to your situation. Say something with regard to mine."

She said, "You are a good man, but isn't it the case that you love this world?"

"How so?" he asked.

She said, "By reciting hadiths," meaning that this, too, is a sort of pomp.

Sofyān said, "I have been lax."

I, 'Abd al-Vāhed, said, "O Lord, be pleased with me!"

Rābe'a said, "Aren't you ashamed to seek the good pleasure of someone with whom you are not pleased?"

Mālek-e Dinār related:

I went to visit Rābe'a. I saw she had a broken jug that she used for ablutions and drinking water. Her reed mat was old and worn, and she had a brick to rest her head on. This hurt me to the core, and I said, "Rābe'a, I have wealthy friends. If you permit, I'll ask them for something for you."

"Mālek," she said, "You're mistaken. Don't I and they have the same provider?"

I said, "Of course."

She said, "Has he forgotten the poor because of their poverty? Does he aid the wealthy because of their wealth?"

I said, "No."

She said, "Since he knows my condition, why should I remind him? He wills it so. We in turn will whatever he wills."

It is related that Hasan of Basra, Mālek-e Dinār, and Shaqiq of Balkh (God most high have mercy upon them) went to visit Rābe'a (God have mercy upon her). The conversation turned on the question of sincerity. Hasan said, "No one is sincere in his claim who is not patient under the blows of his master."

Rābe'a said, "This talk stinks of egoism."

111

Shaqiq said, "No one is sincere in his claim who is not grateful for the blows of his master."

Rābe'a said, "We need something better than this."

Mālek-e Dinār said, "No one is sincere in his claim who does not delight in the blows of his friend."

Rābe'a said, "We need something better than this."

They said, "Now you speak."

Rābe'a said, "No one is sincere in his claim who does not forget the wound of the blow in the contemplation of his desired one.[8] There's nothing strange in this. The women of Egypt did not perceive the wound of the cut while they were contemplating Joseph (peace be upon him).[9] Why should it be strange if someone is like this while contemplating the Creator?"

It is related that one of the sheikhs of Basra came to visit Rābe'a, sat at her bedside, and began to condemn the world. Rābe'a said, "You love the world dearly. If you didn't, you wouldn't dwell on it so much. The buyer is the one who disparages the goods. Were you free of the world, you wouldn't remember it for good or ill. You'll recall that 'Whoever loves a thing, remembers it all the more.'"[10]

It is related that Hasan said, "I was with Rābe'a at the time of the afternoon prayer. She was about to cook something. The meat was in the pot when we started talking. She said, 'This talk is better than putting the pot on to cook.' She left the pot as it was while we performed the evening prayer. She brought dry bread and a jug of water so we could break our fast. She went over to the pot to pick it up. The pot was boiling through the power of the Real most high. Then she poured the food in a bowl, brought it over, and we ate some of the meat. It was a dish the likes of which we had never tasted. She said, 'They prepare such a dish for someone who's risen from prayer.'"

Sofyān-e Sowri said, "One night I was with Rābe'a. She went to the prayer niche and prayed until daybreak. I was praying in the other corner. At dawn she said, 'In thanks for our success, let's fast today.'"

The Devotions of Rābe'a-ye 'Adaviya

"O Lord, if you send me to hell on the morrow of the resurrection, I will reveal a secret such that hell will flee from me, not to return for a thousand years."

"My God, whatever share of this world you have given me, give it to your enemies, and whatever share of the next world you have given me, give it to your friends. You are enough for us."

"O Lord, if I worship you out of fear of hell, burn me in hell. If I worship you in the hope of paradise, forbid it to me. If I worship you for your own sake, do not deprive me of your everlasting beauty."

"O Lord, if you put me in hell on the morrow, I will cry out, 'I have loved you. Is this what they do to lovers?'" A voice called out, "Rābe'a, do not think ill of us. Be assured that we will bring you into the circle of our friends, so you may converse with us."

"My God, my work and my desire, in all this world, is remembering you and in the afterworld, meeting you. This is what is mine—you do as you will."

And nightly she would say, "O Lord, make my heart present or accept my prayers without my heart."

❧   ❧   ❧

When the moment of her death drew near, great people were at her bedside. She said, "For the sake of the Lord's prophets, arise and leave the room." They arose, went out, and closed the door. They heard a voice: *"O soul now in peace, return to your Lord, well pleased and well pleasing. Enter among my servants, enter my garden"* [89:27–31].

Some time passed, and no voice was heard. When they went in, she had died. The sheikhs said, "Rābe'a came to this world and left for the afterworld, never having been arrogant toward the Real most high, never wanting anything, never saying, 'Make me thus' or 'Do such-and-such.'"

113

It is related that she was seen in a dream. She was asked, "Tell us about Monker and Nakir."

She said, "When those young gentlemen came to me and said, 'Who is your Lord?' I said, 'Go back and say to the Real, "Out of so many thousand creatures, you wouldn't forget an old woman. Out of all the world, I have only you. Do I ever forget you that you need to send someone to ask, 'Who is your Lord?'"'"

It is related that Mohammad ebn Aslam of Tus[11] and No'má of Tarsus[12] (God have mercy on them both), who gave water to thirty thousand people in the desert, were both present at Rābe'a's grave. They said, "You, who boasted that you would not bow your head to anyone in the two worlds, what state have you attained?"

A voice replied, "May what I have seen be to my good health!"

∞ 7 ∞
Fozeyl ebn 'Ayāz

The vanguard of the penitent, God's esteemed lieutenant, the sun of generosity and benevolence, the sea of intuitive knowing and scrupulousness, contemptuous of both worlds, the elder of the age, Fozeyl ebn 'Ayāz—God's mercy upon him. He was one of the greatest of the sheikhs, a noble vagabond on the path, praised by his peers, and a refuge for the common folk. He was highly regarded for his austerities and wonders and was without equal in scrupulousness and realization.

This was the beginning of Fozeyl's spiritual life: He had pitched his tent in the middle of the desert between Merv and Abivard.[1] He wore sackcloth, with a woolen hat on his head and prayer beads around his neck. He had many friends, all of them thieves and bandits. Since he was their chief, he divided up whatever money they brought to him. Whatever he wanted, he took as his share. Fozeyl never abandoned the group and expelled anyone who did not serve its interests.

Then, one day, a great caravan was approaching. The travelers had heard rumors of bandits. One merchant in the caravan took all the cash he had and thought, "Let me hide this somewhere. If the caravan is attacked, at least I'll have this cash left."

He went out into the desert. He saw a tent with a man wearing sackcloth sitting inside. The merchant entrusted his gold to the man. "Go into the tent," the man said, "and put it in a corner." The merchant put the gold inside the tent and returned to the caravan.

By the time he got back to the caravan, the bandits had struck and carried off all the cargo. The merchant gathered the personal belongings he had left and set off for the tent. When he got there, he saw the bandits dividing up the haul. "Oh, no!" he said, "I entrusted my money to thieves!"

As the merchant was about to turn back, Fozeyl caught sight of him. "Come here!" he shouted. The merchant went over, and Fozeyl asked, "What's your business here?"

"I've come to get the money I gave you for safekeeping."

"It's right where you put it. Take it."

The merchant went and picked it up.

Fozeyl's friends said to him, "We didn't find any cash in that caravan. How can you give so much of it back?"

Fozeyl replied, "He had confidence in me. Likewise, I have confidence in the Lord most high. I justified his confidence so that perhaps the Lord most high will justify mine."

It is related that in the beginning Fozeyl fell in love with a woman. He used to send her everything he obtained from his banditry. From time to time he would go to see her and weep out of his desire for her. Then, one night, a caravan was passing. In the middle of the caravan someone was reciting this verse: *Is it not time for those who believe to humble their hearts in remembrance of the Lord?* [57:16]. Hasn't the time come for your sleeping hearts to awaken? It was like an arrow piercing Fozeyl's heart. "The time has come! The time has come!" he said. "Indeed, the time is past."

Confused, ashamed, and unsettled, he set off toward some ruins. A group of caravan travelers had alighted there. They wanted to depart, but some of them said, "How can we leave? Fozeyl is on the move."

"I have good tidings for you," Fozeyl said. "He has repented. He flees from you just as you flee from him." Then he wandered about and wept and made amends to his enemies.

Now, there was a Jew in Abivard who would not be satisfied no matter what Fozeyl did. "Now's the time to humiliate the Mohammadans," he told his friends.

To Fozeyl he said, "If you want me to absolve you, haul away the sand dune at such-and-such a place and level the ground."

That sand dune was as big as it could be. Fozeyl hauled it off day and night, until one morning a wind rose up and obliterated the dune. When the Jew saw this, he said, "I have sworn not to absolve you until you give my money back. Now there is some gold under my pillow. Take it and give it to me so I may absolve you."

Fozeyl put his hand under his pillow, pulled out the gold, and gave it to him. "First make me a Muslim," the Jew said.

"What's going on here?" Fozeyl asked.

"In the Torah I read that dirt turns to gold in the hands of one whose repentance is true. I tested this: there was nothing but dirt under my pillow. When it turned to gold in your hands, I realized that your repentance was sincere and your faith was true." The Jew then accepted Islam.

It is related that Fozeyl told someone, "For God's sake, tie me up and take me to the sultan so he can punish me—I deserve a heavy punishment." The man did as he was told and took Fozeyl before the sultan. When the sultan looked at Fozeyl's bearing, he sent him back home with honor.

When Fozeyl reached the door of his house, he burst into tears. Fozeyl's wife asked him whether he was crying because he had taken some blows. "Yes," Fozeyl said, "I have taken a heavy blow."

"Where?" his wife asked.

"In my heart and soul." Then Fozeyl said to his wife, "I intend to go to the Lord's house. If you wish, I will release you."

"God forbid!" his wife said. "I will never be separated from you! I will serve you wherever you are." So, they went to Mecca together. The Real most high made the way easy for them. They settled there and met some of the friends of God. Fozeyl studied with Abu Hanifa (God's mercy upon him) and took instruction from him.

Fozeyl was a superior transmitter of traditions and performed fine austerities. In Mecca the way was opened for him to speak. The Meccans would go to him, and he would preach to them. His spiritual state advanced so far that when his relatives came from Abivard to Mecca to see him, Fozeyl would not open his door to them, but they would not go back.

Fozeyl went up on the roof of the Ka'ba. "Beware, you heedless people!" he said. "May the mighty and glorious Lord grant you wisdom and busy you with some task." Everyone fell to the ground and began to weep. His relatives finally set off for Khorasan, but Fozeyl did not come down from the roof of the Ka'ba.

It is related that Hārun ar-Rashid said to his vizier Fazl-e Barmaki,[2] "Take me to see someone with whom I can put my mind at rest. I'm sick of this pomp and circumstance." Fazl-e Barmaki led him to the house of Sofyān-e 'Oyeyna and called out at the door.

"Who is it?" Sofyān asked.

"The Commander of the Faithful."

"Why didn't you inform me?" Sofyān said. "I would have come to serve you."

When Hārun heard this, he said, "This isn't the man I'm looking for."

"Commander of the Faithful," Sofyān-e 'Oyeyna said, "Fozeyl ebn 'Ayāz is just the man you're looking for."

They went to Fozeyl's house. He was reciting this verse: *Do those who commit evil deeds think that we will consider them equal to those who believe and do good works?* [45:21]. "If we are looking for counsel," Hārun said, "this much is sufficient."

They knocked on his door. "Who is it?" Fozeyl asked.

"The Commander of the Faithful."

"What business does the Commander of the Faithful have with me," Fozeyl said, "and what business do I have with him? He is distracting me."

"Obedience to those in authority is imperative," Fazl-e Barmaki said. "Now shall we enter with your permission or by force?"

"I'm not giving you permission," Fozeyl answered. "Only you know whether you are coming in by force."

Hārun entered. Fozeyl extinguished the lamp so he would not have to see Hārun's face. Hārun groped around with his hands and accidentally touched Fozeyl's. "What soft hands," Fozeyl said, "if only they escape the fires of hell."

Saying this, Fozeyl stood up to pray. Hārun began to weep. "Just say something!" he implored.

When Fozeyl completed his prayers, he said, "Your forefather, the uncle of the Prophet (peace and blessing be upon him) asked the Prophet to make him the ruler over a people. Mohammad answered, 'O uncle, for a moment I will make you the ruler over your self.' In other words, it is better for you to obey the mighty and glorious Lord for one moment than for the people to obey you for a thousand years. *Truly, rulership is remorse on the day of resurrection.*"[3]

Hārun said, "Go on."

"When 'Omar ebn 'Abd al-'Aziz was installed as caliph," Fozeyl continued, "he summoned Sālem ebn 'Abdollāh,[4] Rejā' ebn Heyvat, and Mohammad ebn Ka'b. 'I am tormented by this task,' he said to them. 'What is the prudent thing for me to do?' One of them replied, 'If you wish to be delivered from torment on the morrow, think of the Muslim elders as your fathers. Think of the young men as your brothers, the children as your offspring, and the women as your mothers and sisters.'"

Hārun said, "Go on."

"The lands of Islam are like your house," Fozeyl said, "and the people in that house are like your family. Behave toward them as you would toward your father, your brother, and your children. Visit your father, do good to your brothers, and be generous with your children. I fear for your pretty face lest it be scourged by hellfire and turn ugly. *Many a beaming face goes screaming into the fire, and many a prince is taken prisoner there.*"

Hārun said, "Go on."

"Fear the Lord," Fozeyl said, "and be aware that you must answer to the mighty and glorious Lord. On the day of resurrection the Real most high will interrogate Muslims one by one and demand justice for each one. If an old woman has gone to bed destitute one night, she will seize your robe and stand against you on the morrow."

Hārun fainted from weeping.

"Enough, Fozeyl!" Fazl-e Barmaki said. "You're killing the Commander of the Faithful!"

"Silence, Hāmān!"[5] Fozeyl replied. "You and your people have killed him, not me."

With this Hārun wept even harder. He then said to Fazl-e Barmaki, "He called you Hāmān because he considers me Pharaoh."

He then asked Fozeyl, "Do you have any debts?"

"Yes, I do," Fozeyl said. "I have a debt to the Lord, and it is my devotion. If he calls up that debt, then woe is me!"

"I am talking about debts to people," Hārun said.

"Praise be to God, I have received great bounty from him, and I have no complaint to tell people about."

Hārun then placed a signet ring worth a thousand dinars before Fozeyl, saying, "This is lawful property—I inherited it from my mother."

"These counsels of mine did you no good," Fozeyl said. "Even now you've begun your tyranny and taken up injustice. I call you to salvation, while you call me to take on a heavy burden. I tell you, 'Give whatever you have back to the Lord,' and you give it to another to whom it ought not be given. My words are useless."

Saying this, Fozeyl stood up in front of Hārun and slammed the door.

Hārun left and said, "Ah, what sort of man is this? Fozeyl is a man in the truest sense."

It is related that Fozeyl once hugged his little boy and doted on him, as fathers are wont to do. His child asked, "Father, do you love me?"

"I do," Fozeyl said.

"Do you love the Lord?"

"I do."

"How many hearts do you have?"

"One."

"Can you love two with one heart?"

Fozeyl understood where these words came from; in reality, they told of the jealousy of the Real most high. Fozeyl kept striking his head with his hands and tossed the child aside. He devoted himself to the Real and said, "You are a fine preacher, my little boy."

It is related that one day Fozeyl was standing at 'Arafāt, looking at the crowd and listening to the people's cries and supplications. "Glory be to God!" he said. "If this many people go to a person and ask him for a small gold coin, he will not turn them away disappointed. It is easier for you, generous and clement Lord, to forgive them than for that man to give them a small coin. You are the most generous of the generous. There is hope that you will forgive them all."

It is related that on the night that people gather at 'Arafāt, they asked Fozeyl, "How do you see the state of these people?"

"They would have been forgiven," he said, "if Fozeyl were not among them."

"How is it," they asked, "that we do not see the fearful?"

"If you were fearful, they would not be hidden from you, for only the fearful see the fearful, and only the grief-stricken see the grief-stricken."

"When does a person achieve the utmost in friendship?"

"When it doesn't matter whether gifts are given or withheld."

"What do you say about a person who wants to say, '*I am at your service*' but does not dare for fear that he will say, '*I am not at yours*'?"

"I hope that no one who says '*I am at your service*' will ever be next to anyone who does this and thinks of himself this way."[6]

It is related that they asked Fozeyl, "What is the essence of religion?"

"Reason," he said.

"What is the essence of reason?"

"Forbearance."

"What is the essence of forbearance?"

"Patience."

Imam Ahmad ebn Hanbal related, "I heard Fozeyl (God have mercy on them both) say, 'Whoever seeks leadership becomes inferior.'

"I said, 'Give me counsel.'

"He replied, 'Follow, and be followed.'

"'This is commendable,' I said."

Beshr the Barefoot said, "I asked Fozeyl, 'Which is better, asceticism or contentment?'

"'Contentment,' he said, 'for if someone is content, he will seek no station beyond his station.'"

It is related that Sofyān-e Sowri reported:

I went to see Fozeyl one night, and we were talking about verses of the Qur'an and the stories and the works of holy people. I said, "What a blessed night this is! And what laudable company! Surely, such company is better than being alone!"

"What an evil night this is!" Fozeyl said, "and what wicked company we kept last night!"

"Why?" I asked.

"Because all night you were bound to say something that would please me, and I was bound to answer in a way that would please you. We were both distracted by one another's words and held back from the mighty and glorious Lord. It is better to be alone and to speak privately with the Real."

It is related that Fozeyl saw 'Abdollāh ebn Mobārak coming up to him. Fozeyl said, "Either you go back the way you came, or I will. You come to ply me with a handful of words, and I can do the same to you."

It is related that a man came to pay a call on Fozeyl. Fozeyl asked, "What business brought you here?"

"To receive some comfort and companionship from you."

"By God," Fozeyl said, "this verges on savagery. You have come just so you can deceive me with lies and so I can deceive you. Go back the way you came."

✑ ✑ ✑

"I want to get sick so it won't be necessary to go to Friday prayers or to go near people or to see them."

"If you can, live some place where no one will see you and you will see no one, for this is a great good."

"I am greatly obliged to anyone who passes by me and does not say hello and who does not come to visit me when I am sick."

"When night falls, I am happy because I have an undivided privacy. When morning comes, I am saddened by the loathsomeness of seeing people, for they mustn't come in and confuse me."

121

"Whoever is terrified when alone and feels comfortable with people is far from salvation."

"Whoever reckons his words among his works seldom speaks unless it is about something that is of use to him."[7]

"The tongue of anyone who fears the mighty and glorious Lord is mute."

"When the Real most high loves one of his servants, he bestows on him great sadness. When he despises one of them, he opens this world up before him joyously. If one sorrowful person weeps in the midst of a nation, that whole nation is forgiven for that person's sake."

"A tithe is due on everything, and the tithe of reason is prolonged sorrow." Thus it is that the *Prophet of God (peace and blessing be upon him and his family) was in constant sorrow.*

"As strange as it is that they weep in paradise, it is stranger still that anyone laughs in this world."

"When a dread dwells in someone's heart, nothing passes over his tongue that is not to the purpose. Because of that dread, he burns away lusts and the love of this world and banishes its delights from his heart."

"All things fear anyone who fears the Lord most high."

"The dread and fear of God's servant are equal to his knowledge. The asceticism of God's servant in this world is equal to his delight in the next."

"I have seen no one among this people with more hope in the Lord most high and with more fear of him than Ebn Sirin[8] (God's mercy upon him)."

"If they gave me this entire world, legally and with no strings attached, I would scorn it as much as you scorn a corpse."

"They gathered all evils in a house and made the key to it love of this world. They gathered all virtues in a house and made the key to it hostility to this world."

"It is easy to start with this world, but hard to leave it and escape."

"This world is an asylum and the people in it are like madmen, except that madmen in the asylum are bound by collars and chains."

"By God, if the next world were made of everlasting earthenware and this world were made of transitory gold, it would be right for people to delight in everlasting earthenware. How much more so when this world is made of transitory earthenware and the next world of everlasting gold!"

"No one was given anything of this world that was not deducted a hundredfold from his share of the afterworld, because in the presence of the Real most high you will have what you earn, whatever you do."

"Do not look to soft clothes or delicious food or the pleasures of the moment, lest on the morrow you do not obtain the delight of those clothes or that food."

"People who are alienated from one another resort to etiquette. Whenever etiquette is eliminated, they can look at one another frankly."

"The Real most high sent a revelation to the mountains: 'I will speak to a prophet upon one of you.' All the mountains grew overbearing except Mount Sinai, which lowered its head. It, of course, received the miracle of God's words."

"Whoever values himself will have no share of humility."

"Don't look for these three things, for you'll not find them. Don't look for a scholar whose works balance his learning, for you'll not find him and you'll be stuck without a scholar. Don't look for a person of good works whose sincerity is in keeping with his actions, for you'll not find him and you'll be stuck without any good works. Don't look for a faultless brother, for you'll not find him and you'll be stuck without any brothers."

"The Lord most high curses anyone who expresses friendship toward his brother with his tongue but bears hostility in his heart, and he renders him deaf and blind."

They said, "There was a time when people were hypocritical about everything they did. Now they're hypocritical about everything they don't do."[9]

Fozeyl said, "Loving good works for people's sake is hypocrisy. Performing good works for people's sake is polytheism. Sincerity is when the Real most high protects you from these two characteristics, if he so wills."

"If I swear that I am a hypocrite, I prefer that to saying I am not."

"The essence of piety is being pleased with the Real most high, whatever he may do, and the most deserving of God's pleasure are those who know by realization."

"Those who know the Real most high in the reality of realization worship him with all their might."

"Chivalry is forgiving your brethren."

"The reality of trusting God is having hope in nothing but the mighty and glorious Lord and fearing nothing but him."

"Those who trust God are certain of the mighty and glorious Lord. They neither blame the Lord for anything he does nor complain against him." In other words, they are consistent, inwardly and outwardly, in their submission to God.

"When they ask you, 'Do you love the mighty and glorious Lord?' be silent. If you say no, you are an unbeliever. And if you say yes, your action is unlike the actions of his friends."

"I am seized by shame before the mighty and glorious Lord because of how often I have gone to the toilet." And Fozeyl did not go more than once every three days.

"How many people go into the bathroom and come out pure, and how many people go into the Ka'ba and come out defiled!"

"Battling with the wise is easier than eating sweets with the ignorant."

"Whoever smiles sweetly at a sinner is trying to ruin Islam."

"Whenever anyone curses a beast, the beast responds, 'Amen! Let the curse fall on whichever of us, you or me, is more disobedient to the mighty and glorious Lord.'"

"If I am informed, 'One of your prayers will be answered—ask for whatever you wish,' I will expend that prayer on behalf of the sultan, because if I pray for my own welfare, it is my welfare alone, while the welfare of sultans is the welfare of the people on earth."

"There are two qualities that corrupt the heart—sleeping a lot and eating a lot."

"There are two qualities in you that both come from ignorance. One is that you laugh without seeing something strange. And you give advice without lying awake at night."

"The Real most high states, 'O child of Adam! If you remember me, I will remember you, and if you forget me, I will forget you. The moment when you will not remember me will be imposed on you and not of your own making. Now see how you act.'"

"The Real most high said to the Prophet, 'Give glad tidings to the sinners and tell them that if they repent, I will accept them and inspire fear in the righteous and tell them that if I treat them justly, I will burn them all.'"

Someone asked Fozeyl for counsel. He said, *"Are many divided lords better or the one almighty God?"* [12:39].

∽ ∽ ∽

One day Fozeyl saw his son weighing out gold coins to give to someone. He was cleaning off the grime that had built up in the impressions on the gold. "Son," Fozeyl said, "this is better for you than ten pilgrimages."

Once Fozeyl's son had a blockage of urine. Fozeyl raised his hands and said, "O Lord! By my love for you, deliver him from this illness!"

No sooner had he stood up than his son was cured.

In his devotional prayers, Fozeyl used to say, "O Lord! Have compassion on me, for you have knowledge over me. Do not torment me, for you have power over me."

On occasion, he used to say, "My God! You keep me hungry and you keep me and my family naked and you give me no candle at night. This is how you act with your friends. At what stage did Fozeyl obtain this good fortune?"

It is related that no one had seen a smile cross his lips for thirty years. But on the day his son died, Fozeyl smiled. "Sir," they asked, "what rapture is this?"

"I realized," Fozeyl said, "that the Lord was pleased with the death of this boy. Even I agreed, and I smiled for his pleasure."

At the end of his life, Fozeyl used to say, "There's no cause to envy the prophets, because they also have the grave and the resurrection and hell and the Narrow Bridge[10] before them. In desperation they will say, *'Every man for himself.'* There's no cause to envy the angels either, because their terror is greater than humankind's; they do not suffer the pain of humankind, and I do not need anyone who does not suffer this pain. However, I do envy the person whose mother will never give birth to him."

They say that one day a Qur'an reader came and recited something for Fozeyl. Fozeyl said, "Take this man to my son, so he can recite something for him." To the Qur'an reader Fozeyl said, "Do not recite *The Clamor*. He doesn't have the strength to hear talk of the resurrection."

As fate would have it, the Qur'an reader recited precisely this chapter. When he recited, *"The day of adversity, what is the day of adversity?"* [101:1–2] Fozeyl's son sighed. When he recited, *"It is a day when humankind will be scattered like locusts"* [101:3], Fozeyl's son sighed again and fainted. They examined him and found that the noble child had died.

When the hour of his death approached, Fozeyl had two daughters. He gave his wife some final instructions: "When I die, take these two little girls and carry them to the top of Mount Bu Qobeys. Raise your face to heaven and say, 'O Lord! Fozeyl gave me his final will and said, "As long as I was alive, I looked after these dependents with all my might. Since you have locked me up in the prison of the grave, I return these dependents to you."'"

When they buried Fozeyl, his wife did just as he had told her. She took the little girls to the mountain, made her devotions, and shed many tears. At that very moment, the emir of Yemen passed by there with his two sons. He saw Fozeyl's wife and daughters crying and sobbing. He approached them and said, "What's the matter?"

Fozeyl's wife related the story. "I will give these girls to my sons in marriage," the emir said, "and I will give each of them a dowry of one thousand dinars. Are you satisfied with this?"

"I am," said Fozeyl's wife.

The emir at once ordered his men to bring camel litters and carpets and brocades. He set the girls and their mother in a litter and took them to Yemen. He gathered the nobles and gave the girls to his sons in marriage. *Indeed, God is with the person who is with him.*

'Abdollāh ebn Mobārak (God's mercy upon him) said, "When Fozeyl died, sorrow vanished completely."

∾ 8 ∾
Ebrāhim ebn Adham

Of world and faith the sultan, the phoenix on certainty's mountain, the treasure of the realm of seclusion, the hoard of the secrets of fortune, the king of the greatest clime, nurtured by grace and generosity sublime, the sheikh of the realm, Ebrāhim ebn Adham—God's mercy upon him. He was the most mindful man of his time and the most honest of his age. He had a full portion of the varieties of proper conduct and of the species of mystical truth. He was accepted by everyone. He met many of the sheikhs and followed the great imam Abu Hanifa (God's mercy upon him). Joneyd said, "The key to the sciences of this clan is Ebrāhim ebn Adham."

One day, Ebrāhim approached the great imam. His followers looked at Ebrāhim with contempt. Abu Hanifa (God have mercy on him) said, "Here's our master, Ebrāhim ebn Adham."

"How did he attain this mastery?" they asked.

"He is constantly occupied with the Lord most high," Abu Hanifa said, "while we are distracted by other things."

Ebrāhim was the king of Balkh. This was the beginning of his spiritual life: During his reign, when he had a whole world under his command and forty golden shields were carried before him and forty golden maces behind, he was sleeping one night on his throne. At midnight the ceiling of the room began to shake, as though somebody was up on the roof. "Who's there?" he asked.

"Someone you know," the person answered. "I've lost my camel."

"You ignorant man, why are you looking for a camel on the roof? What would a camel be doing on the roof?"

"You heedless man, are you looking for the Lord while you sit on a golden throne and wear satin clothes? Is looking for a camel on the roof any stranger than that?"

At these words, an awe stirred within Ebrāhim's heart, and a fire was kindled in his heart. He was dumbfounded and grew reflective and sad.

In another account they say that one day there was a general audience at the court. Each of the pillars of state was standing in his place. The slaves were lined up before him. Suddenly an awesome man came through the door, so boldly that none of the servants or retainers had the nerve to ask, "Who are you? What business do you have coming here?" The man kept advancing until he stood in front of Ebrāhim's throne.

Ebrāhim said, "What do you want?"

"I'm stopping over at this inn," the man said.

"This is no inn. This is my palace."

"Who did this palace belong to before this?"

"It belonged to my father."

"Who did it belong to before him?"

"It belonged to somebody or other."

"Who did it belong to before him?"

128

"It belonged to his father."

"Where have they all gone?"

"They all went and died."

"But isn't an inn a place where people come and go?"

He said this and quickly left the palace. Ebrāhim went running after him shouting. "Stop, so I can have a word with you!" The man stopped. "Who are you?" Ebrāhim asked. "Where do you come from? You have kindled a fire in my soul."

"I am a land and a sea, an earth and a sky. I am best known as Khezr."

"Wait here, while I go home and come back."

"The matter is more pressing than that," he said and disappeared.

The burning in Ebrāhim grew hotter, and his pain increased. "What can this be that I saw by night and heard by day?" he said. "Let them saddle my horse so I can go hunting and see where all this leads." He mounted and set off for the desert. He roamed the desert like a crazed man, as though he didn't know what he was doing. In that state he was separated from his troops and wandered far away.

He heard a voice say, "Wake up!" He pretended not to hear. He heard the same voice a second time. The third time he got himself out of there while pretending not to hear. A fourth time he heard a voice say, "Wake up before they wake you up." When he heard these words, he lost all grip on himself.

A gazelle appeared out of nowhere. Ebrāhim gave it his full attention. The gazelle began to speak and said, "They have sent me to hunt you, not you to hunt me. You cannot hunt me. Have you been created to hunt a helpless creature and shoot arrows at it? Don't you have anything else to do?"

"What is going on here?" Ebrāhim thought. He turned away from the gazelle. He heard the same words that he had heard from the gazelle from his saddle pommel. Dread and anxiety welled up within him, and his revelation unfolded. When the Real most high wished to finish things up, Ebrāhim heard the words once again from his collar button. With that, the unveiling was complete, and the empyrean opened up before him. He experienced the rapture of the men of God and attained certainty.

They say that he wept so much that his clothes and his horse were drenched with tears. He repented sincerely and turned off the road. He

129

saw a shepherd, dressed in felt and with a felt hat on his head, driving his sheep forward. Ebrāhim looked at him closely; it was his slave boy. Ebrāhim took off his gold-brocade robe and gave it to the shepherd and presented him with the sheep. He took the shepherd's felt cloak and put it on and set the felt hat on his own head.

After that, he wandered on foot through the mountains and deserts and wept over his sins until he reached Merv. He saw a bridge there. He saw a blind man who was about to walk off the bridge. To keep him from falling, Ebrāhim said, *"God, protect him!"* The blind man stopped, suspended in midair. Some people grabbed hold of him and pulled him back in. They stood staring at Ebrāhim, saying, "What a great man!"

Ebrāhim traveled on from there until he reached Nishapur. He sought some empty, out-of-the-way place so he could devote himself to worship. There is a famous cave there. He dwelled in that cave for nine years, three years in each chamber. Who knows what austerities he endured in that cave day and night? On Thursdays he would come up out of the cave, gather a load of firewood, take it to Nishapur in the morning, and sell it. He would perform the Friday prayer, buy bread with the money he had earned, and give half of it to the poor. He would use the other half and be content with that until the following week. And the circumstances of his life went on in this manner.

It is related that one winter's night Ebrāhim was in the cave. It was a cold night, and he had broken through the ice and performed his ablutions. He prayed until dawn. At dawn, he feared that he would perish from the cold. It occurred to him that he needed a fire or a fur pelt. At exactly that moment, a pelt began to warm his back, and he fell asleep. When he awoke, it was broad daylight, and he got up feeling warm. He wept—the pelt was a dragon with eyes like two huge goblets. A fear welled up in his heart. He said, "O Lord! You sent this to me as a kindness. Now I see it as wrath. I cannot stand it." The dragon began moving and rubbed its face on the ground two or three times in front of him and departed, vanishing from sight.

It is related that when people learned a little about what Ebrāhim was doing, he fled from the cave and set out for Mecca. When Sheikh Abu Sa'id (God sanctify his tomb) went to visit the cave, he said, "Glory to

God! If this cave had been full of musk, it would not give off such a perfume. Because a chivalrous man spent a few days here in true sincerity, the place has become all ease and tranquility."

Ebrāhim then set out for the desert, until one of the eminent men of the faith came to him and taught him the greatest name of the Lord most high. Using that name, Ebrāhim called on the Lord most high. He saw Khezr appear at once. Khezr said, "Ebrāhim, it was my brother Elyās who taught you the great name of the Lord most high." Many words then passed between them. Khezr was Ebrāhim's guide, for he had first attracted him to the path and set him to work.

Ebrāhim continued through the desert. He related:
I reached Zāt al-'Erāq.[1] I saw seventy people dressed in patched frocks. They had given up their lives, and blood was flowing from them. I circled around the group. One of them still had a breath of life left in him. "Young man," I asked, "what is going on?"
He answered, "*O Ebn Adham, your duty is the prayer niche and the water of ablution.* Don't go so far that you are abandoned. Don't come so near that you are afflicted. Don't be one who acts as brashly as this on the carpet of salvation. Fear the beloved who wages war on the pilgrims to the Sacred House and kills them as though they were Byzantine infidels. Know that we were a band of Sufis, and trusting in God, we strode into the desert and resolved not to speak a word or to think of anything but the Lord. We were to move and to rest for his sake and to concern ourselves with nothing but him. When we passed through the desert and reached the sacred precincts, Khezr (the blessings of God upon him) approached us. We greeted him and rejoiced and said, 'Praise be to God that our efforts were appreciated and have not been in vain! The seeker has joined the sought, for a person like this to come to welcome us.' At once, a voice called to our souls, 'Liars and pretenders! Was this what all your promises and vows were about? You forgot us and turned your attention to another. Know this: In payment for this debt, we seize your lives as plunder. We will not make peace with you until we shed your blood.' These noble young men whom you see have all been consumed by this demand for restitution. Ebrāhim beware! If this is what you have in mind, step forward!

131

In our land, bloodshed is forever rife.
In our censers, the aloe's wood is life.
If you don't care for us, then get away!
We'll kill a friend without the will to stay."

Ebrāhim was stunned. "Why have they let you escape?" he asked.

The young man replied, "They said, 'They are ripe. You are still raw. Strive to become ripe, too, and enter after them.'" He said this and gave up the ghost himself.

It is related that it took Ebrāhim fourteen years to cross the desert. The entire way, until he reached Mecca, he prayed and beseeched the Lord. The elders of the sacred precincts found out about this and came out to greet him. He hurried forward ahead of the caravan so that no one would recognize him. The servants came scurrying out before the elders. They saw a man coming ahead of the caravan. They asked him, "Is Ebrāhim ebn Adham nearly here? The sheikhs of the sacred precincts are approaching to greet him."

"What do they want with that godless old man?" Ebrāhim asked.

They raised their hands and slapped him around the head without letting up: "You dare to call such a person godless?! You're the godless one."

"That's exactly what I'm saying," Ebrāhim replied.

When they let him go, Ebrāhim said to his self, "There, had enough? You wanted the sheikhs of the honored sacred precincts to come to welcome you? Praise God that I saw you get what you wanted."

They finally recognized him and apologized. He then took up residence in Mecca, and they turned out to be his friends and companions, but he always ate what he earned himself. Sometimes he carried firewood and sometimes he looked after people's fields.

It is related that when Ebrāhim quit Balkh, he left behind an unweaned son. When the boy grew up, he asked his mother about his father. His mother said, "Your father is lost, but there are indications that he is in Mecca."

"I am going to Mecca," the boy said. "I will perform the pilgrimage to God's house and find my father and strive to serve him." He ordered a proclamation issued: "Anyone who wants to go on the pilgrimage, come forward! I will provide the provisions and transportation." They say that four thousand people gathered. He took them all on the hajj, supplying them with provisions and transportation, in the hope that he might be able to see his father's visage.

When he entered the mosque, he saw people wearing patched frocks. He asked them, "Do you know Ebrāhim ebn Adham?"

"He is our sheikh," they said. "He has gone to the desert around Mecca in search of firewood. He brings a load of firewood every day. He sells it and buys bread and brings it to us."

So, the boy went out into the deserts around Mecca. He saw an old man coming toward him with a heavy load of firewood on his back. The boy was overcome by tears. He held himself back and trailed the old man until he came into the marketplace. The old man kept calling out, *"Who will buy honest goods with honest money?"* A man bought the wood and gave him bread.

Ebrāhim brought the bread to his followers and placed it before them and began to pray. They ate the bread while he prayed. He was constantly instructing his followers, "Stay away from the pretty young boys and women who are not of your family, especially today when there are woman and children here on the pilgrimage. Don't let your eyes wander." They all agreed to this.

When the pilgrims entered Mecca and circumambulated the Ka'ba, with Ebrāhim and his friends walking around it along with them, a handsome young man came up to Ebrāhim. Ebrāhim looked him over very closely while his companions watched. When they saw what was happening, they were shocked. When they completed their circumambulations, they said, "God have mercy on you! You ordered us not to look at any young boy or woman, but you yourself stare at a handsome young boy!"

"You were watching?"

"We were watching."

"Don't let your imaginations get carried away," Ebrāhim said. "We suspect that he is our son from Balkh. When I quit Balkh, I left behind a son still suckling. I know that this young man is that boy."

So his father would not flee from him, the boy never revealed himself. He would come every day and gaze upon his father's face. Acting on his suspicions, Ebrāhim left Mecca with one of his friends and sought out the caravan from Balkh. He came into the middle of the caravan. He saw a tent made of silk brocade with a large chair set in the middle. The boy was sitting on it, reciting the Qur'an. They say that he had reached this verse: *Your possessions and your children are indeed a trial* [64:15].

Ebrāhim burst out crying and said, "Truly spoke my Lord most glorious." He left and came back to his friend. Ebrāhim told him, "Go in and ask that boy, 'Whose child are you?'"

The man went in and asked, "Where are you from?"

"I am from Balkh."

"Whose son are you?"

The boy threw his head forward and buried it in his hands. He was overcome by tears and began to weep. "I am the son of Ebrāhim ebn Adham," he said. He set aside the Qur'an and continued, "I have not seen my father, except for yesterday, and I don't know whether it is him or not. I am afraid that if I say anything, he will run away. He has run away from us before."

His mother was there with him. The dervish said, "Come, so I can take you to see him." They went with him. Ebrāhim was sitting with his friends in front of the Yamāni Pillar.[2] Ebrāhim watched from the distance. He saw his friend with the boy and his mother.

When the woman saw Ebrāhim, she could contain herself no longer. She let out a shout, "There's your father." All of Ebrāhim's friends and all the people started crying together, and the boy fainted from weeping. When he came to, he greeted his father.

Ebrāhim returned his greeting and embraced him and said, "What religion do you follow?"

"The religion of Islam."

"Praise be to God. Do you know the Qur'an?"

"Yes, I do."

"Praise be to God. Have you learned anything of the religious sciences?"

"Yes, I have."

"Praise be to God."

Ebrāhim then asked to leave. The boy would not let go of him, and his mother was calling for mercy. Ebrāhim embraced the boy and raised his face to heaven and said, *"My God, pour your mercy down on me!"* The boy died in his embrace.

His friends asked, "Ebrāhim, what happened?"

"When I embraced him," Ebrāhim said, "love for him stirred in my heart. A voice called out, 'Ebrāhim, do you claim to love us, while you love another and are distracted by him? Do you portion out love in a partnership? Do you instruct your followers not to look at any woman or child, while you cling to this woman and child?' When I heard this voice, I prayed inwardly and said, 'O Lord of might, deliver me! If my love for him will distract me from loving you, either take his life or take mine.' My prayer concerning him was answered."

If this incident strikes anyone as strange, we reply that it did not strike Abraham as strange to sacrifice his son Isaac.

It is related that Ebrāhim said, "At night, I used to be on the lookout for a time when I would find the Ka'ba empty and free of worshipers and could pray for something I needed. I didn't find the opportunity until one night when a heavy rain was falling. I went and seized the chance—it was just Ebrāhim and the Ka'ba. I performed my circumambulations and took hold of the knocker on the Ka'ba's door and asked for immunity from sin. I heard a voice call out, 'You ask me for immunity from sin? All the people ask me for this. If I grant everyone immunity, what will become of my oceans of forgiveness and pardon, of my mercy and compassion? What use will they be?'

"I then said, *'O God, forgive me my sins.'*

"I heard the voice say, 'Speak to me on behalf of the world, not on behalf of yourself. It's better for others to speak on your behalf.'"

In his private devotions, Ebrāhim said, "My God, you know that the eight paradises are paltry next to the kindnesses that you have done for me and next to my intimate remembrance of you and next to the leisure you have given me to meditate upon your greatness."

This was another of his private devotions: "O Lord, deliver me from the debasement of sin to the grandeur of devotion."

And he used to say, "Alas, my God! The one who knows you does not know you. How is it for the one who does not know you?"

It is related that Ebrāhim said, "When I had endured hardship and affliction for fifteen years, I heard a voice say, 'Go, become a servant,

135

then rest easy.' In other words, *Stand firm as you are commanded* [11:112].

It is related that they asked Ebrāhim, "What happened to you that made you leave your kingdom behind?"

"One day," Ebrāhim said, "I was sitting on the throne. They held up a mirror in front of me. I looked in the mirror. I saw my home to be the grave, and in it there was no dear friend or confidant. I saw a distant journey and a long road ahead, and I had no provisions or supplies. I saw a just judge, but I had no case. The kingdom grew cold upon my heart."

"Why did you flee from Khorasan?" they asked.

"Too many people there asked me, 'How did you sleep last night?' and 'How are you today?'"

"Why don't you want a wife?" they asked.

"Does any woman take a husband so he can keep her naked and hungry? I don't take a wife because any woman I marry will be left naked and hungry. If I could, I would divorce myself. How can I make another dependent on me? How can I deceive a woman about myself?"

Ebrāhim asked a dervish, "Do you have a wife?"

"No," the dervish said.

"Do you have any children?"

"No."

"Good, very good."

"How so?"

"The dervish who marries boards a ship, and when a child is born, it sinks."

It is related that one day Ebrāhim saw a poor man crying. "I imagine that you have purchased poverty for free," Ebrāhim said.

"Ebrāhim," the poor man said, "does anyone ever purchase poverty?"

"Well, I have purchased it at the price of the kingdom of Balkh, and I have purchased it very cheap, for it is worth more."

It is related that someone brought Ebrāhim a thousand dinars, saying, "Take them."

136

"I don't take anything from the poor," Ebrāhim said.

"But I am rich."

"Do you need more than you have?"

"Yes."

"Take this back, for you stand at the head of all the poor. Isn't this poverty itself?"

⁓ ⁓ ⁓

These are Ebrāhim's words:

"The hardest situation that I find myself in is when I arrive someplace where people know me. I just have to get out of there. I don't know which is more difficult—putting up with the indignity when you're not recognized or escaping from the dignity when you are."

"We sought poverty and were met by wealth. Other people sought wealth and were met by poverty."

They say that a man brought Ebrāhim ten thousand dirhams. He did not accept it and said, "Do you want to erase my name from among the poor with this much filthy silver?"

It is related that when an inspiration from the unknown descended upon Ebrāhim, he would say, "Where are the kings of the world so they can see what a high position this is and be ashamed of their kingdoms?"

"No one is honest who seeks publicity for himself."

"Sincerity is the honesty of one's intentions toward the Lord most high."

"When a man's heart is not fully present on these three occasions, it is a sign that the door is closed before him: first, when reading the Qur'an; second, when chanting God's name; and third, when praying."

"The mark of the seeker of realization is that his mind is mostly engaged in meditation and reflection; most of his words concern the praise and exaltation of the Real; most of his devotion consists of his

137

good works; and his eyes look mostly at the subtleties of divine might and creation."

"I saw a stone lying on a road, and on that stone was written, 'Turn it over and read.' I turned it over. On it was written, 'When you do not act on what you know, why do you seek what you do not know?'"

"On this path, nothing was harder for me than giving up books, though it has been commanded, 'Do not study.'"

"Those acts that are the most onerous for you today will weigh most heavily on the scales of judgment tomorrow."

"Three veils must be lifted from the pilgrim's heart before the door of good fortune will open before him: First, if the kingdom of both worlds is given to him as an eternal gift, he will not rejoice because he would be rejoicing in created existence. He is still a greedy man, and *the greedy are excluded*. The second veil is that if the kingdom of both worlds belongs to him and is taken from him, he will not sorrow over his bankruptcy because it would be a sign of annoyance, and *the annoyed are chastised*. Third, he will not be deceived by any praise or flattery, for whoever is deceived by flattery has lowly aspirations, and the mean of spirit are veiled. One must have high aspiration."

It is related that Ebrāhim said to someone, "Do you want to be one of God's friends?"

"Yes," he said.

"Do not long for one mote of this world or the afterworld. Turn entirely toward the mighty and glorious Lord and free yourself of all that is not God. Eat lawful foods so that you will not be obliged to stay up all night or to fast by day."

"No one achieves the rank of true believers in prayer, fasting, tithing, or the pilgrimage unless he knows what goes down his throat."

✍ ✍ ✍

They told Ebrāhim, "There is a young man, an ecstatic, who has a lofty spiritual state and performs exquisite austerities."

Ebrāhim said, "Take me there so I may see him." They took Ebrāhim to see him.

"Be my guest," the young man said. Ebrāhim stayed three days and observed the young man's state. It was even greater than what they had said.

Ebrāhim was overcome by envy: "How can I be so despondent," he thought, "while he spends the whole night without rest or sleep? Let me examine his condition myself to see whether any demon has found its way into him or whether all is as unsullied as it ought to be." He said to himself, "One must investigate the basis of his actions." Well, the basis and essence of action are what one eats. They examined what he ate; it was not in conformity with the law. "Great God," Ebrāhim said, "it is a demon!"

He then said to the young man, "I was your guest for three days. Come, be my guest a few days." He brought the young man home and gave him what he himself ate. The young man's spiritual state was lost: his passion was spent, and his love disappeared. The warmth and restlessness left him, and sleeplessness deserted him.

"Now, what have you done to me?" the young man asked.

"What you were eating was not in conformity with the law," Ebrāhim said. "The demon was entering your belly along with that food. When lawful food went down into your belly, the demon had no way back in. The things he showed you were demonic. With this lawful food, the basis of your actions was revealed. Know that the basis of this affair is pure food."

Ebrāhim said to Sofyān, "When people recognize what they're seeking, then everything else, everything they must give in exchange, becomes contemptible in their eyes."

Ebrāhim said to Sofyān, "You are a needy man of little certainty, even though you have great learning."

It is related that one day Shaqiq and Ebrāhim were together. Shaqiq said, "Why do you run away from people?"

"I have embraced my faith," Ebrāhim said, "and I flee from this city to that, from this mountaintop to that, so that anyone who sees me will think that I am a porter or that I am possessed by a demon. Perhaps this way I may bring my belief, safe from Satan's power, to the gateway of death."

It is related that during the month of the fast, Ebrāhim would go out and harvest grain. He would give whatever he was paid to the poor. He prayed all night until daybreak and never slept. They asked, "Why is sleep such a stranger to your eyes?"

"Because I do not rest from weeping for a moment," Ebrāhim said. "Since I'm this way, how can sleep be anything but a stranger to my eyes?"

When he performed his prayers, he spread his hands out over his face. "I am afraid," he used to say, "lest they reject me to my face."

It is related that one day Ebrāhim received nothing. He said, "My God, tonight in gratitude, let me perform four hundred rak'ats of prayer." He received nothing the next night either, nor the third. For seven nights it went like this—no food came to him. He began to feel weak. He said, "My God, would it be appropriate for you to give me something?"

At once, a young man came and asked, "Do you need food?"

"Yes," Ebrāhim said.

The young man took Ebrāhim to his house. When Ebrāhim looked at him closely, he cried out—"What's this?"

"I am your slave boy," the young man said, "and everything I have comes from you."

"I freed you," Ebrāhim said, "and everything you have, I gave you to keep. Permit me to leave."

Later, Ebrāhim prayed, "My God, I swear that after this, I will ask no one but you for anything. I asked for a crust of bread, and you laid this world before me."

It is related that three people were worshiping in a ruined mosque. When they fell asleep, Ebrāhim stood by the door of the mosque until morning. "Why did you do such a thing?" they asked.

"The weather was frigid, and the wind was cold. I took the place of the door, so that your discomfort would be less and whatever discomfort there was would be mine."

It is related that Ebrāhim was on a journey. His provisions were exhausted. He endured it patiently for forty days. He ate flowers and said nothing to anyone, so that none of the brethren would be troubled on his behalf.

It is related that Sahl ebn Ebrāhim[3] said:

I was traveling with Ebrāhim ebn Adham. I fell sick. He spent everything he had on my daily food. I asked him for something. He had a donkey. He sold it and spent the money on me. When I got better, I did not see his donkey. "Where's your donkey?" I asked.

"I sold it," he said.

"I am weak," I said. "What will I ride on? What will I sit on?"

"Sit on my shoulders, brother."

For three stages of the journey, he put me on his shoulders and walked.

It is related that 'Atā Solmā[4] said: "Once Ebrāhim had nothing left to spend on food. For fifteen days, he ate sand."

Ebrāhim said, "For forty years, I have not eaten any fruit from Mecca, and if I were not in my death throes, I wouldn't have said anything or told anyone." He did not eat it because soldiers had purchased some of the lands around Mecca.

It is related that Ebrāhim made the pilgrimage several times on foot without drawing water from the well of Zamzam[5] because the bucket had been purchased with the sultan's money.

It is related that Ebrāhim used to go to work as hired labor and would spend whatever he earned on his friends. One day he performed the evening prayer and bought something. He set off toward his friends. The way was long, and the night was getting late. His friends said, "It's late. Come, let's eat, so he won't be late and keep us waiting again." They ate, performed the night prayer, and went to sleep.

When Ebrāhim arrived, he saw them sleeping. He supposed that they had not had anything to eat and had gone to bed hungry. He quickly lit a fire and kneaded dough from some flour that he had brought. He cooked something for them to eat when they woke up, so they could fast the next day. When his friends woke up, they saw him: his beard was caked with dust and ashes and smoke enveloped him. He was blowing on the fire. "What are you doing?" they asked.

"I found you sleeping," Ebrāhim said. "I figured that you had not eaten anything and had gone to bed hungry. I am fixing some food for you so you can have something to eat when you get up."

"Look," they said, "how he worries about us and how we think about him!"

It is related that Ebrāhim set three conditions whenever anyone asked to follow him. He would say, "First, I serve. And I call the group to prayer. And I divide any favors that come from this world equally among us."

Once a man said, "I won't put up with this!"

"I was amazed at his honesty," Ebrāhim said.

It is related that a person was once accompanying Ebrāhim. He wished to turn back. He said to Ebrāhim, "Sir, make me aware of any faults that you have seen in me."

"I haven't seen any faults in you," Ebrāhim said, "because I have looked upon you with the eyes of friendship. So, of course, everything I have seen of you has pleased me."

It is related that there was a family man. He would go home at evening prayer empty handed, having gone all day without earning a thing. Hungry and utterly depressed, he thought, "What will I say to my wife and children when I come home empty handed?" He kept walking along, sad and filled with pain. He saw Ebrāhim sitting quietly. "Ebrāhim, I envy you," he said, "sitting there so quietly and so at ease."

Ebrāhim said, "Whatever pious acts we have done, whatever devotions God has found acceptable, we give them all to you. Give us your hour of sadness."

It is related that Mo'tasem asked Ebrāhim, "What occupation do you pursue?"

"I have left this world to those who seek it," Ebrāhim said, "and I have handed over the afterworld to those who seek it. I have chosen to remember the Lord most high in this world and to meet the glorious and exalted Lord in the next."

Someone else asked him, "What's your occupation?"

Ebrāhim replied, "Haven't you realized that those who work for the Lord need no occupation?"

It is related that someone said to Ebrāhim, "Hey, you miser!"

"I have given up the governorship of Balkh and abandoned the kingship," Ebrāhim said. "How can I be a miser?"

Then, one day, a barber was trimming Ebrāhim's hair. One of his disciples passed by. "Do you have anything?" Ebrāhim asked.

The disciple set down a purse of gold. Ebrāhim picked it up and gave it to the barber. A beggar came up and asked the barber for something. The barber said, "Take this purse."

"This is a purse of gold!" Ebrāhim said.

"I know that, you miser," the barber said. "The wealthy are wealthy in heart, not in property."

"It's gold!"

"You skinflint! The person I'm giving it to knows what it is."

Ebrāhim said, "I'll never be able to equal that disgrace. There I saw my self having its way."

They asked Ebrāhim, "Since you embarked on this path, has any happiness come your way?"

"Several times," Ebrāhim said. "Once I was in a boat. My hair was long, and my clothes were in tatters. I was in a spiritual state of which the people in the boat were completely unaware. They laughed at me and ridiculed me. There was a joker in the boat who kept coming over and lifting up the hair that hung down my back and slapping me across the neck. I found myself content. I was happy at the humiliation of my self. While this was going on, a wave suddenly rose up and threatened to destroy the boat. They said, 'We must lighten the boat.' One of them said, 'Well, what's this fellow doing among us? Who is he? We should throw him into the sea.' They grabbed me to throw me overboard. The wave receded, and the ship was becalmed. When they grabbed my ear to throw me into the water, I saw my self as I wished it to be.

"On another occasion, I went to a mosque to sleep. They wouldn't leave me in peace, and I was so weak and exhausted that I couldn't resist. They grabbed my feet and dragged me out. The mosque had three steps. When my head landed on each of the steps, it cracked open and started bleeding. There too I saw my self as I wished it to be and was happy. When they threw me down on those three steps and my head cracked open, the secret of one of the world's climes was revealed to me on each step. I thought to myself, 'I wish there were more steps.' I asked them, 'What did I do wrong?' 'You came to steal the mosque's prayer mats,' they replied.

"Another time was when I was imprisoned somewhere. Some joker urinated on me. There too I was happy.

"On another occasion, I was wearing a fur pelt. It was infested with lots of biting insects, and they were gnawing on me. Out of the blue, I remembered the clothes that I had stored away. My self cried out, 'Come on, why suffer so?' There too I saw my lower self as I wished it to be and was happy.

"Another time, I was performing ablutions on the banks of the Tigris. Someone came up and looked at me and spit in my face. He polluted my entire face. I was happy there.

"On another occasion, I was going somewhere, and some people were quarreling with one another. One of them said to his opponent, 'You're more contemptible to me than this worthless Hindu.' There too I was happy."

It is related that Ebrāhim said, "Once I went into the desert, trusting in God to provide for me. For several days, I found nothing to eat. I had a friend, but I said, 'If I approach him, my trust in God will be proven false.' I entered a mosque and uttered, *'I put my trust in the One who lives and does not die'* [25:58].

"An unseen voice called out, 'Praise the Lord who has wiped those who trust in him from the face of the earth!'

"'Why?' I asked.

"'How can anyone be said to trust God when he sets off on a long journey for a bit of food that a friend could legitimately give him and then says, *"I put my trust in the One who lives and does not die?"* He names a lie "trust in God."'"

Ebrāhim said, "Once I saw an ascetic who had put his trust in God. I asked him, 'Where are you from and how do you eat?'

"'This is not mine to know,' he said. 'You must ask the One who provides my daily bread. What business do I have meddling in this?'"

Ebrāhim said, "Once I purchased a slave boy. 'What's your name?' I asked.

   "'Let's see what you call me.'
   "'What do you eat?'
   "'Let's see what you feed me.'
   "'How do you dress?'
   "'Let's see how you dress me.'
   "'What do you do?'
   "'Let's see what you bid me to do.'
   "'What do you want?'
   "'What does a slave have to do with wanting?'

"Then I thought to myself, 'You poor thing! Have you ever in your life been such a servant to the Lord most high? Learn servitude for once from this boy!' I wept so much that I lost consciousness."

It is related that no one ever saw Ebrāhim sit cross-legged. "One day I was sitting this way," Ebrāhim said. "I heard a voice say, 'Ebn Adham! Do servants sit this way before their lord?' I sat up straight and repented: 'I will not sit like that again!'"

It is related that Ebrāhim was once asked, "Whose servant are you?" He went into spasms, fell down, and began to roll around in the dirt. Then he got up and recited this verse from the Qur'an: *Does not everything that exists in heaven or on earth come to serve the Compassionate?* [19:93].

   "Why didn't you answer at first?" they asked him.

   "I was afraid that if I said, 'I am his servant,' he would ask me about the duties of servitude and say, 'How have you fulfilled your duties in serving me?' If I said that I am not...how can one even say this? I can never say this."

It is related that Ebrāhim was asked, "How do you spend your days?"

   "I have three horses tied up," Ebrāhim said. "When some blessing appears, I mount the horse of thanks and ride out to meet it. When disaster strikes, I mount the horse of patience and go out to meet it. And when a cause for devotion appears, I mount the horse of sincerity and ride forth."

It is related that Ebrāhim said, "If you do not want to make your wife like a widow or your children like orphans, if you do not want to sleep with dogs in the garbage dumps at night, then do not long to be given a place in the ranks of true believers." These words ring true coming from this privileged man, who left kingship behind to get there.

It is related that one day a group of sheikhs were sitting together. Ebrāhim intended to join them. They did not give him leave to enter: "The stench of kingship still comes from you." In spite of all his labor, they say this to him! I don't know what they will say to others.

It is related that Ebrāhim was asked, "Why are hearts veiled from the Real?"
    "Because they love everything the Lord most high loathes. They have turned away from the eternal garden to this transitory pile of ashes. They have bid farewell to the workshop of everlasting life and lasting bliss and have fallen short of the kingdom and the life that do not decay."

It is related that someone said, "Give me counsel."
    Ebrāhim said, "Remember the Lord and put created things aside."

Someone else asked for counsel.
    Ebrāhim said, "Open what is closed. Close what is open."
    "Clarify this."
    "Open the closed purse, and close the open mouth."

Ahmad-e Khezruya related: "To a man circumambulating the Ka'ba, Ebrāhim said, 'You will not attain the rank of the pious until you pursue these six tasks: Close the door of blessing in front of you and open the door of hardship. Close the door of grandeur and open the door of abjection. Close the door of sleep and open the door of wakefulness. Close the door of wealth and open the door of poverty. Close the door of hope and open the door of death. Close the door of unrighteousness and open the door of preparing for the death that lies before you.'"

It is related that Ebrāhim was receiving visitors. A man came and said, "Sheikh, I have done a great injustice to myself. Tell me something so I can take control of myself."

"If you will adopt six habits from me, you will never again suffer loss," Ebrāhim said. "First, when you want to commit a sin, do not eat of his sustenance."

"But everything in the world is his sustenance. How will I eat?"

"Is it good to eat of his sustenance and rebel against him? Second, when you want to commit a sin, leave the kingdom of the Lord most high."

"These words are even more difficult. Since God's dominion encompasses east and west, where will I go?"

"Is it good to dwell in his kingdom and rebel against him? Third, when you commit a sin, find a place where the Lord most high will not see you."

"How can this be? He knows all secrets."

"Is it good that you eat his sustenance and dwell in his kingdom and have no shame before him? Will you sin in his sight? Fourth, when the angel of death comes to seize your life, say, 'Give me a reprieve so I may repent.'"

"He will not grant this to me."

"Well, if you are unable to put off the angel of death for even a moment, you can still repent before he comes. Fifth, when Monker and Nakir come to you, drive them both off."

"I will never be able to."

"Then prepare yourself to answer them now. Sixth, on the morrow at the resurrection, when the order comes, 'Take the sinners to hell,' don't go."

"Is it possible for me to stand up against the angels?" Then, the man said, "What you have said is done." He repented then and there. He remained repentant for six years until he departed from this world.

It is related that Ebrāhim was asked, "Why has the Lord most high said, 'Call on me; I will answer' [40:60]? We recite this, and no answer comes to our prayer."

Ebrāhim said, "It is because you know the Lord most high and holy but do not obey him. You recognize his Messenger but do not follow his tradition. You read the Qur'an but do not act on it. You feed on his blessings but do not give thanks. You know that paradise has been arrayed for the sake of the obedient but do not seek it, and you know that hell has been created for sinners with yokes and chains of fire but do not fear it and flee from it. You know that Satan is the enemy but do not oppose him. You know that death exists but do not prepare for it. You bury your parents and children but learn no lesson from it. You do not give up your own faults but are always preoccupied with others'. How should the prayers of someone like this be granted an answer? All his tolerance for you is the result of his attributes of patience and mercy and is reserved for the day of punishment."

It is related that they asked, "When a man gets hungry and has nothing, what should he do?"

"Be patient, one, two, three days," Ebrāhim said. "Let him be patient for ten days and die. The blood debt will be on his killer."

It is related that they said, "Meat is expensive."

"Let's make it cheap," Ebrāhim said.

"How?"

"Let's not buy it or eat it."

It is related that one day Ebrāhim invited some of his followers for a visit. They had to wait for someone. "He is a troublesome man," one of the guests said.

"People usually eat the bread before the meat," Ebrāhim said. "Are you going to eat the meat before the bread?"

It is related that Ebrāhim, his clothes in tatters, intended to go to the baths, but they did not let him in. He had a moment of insight. "If they won't let you into Satan's house empty handed," he said, "how will they let you into the house of the Compassionate?"

It is related that Ebrāhim reported:

Once I went into the desert, trusting in God to provide for me. I found nothing to eat for three days. The devil came up and said, "Did you leave behind the kingship and all that comfort so you could go on the pilgrimage hungry? One can also go on the pilgrimage in pomp and splendor."

I said, "My God, do you assign the enemy to your friend to torment him? I can cross this desert with your aid."

I heard a voice say, "Ebrāhim, throw out everything you have in your pockets so I may bring forth what is hidden."

I put my hand in my pocket; four small, silver coins that I had forgotten about were still in there. When I threw them away, the devil backed away me, and food appeared from out of the hidden realm. It was clear that the devil hovers around those who hold on to this world.

It is related that Ebrāhim said: "Once I went out to gather the harvest. Every time I filled my skirt with grain, they would beat me and take it away. They did this forty times. The forty-first time, they did not. I heard a voice say, 'These forty times are in recompense for the forty golden shields that they used to carry before you.'"

It is related that Ebrāhim said: "Once I was tending a garden. The owner of the garden came and said, 'Bring me sweet pomegranates.' I brought him a plateful; they were sour. 'Bring me sweet pomegranates,' he said. I brought him another plateful; they were still sour. 'Praise be to God!' he said. 'You've been in the garden all this time and you still can't tell sweet pomegranates from sour?'

"'I tend the garden,' I said, 'but I don't know the flavor of pomegranates since I haven't tasted them.'

"'You're such an ascetic,' the man said, 'that I suspect that you must be Ebrāhim the son of Adham.' When I heard this, I left the place."

It is related that Ebrāhim said:

One night I dreamt that I saw the angel Gabriel (peace be upon him). He came to earth from heaven with a piece of paper in his hand. I asked him, "What do you want?"

"I am writing down the names of the friends of the Real," he said.

"Will you write my name down too?" I asked.

"You are not one of them."

"But I love the friends of the Real."

Gabriel thought for a moment. Then he said, "I have been commanded, 'Record Ebrāhim's name first.'"

On this path, hope emerges from despair.

It is related that Ebrāhim said:

One night in the mosque of the Holy Sanctuary, I hid myself by rolling up in a reed mat, because the caretakers would not allow anyone to spend the night in the mosque. When a watch of the night had passed, the door of the mosque opened, and an old man wearing sackcloth entered, together with forty others all dressed the same. The old man went into the prayer niche, performed two rak'ats of prayer, and leaned his back against the niche. One of the others said to him, "There's someone in the mosque tonight who is not one of us."

The old man smiled and said, "It's the son of Adham. For forty days and nights now he has not enjoyed the sweetness of worship."

When I heard this, I came out and said, "Give me a true sign. For the Lord's sake, you must tell me why this is."

He said, "On a certain day in Basra, you bought some dates. A date fell on the ground—you thought it was one of yours. You picked it up and put it with your dates."

When I heard these words, I went to see the date seller and asked his forgiveness. He forgave me and said, "Since this affair is so delicate, I give up selling dates." He repented of that business, closed up shop, and entered into God's work. In the end, he became one of the Substitutes.[6]

It is related that Ebrāhim was going somewhere one day. A soldier came up and said, "Who are you?"

"A servant," Ebrāhim said.

"Which way is the village?"

Ebrāhim pointed to the graveyard.

The soldier said, "Are you making fun of me?" and gave Ebrāhim several lashes across his head and split it open. The blood began to flow. Then he threw a rope around Ebrāhim's neck and led him off.

The men in the town had heard that Ebrāhim was coming and had come out to welcome him. When they saw what was going on, they said, "Hey, you idiot! This is Ebrāhim the son of Adham, and he is the friend of the Lord most glorious."

The soldier fell at Ebrāhim's feet and asked for forgiveness. He asked, "When I was splitting your head, were you praying for me?"

"Yes," Ebrāhim said, "you deserved a good prayer for that deal you made with me. I was praying because my share of the deal you made would be paradise. I did not want yours to be hell."

"Why did you say, 'I am a servant'?"

"Who is not a servant of the Lord?"

"Why did you point to the graveyard when I was looking for the village?"

"Because every day the graveyard becomes more populous, and the village becomes more desolate," Ebrāhim said.

It is related that one of the friends of the Real said: "I saw the heavenly host in a dream, each one of them with skirts and sleeves filled with pearls. I asked, 'What is going on?'

"They said, 'Some idiot split open the head of Ebrāhim the son of Adham. When they brought him to paradise, it was commanded: "A boor split open our friend's head. Scatter these jewels over him." They scattered them, and all the people of heaven gathered them up. We got a few too.'"

It is related that Ebrāhim once passed by a drunk. The drunk's mouth was polluted with wine. Ebrāhim brought some water and washed his mouth out. Ebrāhim used to say, "If you leave any mouth that may have mentioned the name of Lord most high polluted, it is an act of disrespect."

When the drunk awoke, people told him, "The ascetic of Khorasan washed your mouth out."

The man said, "I, in turn, repent."

Later, in a dream, Ebrāhim was told, "You washed his mouth out for our sake. We washed your heart."

It is related that Suri[7] says: "I was with Ebrāhim at the Holy Sanctuary. We performed several rak'ats of prayer during the afternoon siesta under a pomegranate tree. I heard a voice from that tree say, 'Abu Eshāq! Honor us and eat some of these pomegranates.' Ebrāhim bowed his head. Three times the tree said the same thing. Then Ebrāhim got up and picked two pomegranates. He ate one and gave one to me. The tree was small, and the pomegranate sour. When I returned, I came upon that tree once—it had grown tall, and its pomegranates were

151

sweet. It used to bear pomegranates twice a year. The people called that tree the Pomegranate of the Pious, through the blessing of Ebrāhim the son of Adham. The pious used to rest in the shade of that tree and talk."

It is related that Ebrāhim was sitting on a mountain with an eminent person and talking. He asked Ebrāhim, "What is the sign of a person who has attained perfection?"

"When he tells the mountain, 'Go,' it starts to move." At that instant the mountain started moving. "O mountain,' Ebrāhim said, "I wasn't talking to you, but I'll take you as an example. Be calm."

The mountain at once became still.

It is related that Rejā says: "I was with Ebrāhim in a boat. A strong wind rose up and the world turned dark. 'Alas,' I said, 'don't let the ship sink!'

"A voice came from the air saying, 'Don't be afraid of sinking. Ebrāhim ebn Adham is with you.' In a moment, the wind let up, and the dark world turned light."

It is related that Ebrāhim was once sitting in a boat. A mighty wind rose up. The boat was about to sink. Ebrāhim then looked around—he saw a small book containing a section of the Qur'an hanging from a plank. He said, "My God, will you drown us while your book is in our midst?" The wind immediately died down, and a voice came down saying, "I will not do it."

It is related that Ebrāhim once wanted to board a boat. He had no money. They said, "Everyone must pay one dinar."

Ebrāhim performed two rak'ats of prayer and said, "My God, they are asking me for something, and I have nothing." On the spot, the sand on the riverbank all turned to gold. Ebrāhim picked up a fistful and gave it to them.

It is related that one day Ebrāhim was sitting on the banks of the Tigris, stitching his worn cloak. Someone came up and asked, "What did you get for giving up the kingdom of Balkh?"

Ebrāhim's needle fell into the water. He made a sign to the fish to give him back his needle. A thousand fish raised their heads from the water, each one holding a golden needle in its mouth. "I want my own needle," Ebrāhim said. A weak little fish brought up the needle, holding it in its mouth. "This was the least thing that I received for leaving the kingdom of Balkh behind. You know the others."

It is related that one day Ebrāhim arrived at a well. He lowered the bucket. The bucket came up full of silver. Ebrāhim tipped it out and lowered it into the well again. It came up full of gold. He lowered it again. It came up full of pearls. He tipped it out again and had a moment of joy. "My God," Ebrāhim said, "you lay a treasure before me, but you know that I won't be deceived by it. Give me water so I may perform my ablutions."

It is related that Ebrāhim was going on the pilgrimage once. There were others with him. They said, "There is no one among us with a mount or provisions."

"Hold firm to the Lord for your sustenance," Ebrāhim said. "Then look at that tree. If you crave gold, it will turn to gold."

They looked. All the camel thorn trees had turned to gold by the power of the Lord most high.

It is related that one day Ebrāhim was traveling with a group of dervishes. They arrived at a fortress. There was a lot of firewood in front of the fortress. "Let's stay here tonight," they said. "There's lots of firewood to build a fire." They lit the fire and sat in the firelight. Everyone was eating plain bread, and Ebrāhim stood praying.

"I wish we had some lawful meat," someone said, "to roast on this fire."

Ebrāhim bowed low and said, "Our Lord is capable of giving us lawful meat." He said this and stood up to pray.

Just then, a lion roared. They saw a lion coming, dragging an onager. They took it and killed it, cut it up, and ate it. The lion sat there watching them.

It is related that when Ebrāhim's life came to end, he disappeared, so that no one knows precisely where his grave is. Some say, "It is in Baghdad," and some say, "It is in Syria," and some say, "It is there where the city of Prophet Lot (peace be upon him) was leveled to the ground. He fled there to escape people and there he died."

It is related that when death came to Ebrāhim, a hidden voice called out, "Know that the peace of the world has died." All the people of the time were shocked when they heard this message, wondering, "What will happen now?" until the news came: "Ebrāhim has gone from this transitory abode to the everlasting palace."

∽ 9 ∽

Beshr al-Hāfi, the Barefoot

Warrior on the field of determination, provisioner at the portico of contemplation, laborer in the workshop of guidance, perfect master at the court of self-reliance, reigning over the realms of purity, Beshr al-Hāfi the Barefoot—God's mercy upon him. He had a mighty determination and an exalted rank, although he was one of the common people. He was a follower of Fozeyl ebn 'Ayāz and was the disciple of his maternal uncle 'Ali-ye Khashram.[1] Beshr was a scholar of the principles and branches of the law. He was born in Merv, but he spent his life in Baghdad and lived under hard circumstances.

This was the beginning of his conversion: One day he was walking around drunk. He saw a piece of paper that had fallen on the road, and on it was written, "In the name of God, the Merciful and Compassionate." He immediately bought a fine perfume and anointed the piece of paper and kissed it and rubbed it against his eyes. He put it in a place of great honor.

That night an eminent person had a dream. He was told, "Go and inform Beshr: '*You anointed our name, so we anoint you. You glorified our name, so we glorify you. You purified our name, so we purify you. By my might, I shall anoint your name in this world and the next!*'"

That eminent person thought, "He's a degenerate man. I am seeing something amiss." He performed his ablutions and prayed and went back to sleep. He heard the same words a second time and a third. At dawn he got up and went in search of Beshr. They told the sheikh, "He's at a drinking party." The sheikh went as far as the door of the tavern. Beshr was drunk. The sheikh said, "Tell Beshr that I have a message for him."

Beshr replied, "Go and ask him whom the message is from."

"It is a message from the mighty and glorious Lord," the sheikh said.

Beshr began to weep and asked, "Does he reproach me?"

"No."

"Wait while I speak with my friends," Beshr said. He went before his friends. "Friends, I have been called," he said. "I am going and bid you farewell. You will never see me doing this sort of thing again." So it was that no one ever heard his name without some comfort touching his heart. Beshr came out of the tavern just as he was—a wreck, bareheaded and barefoot—and made his repentance. He embarked on the path of renunciation and with high aspiration appealed to the good fortune of God's friends.

Beshr never wore shoes on his feet again and so they called him Hāfi, meaning "the barefoot." They asked him, "Why don't you wear shoes?"

"The day I made my peace," he said, "I was barefoot. Now I'm ashamed to wear shoes. What's more, the Real most high states, 'I have made the earth your carpet.'[2] It's not good manners to walk on kings' carpets with your shoes on."

Some of the companions of the intimate realms were like this: They would not urinate on a clump of dirt or spit on the ground. They saw the secret of God's light in all things. Beshr was the same way. Indeed, the light of God becomes the wayfarer's eye. Those without insight see nothing but themselves, but those whose eyes have become the mighty and glorious Lord see nothing but the Lord. So it was that the Prophet (peace and blessing be upon him) walked on tiptoe behind Sa'laba's[3] funeral bier and said, "I am afraid to step on the angels." Who are those angels? They are the light of God. *The believer sees by the light of God.*[4]

It is related that Ahmad ebn Hanbal often went to visit Beshr and was his devoted disciple. Ebn Hanbal's students used to say, "You are a scholar of hadith, of the law and legal argument, and you have no peer in the various sciences. Is it appropriate for you to go see an untamed wild man every hour of the day?"

"Yes," Ebn Hanbal said, "I know all the disciplines that you counted off better than he, but he knows the Lord most glorious better than I."

So, he would go visit Beshr and say to him, "Tell me about my Lord."

It is related that one night Beshr was going home. He stopped bewildered with one foot inside the door and one foot out and remained there until dawn. Others say that Beshr's sister had a premonition that he was coming to see her that night. She was waiting for him. All of a sudden, he showed up, frenzied and intoxicated. He wanted to go up on the roof. He climbed several steps and stopped and remained there bewildered until morning. When it was time for prayer, he came down and went to the mosque and prayed and returned to his sister's house. His sister asked, "What happened?"

"It occurred to me," Beshr said, "that there are several people in Baghdad named Beshr—one is a Jew, one a Zoroastrian, one a Christian. My name is also Beshr. I have been fortunate and received Islam. What did those others do to get tossed aside? What did I do to be so fortunate? I was left bewildered at the wonder of this."

It is related that Belāl-e Khavvās[5] said:

I was traveling through the desert country of the Israelites. Someone fell in alongside me. It occurred to me that it was Khezr. I said, "For God's sake, who are you?"

He said, "I am Khezr, your brother."

I asked, "What do you say about the imam Shāfe'i?"

"He is one of the supports of the world."

"What do you say about Ahmad-e Hanbal?"

"He is one of the righteous."

"What do you say about Beshr?"

"After him, there won't be another like him."

It is related that Abu 'Abdollāh ebn Jallā says, "I met Zu'n-Nun, who had the expressions. I met Sahl, and he had the wordless teachings. I met Beshr, and he had scrupulousness. They asked me, 'To which of the elders do you most incline?'

"'To Beshr ebn al-Hāres,' I said, 'for he is our teacher.'"

Beshr said, "I memorized seven chests of books on hadith. I buried them in the ground." He did not transmit hadith and said, "I do not transmit them because I find no appetite for silence within me. If I find an appetite for silence, I will transmit them."

It is related that they said to Beshr, "Baghdad has a mixed population, and most of the food in it is unlawful. What do you eat?"

"What you eat."

"So, how did you attain this spiritual station?"

"By a morsel smaller than any morsel and by a hand less grasping than any hand. The person who eats and weeps is not the same as the one who eats and laughs." Then Beshr added, "The licit does not admit any excess."

Someone asked him, "What should I have to go along with my bread?"

"Good health," Beshr replied.

It is related that for a period of forty years he longed for roast lamb but could not afford it. And they say that for years he craved beans but did not eat them. It is related that he never drank water from canals that sultans had excavated.

An eminent person said, "I was with Beshr during a very hard cold snap. I found him naked and shivering. I said, "Abu Nasr! What are you doing?"

"'I remembered the poor,' he said. 'I didn't have the money to comfort them. I am empathizing with them in body.'"

They asked Beshr, "How did you attain this spiritual station?"

"By hiding my condition from everyone but the mighty and glorious Lord all my life."

"Why don't you preach to the sultan? We are oppressed."

"The Lord knows and sees. He is too great for that. I consider him too great for me to mention him in front of someone who knows him, much less in front of someone who doesn't know him."

Ahmad ebn Ebrāhim the Perfumer[6] said:

Beshr told me to tell Ma'ruf: "When I have prayed, I will come to see you." I delivered the message.

I waited until we had performed the noon and afternoon prayers, the evening prayer, and the night prayer. Then Beshr picked up his prayer rug and set out. When he reached the Tigris, he walked across the water and went to see Ma'ruf. They talked together until morning. Then Beshr returned, and he walked across the water the same way. I fell at his feet and said, "Pray for me." He prayed for me and said, "Don't reveal this." I didn't say anything to anyone as long as he was alive.

It is related that there was a group of people with Beshr, and he was talking about acceptance. Someone said, "Abu Nasr, you do not accept anything from people because of your sense of dignity. If you are true in your renunciation and have turned away from this world, take something from people in secret and give it to the poor. Abide in your trust in God and take your own food from the unknown."

These words were hard for Beshr's followers to take. Beshr said, "Hear the answer. Know that dervishes are of three types. One type are those who never ask for anything, and if people give them something, they do not accept it. These are the people of the spirit, for when they ask the mighty and glorious Lord for something, he gives them whatever they want. If they make an oath to the Lord, he fulfills it immediately. Another type are those who never ask for anything, and if people give them something, they accept it. These people are in the middle. Through the Lord most high, they dwell in their trust in God. They are the ones who will sit at the everlasting banquet in the holy presence. Another type are those who sit patiently and preserve their moment of rapture. They reject claims and causes."

When that Sufi heard the answer, he said, "I accept these words. May the Lord accept you."

Beshr said, "I came upon 'Ali-ye Jorjāni[7] at a spring of water. When he saw me, he said, 'What sin have I committed that I have seen a human being today?' and ran away.

"I ran after him. I said, 'Counsel me.'

"'Embrace poverty,' he said, 'and live patiently. Regard passion as your enemy and oppose your lusts. Make your house today emptier than the grave. If your house is like that, you will reach the Lord happy and refreshed on the day they lay you in the grave.'"

It is related that a group came to see Beshr from Syria. "We are planning on going on the pilgrimage," they said. "Would you like to go with us?"

"On three conditions," Beshr said. "One is that we will take nothing with us. Nor will we ask anyone for anything. And if we are given anything, we will not accept it."

"We can do the first two," they said, "but not accepting something if it is given to us, that we can't do."

"Then you are trusting in the pilgrims' provisions."

The explanation for these words is what Beshr said in reply to that Sufi: "If you had decided in your heart that you would never accept anything from people, then this would have been trusting the Lord."

It is related that Beshr said:

One day I came into the house. I saw a man. I said, "Who are you to enter without my permission?"

He said, "I am your brother Khezr."

"Pray for me," I said.

"May the Lord most high make obedience and devotion easy for you."

"Go on," I said.

"May he conceal your devotion from you."

It is related that someone was consulting with Beshr. "I have two thousand dirhams, lawfully earned. I want to go on the pilgrimage."

"You are going sightseeing," Beshr said. "If you're going to please the Lord, pay some poor people's debts. Or give the money to an orphan or a man with a family, for the comfort that they will feel in their hearts is nobler than a hundred pilgrimages."

"I want to go on the pilgrimage more," the man said.

"Because you did not earn this money appropriately, you won't be at peace until you spend it inappropriately."

It is related that Beshr was passing by a graveyard. He said: "I saw that the dead in the graveyard had come up on top of their graves and were quarreling over how to divide something between them. 'O Lord,' I said, 'let me know what is going on here.'

"I heard a voice say, 'Ask them.'

"I asked them. They replied, 'A week ago, one of the true believers of the faith passed by and recited *"Say, He is the Lord, the Unique"*

159

three times and gave us the spiritual reward for it. We've been divvy-ing up the reward for a week now and still haven't finished.'"

It is related that Beshr said: "I dreamt I saw Mohammad (peace and blessing be upon him). He said to me, 'Beshr, do you have any idea why the Real most high chose you from among your peers and elevated you to your rank?'

"I said, 'No, Messenger of God, I do not.'

"'It was because you followed my way of life and honored the pious and counseled your brethren and loved my companions and the members of my family. For these reasons, I have raised you to the sta-tus of the nobles.'"

Beshr said: "One night I saw 'Ali (peace be upon him) in a dream. 'Commander of the Faithful,' I said, 'give me a piece of advice.'

"'How good it is,' he said, 'for the wealthy to have pity on the poor in search of divine recompense. It is even better for the poor to treat the rich with disdain and to put their trust in the generosity of Creator of the world.'"

❧ ❧ ❧

It is related that Beshr said to his followers, "Travel, for water is sweet when it flows, and when it settles, it stagnates."

"Tell anyone who wants to be held dear in this world to avoid three things: Do not ask created beings for what you need. Do not speak evil to anyone. And do not accept anyone's hospitality."

"Anyone who is fond of being recognized by people will not enjoy the sweetness of the afterlife."

"If contentment is no more than living honorably, it is enough."

"If you are fond of having people recognize you, this fondness is the start of loving the world."

"You will never enjoy the sweetness of devotion until you put up an iron wall between yourself and your lusts."

160

"Three acts are the hardest of all: generosity when empty handed, scrupulousness in private, and speaking out before someone you fear."

"Scrupulousness is when you leave doubts completely behind and forestall the calculations of the self at every instant."

"Renunciation is a king who alights only in an empty heart."

"Sorrow is a king who, when he alights somewhere, is not content to have anyone else alight beside him."

"The noblest things that have been given to God's servants are realization and patience in poverty."

"If the Lord has special favorites, they are the knowers in realization."

"The pure are those whose hearts are pure with the Lord."

"The realized are a folk whom no one knows but the Lord most high and whom no one holds dear but for the sake of the Lord most high."

"Tell anyone who wants to taste freedom, 'Keep the innermost self pure.'"

"Whoever acts honestly for the sake of the Lord will be terrified of people."

"Greet the children of this world by refusing to greet them."

"Paying attention to the miserly hardens the heart."

"Among brethren, forgoing etiquette is etiquette itself."

"I have never sat down with anyone—nor has anyone sat down with me—when it was not certain that when we separated, we both would have been better off if we had not sat down together."

"I detest death, and no one detests death unless he is in doubt."

"You will not be whole until your enemy feels safe from you."

"If you do not serve the Lord, at least do not rebel against him."

It is related that someone came to see Beshr and said, *"I put my trust in God!"*

"By God, you are lying," Beshr said. "If you had put your trust in him, you would have been content with what he did and does."

"If you feel some pride in speaking, be silent. When you feel pride in silence, speak."

"If you spend your entire life in this world bowing down in thanks, you will still not have offered sufficient thanks for the fact that he mentioned you among his friends. Strive to be one of his friends."

✍   ✍   ✍

When it came time for Beshr to die, he was in great anxiety. They said, "You don't really love life, do you?"

"No," Beshr answered, "but going into the presence of the King of Kings is a difficult business."

It is related that during Beshr's mortal illness, someone came in and complained of the poverty of his life. Beshr gave him the shirt that he himself was wearing. He borrowed another shirt and died in it.

It is related that as long as Beshr was alive, no animal dropped dung in Baghdad out of respect for him because he used to walk barefoot. One night a man's animal defecated. The man cried out, "Beshr is no more!"

People looked into the matter carefully, and it was so. "How did you know?" they asked.

"Because as long as Beshr was alive, there was no dung in all the streets of Baghdad. I saw that what my animal did was out of the ordinary. I realized that Beshr was no more."

After his death, Beshr was seen in a dream. "What has the mighty and glorious Lord done with you?" he was asked.

Beshr said, "He reproached me and asked, 'Why were you afraid of me in the lower world? Didn't you realize that generosity is my attribute?'"

Someone else saw Beshr in a dream and asked, "What did the Real most high do with you?"

Beshr said, "He forgave me and said, 'You, who did not eat for my sake, eat! You, who did not drink for my sake, drink!'"

Someone else saw Beshr in a dream and asked, "What did the mighty and glorious Lord do with you?"

"He forgave me," Beshr said. "He permitted me one half of paradise. 'Beshr,' He said, 'know that if you had prostrated yourself to me in fire, you would not have offered sufficient thanks for the fact that I gave you a place in the hearts of my servants.'"

Someone else saw Beshr in a dream and asked, "What did the Mighty and Glorious Lord do with you?"

Beshr said, "The edict came down: 'Welcome, Beshr! At the hour your life was taken from you, there was no one on the face of the earth more beloved to me than you.'"

It is related that one day a woman came to see the imam Ahmad ebn Hanbal. "During the summer," she said, "I spin cotton on the roof on my house by the light of the sultan's torches. The caliph's people allow spinning by this light. Is it proper or not?"

Ahmad asked, "Who has made you worry about this sort of question?"

"I am the sister of Beshr ebn Hāres," she said.

Ahmad wept sorrowfully. "Such mindfulness comes from his family," he remarked. Then he said, "It is not proper. Be careful! Take heed that your pure honor is not muddied. Follow that pure guide, your brother, until you get to the point that even if you want to spin by the light of their torches, your hand will not obey you. Your brother was that way: whenever he stretched out his hand toward food of doubtful purity, his hand would not obey him. He used to say, 'I have a sultan that they call the heart. Mindfulness is its desire. I do not dare oppose it.' Peace be upon anyone who follows right guidance."

∞ 10 ∞
Zu'n-Nun of Egypt

Leader in seeking the public's blame, the light of resurrection's acclaim, the demonstration of detachment and dignity, the sultan of realization and unity, the proof that *"Poverty is my pride,"*[1] the axis of his age, Zu'n-Nun of Egypt—God's mercy be upon him. He was a king among the followers of the way and a traveler on the path of affliction and blame. He had a precise insight into the secrets of unity, a perfect conduct, and a multitude of austerities and wonders. Most of the people of Egypt called him a heretic, while some were astonished by what he did. As long as he was alive, everyone was skeptical of him. So thoroughly did he conceal himself that no one was aware of his true state until he died.

This was the cause of Zu'n-Nun's conversion. He was informed that in a certain place there was a devout recluse. Zu'n-Nun related:

I set out to visit him. I saw him hanging from a tree, saying, "Body, help me to obey. Otherwise, I will leave you like this until you die of hunger." I was overcome by tears. The recluse heard the sound of my weeping and asked, "Who is it that has mercy on one whose shame is meager and whose sins are many?"

I went up to him and greeted him. "What is going on here?" I asked.

"This body of mine," he said, "will not leave me in peace to obey the Real most high, and it wants to associate with people."

"I thought you had shed a Muslim's blood or committed a mortal sin."

"Haven't you realized that if you mix with people, everything else follows?"

"You are an awesome ascetic."

"Do you want to see someone more ascetic than I?"

"I do."

"Climb this mountain."

When I climbed the mountain, I saw a young man at the door of a meditation cell, with one foot inside the doorway and one foot out. He had cut off the foot that had stepped outside the cell, and worms were gnawing on it. I went up to him and greeted him and asked him his story.

"One day I was sitting in this cell," he said. "A woman passed by. My heart inclined to her and demanded that I go out after her. I set one foot outside the cell. I heard a voice say, 'Have you no shame? After worshiping and obeying the mighty and glorious Lord for thirty years, you now obey Satan?' I amputated the foot that had stepped outside the cell, and I sit here waiting to see what will unfold and what they will do with me. What business has brought you to see sinners? If you want to see a true believer in the Lord, go to the top of the mountain."

I was unable to climb the mountain because of its height, but I asked for information about this man. They said, "For some time, a man has been worshiping on that mountain. One day somebody was debating with him, claiming, 'Daily sustenance must be acquired.' The man took an oath: 'I will eat nothing that needs to be acquired from the created world.' Several days passed. He ate nothing. The Real most high sent bees to fly around him and give him honey."

Zu'n-Nun said, "When I saw these things, I realized that the mighty and glorious Lord will look after the affairs of anyone who trusts in him and will not let his pain go to waste. Then, as I was coming down the road, I saw a blind little bird in a tree. I thought, "Where does this helpless creature get food and water?" It immediately flew down from the tree, struck its beak against the ground, and two bowls appeared—one of gold and one of silver, one filled with sesame seeds and the other with rose water. The bird ate the sesame seeds and drank the rose water and flew back to the tree. The bowls vanished. When I saw that, all at once I felt the confidence to trust in God."

Zu'n-Nun then continued on past several way stations. At night he entered a ruined building. He found a small pot of gold there. A board had been laid across the top of the pot, with the name of the mighty and glorious Lord written upon it. Zu'n-Nun's companions divided the gold. Zu'n-Nun said, "Give me the board. It has the name of my friend written on it." He took the board and kept kissing it. By its blessings he reached the point that one night he dreamt that they said to him, "Zu'n-Nun, everyone was satisfied with gold and jewels, thinking them precious. You were seeking something loftier than that—our name. We have therefore opened the door of knowledge and wisdom before you."

Zu'n-Nun then returned to the city. He related:

One day I was out walking and came to the bank of a river. I saw a palace at the edge of the water. I went and performed my ablutions. When I finished, without thinking, I glanced at the roof of the palace. I saw a young maid standing on the palace's parapets, as beautiful as she could be. I wanted to test her. I said, "Young maid, whom do you belong to?"

"Zu'n-Nun," she replied, "when I saw you from afar, I thought that you were a madman. When you came closer, I thought you were a scholar. When you came even closer, I thought you were a mystic. Then I looked closely—you weren't any of those."

"How so?" I asked.

"If you were a madman, you wouldn't have performed ablutions. If you were a scholar, you wouldn't have looked at a woman outside of your family. If you were a mystic, your eyes wouldn't have glimpsed anything but the Real."

She said this and disappeared. It was clear to me that she was not human—she was a warning. My soul caught fire. I hurled myself toward the river. A group of people were sitting in a boat. I went along with them. There was a merchant in the boat, and one of his jewels had gotten lost. They all agreed that I had it. They humiliated me and tortured me. I was silent. When things had gone beyond all bounds, I said, "O Lord, you know." A thousand fish raised their heads from the river, each one holding a jewel in its mouth.

Zu'n-Nun took one and gave it to the merchant. When the people in the boat saw this, they fell at his feet and asked for forgiveness. This is why they named him Zu'n-Nun, "the master of the fish."

There was no end to his devotions and austerities. It reached the point that he had a sister who had attained such realization from serving him that one day she was reciting this verse: "*We shaded them with clouds and sent manna and quails down to them*" [7:160]. She said, "My God, you sent manna and quails to the Israelites, so why not to the followers of Mohammad? By your lordship, I will not rest until you rain down manna and quails." Manna and quails began to rain down at once. She ran out of the house, turned toward the desert, and was never found again.

It is related that Zu'n-Nun used to roam through the mountains. He related:

I saw some afflicted people huddled together. I asked, "What has happened to you?"

They said, "There is a recluse there in a meditation cell. He comes out once a year and breathes on people. All are cured, and he goes back into his cell until the next year."

I, too, waited until he came out. I saw a lean and sallow man, his eyes sunk into their sockets. The mountain shook with his awesomeness. Then he looked upon the people with compassion, looked to the heavens, and breathed on them once. Instantly, they were all cured. As he was about to enter his cell, I grabbed the hem of his robe and said, "For God's sake, you cured their external illness. Cure my inner one as well."

He looked at me and said, "Zu'n-Nun, take your hand off my robe, for the friend is watching you from the zenith of majesty and glory! When he sees that you have appealed to someone besides him, he will turn you over to that person and turn that person over to you." He said this and entered his cell.

It is related that one day his friends found Zu'n-Nun crying. "Why are you crying?" they asked.

"Last night during my prostrations," he said, "I fell asleep. I saw the most glorious Lord in a dream. He said, 'Abu'l-Feyz, I created humankind. They were divided into ten parts. I displayed this world to them. Nine-tenths of them turned to this world. The tenth part was also divided by ten. I displayed paradise to them. Nine-tenths turned to paradise. The remaining tenth was again divided by ten. I placed hell in front of them. Nine-tenths shied away and scattered, terrified of hell. Thus, one part remained that was neither deceived by the world nor inclined toward paradise nor afraid of hell. I said, "You are my servants! You did not look at this world and did not hope for paradise and did not fear hell. What do you seek?" They lowered their heads and said, "You teach us what we desire. You know what we want."'"

It is related that a child came to Zu'n-Nun and said, "I have a legacy of a hundred thousand dinars. I want to spend them in your service."

Zu'n-Nun asked, "Are you of age?"

"No," he said.

"It's not right to spend the money you need to live on. Wait until you are of age."

When the child came of age, he converted at the sheikh's hands. He spent so much gold on the Sufis that none was left. One day some urgent business came up that required a bit of gold, but there was nothing. The young man said, "Where is there another hundred thousand dinars for me to spend in the service of these dear people?"

The sheikh heard this. He realized that the young man had not yet reached the truth of this affair, for the world still held some importance for him. He called the young man and said, "Go to the shop of this apothecary and tell him to give you three drams of a certain medicine." The young man went and brought the medicine. The sheikh then told him, "Grind it in a mortar and then pulverize it with oil. Make three pellets from it, pierce each one with a needle, and bring them to me."

The young man did as he was told and brought the pellets to Zu'n-Nun. The sheikh rubbed them in his hands and blew on them. They turned into three rubies, the likes of which no one had ever seen. He said, "Take these to the market, have them priced, and bring them back."

The disciple took them to the market and had them weighed. Each one was priced at a thousand dinars. He came back and told the sheikh. Then Zu'n-Nun said, "Put them in the mortar, crush them into powder, and throw it in the water. And know that dervishes do not hunger for bread but choose hunger for themselves."

The young man repented and awoke: in his heart, the world had no value.

It is related that Zu'n-Nun said:

For thirty years, I summoned the people to God, and only one person came to the Lord's court as he ought. It happened like this: One day a prince entered the mosque with his retinue, and I spoke these words: "No one is more foolish than a weak man who tangles with a strong one."

The prince came up and said, "What is this you're saying?"

I replied, "Humankind is a weak thing, but it gets tangled up with a powerful Lord."

The young man's complexion changed. He got up and left. The next day he returned and asked, "What is the path to the Lord most high?"

168

"There is a lesser and a greater path," I said. "If you desire the lesser path, bid farewell to sin, farewell to this world, and farewell to lust. If you desire the greater path, abandon everything other than the Real and empty your heart of all things."

He said, "By God, I choose nothing but the greater path." So, the next day he donned the woolen cloak and came and set to work until he became one of the Substitutes.[2]

Abu Ja'far the One-eyed[3] said, "I was with Zu'n-Nun, and stories were being told about the devotions of inanimate objects. A bench had been placed in the room. Zu'n-Nun said, 'For the friends of God, the devotions of inanimate objects are like this: If this very moment I tell this bench, "Walk around the room," it will begin to move.'

"At once, the bench began to move and walked around the room and returned to its place. A young man was present. When he saw this, he wept until he died. They washed his body on that very bench and buried him."

It is related that one day someone came to see Zu'n-Nun and said, "I have a debt, but I don't have any money." Zu'n-Nun picked a stone up from the ground and gave it to him. The man took the stone to the market. It had turned into an emerald. He sold it for four hundred dirhams and paid off the debt.

It is related that there was a young man who was constantly disparaging the Sufis. One day Zu'n-Nun gave him his ring and said, "Go to the baker and pawn it to him for one dinar."

The young man took the ring from Zu'n-Nun and took it to the baker. The baker would not take it in pawn. The young man returned to the sheikh and said, "He won't take it for more than one dirham."

"Take it to the jeweler," Zu'n-Nun said, "so he can price it." The young man took it, and the ring was priced at two thousand dinars. He brought it back and told Zu'n-Nun. The sheikh said, "Your knowledge of the state of the Sufis is like the baker's knowledge of this ring." The young man repented and stopped disparaging the Sufis.

It is related that Zu'n-Nun wanted to eat vinegar beef stew for ten years but never did. On the eve of the holiday, his self said, "How about giving me vinegar beef stew tomorrow as a holiday gift?"

Zu'n-Nun said, "Self, if you help me recite the entire Qur'an tonight in two rak'ats of prayer, I will give you vinegar beef stew to eat tomorrow." His self agreed.

The next day when Zu'n-Nun was done with his holiday prayers, they brought him vinegar beef stew. The sheikh picked up a tidbit to put in his mouth, turned it over, put it back in the bowl, and stood up to pray. Later a servant asked, "Sheikh, what was that all about?"

"The moment I picked up the tidbit of stew," Zu'n-Nun said, "my self cried, 'At last, I have reached my goal!' I said, 'You won't reach it!' and put it back."

They say that within the hour someone came with a whole pot of vinegar beef stew. He set it before the sheikh and said, "Sheikh, know that I am a porter with a family. For some time my family has been after me for vinegar beef stew, but I hadn't gotten around to it. Then, last night on the eve of the holiday, I prepared it. Today I fell asleep for a while. I saw the Prophet (peace and blessing be upon him) in a dream. He said, 'Do you want to see me on the morrow of the resurrection?'

"'Yes, O Messenger of God,' I said.

"'Take this pot of vinegar beef stew and bring it to Zu'n-Nun. Give him my greetings and say, "Mohammad, the Messenger of God, intercedes for you—avail yourself of a few bites of this stew and pacify your self."'"

Zu'n-Nun wept and said, "I obey."

It is related that when Zu'n-Nun's spiritual labors were highly advanced, the people of Egypt accused him of heresy. They informed Motavakkel,[4] the caliph of the time, about what he was doing. The caliph then sent someone to Egypt to summon him. Zu'n-Nun came to Baghdad, and they put him in fetters. When he reached the caliph's court, there was an old woman sitting there. She came up to him and said, "Be careful! Don't fear him, for like you, he is also one of the Lord's servants. He can do nothing until the mighty and glorious Lord wills it."

Zu'n-Nun then said, "Along the way I saw a water carrier, clean and well dressed. He gave me some water, and I made a sign to someone who was with me to give him a dinar. The water carrier would not take it and said, 'You are a prisoner in chains, a stranger. It would not be chivalrous of me to take anything from such a person.'"

Then the order came: "Take him to prison." They took Zu'n-Nun to prison, and he remained in captivity for forty days. Each day the sister of Beshr the Barefoot sent him a loaf of bread. The day he left prison, all forty loaves remained. Beshr's sister said, "You know that these loaves were ritually clean and would have put you under no obligation to us. Why didn't you make use of them?"

Zu'n-Nun said, "The plate was not clean." In other words, it had passed through the jailer's hands.

When he came out of prison, he fell down and cracked open his forehead. A lot of blood flowed, but none of it touched his face or hair or clothes. The blood that hit the ground all disappeared at the command of the mighty and glorious Lord.

Then they led him before the caliph and asked him to explain the things he said. He gave a good account of them. Motavakkel wept, and all of the pillars of state were astonished at Zu'n-Nun's fluency and eloquence. So it was that the caliph became his disciple and sent him back to Egypt honored and revered.

It is related that Ahmad-e Salmā[5] said, "I was with Zu'n-Nun. I saw a golden basin set before him, and they were putting sweet perfumes of musk and ambergris around him. In a state of expansion, he said to me, 'The perfumes they burn near kings are just like these.' I was terrified and stepped back. Zu'n-Nun then gave me a dirham; I used it to pay my expenses as far as Balkh."

It is related that Zu'n-Nun had a disciple. He had kept forty forty-day fasts and forty times he had stood on the plain of 'Arafāt and for forty years he had stayed awake through the night. For forty years he had kept watch over the chamber of his heart. One day he came to Zu'n-Nun and said, "Sheikh, I have done all this, and in spite of it, the friend has yet to speak to me, has yet to look at me, has yet to acknowledge me in the least—nothing of the unseen world is revealed. I'm not praising myself with what I say; I am just describing the way I am. I performed everything that is within my all-too-powerless capacity. Even so, I do not complain of the Real, for still my heart and soul seek to serve him. I am just expressing my sadness at my misfortune and telling the story of my unlucky life. Nor am I saying that my heart has grown weary of devotion—God forbid!—but I fear that the rest of my life will be like this. I have been knocking hopefully at the door for a whole lifetime without hearing any voice respond. It is hard on me. Now you are the physician of the sorrowful and you know the cure. Remedy my helplessness."

Zu'n-Nun said, "Go and eat your fill tonight. Don't perform the night prayer. Sleep all night long. If the friend doesn't come in grace, perhaps he'll come in retribution. If he doesn't look on you with compassion, he may look on you with contempt."

The dervish went and did as he was told. But his heart would not allow him to skip his prayers. He performed the night prayer and went to sleep. He saw the Prophet (peace and blessing be upon him) in a dream. The Prophet said, "The friend sends you greetings and says, 'Unmanly and effeminate is the one who comes to his court and is soon sated. The fundamental thing is to persevere in one's work and to stop laying blame.' The Real most high declares, 'I place your forty-year desire in your embrace, and whatever you desire, I deliver unto you. But convey our greetings to that pretentious bandit and tell him, "You lying bandit, you pretender! If I don't make you the disgrace of the entire world, then I am not your Lord. Do not deceive the lovers and underlings of our court again!"'"

When the disciple awoke, he wept. Then he got up and set off to see Zu'n-Nun and told him what had happened. When Zu'n-Nun heard that the Lord most high had sent him his greetings and called him lying and pretentious, he sobbed and wailed with happiness.

If anyone asks, "How can it be right for a sheikh to say to his disciple, 'Skip your prayers and sleep,'" we reply, "They are doctors." There are times when the doctor cures with poison; since Zu'n-Nun knew that this would relieve his disciple's condition, this is what he ordered for him, for he recognized that the disciple was protected and would not be able to skip his prayers. Thus the Real, glorious and exalted, ordered Abraham (peace and blessing be upon him) to sacrifice his son. He knew that he would not do it. There are things on the path that do not appear to square with the externals of the religious law. Thus, he gave Abraham a command, but he did not want him to carry it out. And thus too when Khezr (peace be upon him) killed the young boy: God did not command it, but he wanted him to do it.[6] But anyone who has not reached this rank and sets foot here is an atheist and heretic unless everything he does follows the dictates of religious law.

It is related that Zu'n-Nun said:

I saw an Arab circling the Ka'ba. He was lean and sallow and wasted away. I asked, "Are you a lover?"

"Yes," he said.

"Is the beloved close to you or far away?"

"Close."

"Does he favor you or oppose you?"

"He favors me."

"Glory be to God," I said, "the beloved is close to you and favors you, and you're so thin!"

He replied, "You worthless fool! Haven't you realized that the torment of favor and proximity are a thousand times harder than the torment of opposition and distance."

It is related that Zu'n-Nun said, "During some of my travels, I met a woman. I asked her about the limits of love. She said, 'You worthless fool! Love has no limits.'

"'Why?' I asked.

"'Because the beloved has no limits,' she replied."

It is related that Zu'n-Nun went to see a brother, one of those folk renowned for love. He saw him suffering from affliction. Zu'n-Nun said, "He does not love anyone who makes himself famous for loving him."

The brother replied, *"I seek God's forgiveness and repent to him."*

It is related that Zu'n-Nun fell sick. Someone came to visit him on his sickbed. "The friend's ailment is sweet," the man said. Zu'n-Nun was highly offended. "If you knew him," he said, "you wouldn't mention his name so glibly."

It is related that Zu'n-Nun once wrote a letter to a friend: "May the Real most high cover us both with the veil of ignorance. Behind that veil, let him reveal whatever pleases him, for there are many who are veiled whom he regards as his enemies behind the veil."

It is related that Zu'n-Nun said:

I was on a trip. I arrived at a field covered with snow. I saw a Zoroastrian scattering millet. I asked the Zoroastrian, "Why are you scattering these seeds?"

"The birds can find no seed today," he said. "I am scattering these seeds for them to peck at. Perhaps the Lord most high will have mercy on me."

"The seed that a stranger scatters bears no fruit," I said.

"If he does not accept them, at least he sees what I am doing. This is enough for me."

I went on the pilgrimage. I saw that Zoroastrian lovingly circling the Ka'ba. When he saw me, he said, "Zu'n-Nun, you see that he accepted the seed. It bore fruit, and he brought me to his house."

I was overjoyed. "O Lord," I said, "you sell forty years of Zoroastrianism cheaply for a handful of millet."

An unseen voice called out, "The Real most high calls whom he calls without reason and when he drives them away, he drives them away without reason. Leave it be, Zu'n-Nun, for the action of *He who acts as he chooses* [85:16] does not square with the analogies of your reason."

It is related that Zu'n-Nun said, "I had a poor friend who died. I saw him in a dream. 'What did God do with you?' I asked.

"My friend replied, 'He forgave me and said, "I forgave you because with all your needs you took nothing from the lowly of this world."'"

It is related that Zu'n-Nun said, "I never ate or drank my fill, so I did not sin against the Lord and felt no intention to sin."

It is related that when Zu'n-Nun was about to pray, he would say, "O Lord, with what foot shall I come to your court? With what eye shall I look in your direction? With what tongue shall I speak of you? I made my capital out of bankruptcy, and I came to your court. When it was necessary, I put aside my modesty."

He would repeat, "God is most great" and then say, "If any sorrow arises and befalls me today, I will tell it to him. If any sorrow befalls me on the morrow, whom will I tell it to?"

In his private devotions he would constantly repeat, "O Lord, do not torment me with the disgrace of the veil." And he would say, "Glory be to the Lord who veils the realized knowers from all the creatures of this world with the veils of the afterworld and who veils them from all the creatures of the afterworld with the veils of this world."

✍ ✍ ✍

"The most difficult of veils is the vision of the self."

"Wisdom does not settle in the belly full of food."

"Asking for forgiveness without refraining from sin is the repentance of liars."

"Happy is the person whose heart's watchword is scrupulousness, whose heart is purified of lust, and who reckons with his self in everything he does."

"Bodily health is in eating sparingly. Spiritual health is in sinning sparingly."

"There is nothing surprising about the person who suffers hardship and bears it patiently. What is surprising is the person who suffers affliction and is pleased."

"As long as people are fearful, they are on the path. When fear leaves their hearts, they are lost."

"A person is on the right path when he fears the mighty and glorious Lord. When fear abandons his heart, he falls from the path."

"The servant's fear of poverty is the sign that the mighty and glorious Lord is angry with him."

"Six things corrupt people: first, weak intention in the work of the afterworld; second, their bodies are in hock to Satan; third, great hopes have prevailed over them in spite of death's imminence; fourth, they have chosen to please creatures instead of pleasing the Creator; fifth, they have followed their desires and abandoned the customs of the Messenger (peace be upon him); and sixth, they have justified themselves by appealing to the lapses of the early Muslims, either burying their virtues or imposing their own corruption on them."

"Even if the aspiring are misguided, they are close to salvation. Even if the willful are righteous, they are hypocrites." In other words, the aspiring do not have the will to bow down to anything, for they have no desire. The willful are soon contented and alight somewhere.

"Only those people whose hearts yearn for piety and who rejoice in remembering their Master's name are truly alive."

"Make friends with one who is unchanged by your changes."

"If you want to be a good companion, act with your friends the way Abu Bakr (may God be pleased with him) acted with the Prophet (peace and blessing be upon him). He opposed him in matters neither of religion nor the world. The Real most high thus called him his companion."

"It is an indication of the love of the mighty and glorious Lord when one follows Mohammad, the Lord's beloved, in ethics, actions, mandates, and customs."

"I've seen no doctor more ignorant than one who treats drunks when they are drunk." In other words, talking with someone who is drunk on this world is useless. Thus Zu'n-Nun said, "There's no remedy for the drunk except for him to sober up. Then he is treated with repentance."

"The Real most high does not honor his servant with any honor more honorable than showing him the lowliness of his self. And he does not dishonor any servant with any dishonor more dishonorable than veiling him so he cannot see the dishonor of his self."

"A good aid in refraining from lusts is keeping guard over eye and ear."

"If you are on familiar terms with created beings do not hope to be on familiar terms with the Lord."

"I've seen nothing more conducive to sincerity than seclusion. Whoever takes up seclusion sees nothing but the mighty and glorious Lord. Whoever loves seclusion has fastened himself to the pillar of sincerity and has grasped one of the supports of honesty."

"You must attain what you seek with the first step." In other words, if you do not attain anything, it indicates that you have not yet taken a step on this path. As long as one atom of your being remains, you have no standing on the path.

"The sins of the intimates are the good deeds of the pious."

"When the carpet of glory is unrolled, all sins, from the first to the last, are effaced by its fringes and obliterated."

"The spirits of the prophets were hurled into the arena of realization, and the spirit of our Messenger (peace and blessing be upon him) outstripped them all to reach the garden of unity."

"One who loves the Lord is not given the goblet of love until he burns away the blood in his heart and succeeds in cutting it out."

"Know that the fear of hellfire is like a drop of water thrown into the great ocean compared to the fear of separation. I do not know anything that so seizes the heart as the fear of separation."

"Everything has a punishment, and the punishment for love is neglecting to remember the mighty and glorious Lord."

"This is the Sufi: when he speaks, his speech is all an explanation of the realities of his state." That is to say, he says nothing that he is not. When he is silent, his conduct expresses his condition. With the severing of attachments, his condition speaks for itself.

They asked Zu'n-Nun, "Who is a realized knower?"
He said, "He is a man from among them and yet separate from them."

"The realized become more humble every hour because every hour they draw closer."

"To be realized is in the dread, not the description." In other words, if someone describes himself in terms of realization, then he is not realized, for if he were, he would be terrified to say so. *Among God's servants, only the wise fear him* [35:28].

"The realized must not remain in one state. Every hour a different state comes down to them from the unseen realm, so that they have many states, not just one."

"The civility of the realized is superior to all other forms of civility, for realization teaches them manners."

"Realization has three aspects: first is the realization of God's oneness, and this pertains to the generality of believers. Second is the realization of proof and explanation, and this pertains to philosophers, preachers, and scholars. Third is the realization of the attributes of singularity, and this pertains to God's friends, those who witness the Real in their hearts so that he reveals to them that which he reveals to no worldling."

"The reality of realization is God's communication of spiritual secrets through that which is linked to the subtleties of the lights of realization." In other words, one can see the sun even in the light of the sun.

"Beware! Do not presume to realization!" In other words, if you are presumptuous, you are a liar. Another sense of it is that if you are presumptuous, you are either telling the truth or lying. If you are telling the truth, the righteous do not praise themselves. So it is that the mightiest of the righteous Abu Bakr (may God be pleased with him) said, *"I am not the best of you."* In this regard, Zu'n-Nun said, *"The greatest of my sins is my knowledge of him."* And if you are lying, the liar does not know realization. Another sense of it is this: Don't say, "I have realized," so he may speak.

"The more one knows the Lord, the more intensely one is bewildered by him." For the closer one is to the sun, the more one is dazzled by it, until the point that one no longer exists.

178

Intimates have the greater bewilderment,
for they well know the imperial punishment.

So it is that they asked Zu'n-Nun about the attributes of the realized. He said, "The realized are seers without knowledge, without eye, without information, without contemplation, without attribute, without revelation, and without veil. They are not themselves; they are not in themselves. Indeed, what they are, they are in the Real. Their motion is driven by the Lord, and their words are the words of the Real that flow from their tongues, and their vision is the vision of the Real that has found its way into their eyes." Then Zu'n-Nun said, "The Prophet (may God bless him and give him peace) revealed this quality and spoke through the Real most high when he said, 'When I, who am the Lord, love a servant, I am his ears so he can hear me, I am his eyes so he can see me, I am his tongue so he can speak to me, and I am his hands so he can reach me.'"

"Renunciants are the kings of the afterworld, and the realized are the kings of renunciants."

"The sign of the Lord's love is that you abandon whatever distracts you from the mighty and glorious Lord, until only you and the Lord's work remain."

Then Zu'n-Nun said, "Four things are symptoms of the diseased heart: first, it does not find sweetness in devotion. Second, it does not fear the mighty and glorious Lord. Third, it does not see a warning in things. And fourth, it does not understand the learning that it hears."

"The sign that a man is attaining the stage of true servitude is that he opposes desire and abandons lusts."

"Devotion is being his servant under all circumstances, just as he is your Lord under all circumstances."

"Learning exists, but acting on learning is lacking. Action exists, but acting in sincerity is lacking. Love exists, but honesty in love is lacking."

"The masses repent from sin, while the elite repent from negligence."

"There are two kinds of repentance: the repentance of penitence and the repentance of compliance. The repentance of penitence is when God's servant repents out of fear of the punishment of the Lord. The repentance of compliance is when God's servant repents out of shame before the Lord."

"Every limb has its own form of repentance. The repentance of the heart is to resolve to abandon forbidden desires. The repentance of the eyes is to shut them to forbidden things. The repentance of the hands is to give up grasping after prohibited objects. The repentance of the feet is not to go to prohibited places. The repentance of the ears is to stop them from hearing worthless talk. The repentance of the belly is to avoid eating illicit foods. The repentance of the private parts is to avoid obscene acts."

"Fear is the guardian of action, and hope, the beneficent intercessor."

"Fear must be stronger than hope, for if hope is predominant, the heart is confused."

"Let them seek what they need with the tongue of poverty, not the tongue of authority."

"I prefer abiding, perplexed poverty to abiding, conceited purity."

"Remembrance of the mighty and glorious Lord is food for my soul, praising him is wine for my soul, and shame before him is clothing for my soul."

"Shame is an awe in the heart, with a terror at the things you have done that are not to be done."

"Love makes you speak, shame makes you silent, and fear makes you uneasy."

"Piety is not polluting the outer being with sin or the inner being with nonsense while standing firm with the Lord."

"Honest are those whose tongues speak properly and truthfully."

"Honesty is the sword of the mighty and glorious Lord. This sword never passes through anything without slicing it."

"Honesty is a sorrowful language, and speaking the truth is eloquent."

"Watchfulness is when you give priority to what the Real has chosen." In other words, you prefer what is best and you esteem what the mighty and glorious Lord has esteemed. When the least thing is born of you because of this preference, you do not even glance at it from the corner of your eye. You see it as the grace of the Real and not your own doing. You show no regard for the world and what is accounted wise. You throw even that away and do not see yourself as playing any role in this rejection.

"Ecstasy is a secret in the heart. Listening to music and poetry is a divine inroad through which the Lord incites hearts and makes them greedy to seek him. Whoever listens to them through the Lord finds his way to the Lord, but whoever listens to them through the self falls into heresy."

"Trust in God is leaving the service of many lords and entering the service of the one Lord and severing subsidiary causes."
　　They said, "Explain this further."
　　Zu'n-Nun said, "Trust in God is maintaining the attribute of servitude in oneself happily and relinquishing the attribute of lordship."

"Trust in God is relinquishing deliberation and abandoning one's own powers and wiles."

"Someone endowed with intimacy is terrified by this world and its creatures, except for the friends of the Real, because intimacy with his friends is intimacy with the Real."

"When he casts his friends into the joy of intimacy, it is as though he were speaking with them in paradise in the language of light. When he casts them into the joy of awe, it is as though he were speaking with them in hell in the language of fire."

"This is the least degree of intimacy for those captivated by the Lord most high: If they are burned in hellfire, their aspiration does not lessen one iota, for they are intimate with him."

"The mark of intimacy is not becoming intimate with people."

"The key to devotion is meditation. The sign of achieving it is opposition to the self and lust, and opposition to them is forsaking desires. Whoever perseveres in meditating in his heart sees the unseen world in his spirit."

"Acceptance is rejoicing at heart over fate's bitterness and forsaking choice before fate is fulfilled and feeling no bitterness after fate is fulfilled and bubbling with love in the midst of affliction."

They asked, "Who is most knowledgeable of his own self?"
　　Zu'n-Nun said, "Whoever accepts what has been allotted."

"Sincerity is not complete unless there is honesty and patience in it. Honesty is not complete unless there is sincerity and constancy in it."

"Sincerity is guarding devotion from the enemy so he does not ruin it."

"There are three indications of sincerity: first, one considers praise and censure as one and the same; second, one forgets to look at one's good works; and third, one does not consider any reward necessary in the afterworld for those good works."

"I have not seen anything more difficult than sincerity in seclusion."

"Whatever is seen by the eyes is related to learning. Whatever is known by the heart is related to certainty."

"Three things are among the indications of certainty: first, looking to the Real in all things; second, resorting to the Real in all actions; and third, seeking his aid in all situations."

"Certainty invites one to limit expectations. Limiting expectations invites one to renunciation. Renunciation invites one to wisdom. And wisdom leads to looking clearly at outcomes."

"Patience is the fruit of certainty."

"A little certainty is greater than this world, for a little certainty inclines the heart to love of the other world and with a little certainty the heart studies the entire empyrean of the other world."

"The mark of certainty is to oppose people often during one's life and to forsake praising them if they give gifts and not to bother rebuking them if they give nothing."

"Anyone who grows intimate with people resides on the carpet of the Pharaoh's followers. Anyone who fails to listen attentively to certainty falls short of sincerity. But if the Real and he alone comes to anyone as his share of all things, then he has nothing to fear, even if everything he has passes away except the Real, since this results in the presence of the Real."

"Every pretender there is, is veiled by his pretense from the vision and words of the Real. If the Real is present to a person, he has no need of pretense. If the Real is absent, this is where the pretense comes from, for pretense is the sign of those who are veiled."

"There has never been a disciple more obedient to his teacher than the Lord.[7] The mighty and glorious Lord dignifies the external motions of anyone who observes him in the passing thoughts of his heart. Anyone who is afraid flees to the Lord, and anyone who flees to the Lord obtains salvation. Anyone who is content rests easy with the people of his time and becomes superior to them all. Anyone who trusts in God becomes secure. Anyone who takes pains over what is unnecessary to his task loses what is necessary to it. The heart of anyone who fears the mighty and glorious Lord melts away, and the Lord's love becomes firmly fixed in it, and his reason becomes perfect. Anyone who seeks greatness has undertaken a great risk, but anyone who knows the value of what he strives for will look with contempt on the value of what he has to expend."

"If anyone feels little regret before the Real, it is a sign that the Real has little value to him."

"Do not associate with anyone whose outer appearance does not indicate his inner state."

"Do not grieve over the goal while remembrance of the One adored exists."

"Whoever truly recalls the Lord forgets anything other than him. If anyone forgets all things in remembrance of the Lord most high, he will watch over all things for him and will be his compensation for all things."

They asked, "How did you recognize the Lord?"

Zu'n-Nun said, "I recognized the Lord by the Lord and creation by the Prophet." That is to say, God and the light of God: the Lord is the Creator; the Creator can be known by the Creator. The light of the Lord is creation, and the essence of creation is the light of Mohammad (may God bless him), and thus creation can be known by Mohammad (peace be upon him).

They asked, "What do you say about creation?"

He said, "All creation lives in terror, and remembering the Real in the midst of the terror-stricken is absence."

They asked, "When does the servant entrust himself to God?"

He said, "When he comes to regret his self and his actions and takes shelter in the mighty and glorious Lord and is no longer attached to anything but the Real."

They said, "With whom shall we associate?"

He said, "With one who has no property, who does not repudiate you under any circumstances, and who is unchanged by your changes, even if they are great. The more you change, the more you need a friend."

They said, "When does the path of fear become easy for God's servant?"

He said, "When he accounts himself ill and avoids all things for fear of prolonging the illness."

They said, "How does God's servant become worthy of heaven?"

He said, "By five things: constancy that is unchanging, exertion that does not go astray, contemplation of the Lord in public and private, expectation of death in gathering provisions for the road, and taking account of oneself before accounts are rendered."

They asked him about the mark of fear.

He said, "It is the fear of the Lord keeping one safe from all other fears."

They said, "Who is most self-possessed of people?"

He said, "The one who holds his tongue."

They said, "What is the sign of trust in God?"

He said, "Cutting off desire for created things."

They asked him again about the mark of trust in God.

He said, "It is repudiating the powerful and stripping away causes, casting the self into servitude and ousting it from lordship."

They said, "When does seclusion come out right?"

He said, "When one is secluded from one's self."

They said, "Who suffers most?"

He said, "The most ill-tempered people."

They said, "What is this world?"

He said, "Whatever distracts you from the Real."

They said, "Who is lowly?"

He said, "One who does not learn the path to the Lord."

It is related that Yusof ebn al-Hoseyn asked Zu'n-Nun (God have mercy on them both), "With whom should we associate?"

Zu'n-Nun said, "With one who doesn't meddle with 'me' and 'you.'"

"Give me counsel," Yusof said.

"Be the Lord's friend," Zu'n-Nun said, "in attacking the self; do not be the self's friend in attacking the Lord. Hold no one in contempt,

even if he is a polytheist; consider his outcome, for it may be that realization will be stripped from you and given to him."

Someone asked him for counsel. Zu'n-Nun said, "Appoint your inner
being to the Real and give your outer appearance over to people. Be
dear to the mighty and glorious Lord, so he will make you independent
of people."

"Go on," they said.

"Do not choose doubt over certainty. And never be pleased with
your self, so it may not rest easy. If some hardship should confront you,
endure it patiently and be an attendant at God's court."

Someone else asked him for advice. Zu'n-Nun said, "Don't send your
aspirations before or behind."

"This needs to be explained," they said.

"Don't think about what has passed or what is yet to come. Spend
yourself on the moment."

They asked, "Who are the Sufis?"

"They are the people," Zu'n-Nun said, "who choose the Real most
high over everything and whom the Real chooses over everyone."

Someone said, "Guide me to the Real."

Zu'n-Nun said, "If you're seeking guidance to him, this is beyond
all reckoning. If you're seeking proximity, it is in the very first step."
These words have been explained before.

Someone said to Zu'n-Nun, "I love you."

Zu'n-Nun said, "If you know the Lord, the Lord is enough for
you. If not, seek someone who knows him to guide you to him."

They asked him about the end of realization. He said, "This is the sign
of anyone who reaches the end: how he is, is just as he is; where he is,
is just the same as before."

They asked, "What is the first station that the seeker of realization sets
out toward?"

Zu'n-Nun said, "Bewilderment; after that, poverty; after that,
unity; and after that, life."

They asked about the actions of the realized.

Zu'n-Nun said, "He looks to the Real under all circumstances."

They asked about the perfection of the knowledge of the self.

He said, "Being suspicious of the self and never thinking well of it."

"The realities of hearts are in forgetting the share of selves."

"The person furthest from the mighty and glorious Lord is the one who outwardly alludes to him the most." In other words, one keeps it hidden. Thus, it is related of Zu'n-Nun that he said, "For seventy years, I walked in unity, seclusion, detachment, and affirmation and out of all of this, I laid hold of nothing but a conjecture."

ᕀ ᕀ ᕀ

It is related that when Zu'n-Nun succumbed to mortal illness, they asked, "What do you desire?"

"That before I die," he said, "I know him, if only for a moment." Then he recited this verse:

Fear made me ill, and yearning consumed me.
Love laid me low, and God brought me to life.

One day he was delirious. Yusof ebn al-Hoseyn said, "While you're in this condition, give me a parting piece of advice."

Zu'n-Nun said, "Associate with someone whose outward appearance puts you at peace and whose sight teaches you about the Lord."

During his death throes, they said, "Give us a final testament."

Zu'n-Nun said, "Don't distract me. I am astonished by his benevolence." And then he died.

That night seventy people dreamt they saw the Prophet (peace and blessing be upon him). He said, "The friend of the Lord Zu'n-Nun will come. We have come to welcome him."

When he died, this was written upon his forehead in green: *"This is the beloved of God—he died in the love of God. This is the martyr of God—he died by the sword of God."*

When they lifted up his funeral bier, birds spread their wings above him and shaded him, for the sun was very hot. As they carried his bier down the road, a muezzin was sounding the call to prayer. When he reached the words of the testimony of faith, Zu'n-Nun raised a finger. A shout rose up from the people: "Can he be alive?" They set his bier down. No matter how much they tried to force down the finger that he had raised, it would not be bent back into place. After that, they buried him. When the people of Egypt saw what he was like, they were put to shame and they repented of the injustice that they had done him.

✑ 11 ✑
Bāyazid of Bestām

The sultan of the realized, the decisive argument for the seekers of truth, the divine caliph, the infinite pillar, fully matured in the world of disappointment, the master of the age, Abu Yazid of Bestām—God's mercy be upon him. He was the greatest of the sheikhs and the mightiest of God's friends. He was the proof of the Lord and caliph in reality. He was the axis of the world and the ground of its supports. His austerities and wonders were many. He had a penetrating vision into spiritual secrets and realities and a profound earnestness. He was constantly at the way stations of proximity and awe, and he was drowned in the fire of love. He always kept his body engaged in struggle and his heart in contemplation. His accounts of the hadith were outstanding. No one before him had the ability to infer the meanings of the path that he did.

In this way one can say that it was he who wholly dominated the field. His perfection is so apparent that Joneyd (God's mercy be upon him) said, "Bāyazid among us is like Gabriel among the angels." Joneyd also said, "The final arena for pilgrims entering into unity is Bāyazid's starting point. All true believers who reach the start of his tracks turn back, collapse, and disappear." The proof of this is what Bāyazid himself said, "Two hundred years will pass over a garden before a rose like us blossoms again." Sheikh Abu Sa'id ebn Abi'l-

Kheyr (God have mercy upon him) said, "I saw eighteen thousand worlds filled with Bāyazid, but he was not there." What Bāyazid is, is effaced in the Real.

It comes down to us that Bāyazid's grandfather was a Zoroastrian, and his father was one of the eminent men of Bestām. Bāyazid's revelations were with him even from his mother's womb. They relate that his mother said, "Whenever I put any morsel in my mouth that was the least bit questionable, he would squirm in my womb until I spit it out."

This statement is confirmed by what Bāyazid himself said when he was asked, "What is the best thing for a person on this path?"

"Innate good luck."

"If he does not have that?"

"A knowing heart."

"If he does not have that?"

"A seeing eye."

"If he does not have that?"

"A hearing ear."

"If he does not have that?"

"Sudden death."

It is related that his mother sent him to school, and when he came to this verse in the sura *Luqmān*—*Give thanks to me and to your parents* [31:14]—he asked his teacher what it meant. When the teacher explained it to him, he was deeply affected. He set down his writing tablet, asked to be excused, and went home.

His mother said, "Teyfur, why have you come home? Is there some excuse for this? Did they give you a prize?"

"No," he said. "I came to the verse in which the Real most high commands me to serve him and to serve you. How can I manage two houses? This verse has cut me to the quick. Either ask the Lord to make me entirely yours, or give me to the Lord so I can be entirely his."

His mother said, "I give you over to the Lord's work and surrender my claim on you."

Then Bāyazid left Bestām[1] and wandered in the Syrian desert for thirty years. He practiced asceticism and was constantly undergoing sleeplessness and hunger. He served 113 elders and learned something useful from all of them, among them Ja'far as-Sādeq (may God be pleased with him).

It is related that one day Bāyazid was with Ja'far as-Sādeq. He said, "Get that book down from the shelf."

"What shelf?" Bāyazid asked.

"You've been here for some time. Haven't you seen this shelf?"

"No. What business do I have raising my head in your presence? I didn't come here to look around."

"Since this is the way it is, go back to Bestām. Your work is complete."

It is related that they pointed out to him that there was a great elder in a certain place. Bāyazid went to see him. As Bāyazid approached, the elder spat in the direction of Mecca. Bāyazid immediately turned back without seeing him. "If he had taken even one step on the path," Bāyazid said, "no transgression of religious law would have overtaken him."

It is related that there were forty steps from Bāyazid's house to the mosque. Out of respect for the mosque, he would never spit on this route.

It is related that it took Bāyazid twelve years' time to reach the Ka'ba. Every few steps he would unroll his prayer rug and perform two rak'ats of prayer and say, "This is not the vestibule of some king of this world that one can run through in a straight shot."

He then went to the Ka'ba, but he did not go to Medina all that year. "It would not be proper," he said, "to make the Prophet (peace and blessing be upon him) tag along on this visit. We will make the pilgrimage to him separately."

He went back, and the following year he undertook the pilgrimage to Medina. As he was coming down the road into the city, a great crowd of people followed him. When he left, the people came out behind him. Bāyazid looked and asked, "Who are they?"

"They will keep you company," he was told.

"O Lord," he said, "I ask you not to veil yourself from me with your creatures!"

So, he wished to eliminate their affection for him from their hearts and to remove from their path the trouble he might cause them.

He performed the morning prayer, looked at them, and said, *"Verily I am God, and there is no god but me! Worship me!"*

"This man has got to be crazy," they said. They left him and went away.

Bāyazid had spoken to them there with the tongue of the Lord most high. This is what they call *"speaking through his Lord."*

He then found a skull on the road. On it was inscribed this verse: *Deaf, dumb, and blind, they shall not return* [2:18]. He cried out and fell down and kissed the skull and said, "It must be the head of a Sufi who was effaced in the Real and obliterated. He has no ear to hear the words of the Real, no eyes to see the unending beauty, no tongue to sing his mighty praises, and no mind to comprehend even a mote of realization. This verse is about him."

Zu'n-Nun of Egypt sent a disciple to serve Bāyazid (God have mercy on them both) with this message: "Bāyazid, you sleep all night and lounge about at ease. The caravan is about to pass you by!"

The disciple came and delivered the message. Bāyazid replied, "Tell Zu'n-Nun that the complete person is one who has slept all night and by dawn has alighted at the next way station before the caravan has arrived."

When Zu'n-Nun heard this, he wept and said, "May he be blessed! Our mystical states have not advanced to this degree. He will be the path through this desert and the inner journey in this way of life."

It is related that on his way to the pilgrimage, Bāyazid had a camel on which his provisions and saddle had been loaded. Someone said, "This poor camel! His load is so heavy. It really is cruel."

Bāyazid said, "Young man, it's not the camel that carries the load. Take a look. Is there any load on the camel's back?"

When the young man looked closely, the load was a handspan above the camel's back. "Praise be to God," he said, "this is a strange business!"

"If I keep my true state hidden from you," Bāyazid said, "you start wagging your tongue to blame me. If I reveal it, you can't take it. What's to be done with you?"

191

Then, after he had gone and performed the pilgrimage to Medina, it occurred to him to go pay his respects to his mother. He set off with a group of people toward Bestām. The rumor of his visit went around Bestām, and the townspeople came out to greet him. Bāyazid was on the verge of being so distracted by their kind attentions that he would have been held back from the Real. When he entered the city, he got a loaf of bread from a shop and ate it—and this during the month of the fast! When the people saw this, they all quickly backed away.

"Did you see," Bāyazid said to his followers, "how all the people rejected me when I followed one of the fine points of the law?"[2]

Then, at dawn, he went to the door of his mother's house and listened. He heard his mother performing her ablutions, as she prayed, "My God, protect my wanderer! Let the hearts of all the sheikhs hold him dear. Grant him good health."

Bāyazid wept when he heard this. He knocked on the door.

"Who is it?" his mother asked.

"Your wanderer," he replied.

His mother started crying and opened the door. "O Teyfur," she said, "my eyes have grown weak from weeping so much in your absence. My back is bent double from grieving so much over you."

It is related that he said, "The act that I considered the least important was greater than all my other acts combined, and that was pleasing my mother." He continued, "What I was searching for in all my austerities and struggles and wanderings, I found in this: One night my mother asked me for water. There was no water in the pitcher or jug. I went to the stream and brought back some water. My mother had fallen asleep. It was a cold night. I held the pitcher in my hand. When she awoke, she realized what had happened and called for me. She saw how the pitcher had frozen to my hand.

"'Why didn't you put it down?' she asked.

"I said, 'I was afraid that you would wake up and I would not be here.'

"Another time she said, 'Close that half of the door!' Until dawn I weighed whether I should close the right half or the left, so I wouldn't disobey my mother. At dawn, what I was searching for came in through the door."

It is related that when he was coming back from Mecca, he arrived in Hamadan. He had purchased an egg spiced with saffron. He tied a little of it in a corner of his robe and took it to Bestām. When he unwrapped it, he saw that a few ants had gotten mixed in. He said, "I have made them homeless." He got up and took them back to Hamadan and set them back in their colony.

Until someone has taken *glorying in God's commandment* to this extreme, he will not attain this degree of *compassion toward God's creatures*.

It is related that Bāyazid said: "For twelve years, I was the blacksmith of my self. I put it in the furnace of asceticism and heated it with the fire of austerity. I placed it on the anvil of scorn and pounded it with the hammer of reproach, until I made a mirror of myself. For five years, I was my own mirror, and I polished it with every kind of worship and devotion. Then for one year, I gazed at it respectfully. I saw a sash around my waist, made of reliance on my own devotion, of self-satisfaction with my own works, and of pride and coquetry. I strove for another five years, until the sash was cut. I converted to Islam again. I looked closely: I saw that all created beings were dead. I said 'God is great' four times over them and turned away from their coffins. Without troubling any created thing, I attained the Real with the aid of the Real."

It is related that whenever he arrived at the door of the mosque, he would stand there awhile and weep. They said, "What's going on?"

Bāyazid said, "I perceive myself as a menstruating woman who fears that the mosque will be defiled if she enters."

It is related that he once resolved to perform the pilgrimage. He went a few stages down the road and came back. "You have never broken one of your resolutions," they said. "How did this happen?"

"I saw a black man on the road with a sword drawn. He said to me, 'If you turn back, fine. If not, I'll cut off your head.' Then he said, 'You have left the Lord behind in Bestām and set off for the Ka'ba.'"

It is related that Bāyazid said: "A man came up to me and asked, 'Where are you going?'

"'On the pilgrimage,' I said.

193

"'What do you have?'

"'Two hundred dirhams.'

"'Give them to me and circumambulate me seven times. This is your pilgrimage.'

"I did so and returned."

When Bāyazid's affairs had risen aloft and his words were incomprehensible to superficial people, he was expelled from Bestām seven times. Bāyazid kept asking, "Why do you expel me?"

"Because you are an evil man."

"What a fine town this must be, where Bāyazid is the evil one!"

It is related that one night Bāyazid went up to the roof of his meditation cell to chant God's name. He stood on the top of the wall and said nothing until dawn. The people looked at him. Blood was coming from him instead of urine. "What's going on?" they asked.

"I have remained idle here until dawn for two reasons. One is that I let slip a certain word when I was a child. The other is that such a grandeur cast its shadow over me that my heart was stunned. If my heart had come to, my tongue would have failed. If my tongue had moved, my heart would have failed. I continued in this state all night until daybreak."

It is related that when the sheikh would retire for worship or meditation, he would go into the house and close every opening securely. He used to say, "I'm afraid that some voice will disturb me." This was merely an excuse.

'Isā of Bestām[3] says, "I followed Bāyazid for thirteen years without hearing a single word from him. It was his habit to prop his head on his knees."

Sheikh Sahlaki[4] says, "This was when he was in a state of contraction. But in a state of expansion, they used to get many useful sayings from him."

Once in a private place, the words *Glory be to me! How great is my nature!* slipped from Bāyazid's tongue. When he came to his senses, his disciples said, "You spoke these words."

The sheikh said, "May the mighty and glorious Lord be your enemy if you hear this again and do not rip me to shreds!" Then he gave everyone a knife, so they would kill him if he spoke those words again. It happened that Bāyazid said the same thing again, and his followers were determined to slay him. They saw the room fill with Bāyazid, as though he occupied every corner of it. They stabbed with their knives, but it was like someone stabbing water. After some time passed the image shrank, until Bāyazid appeared no bigger than a sparrow sitting in the prayer niche.

His followers told the sheikh what happened. He said, "Bāyazid is this that you see. That was not Bāyazid." He continued, *"God the all-powerful declares himself through the tongue of his servant."*

If anyone should ask, "How was that?" we will say, "It was just as Adam (peace be upon him) was in the beginning when he rubbed his head against the heavens. Gabriel (peace be upon him) touched Adam with his wing, so he would be a bit shorter than that. Since it is right for large forms to become small, so is the opposite right. Just as a child in his mother's womb weighs, for example, four pounds, when he reaches adolescence, he can weigh two hundred pounds. Or just as Gabriel (peace be upon him) was manifested to Mary in the form of a man. What happened to Bāyazid was the same way. But until someone truly reaches that point, explanation is worthless."

It is related that once Bāyazid took a red apple, looked at it closely, and said, "This is a divine apple."

In his innermost self, a voice spoke out: "Bāyazid, aren't you ashamed to apply our name to a piece of fruit?" For forty days, the name of the Real most high was forgotten in his heart.

"As long as I live," he said, "I swear I will not eat fruit from Bestām."

Bāyazid said:

One day I was sitting around, and it occurred to me, "Today I am the spiritual guide of our time and the eminent man of the age." When I thought this, I knew that I had made a tremendous blunder. I got up and set off on the road to Khorasan. I took up residence in a way station and took an oath: "I will not get up from here until the Real most high sends someone to me to show me to me."

I stayed there for three whole days and nights. On the fourth day, I saw a one-eyed man, coming toward me on a she-camel. When I looked at him closely, I saw the traces of awareness on his face. I made a sign for the camel to stop. At once its feet sank into the earth.

The man looked at me and said, "Are you bringing me here so I'll open my bad eye and close my good one, so I'll drown Bestām along with Bāyazid and all its people?"

I fainted away. Afterward I said, "Where are you coming from?"

"Since the moment you took the oath," he said, "I have come nine thousand miles." Then he added, "Beware, Bāyazid! Watch over your heart!" He wheeled about and left.

It is related that Bāyazid lived next to a mosque for forty years. He kept the clothes he wore to the mosque separate from those he wore at home and kept them both separate from those he wore for ablutions. For forty years he never leaned his back against any wall except those he shared with the mosque and the hospice. He would say, "The Real most high will ask about the most minor things, and this is more than a minor thing."

Bāyazid said, "For forty years, I didn't eat what people ate." In other words, "My food came from someplace else."

He said, "For forty years, I stood guard over my heart. When I looked closely, I saw the sash worn by polytheists tied around my waist." His polytheism consisted of paying attention to something other than the Real—the heart in which no polytheism remains is inclined to nothing but the Real. As long as it is attracted to another place, polytheism remains.

He said, "For forty years, I was guardian over my heart. When I looked closely, I saw servitude and lordship, both from the Real."

He said, "For thirty years, I was seeking the mighty and glorious Lord. When I looked closely, I saw that he was the seeker and I the sought."

He said, "For thirty years now, every time I have wanted to mention the Lord most high, I have cleansed my mouth and tongue with three drinks of water, for the sake of glorifying the Real."

Abu Musā[5] asked Bāyazid, "What did you consider to be the most difficult task on this path?"

He said, "For some time, I used to take my self to his court, and it would weep. When the Real came to help, my self would take me and laugh."

It is related that in the end Bāyazid's labors reached the point that whatever passed through his mind would immediately appear before him. And when he mentioned the mighty and glorious Lord, blood would come from him instead of urine.

One day a group of people came to see Bāyazid. He lowered his head and then raised it and said, "Since dawn, I've been searching for a seed to give you that you would be able to plant. I haven't found it."

It is related that Abu Torāb had a disciple who was very passionate and prone to ecstatic visions. Abu Torāb would constantly say, "Given the way you are, you ought to go see Bāyazid."

One day the disciple said, "Why should someone who sees Bāyazid's Lord a hundred times each day bother with Bāyazid?"

"When you see the Lord," Abu Torāb said, "you see him according to your capacity. When you see him in Bāyazid's presence, you see him according to his capacity. The difference is in the eye. Will he not manifest himself once before Abu Bakr (may God be pleased with him) and once before the rest of creation?"

These words touched the disciple's heart, and he said, "Get up, let's go."

They both came to visit Bestām, but the sheikh was not at home. He had gone to get water, and they went after him. They saw the sheikh coming toward them, with a pitcher of water in his hand, wearing an old fur cloak. When Bāyazid's eyes fell on Abu Torāb's disciple, and the disciple's eyes fell on the sheikh, the disciple suddenly trembled, collapsed, and died.

Abu Torāb said, "O Sheikh! Death at a single glance?"

"Abu Torāb," Bāyazid said, "there was something in the nature of this young man that it was not yet time to reveal. On beholding me, that spirit was revealed all at once. He couldn't take it and succumbed. The same thing happened to the women of Egypt. They couldn't deal with Joseph's beauty. They all cut their hands at once and were unaware of it."[6]

Yahyā-ye Mo'āz of Rey wrote a letter to Bāyazid (may God have mercy on them both): "What do you say about someone who drank a cup of wine and became drunk on eternity without beginning or end?"

Bāyazid wrote back: "There is a man here who drinks up the sea of eternity without beginning or end in a single day and cries out, 'Is there any more?'"

Yahyā also wrote: "There is a secret between you—Bāyazid—and me. But our rendezvous is in paradise in the shadow of the Tubā tree." He had sent a loaf of bread along with the letter. "The sheikh must consume this loaf, for I have kneaded it with the water of Zamzam."

Bāyazid wrote back. He mentioned the secret between them and continued: "Where there is recollection of the Real, there is both paradise and the shadow of the Tubā tree. I did not consume that loaf of bread, because you told me that you kneaded it with the water of Zamzam, but you didn't tell me what seeds you planted."

When Yahyā heard this, longing for Bāyazid overwhelmed him, and he went to visit him. He arrived there at the time of the night prayer. Yahyā related: "I didn't want to bother the sheikh until dawn. I heard that he was in the graveyard, busy with his devotions. I went to the graveyard and watched him standing on two toes until daybreak. I was astonished at what he was doing and listened to him. All night he was busy conversing and talking back and forth. When morning broke, he murmured, *'Protect me from asking you for this spiritual station.'*"

Then Yahyā went forward, greeted Bāyazid, and asked him about that nocturnal revelation. Bāyazid said, "They counted off twenty-odd spiritual stations to me, and I said, 'I don't want any of these—they are all stations of veiling.'"

While Bāyazid had reached the end point, Yahyā was a mere beginner. He asked, "Sheikh, why didn't you ask for realization? He is the King of Kings and has said, 'Whatever you wish for, just ask.'"

Bāyazid shouted, "Be quiet, Yahyā! I would become jealous of myself if I knew him. I don't want anyone to know him but himself. Where there is realization of him, what business do I have interfering? He himself, Yahyā, desires that no one know him but himself."

198

"By the might of the Lord," Yahyā said, "give me a share of the victory that was yours last night!"

Bāyazid said, "If they give you the purity of Adam, the sanctity of Gabriel, the friendship of Abraham, the passion of Moses, the purity of Jesus, and the love of Mohammad (peace and blessing be upon them all), then beware! You will not be content and you will seek what is beyond, for there are affairs beyond this. Aspire and bow your head down to nothing. You will be veiled by whatever you submit to."

Ahmad ebn Harb[7] sent a prayer mat to Bāyazid for him to pray on at night. Bāyazid said, "I have gathered together the devotion of the denizens of heaven and earth and put that in my pillow and placed it under my head."

It is related that Zu'n-Nun sent a prayer rug to Bāyazid. He sent it back, asking, "What use do I have for a prayer rug? I could use a cushion. Send me one to lean on." In other words, his work had gone beyond prayer and reached the final stage.

When Zu'n-Nun heard this, he ordered a finely worked pillow and sent it to the sheikh. Bāyazid sent this back too—by this time he had melted away and was no more than skin and bones. He said, "Whoever has the kindness and generosity of the Real as his support takes neither comfort in created pillows nor has any need of them."

It is related that he said: "One night I was in the desert and had wrapped my head in my robe. I had a nocturnal emission, and it was bitterly cold. I wanted to wash, but my self was lazy and said, 'Wait until day-break when the sun comes up. Wash then.'

"When I saw my self's laziness, I realized that I was deferring my prayers. I broke the ice with my robe then and there and washed. In this way I remained wrapped in my robe—it froze solid—until the air grew warm. I kept my self in this torment all winter. Before daybreak, I used to faint seventy times to punish it for its laziness."

It is related that Bāyazid was passing through the graveyard one night. A young man from one of the great families of Bestām was playing a lute. When the young man approached the sheikh, Bāyazid said, *"There is no power or might but in God."* The young man smashed his lute over Bāyazid's head, breaking them both. Bāyazid went back to the shrine.

First thing in the morning, Bāyazid gave his servant the price of the lute and a plate of sweets and sent him to see the young man. He offered his apologies: "Tell the young man that Bāyazid apologizes and says, 'Last night you broke your lute over our head. Take this pouch of money and buy another. Eat these sweets, so that the sadness of breaking it and the bitterness of its loss will leave your heart.'"

When the young man saw what had happened, he came and fell at Bāyazid's feet and repented and wept profusely. By the grace of the sheikh's character, several other young men repented with him.

It is related that one day Bāyazid was walking along with his followers. A dog was coming toward them down a narrow street. The sheikh turned back and yielded the street to the dog. A skeptical thought crossed a disciple's mind: "The Real most high has honored humankind. The sheikh is the sultan of the realized. In spite of such high standing and a group of honest disciples, he yielded the way to a dog, preferring it to them. How is this?"

"Oh, my dears," Bāyazid said, "the dog spoke to Bāyazid in a mute language. It said, 'In the time before time, how did I fall short and how did you excel that I should be dressed in dog fur and you should be draped in the royal robe of the sultan of the realized?' When this thought came to my innermost soul, I yielded the way to the dog."

It is related that one day Bāyazid was out walking. A dog came up alongside him, and the sheikh pulled his robe out of the way. The dog said, "If I am dry, there's no quarrel between us. If I am wet, a thorough washing will square things between us. But if you tug back your robe, you won't get clean, even if you wash in the seven seas."

"Your filthiness is on the outside," Bāyazid said. "Mine is on the inside. Come on, let's put the two together. Perhaps by adding them together, cleanliness will result for both of us."

"You're not fit to accompany me," the dog said. "I am rejected by the people, while you are accepted. Anybody who catches up with me hits me with a stone, but anybody who meets you says, 'Greetings, O Sultan of the Realized!' I never set aside a single bone for tomorrow, but you keep a whole barrel of wheat."

Bāyazid said, "I am not fit to accompany a dog. How can I be fit to accompany the Eternal and Everlasting?"

Praise to the Lord who educates the best of his creatures by way of the least of them.

Bāyazid related: "Doubt beset me, and I despaired of my devotion. I said, 'Let me go to the market and buy an infidel's sash and tie it around my waist.' There was a sash hanging up on display in the market. 'How much?' I asked.

"'A thousand dinars.'

"I was downcast. A voice called out, 'Don't you know that a sash to tie around the waist of someone like you couldn't sell for less than a thousand dinars?' I rejoiced at heart—I knew that the Real most high had some consideration for me."

It is related that there was an ascetic among the eminent people of Bestām, widely accepted and with many followers. He was never absent from Bāyazid's circle. One day he said, "Sheikh, for thirty years I have fasted during the day and kept vigil at night, but I have not found a trace of the knowledge that you speak of, even though I love it and believe in it sincerely."

"If you fast and pray for three hundred years," Bāyazid said, "you will not catch the slightest whiff of this tradition."

"Why?"

"Because you are veiled by your self."

"What's the remedy?"

"It's mine to tell you, but you won't accept it."

"I'll accept it. I've been seeking it for years."

"Go, this very hour, and shave off your hair and beard. Throw out these clothes of yours. Put on a coarse woolen loincloth and go sit in the most visible place in the neighborhood where you are best known. Fill a feedbag with walnuts and place it in front of you. Gather the children around you and tell them, 'I'll give a walnut to anyone who slaps me. And I'll give two walnuts to anyone who slaps me twice.' Go around the city, until all the children slap you across the neck. That will be your cure."

"Good Lord! There is no god but God!"

"If a nonbeliever says these words, he becomes a believer, but with these words, you have become a heathen."

"Why?"

"Because when you said these words, you were exalting yourself, not the Real."

"I cannot do this. Order me to do something else."

"This is your cure. I told you, you wouldn't do it."

It is related that Shaqiq's student resolved to undertake the pilgrimage. Shaqiq said, "Pass by Bestām and take the opportunity to pay a visit to Bāyazid."

When the disciple came to pay his respects to Bāyazid, the sheikh asked, "Whose disciple are you?"

"I am the disciple of Shaqiq of Balkh."

"What does he say?"

"He has been freed of the created world and abides according to the rule of trust in God. He says, 'If the heavens and earth turn to iron and brass and no rain comes from the heavens and nothing grows from the earth and all the world's creatures become my dependents, I will not turn away from my trust in God.'"

"What a hardened polytheist he is! Bāyazid won't fly to the city of that polytheist, even if he turns into a crow! When you go back, tell him, 'Don't test the mighty and glorious Lord for two loaves of bread. When you're hungry, take two loaves from your own kind and set aside your program of trust in God, lest the entire city and province are leveled to the ground because of your misfortune.'"

That man turned back because of the harshness of these words and went to see Shaqiq. Shaqiq said, "You're back soon!"

"You told me to go visit him, and this is what happened!" And he told him the story.

Shaqiq saw that he was to blame for these words. They say that he had four hundred assloads of books. Although he was truly eminent, the eminent often have the greatest opinion of themselves.

Shaqiq said, "Didn't you ask him, 'If he's like this, how are you?'"

"No."

"Go back and ask."

The disciple returned and went to see Bāyazid.

The sheikh said, "You're back?"

"I was sent to ask you: 'If he's like this, how are you?'"

"Look, another bit of foolishness!" Bāyazid said. "If I tell you how I am, you will not understand."

"If the sheikh sees fit, have it written down somewhere, so I will not have wasted my time coming such a long way."

"Write: 'In the name of God the merciful and compassionate—this is Bāyazid.'" He folded up the piece of paper and gave it to the disciple.

In other words, Bāyazid is nothing. He has no attributes, so how can he be described? Bāyazid is an invisible mote—what sense does it make to ask, "How is he? Does he have trust in God or sincerity?" These are all creaturely attributes. *Mold yourself to God's molds*—this is what's needed, not being a locus for trust in God.

The disciple left. Shaqiq had fallen ill and was on the verge of death. He was waiting for Bāyazid's response. The disciple arrived in the nick of time and gave him the piece of paper. When Shaqiq had studied it, he said, *"I bear witness that there is no god but God and Mohammad is his servant and messenger."* He became a Muslim, purified of his high opinion of himself. He repented of it and died.

It is related that Ahmad-e Khezruya and a thousand of his disciples came to visit Bāyazid. Every one of them could walk on the water and fly through the air. Ahmad said, "Whichever one of you can endure meeting Bāyazid face to face, come along. If you cannot, wait outside while we go in and visit him."

Every one of the one thousand went in. Each of them had a walking stick. They left them in the vestibule in a place called the walking-stick room. One of them said, "I don't have the strength to meet him. I'll watch over the walking sticks in the vestibule."

When Ahmad and his followers went before Bāyazid, Bāyazid said, "Bring in the best one among you." So they brought the disciple in from the vestibule.

Bāyazid said to Ahmad, "How long will you travel and wander around the world?"

"Water stagnates when it stands in one place," Ahmad said.

"Why don't you become the ocean so you won't stagnate and be polluted?"

Then Bāyazid began to speak. "Come down a notch," Ahmad

203

said. "We can't understand you." He said this seven times before they understood what Bāyazid was saying.

When Bāyazid fell silent, Ahmad said, "Sheikh, I saw the devil hanging from a gallows at the end of your street."

"Yes," Bāyazid said, "he had promised us not to roam around Bestām. Now he tempted someone and suffered capital punishment for it. It is customary to hang the thief on a gallows in front of the king's court."

Someone asked Bāyazid, "We see a group of people in front of you who look like women. Who are they?"

"They are angels," he said, "who come to ask me about the spiritual sciences, and I answer their questions."

It is related that Bāyazid said:

One night in a dream, I saw the angels from the lowest sphere of the heavens come to me and say, "Arise, so we may commemorate the mighty and glorious Lord."

I said, "I have no tongue to commemorate him."

The angels of the second sphere came to me. They said the same thing, and I gave the same answer. It went on this way until the angels of the seventh and highest sphere came down, and I gave the same answer. "When will you have a tongue to commemorate him?" they asked.

I answered, "When they are consigning the people of hell to live in hell and the people of paradise to paradise, when the day of resurrection is under way, Bāyazid will circle the throne of the mighty and glorious Lord and say, 'God, God!'"

Bāyazid said, "One night my room was bathed in light. I said, 'If you are Satan, I am too dear, my aspiration too high, for you to have any desire for me. If you are one of the great ones, let me proceed from the abode of service to the abode of favor.'"

It is related that one night Bāyazid found no relish in his devotions. He said to his servants, "Go look to see what's in the house." They looked around and found a bunch of grapes. Bāyazid said, "Give them to someone. Our house is not a grocery store." When this was done, he had a moment of joy.

It is related that the sheikh had a Zoroastrian neighbor. He had a suck-ling child who cried all night for fear of the dark, since the man did not own a lamp. Every night Bāyazid would pick up his lamp and take it to the neighbor's house, so the child would quiet down. When the Zoroastrian returned from a trip, the child's mother told him the story of what Bāyazid had done. "Now that the sheikh's light has come," the neighbor said, "it would be a pity if we were to go back to our dark-ness." He came at once to Bāyazid and converted to Islam.

It is related that a Zoroastrian was told to convert to Islam. He said, "If Islam is what Bāyazid does, I don't have the strength for it and I can't do it. If it's what you do, I don't have any need of it."

It is related that Bāyazid was sitting in the mosque. Suddenly he said, "Get up—let's go welcome one of the Lord's friends." When they reached the city gate, Ebrāhim of Herat[8] was coming, riding a donkey.

Bāyazid said to him, "I heard a voice in my heart say, 'Get up and welcome him and be our intermediary.'"

Ebrāhim said, "If you were made the intermediary for everyone, from the first to the last, it would still amount to no more than a hand-ful of dust." Bāyazid was astonished by his words.

When it was time to eat, some fine food was brought out. Ebrāhim said to himself, "What food the sheikh eats!" Bāyazid knew what he was thinking. When they were finished eating, Bāyazid took Ebrāhim by the hand and led him aside. He touched a wall—a door swung open, and an endless sea appeared. "Come," Bāyazid said, "let's enter this sea."

Ebrāhim was afraid and said, "I have not reached this stage."

Then Bāyazid said, "The barley that you brought from the desert and baked into bread and stored in your pouch was barley that animals had eaten and spit out. You've made it into bread and you're eating it." When they looked into the matter closely, that was exactly how it was. Ebrāhim repented and asked for forgiveness.

Someone said to Bāyazid, "I saw you standing next to so-and-so's funeral bier in Tabaristan,[9] holding hands with Khezr. While prayers were being said over the bier, you were seen flying through the air."

"You've told the truth," Bāyazid said.

205

It is related that a crowd of people came to visit the sheikh. Fearing a drought, they moaned and wept and said, "Pray for the Real most high to send rain."

The sheikh bowed his head and then looked up and said, "Go fix up your gutters. Rain is on its way." It immediately began to rain and continued to do so all day and night.

It is related that one day Bāyazid stretched out one of his legs. A disciple stretched out his leg too. Bāyazid folded his leg back under him. The disciple was unable to fold his leg back under him, no matter how much he tried. His leg remained in that position for the rest of his life. This came from thinking that when Bāyazid swung his leg down, it was just as other people do.

It is related that Bāyazid once swung his leg down from the platform. A scholar got up to go. He stepped on the sheikh's foot. "You fool," they said, "why have you done this?"

"What are you talking about?" he replied. "His babblings have congealed in his foot!"

Afterward the scholar's foot developed gangrene, and they say that this illness infected several of his children. An eminent man was asked, "How is it that when someone has committed a sin, its punishment infects another? What does this mean?"

"When a man is a strong archer," he answered, "his arrow travels faster and farther."

It is related that a skeptic came to visit Bāyazid and asked him to explicate a certain difficult problem. The sheikh saw the skepticism in him. He said, "There is a cave on a certain mountain, and one of our friends lives inside. Ask him to explicate it for you."

The skeptic got up and went to the cave. He saw a mighty dragon, as terrifying as it could be. He fainted and soiled himself. Wild with panic, he threw himself out of the cave, leaving his shoes behind.

He went back to see Bāyazid and fell down at his feet and repented. Bāyazid said, "Glory be! You can't keep track of your shoes or your cleanliness, all because of the awesomeness of one of God's creatures. How could you have kept track of the explication of the awesomeness of the Creator, when you came here skeptically asking me to explicate these words for you?"

It is related that a Qur'an reader was skeptical about Bāyazid, because he experienced mighty things, while the poor Qur'an reader was denied them. He said, "I will practice the same behavior and austerities that Bāyazid does; he says things that are alien to us."

Bāyazid was aware of all this. One day the Qur'an reader set off to see Bāyazid. The sheikh entrusted the Qur'an reader with a single breath of his spiritual grace. The Qur'an reader lost his grip on himself for three days and soiled himself. When he came to, he washed and went to see Bāyazid to apologize. Bāyazid said, "Didn't you realize that they don't put an elephant's load on a donkey's back?"

It is related that Sheikh Sa'id of Meykhurān[10] came to see Bāyazid and wanted to put him to the test. Bāyazid handed him over to one of his disciples, whose name was Abu Sa'id Rā'i the Shepherd.[11] "Go see him," Bāyazid told Sheikh Sa'id. "I have given him the province of miracles as a land grant."

When Sa'id went there, he saw Rā'i in the desert praying, while wolves watched herd over his sheep. When Rā'i was finished praying, he asked, "What do you want?"

"Warm bread and grapes."

Rā'i had a piece of wood in his hands. He broke it in half. He put one half down beside himself and the other half beside Sa'id. They immediately brought forth grapes—those beside Rā'i were white and those beside Sa'id were black. Sa'id said, "Why are those beside you white and these beside me black?"

Rā'i said, "Because I asked for mine certain I would get them, while you were merely testing me. Everything will have a color to fit its circumstances."

Rā'i then gave Sa'id of Meykhurān a blanket and said, "Take care of it." When Sa'id went on the pilgrimage, he lost it on the plain of 'Arafāt. When he returned to Bestām, he saw it with Rā'i.

It is related that they asked Bāyazid, "Who was your spiritual guide?"

"An old woman," he said. "One day I was so in the throes of yearning and unity that I was as weak as a hair. With no idea where I was going, I went into the desert. An old woman came up to me with a sack of flour. She said, 'Carry this sack for me'—and I was in such a state that I couldn't even carry myself. I made a sign to a lion. It came over, and I put the woman's sack on its back. I said to the old woman, 'If you go to the city, who will you say you saw?'—and didn't I just want her to know who I was?

"'I saw a cruel showoff,' she replied.

"'Huh? What are you saying?'

"'Huh yourself! Is this lion responsible for its actions or not?'

"'No.'

"'When the mighty and glorious Lord did not make it responsible for its actions and you do, isn't that cruel?'

"'It is.'

"'And in spite of all of this, you still want the people in the city to know that this lion obeys you and that you perform miracles? Isn't this showing off?'

"'Yes,' I said. I repented and sank from the highest high to the lowest low. These were the words of my guide."

After that, whenever a wondrous sign or miracle came to him, he would ask the Real most high to confirm it. Then a golden light would immediately appear, with a green writing on it that read: *There is no god but God: Mohammad is the Prophet of God; Noah is the Confidant of God; Abraham is the Friend of God; Moses is the Spokesman of God; Jesus is the Spirit of God* (peace and blessing be upon them all). With these five witnesses, he would accept the miracle. It eventually reached the point that even these witnesses were not necessary.

Ahmad-e Khezruya said, "I saw the mighty and glorious Real in a dream. He said, 'All people seek what they are looking for from me, except Bāyazid, who seeks me from me.'"

It is related that Shaqiq of Balkh and Abu Torāb of Nakhshab came to visit Bāyazid. Bāyazid called for food. One of his disciples stood to wait on them. Abu Torāb said, "Join us."

"I am fasting," the disciple said.

"Eat and take the spiritual reward for one month's fast," Abu Torāb said.

"This fast cannot be broken."

Shaqiq said, "Break the fast and take one year's wages."

"It cannot be broken."

"Leave him be," Bāyazid said. "He is banished from the presence."

Not long after that, the disciple was captured as a thief, and both his hands were cut off.

It is related that one day in the congregational mosque Bāyazid stuck his walking stick in the ground. It fell over and knocked against an old man's cane. The old man bent over and picked up the sheikh's walking stick. Bāyazid went to the old man's house and asked his pardon. "You bent down," he said, "to pick up a cane."

It is related that someone came in one day and asked Bāyazid a difficult question about shame. Bāyazid answered his difficulty. The dervish melted away. A disciple came in and saw a pool of golden water standing there. "Sheikh, what is this?"

"Someone came in through the door and asked about shame and I answered him. He couldn't take it and turned to water for shame."

It is related that Bāyazid said: "Once I came to the Tigris. The river drew back its waters. I said, 'I will take no pride in this when they will ferry me across for one small coin. I will not lose thirty years of my life for this amount. I need the Munificent, not the marvelous.'"

It is related that Bāyazid said: "I wanted to ask the Real most high to absolve me of the responsibility of supporting women. Then I thought, 'This is not a proper thing to ask. The Prophet (peace and blessing and salutations be upon him) did not ask for it.' Out of my respect for the Prophet, the Real most high absolved me of this responsibility. What's the difference between a woman and a wall to me—they're one and the same."

It is related that Bāyazid was praying behind an imam. Then the imam asked, "Sheikh, you don't work a paying job and you don't ask anyone for anything. How do you eat?"

"Wait while I make up this prayer," Bāyazid said. "It's not right to pray behind somebody who does not know the Provider."

Once Bāyazid saw someone praying in a mosque. He said, "If you imagine that prayer is the means to attain the Real most high, you're mistaken. It's all a chimera, not a communion. If you don't pray, you'll be an infidel. If you regard it as even slightly reliable, you're a polytheist."

It is related that Bāyazid said: "There's the person who comes to see me, and the fruit is only curses, and then there's the person who comes to see me, and the benefit is compassion."

"How is that?"

"If someone comes and a state overwhelms me that makes me lose myself, he speaks ill of me and starts cursing. If someone else comes and sees that the Real has overwhelmed me, he excuses it. The fruit of that is compassion."

Bāyazid said, "I wish that the day of resurrection would come sooner, so I could pitch my tent facing toward hell. When hell sees me, it will be humiliated, and I will be the means of comforting the people."

Hātem the Deaf used to tell his disciples, "On the day of resurrection, anyone of you who does not intercede on behalf of those bound for hell is no disciple of mine."

They reported these words to Bāyazid. He replied, "I would say that my disciple is the one who stands beside hell and takes the hand of those being led there and sends them to paradise and goes to hell in their place."

They asked, "With all the honor that the Real most high has shown you, why don't you call people to the Lord?"

Bāyazid said, "How can Bāyazid carry off the person whom he has bound?"

An eminent person went to see Bāyazid. He saw him sunk in meditation. When Bāyazid raised his head, the eminent man asked, "Sheikh, what did you do?"

"I bowed my head to my extinction and raised it to the subsistence of the Real."

It is related that one day as Bāyazid was preaching from the pulpit, he recited this verse: *They do not esteem God as he merits* [6:91]. He struck his head so hard against the pulpit that he blacked out. Later he said, "Since you were aware of this, why did you lead this mendacious liar to the point where he would claim to know you?"

A disciple saw Bāyazid trembling. "Sheikh, why do you move like this?" he asked.

Bāyazid said, "One must walk the path of sincerity for thirty years, sweep the dung hills with his beard, and prop his head on the knee of grief before one can know the movements of true believers. You just got up out of bed a couple of days ago and you want to be let in on their secrets?"

It is related that once in Byzantium the army of Islam was exhausted and was near defeat at the hands of the unbelievers. The soldiers heard a voice: "Bāyazid, help!" A fire appeared from the direction of Khorasan. A panic spread through the opposing army, and the army of Islam was victorious.

It is related that a man came to see Bāyazid. Bāyazid had his head bowed. When he raised it, the man asked, "Where were you?"

"In the presence."

"I was there just now. I didn't see you."

"You're telling the truth, but I was within the veil and you were without. Insiders and outsiders cannot see one another."

Bāyazid said, "Know that anyone who reads the Qur'an but is not present at Muslims' funerals and does not visit the sick and does not inquire after orphans and still claims to be of this tradition is a mere pretender."

Someone said to Bāyazid, "Purify your heart so I may speak with you."

"For thirty years," Bāyazid said, "I've been asking the Real most high for a pure heart and I haven't gotten one yet. Where am I going to get a pure heart to talk to you for an hour?"

Bāyazid said, "People imagine that the path to the Real most high is more luminous than the sun. For many years I have asked him for an opening onto this path the size of a pinprick. It hasn't happened."

It is related that on the days when hardship did not befall him, Bāyazid used to say, "My God, you sent bread. Bread needs stew. Send hardship, so I can eat my bread with stew."

One day Abu Musā asked Bāyazid, "How are your mornings?"
Bāyazid said, "I have neither mornings nor evenings."

Bāyazid said: "The voice spoke in my breast: 'O Bāyazid, our treasuries are full of acceptable devotions and approved services. If you want us, bring us something we do not have.'
"I said, 'O Lord, what is there that you do not have?'
"He said, 'Helplessness and inability, need and lowliness, poverty and defeat.'"

Bāyazid said, "I went to the desert. Love had rained down, and the earth was wet. Just as the foot sinks into snow, it sank into love."

Bāyazid said, "I saw nothing in prayer but the body standing erect and nothing in fasting but the stomach's hunger. Everything I have comes from his favor, not from my actions." He continued, "Nothing results from effort and acquisition, and the tradition that I follow is greater than both worlds. But the fortunate servant is one who is walking along—suddenly his foot sinks into a treasure, and he becomes rich."

Bāyazid said, "For every disciple who enters into my service, I must come down a bit lower and speak according to his power of understanding."

It is related that when Bāyazid used to speak of the attributes of the Real, he was happy and quiet. When he spoke of his essence, he would spring up, start jumping about and say, "He is coming, he is coming—he is gone."

Bāyazid saw a man who was saying, "I am astonished by anyone who knows him and does not worship him."
Bāyazid said, "I am astonished by anyone who knows him and worships him." In other words, it is astonishing that such a person remains alive to worship him.

It is related that Bāyazid said: "The first time I went on the pilgrimage, I saw a house. The second time I went to the house, I saw the Lord of the house. The third time I went, I didn't see the house or the Lord of the house." In other words, "I was so lost in the Real, I was not aware of anything. If I saw anything, I saw the Real."

The proof of these words is that someone went to Bāyazid's house and called out. The sheikh asked, "Whom are you looking for?"

He answered, "Bāyazid."

He said, "There's no one home but the Lord."

Another time, someone went to his house. The sheikh asked, "Whom are you looking for?"

He answered, "Bāyazid."

"Poor Bāyazid! I have been looking for him for thirty years and I haven't found a trace of him yet."

They reported these words to Zu'n-Nun. He said, "May the mighty and glorious Lord forgive my brother Bāyazid. He is lost in the crowd that is lost in the Lord."

It is related that they said to Bāyazid, "Tell us something about your self-mortifications."

"If I tell you the greatest of them," Bāyazid said, "you will not be able to stand it. As for the least of them, let me say that one day I ordered my self to do something. It was stubborn. I didn't give it water for a year. 'Either submit or die of thirst,' I said."

Bāyazid asked, "What do you say about someone whose veil is the Real?" In other words, as long as he knows that it is the Real, it is a veil. For it to be true unveiling, he must not remain, nor what he knows.

Bāyazid was so submerged that for twenty years he had a disciple who was never separated from him, and everyday Bāyazid would call him and ask, "What is your name, my son?"

One day the disciple said to Bāyazid, "Are you mocking me? I have been in your service for twenty years, and every day you ask me my name."

"I'm not mocking you, son," Bāyazid said. "But his name has come and removed all other names from my heart. I learn your name and forget it again."

It is related that Bāyazid was asked, "How did you attain this rank and reach this station?"

Bāyazid said, "When I was a child, I went outside of Bestām one night. The moon was shining, and the world was at rest. I saw a presence, beside which the eighteen thousand worlds seemed no more than a mote of dust. A burning came over me, and a mighty ecstasy overwhelmed me. 'O Lord,' I said, 'such a grand court and so deserted! Such a splendid workshop and so hidden!'

"After I said this, a hidden voice called out, 'The court is not deserted because no one comes, but because I do not want them. Not every grubby face is worthy of this court.'

"I resolved to beg on behalf of all created beings. Again, a thought occurred to me: 'The position of intercessor belongs to Mohammad (peace and blessing be upon him).' I discreetly held my peace.

"I heard a voice address me, 'For this one discretion, we have exalted your name. Until the resurrection, they will say, "Bāyazid, Sultan of the Realized!"'"

In the presence of Abu Nasr-e Qosheyri,[12] they said, "Bāyazid told this story: 'Last night, I wanted to ask his beneficent lordship to paint over the sins of everyone, from first to last, with his forgiveness. But I was ashamed to refer such a great request to his beneficent presence and to usurp the office of intercession, which belongs to the founder of religious law. I discreetly held my peace.'"

Qosheyri said, *"For this high aspiration, he obtained what he obtained*—he flew to the zenith of nobility."

It is related that Bāyazid said: "All my life, I needed to make one prayer that would be worthy of his presence, and I never did. One night I performed four rak'ats of prayer between the evening prayer and dawn. Every time I finished, I told myself that something better than this was needed. As daybreak approached, I still had not succeeded. 'My God,' I said, 'I have tried to make these prayers worthy of you, but they were not. They were worthy of Bāyazid. Now you have many who do not pray—consider Bāyazid one of them.'"

Bāyazid said: "After forty years of austerities, one night the veil was lifted. I cried out for them to make way for me. A voice addressed me,

'No audience will be granted to you with the jug and old fur cloak you have.' I threw aside my jug and cloak.

"I heard a voice say, 'Bāyazid, tell these claimants: "After forty years of austerities and self-mortifications, Bāyazid, with his broken jug and tattered cloak, was not granted an audience until he threw them away. With all the attachments you cling to, you have made the path into a lure for the desires of the self. Never, God forbid, no, never shall you be received!"'"

It is related that someone was keeping an eye on the sheikh at dawn to see what he would do. He said "God" once and collapsed with blood flowing from him. "What happened?" they asked.

Bāyazid replied, "A voice called out: 'Who are you to talk with us?'"

It is related that one night Bāyazid stood on his toes from the evening prayer until dawn. A servant was watching what was going on. Blood dripped on the ground from Bāyazid's eyes. The servant was astonished. In the morning, he asked the sheikh, "What happened? Share it with us."

Bāyazid said, "With the first step I took, I arrived at the celestial throne. The throne looked to me like a hungry wolf with spittle dripping from its lips. 'O throne,' I said, 'they show the way to you by saying, *"The Merciful is firmly established on his throne"* [7:54]. Come, let's see what you have!'

"The throne replied, 'Is there any place for talk like this? They also show me the way to you by saying, *"I am in their broken hearts."*[13] The celestial beings search for him among the earthlings, and the earthlings seek him among the celestial beings. The old seek him from the young, and the young from the old. The ascetic seeks him from the drunkard, and the drunkard from the ascetic.'"

Bāyazid continued, "When I reached the station of proximity, they said, 'Ask!'

"I said, 'I have nothing to ask. You ask for something on my behalf.' I said, 'I want you and you alone.'

"'As long as an atom of Bāyazid remains,' they said, 'this request is impossible: *Leave yourself and come to us.'*

215

"'I cannot go back without some tidbit,' I said. 'I will be presumptuous.'

"'Speak!'

"'Be merciful to all creatures!'

"'Look back!' I looked back: I saw no created thing that did not have an intercessor. The Real looked to be much more well-disposed toward them than I. I fell silent. Then I said, 'Have mercy on Satan.'

"'You are indeed presumptuous. Silence! He is made of fire. The fiery needs the fire. Try not to bring yourself to the point where you deserve fire—you won't have the strength for it.'"

It is related that Bāyazid said, "The Real most high brought me into his presence in two thousand stages. At each of these stages, a kingdom was presented to me. I accepted none of them. At last, he said to me, 'Bāyazid, what do you want?'

"'Not to want anything,' I said."

Whenever someone asked Bāyazid to pray for him, the sheikh used to say, "O Lord, they are your creatures, and you are their creator. Who am I to stand in between as an intermediary between you and your creation?" And to himself he used to say, "He is the knower of secrets. What business do I have meddling?"

Someone came to see Bāyazid and said, "Teach me something that will be the means of my salvation."

"Remember two things," Bāyazid said. "This amount of learning will be enough for you. Know that the Real most high knows all about you and sees everything that you do. And know that the Lord has no need for your good works."

One day Bāyazid was walking along. A young man followed him step for step, saying, "This is the way they walk in the sheikh's footsteps." Bāyazid was wearing an old fur cloak, and the young man said, "Sheikh, give me a piece of your cloak, so your blessings will come to me."

"Even if you wear Bāyazid's own skin," the sheikh said, "it will do you no good, until you work like Bāyazid."

One day Bāyazid saw someone distraught who kept saying, "My God, look upon me!"

In a frenzy, his sense of honor outraged, Bāyazid cried out, "Are you so pretty that he should look at you!?"

"Sheikh, I'm begging for that glance so I can be pretty."

Bāyazid was very pleased. "You've spoken well," he said.

It is related that Bāyazid was talking about the truth one day and bit his lip. He said, "I am the wine, the drinker, and the serving boy, all in one."

It is related that Bāyazid said: "I removed seventy infidel sashes from around my waist. Only one remained. However much I tried, it would not come undone. I cried out, 'My God, give me the strength to remove this one too!'

"A voice replied, 'You have removed all the sashes. This one is not yours to remove.'"

مه مه مه

Bāyazid said, "I knocked on the door of the Real with every hand—until I knocked with the hand of misfortune, it was not opened. I asked for admittance with every tongue—until I asked with the tongue of sorrow, it was not granted. I walked his path on every foot—until I walked on the foot of abjection, I did not reach the way station of grandeur."

"For thirty years, I used to say, 'Do this, give me that.' When I reached the first step of realization, I said, 'My God, you be me and do whatever you wish.'"

"Once I was performing my devotions in his court and said, *'How does the traveler reach you?'* I heard a voice say, *'Bāyazid, finalize the divorce from yourself, and then say, "God."'*"

"I worshiped the Lord for thirty years. When I fell silent, I looked; my veil was the mention of his name."

"If the Real most high asks me to account for my seventy years, I will ask him to account for seventy thousand. It is seventy thousand years

217

since he said, *'Am I not your Lord?'* [7:172] and threw everything into a tumult of saying yes. All the uproar in heaven and earth comes from yearning for that *Am I not*. After thinking this, a voice came to me: 'Hear the answer! On the day of reckoning, we will rip you limb from limb, pulverize you, and give a vision to each mote. We will say, "Behold the account for seventy thousand years—we place the sum and remainder in your embrace.""'

"If the eight heavens open up within my cottage and the province of both worlds is granted to me, I still won't hand over the one breath that arises from my soul at dawn in yearning for him. Indeed, I equate one breath that I exhale in suffering for him with the kingdom of the eighteen thousand worlds."

"If he does not show his face in paradise on the morrow of the resurrection, I will cry and wail so much that the residents of the seven circles of hell will forget their torment because of my tears and moans."

"Everyone who existed before us bowed down to something. We bow down to nothing and have sacrificed ourselves entirely to him. We do not desire ourselves for the sake of ourselves—the earth and the seven heavens would collapse in a heap if one mote of our attributes came into plain view."

"He desired to see us, but we did not desire to see him." In other words, the servant has no desire.

"For forty years I turned to God's creatures and called them to the Real, and no one responded. I turned away from them and entered the presence. I saw them all there before I arrived." In other words, "I realized that the Real's concern for his creation was greater than mine. It was what I desired—with one act of concern, the Real most high brought them all to himself before me."

"I came out of Bāyazid-ness, as a snake sheds its skin. Then I looked closely: I saw the lover and beloved as one, for in the world of unity one can see everything as one."

"They called out through me within me: 'O you, me.'" In other words, he reached the stage of extinction in God.

"I left several thousand stages behind me. When I looked closely, I found myself at the stage of the word 'God.'" In other words, there is no way into the depths of the meaning of "God."

"For thirty years God was my mirror. Now, I am my own mirror." In other words, "Whatever I was, I no longer remained—'I' and 'the Real' is polytheism. When I no longer remained, the Real most high was his own mirror. When I say, 'Now I am my own mirror,' the Real is speaking with my tongue, and I have disappeared."

"I lived near this court for years. In the end, my share turned out to be nothing but awe and amazement."

"I entered the court of grandeur, but it wasn't crowded at all. The people of this world were busy with this world and veiled behind it. The people of the afterworld were busy with the afterworld, and the pretenders with their pretense. Among the masters of Sufism and the path, some folks were busy with eating and drinking, and some with music and dance. Those who were advanced on the path, the vanguard of the army, were lost in the desert of amazement and drowned in the sea of helplessness."

"For a while I circumambulated God's house. When I reached the Real, I found the house circumambulating me."

"One night I was searching for my heart and did not find it. At dawn I heard a voice say, 'Bāyazid, are you searching for something other than us? What business do you have with your heart?'"

"The true believer is not one who goes chasing after something. Whatever he wants comes to him anywhere he is. He hears the answer from anyone he talks to."

"The Real most high brought me to the point where I saw the entire created world between my own two fingers."

219

"The disciple is given the sweetness of devotion. When he is happy with that, his joy veils him from his proximity."

"The least station of the realized is having the attributes of the Real within them."

"If they burn me in hellfire in place of other creatures, and if I bear it patiently because I claim to love him, I have still done nothing. And if he forgives me and all other creatures because of his attributes of mercy and compassion, it is still no great thing."

"Repent of sin once, repent of devotion a thousand times." In other words, conceited devotion is a thousand times worse than sin.

"The rank of perfection for the realized is burning in love."

"Claiming knowledge of pre-eternity is proper for someone who first sheds the light of the essence upon himself."

"I regarded this world as the enemy and drew near the Creator and chose the Lord over his creatures, until the love of the Real so took possession of me that I regarded my being as the enemy. When I removed these inconveniences from in between, intimacy with God's enduring grace was mine."

"The Lord most high has some servants who will cry out for help if paradise, in all of its splendor, is presented to them, just like the denizens of hell."

"The true devotee and the honest worker are those who strike off the head of all their desires with the sword of striving. All their lusts and cravings are obliterated in their love of the Real. They love what the Real wants, and they desire him as their sweetheart."

Bāyazid asked, "Doesn't the Lord most high take his servants to paradise because he is pleased with them?"
      "Yes," they replied.
      "When he is pleased with them, what will they do with paradise?"

"A mote of his sweetness in a heart is better than a thousand palaces in the highest paradise."

"His singularity renders many strong people weak and many weak ones strong."

"If you attain extinction, return to the basis of the primal extinction, until you reach this tradition. Otherwise, this piety and asceticism are just a breeze blowing over you."

"Those who know the Lord are heaven's reward, and heaven is their torment."

"Sin will not harm you as much as disrespect and contempt for your fellow Muslim."

"For the people of this world, this world is pride within pride. For people of the afterworld, the afterworld is joy within joy. For the people of realization, the love of the Real is light within light."

"In seeing with the eye, action is ready money. In contemplation, everything is the readiest of ready money."

"For the realized, devotion is holding the breath."

"When the realized fall silent, their desire is to speak with the Real. When they close their eyes, their goal is to look upon the Real when they open them. When they lower their heads to their knees, their quest is to not raise them again until Esrāfil blows his trumpet, so great is their hope in the Real most high."

"Ride on the heart while walking with the body."

"The sign of knowing the Real is fleeing from his creatures and falling silent in his realization."

"Dominion will not be withheld from those who are afflicted by the Real, and they will not bow down before either world."

"His love entered and removed everything except him. It left no trace of anything else—the one remained, just as he is the One."

"The perfection of the realized is burning in the love of the Real."

"On the morrow the people of paradise will go to pay their respects. When they come back, forms will be offered to them. Anyone who chooses a form will not be allowed to pay his respects again."

"Nothing is better for God's servant than to be without anything— neither renunciation nor learning nor good works. When he is without anything, he is with everything."

"This story must be written in pain—the pen isn't good for anything."

"The realized must speak so much of realization and run so far through its streets that no realization remains and the realized arrive. Then what they know will be their deputy. The realized will not attain realization until they forget what they know."

"It is fitting to seek knowledge and information from someone who goes from knowledge to the Known and from information to the Informer. But anyone who studies for self-glory, seeking to adorn himself and advance his position so he will be accepted by creatures, will move further from him each day and be ever more abandoned."

"What value does this world have that anyone should fancy that passing beyond it is any great task?"

"It is impossible for anyone to know the Real and not to love him. Realization without love is worthless."

"You will hear a voice from streams of flowing water, asking how they should proceed. When they reach the sea, this voice falls silent. The sea neither gains nor loses from their coming and going."

"He has servants who become nonexistent if they are veiled from him for an instant in this world, and how can the nonexistent worship?"

"Whoever knows the Lord cannot move his tongue to utter any word except to mention the Real."

"The least thing necessary for the realized is that they free themselves of possessions and property. The Real is such that if you dedicate both worlds to loving him, it's still a meager thing."

"The spiritual reward of the realized is from the Real in the Real."

"The realized seek their place in clear vision and speak not a whisper about the essence. If a hundred thousand people, with their progeny and descendants in generations without number, stretching from heaven to earth, and a hundred thousand of the most esteemed angels, like Gabriel and Michael (peace be upon them) should all be born in a corner of their hearts, the realized would think nothing of such beings compared to the existence of their realization of the Real and would be completely unaware of all their comings and goings. If it is contrary to this, they are not realized, but mere pretenders."

"The realized knower sees the known, while the scholar abides with the world. The scholar says, 'What will I do?' while the knower says, 'What will he do?'"

"Paradise has no importance for the friends of the Real. Although the lovers are abandoned in love, their affairs are nevertheless attended to, for whether sleeping or awake, they are both the seekers and the sought. They are not burdened by their loving and seeking. They are overwhelmed by contemplation of the Real—for the lover, being aware of love is a penalty. Looking to one's own seeking in the face of the sought is rebellion on the path of love."

"The Real knows all about the hearts of his friends. Having seen that some hearts were unable to bear the burden of realization, he busied them with worship."

"Only those porters of the Real who have been abased by self-mortification and disciplined by contemplation pick up the burden of the Real."

223

"If only God's creatures could recognize themselves! With this self-recognition, their realization would be complete."

"Strive to capture a single moment when you see nothing but the Real in heaven and earth." In other words, strive until your entire life is made good in that moment.

"Three qualities are given to distinguish someone who loves the Real: a generosity like the sea's, a kindness like the sun's, and a humility like the earth's."

"Pilgrims at Mecca circumambulate his house with their bodies and pray for long life. Lovers circumambulate his throne with their hearts and pray to meet him."

"In knowledge, there is a knowledge that scholars do not know, and in piety, a piety that the pious do not know."

"He will make a pharaoh of whomever he chooses in order to torment him."

"All this talk and busyness, shouting, motion, and desire take place outside the veil. Within the veil, there is silence, peace, calm, and awe."

"This daring lasts only while a gentleman is absent from the Real and loves himself. When the presence is obtained, what place is there for all this chatter?"

"Associating with good people is better than doing good, and associating with evil people is worse than doing evil."

"One must do all things in striving—then one must see the grace of the mighty and glorious Lord, not one's own doing."

"Anyone who knows the mighty and glorious Lord does not have to ask and never did. Anyone who does not know him will not understand the words of one who does."

"The realized is one whose fountain nothing ever taints. Any muddiness that enters it becomes limpid."

"Fire torments the person who does not know the Lord, but those who know the Lord torment fire."

"Whatever exists can be obtained with two steps: the first tramples on one's own shares, and the second embarks on the commandments of the Real. You pick one foot up and set the other down."

"Anyone who abandons desire attains the Real."

"Anyone who is near the Real has everywhere and everything, because the Real most high is everywhere and has everything."

"Whoever knows of the Real is ignorant, and whoever is ignorant in the Real knows."

"The knower flies, while the ascetic walks."

"Anyone who knows the Lord torments fire, and fire torments anyone who does not know him. Anyone who knows the Lord rewards paradise, and paradise is his punishment."

"The realized are happy with nothing but union."

"The hypocrisy of the realized is better than the sincerity of the disciple."

"They relate that Abraham and Moses and Jesus (the blessings of the Compassionate be upon them) said, 'O Lord, make us part of Mohammad's community.' Do you think that they yearned for the disgraceful deeds of these petty power-mongers? Far from it! Rather, they saw certain people in this community whose footsteps sank beneath the earth, while their heads surpassed the loftiest heights—and these people were lost among them."

"The portions of God's friends vary in degree according to four names, and each group rests upon one of the names of the mighty and glorious Lord and is based on his words—*He is the first and the last, the outer and the inner* [57:3]. The more their portion was determined by the outer, the more they were concerned with the external miracles of his power. Whoever's portion was determined by the inner was concerned with what emerges from the lights and secrets. Whoever's portion was determined by the first had the job of striking out in advance. And whoever's portion was determined by the last was occupied with the future and with things to come. Unveiling came to each of them according to their strength."

"If all the good luck that people enjoy is entrusted to you, do not accept it. And if all the bad luck crosses your path, do not despair. *Be, and it was* [2:117] is the business of the mighty and glorious Lord. If anyone looks into himself and sees that his worship is sincere, can give an account of the purity of his unveiling and sees that his soul is not the most wicked of souls, his account will be clear."

"Anyone whose heart dies in a preponderance of lust will be wrapped in a shroud of damnation and buried in the earth of regret. Anyone who kills his self by standing aloof from lusts is wrapped in a shroud of compassion and buried in the earth of well-being."

"Anyone who attained the Real attained him only by maintaining reverence. Anyone who fell from the path fell only by abandoning reverence."

"No one can ever understand this tradition by seeking, but no one understands it but the seekers."

"When a disciple shouts and clamors, he is a pond. When he falls silent, he becomes a sea full of pearls."

"Either appear the way you are, or be the way you appear."

"If anyone's reward from the mighty and glorious Lord is put off until tomorrow, he has not served him today. The reward for every breath of striving is granted immediately."

"Knowledge is an excuse, realization is a deception, and contemplation is a veil. So how will you attain the thing you seek?"

"The heart's contraction is in the breath's expansion, while the heart's expansion is in the breath's contraction."

"The self is an attribute that can only ever be nurtured in vain."

"Life is in knowledge, ease is in realization, and sustenance is in remembrance."

"Yearning is the palace of lovers. In that palace, a throne is erected of the punishment of separation, and a sword is unsheathed of the terror of alienation. A stalk of the narcissus of union is given to the hand of hope, but every moment, they strike off a thousand heads with that sword." And Bāyazid said, "Seven thousand years have passed, and that narcissus is still fresh and verdant, for the hand of no hope has touched it."

"Realization is knowing that the motion and quiescence of the created world are the Lord's."

"Trust in God is reducing life to a single day and throwing concern for tomorrow clean away."

"Abundant remembrance is not a matter of the number of times you mention God's name, but of being present without inattentiveness."

"Love is not caring for this world or the next."

"Except in questions of detachment and unity, the disagreements among scholars are a blessing."

"Hunger is a cloud that rains down only the rain of wisdom."

"The people farthest from the Real are those who allude to him the most."

"The ones nearest the Real are those who most bear the people's burdens and maintain a pleasant disposition."

"Forgetting the self is remembering the Real. Anyone who knows the Real through the Real is alive, and anyone who knows the Real through his self perishes."

"The heart of the realized is like a candle in a lantern made of pure glass whose rays illuminate the entire celestial world. What does it fear of the darkness?"

"People perish from two causes: one is not respecting people, and one is not acknowledging their debt to the Real."

They asked, "What is the obligatory and what is the laudable?"

Bāyazid said, "The obligatory is keeping company with the Lord, and the laudable, abandoning this world."

It is related that a disciple was going on a trip. He said to the sheikh, "Give me a parting piece of advice."

"I recommend three traits. When you are in the company of an ill-natured person, absorb his ill nature into your good one, so your life will be well disposed and well regarded. When someone does you a favor, first give thanks to the Lord and only then to the person, for the Real made his heart kind toward you. And when misfortune confronts you, acknowledge your weakness quickly and ask for help—you cannot endure patiently, and the Real fears nothing."

They asked him about renunciation. Bāyazid said, "Renunciation is worthless. I was a renunciant for three days: on the first day rejecting this world; on the second, the afterworld; and on the third, whatever was not the Lord. A voice called out, 'Bāyazid, don't you have enough strength for us?'

"'This is what I desire,' I said.

"The words 'You have attained it! You have attained it!' reached my ears."

"The perfection of my contentment with him has reached such an extent that if he raises one of his servants forever to the highest heights and abases me forever to the deepest depths, I will be more content than that servant."

They asked Bāyazid, "When does God's servant attain the rank of perfection?"

Bāyazid said, "When the servant recognizes his own faults and aspires to nothing in the created world, then the Real will draw him near to himself to the extent of his aspiration to him and his distance from his self."

They said, "You command us to renunciation and worship but don't do much of this yourself!"

Bāyazid cried out, "Renunciation and worship have been severed from me!"

They asked, "What is the path to the Real like?"
"Get off the path, and you have reached the Real."

They asked, "How can one attain the Real?"
"Through blindness, deafness, and dumbness."

They said, "We have heard the words of many guides, but none are greater than yours."

"They used to talk about the sea of pure behavior, while I talk of the sea of the pure tradition. They talk in confused terms; I talk in pure ones—and the confused does not clarify the confusion. They said, 'We and you!' We say, 'You and you!'"

Someone asked for a parting piece of advice. Bāyazid said, "Look at the heavens." He looked up. "Do you know who created this?" Bāyazid asked.

"I do," he said.

"The One who created this is aware of you wherever you are. Be on your guard."

Someone said, "These seekers never rest from their traveling."
"The goal abides—it is no traveler. It's impossible to seek the abiding on a trip."

They asked, "Whom shall we follow?"
"Someone who asks after you when you are sick, who accepts your repentance when you sin, and from whom nothing that the Real knows about you is hidden."

Someone asked, "Why don't you pray at night?"
"I don't have the leisure to pray. I wander through the celestial sphere, and wherever someone has fallen, I take him by the hand." In other words, "I work within myself."

229

They asked, "What is the greatest mark of the realized?"

"They eat with you as they flee from you. They buy from you as they sell back to you. At night, their heart rests upon the pillow of intimacy among the holy vanguard."

"The realized are those who dream of nothing but the mighty and glorious Lord, who conform to no one but him, and who reveal their innermost self to no one but him."

They asked Bāyazid about commanding good and forbidding evil. He said, "You are in a country where there is no commanding good or forbidding evil. Both of these pertain to the country of created beings. In the presence of unity, there is neither commanding good nor forbidding evil."

They asked, "How does a true believer know that he has truly attained realization?"

"When he passes away beneath the awareness of the Real and abides upon the plane of the Real, without self or others. Then he is both extinct and subsistent, subsistent and extinct, dead in life, alive in death, veiled in unveiling, unveiled in veiling."

They said, "Sahl ebn 'Abdollāh (God have mercy upon him) talks about realization."

Bāyazid said, "Sahl has gone to the edge of the sea and fallen in the eddies."

"Sheikh, what is it like for one who is drowned in the sea?"

"He stops chatting about what regards created beings or concerns the two worlds: *One who knows God is mute*."

They asked, "What does it mean to be a dervish?"

"It means that someone stumbles across a treasure in the corner of his heart, a treasure they call the disgrace of the afterlife, and in that treasure he finds a pearl they call love. Whoever finds that pearl is a dervish."

They asked, "How does a true believer reach the Lord?"

"Poor creature, does he ever reach him?"

They asked, "How did you attain what you attained?"

"I gathered together all the equipment of this world, bound it with the chain of contentment, put it in the catapult of sincerity, and launched it into the sea of despair."

They asked, "How old are you?"

"Four years old."

"How is that?"

"For seventy years I was within the veils of this world. But for four years, I've been seeing him—and don't ask about that. The period of veiling doesn't count as life."

Ahmad-e Khezruya said to Bāyazid, "I will never reach the end of repentance."

Bāyazid said, "The end of repentance has a certain majesty, and majesty is an attribute of the Real. How can a created thing get a hold on it?"

They asked Bāyazid about prayer. He said, "It's a connection, but there's nothing to connect except after a breaking."

They asked, "What is the path to the Lord like?"

"Disappear from the path, and you are joined to God."

They asked, "Why do you praise hunger?"

"If Pharaoh had been hungry, he never would have said, '*I am your Lord most High*'" [79:24].

"The self-important will never catch a whiff of realization," Bāyazid said.

"What is the mark of the self-important person?" they asked.

"He does not see a soul in the eighteen thousand worlds more wicked than his own."

"You go across water!" they said.

"A piece of wood goes across water."

"You fly through the air!"

"A bird flies through the air."

"You go to the Ka'ba in a single night!"

"A magician goes from India to Mount Damāvand in a single night."

Then they asked, "What do true believers do?"

"They attach their hearts to no one but the mighty and glorious Lord."

They asked, "What were you like during your self-mortifications?"

"I was in the prayer niche for sixteen years, and I saw myself as a menstruating woman."

"I finalized my divorce from this world and went to the One alone and stood before the presence and said, 'O Lord, I have no one but you, and when I have you, I have all.' When he recognized my sincerity, the first favor that he did was to remove the debris of my self from before me."

"The Real most high ordered the commanding of good and the forbidding of evil. Those who followed his order received the robe of honor and were preoccupied with it. I asked for nothing from him but him."

"I remembered him as much as all the people together remembered him, until it reached the point where my remembrance was his remembrance. Then the knowledge of him charged toward me and obliterated me. It charged again and brought me to life."

"I fancied that I loved him. When I looked closely, his love for me was far ahead."

"Everyone drowned in the sea of works, while I drowned in the sea of reverence." In other words, others saw their own austerities, while he saw the care of the Real.

"People took their knowledge from the dead. I took mine from the living who will never die."

"Everyone speaks to the Real, but I speak from him." Therefore, he said, "Nothing was harder for me than submitting to knowledge," that is, the knowledge of external teaching.

"I summoned the self to the Lord: it did not answer, and I abandoned it and went to the presence alone."

"My heart was carried off to heaven. It wandered through the heavenly spheres and came back. I said, 'What did you bring?' It said, 'Love and contentment, for these two were king.'"

"When I knew the Real through my own learning, I said, 'If everything in its capacity is not enough for you, nothing in anyone's capacity is enough for you.'"

"After I mustered all my limbs to serve him, whenever any one of them got lazy, I would busy myself with another, until it became Bāyazid."

"I wanted to know what would be the harshest punishment for my body. I saw nothing worse than indifference. Hellfire doesn't do to people what a bit of indifference does."

"I have been praying for years, and with every prayer, I have believed with all my soul that I am a Zoroastrian and want to cut the infidel sash."

"Women's affairs are better than ours; they wash once a month because of impurity, while we have not washed during our entire life because of purity."

"If *bā yazid*—meaning 'with increase'—can be properly derived from Bāyazid throughout my life, then there is nothing to fear."

"I would prefer them to ask, 'Why didn't you?' instead of 'Why did you?' tomorrow on the plain of resurrection." What Bāyazid means is, "Unless worship passes over me without my interference, whatever I do concerning him is my I-ness, and I-ness is polytheism, and polytheism is the worst sin."

"The Lord most high knows all about the innermost souls of his creatures. He sees emptiness in every soul he examines, except in Bāyazid's soul, which he sees to be full of himself."

233

"How many people are near us and yet far away! How many are far from us and yet near by!"

"I dreamt that I asked for more from the Real most high after unity. When I awoke, I said, 'O Lord, I do not want any more after unity.'"

"I saw the mighty and sublime Real in a dream. He said to me, 'Bāyazid, what do you want?'

"I said, 'I want what you want.'

"He said, 'I am yours just as you are mine.'"

"I saw the Real most high in a dream and asked, 'What is the path to you like?'

"He said, 'Say farewell to yourself, and you have attained me.'"

"People think that I am someone like them. If they see my qualities in the hidden realm, they will perish."

"My case is like that of the sea: its depth is not visible, and its beginning and end are not evident."

Someone asked Bāyazid, "What is the empyrean?"

"It is I."

"What is the throne?"

"It is I."

"What is the tablet and the pen?"

"It is I."

"Does the mighty and glorious Lord," they asked, "have servants comparable to Abraham, Moses, and Mohammad (peace and blessing be upon them)?"

"They are all I."

"They say that the mighty and glorious Lord has servants comparable to the angels Gabriel, Michael, Esrāfil, and Azrā'il (peace be upon them)."

"They are all I."

The man fell silent.

Bāyazid said, "Yes, whoever is obliterated in the Real has attained the reality of whatever exists. All is the Real. If that person does not exist, the Real sees himself entirely. This is not strange."

The Ascension of Bāyazid

Bāyazid said:

After the Real raised me to the rank of independence from all beings and illuminated me with his light, revealed his marvels and secrets to me and manifested his majesty and essence to me, I looked upon him with the eye of certainty. I looked upon myself through the Real and meditated upon my attributes. My light was darkness next to the light of the Real. My glory became absolute abasement next to the glory of the Real. My grandeur disappeared next to the grandeur of the Real. There all was purity—here all was muddiness.

When I looked again, I saw my being in his light—I recognized my glory in his glory and grandeur. Everything I did, I was able to do through his power. His light shone in my bodily form. Everything my bodily eyes perceived, they perceived through him. I looked through the eyes of justice and truth. All worship was from the Real, not from me. And I had fancied that I myself worshiped him!

I said, "O Lord, what is this?"

"I am all that," he said, "and it is nothing other than me. In other words, you are the agent of actions, but I am the one who gives you power and capability. Until my grace shows itself, nothing results from you or your devotion."

He then sewed my eyes shut, so I could not see any intermediary, not even myself. He taught the glance to fix on the source of his action and essence. He obliterated me through his being—he made me permanent in his permanence, and he made me powerful. He revealed to me the selfness of himself without the inconvenience of my being. Thus, the Real increased my reality, and I looked from the Real to the Real and saw the Real in reality.

There I stopped and rested. I plugged the ear of effort and pulled the tongue of need back into the mouth of undesire. I put aside acquired knowledge and removed the annoyance of the sensual self. For a time I remained without means. With the hand of success, I swept away frivolities from the path of principles. The bounty of the Real came over me—he gave me the pre-eternal knowledge and bestowed speech on my tongue by his grace. He created my eye through his own light—I saw all beings in the Real.

When I made my private devotions to the Real with the tongue of grace and obtained a knowledge of the knowledge of the Real and looked upon him with his light, he said, "Bāyazid, without all you are with all, and without means you are with means."

"O Lord," I said, "do not let me be deluded by this. Do not let me feel that with my being I can do without you. It is better for you to be me without me than for me to be myself without you. When I speak with you in you, it is better than speaking to my self in your street without you."

He said, "Now heed the law. Do not set foot beyond the limits of what is commanded and forbidden, so your effort may be worthy of our thanks."

I said, "Because this is my desire and the certainty of my heart, it is better if you thank yourself than your servant. But if you blame, you are free of fault and defect."

He asked me, "Whom did you learn from?"

I said, "The one who asks knows better than the one who is asked— he is the desired and the desirous, the answered and the answerer."

When he saw the purity of my innermost self, then my heart heard the voice of his satisfaction, and he stamped me with joy. He illuminated me and made me pass beyond the darkness of the self and the murkiness of human nature. I realized that I live through him and unrolled the carpet of joy in my heart through his bounty.

He said, "Ask for whatever you wish."

"I want you," I said. "You are more bounteous than your bounty and greater than your generosity. I am content with you from you. When you possess me, I roll up the edict of bounty and generosity. Do not keep me from you and do not bring me anything besides you."

For a time he did not answer me. Then he crowned me with miraculous power and said to me, "You speak the real and seek the reality about what you saw of the Real and heard of the Real."

"If I saw," I said, "I saw in you and if I heard, I heard in you. First you heard, then I did."

And I sang his praises. Thus, he filled me with his greatness, until I flew through the courtyards of his majesty and saw the wonders of his creation. When he realized my weakness and recognized my need, he strengthened me with his strength and adorned me with his finery; he crowned me with miraculous power and opened the door of the palace of unity before me.

When I became aware that my attributes were ripened in his attributes, he named me through his presence and honored me with the selfness of himself. Unity emerged, duality departed. He said, "What pleases you pleases us. Your speech is incorruptible, and no one can hold your I-ness against you."

Then he made me taste the pangs of jealousy and brought me back to life. I emerged pure from the furnace of testing. Then he said, *"Who rules the kingdom?"*

"You," I said.

"Who holds sway?"

"You."

"Who decides?"

"You."

Since these were the very words that he heard in the beginning, he wished to show me once again: "If my mercy had not come first, people would have never been at ease; if not for my love, my destructive power would have carried off everything from the world." By way of omnipotence, he looked at me with a vanquishing gaze. Once again, no one saw the slightest trace of me.

When I launched myself intoxicated into every valley, when I melted my body with jealous fire in every crucible, when I spurred the questing horse into space, I saw no prey better than need and saw nothing better than helplessness and saw no candle more luminous than silence and heard no word better than wordlessness. I took up residence in the palace of stillness and donned the stomacher of patience. When things came to a head, he saw me devoid of the sickness of human nature, inside and out. He opened a rift of relief in my dark breast and gave me a language of detachment and unity.

Thus, I now have a tongue of eternal grace and a heart of holy light and an eye of divine making. I speak with his aid, and I grasp with his strength. Since I live through him, I will never die. Since I have attained this stage, my allusions are eternal, and my devotions are everlasting. My language is the language of unity. My spirit is the spirit of detachment. I do not speak of myself as a narrator; nor do I speak to myself as a preacher. He makes my tongue what he wishes, and I am an interpreter in between. In reality, he is the speaker, not I.

Now, when he made me great, he said to me, "The people want to see you."

"I don't want to see them," I said, "but if you would like to bring me out before the people, I will not oppose you. Adorn me with your singularity, so when the people see me, they will look upon your making. They will have seen the maker—I will not be there."

He granted me this wish and crowned me with miraculous power and made me pass beyond the stage of human nature. He then said, "Come before my creatures." I took a step outside the presence. With the second step, I collapsed. I heard a voice say, "Bring back my friend—he cannot exist without me and knows no way but me."

And Bāyazid said:

When I reached singularity—and that was the first moment I looked upon unity—I ran through that valley for years with the feet of understanding, until I turned into a bird; its eyes were oneness, its wings eternity. I flew through the air of how and thus. When I became absent from created things, I said, "I have reached the Creator."

Then I looked out across the valley of divinity. I drank of such a goblet that I will never slake the thirst of its memory for all eternity. I flew through the space of his singularity for thirty thousand years; for another thirty thousand years I flew through godhood and through uniqueness for thirty thousand more. When ninety thousand years elapsed, I saw Bāyazid, and everything I saw was all I. Then I crossed four thousand deserts and reached the end. When I looked closely, I saw myself at the initial stage of the prophets. So long had I traveled then in that endlessness that I said, "No one has ever reached beyond this rank, and there is nothing superior to that station." When I looked carefully, I saw my head resting on the foot of a prophet. Then it became clear that the final state of God's friends is the initial state of the prophets—the final state of the prophets has no limit.

Then my spirit passed beyond the entire empyrean, and heaven and hell were revealed to it. It paid no attention to anything and could not tolerate anything that came before it. My spirit did not reach the soul of any prophet without greeting him. When it reached the soul of Mohammad (peace and blessing be upon him), it saw there a fire, endless like a hundred thousand seas, and a thousand veils of light. If I had

238

set foot into the first sea, I would have burned up and blown away on the wind.

Thus, in the end, I was so stupefied by awe and terror that nothing of me remained. Although I was just about able to see the ropes holding the tent of Mohammad the Messenger of God, I did not have the nerve to attain to Mohammad, even though I had attained the Real.

That is to say, anyone can attain the Lord most high according to his strength, for the Real is with all. Mohammad, however, is the guardian at the door of the private chamber. Thus, until you have crossed the valley of *"There is no god but God,"* you do not come to the valley of *"Mohammad is the messenger of God."* In reality, both valleys are one. I expressed this same idea before when I said that the disciple of Abu Torāb used to see the Real but could not bear Bāyazid's vision.

Bāyazid continued:

I said, "My God, everything I saw was all I. There is a path to you for me by means of my I-ness, but there is no way for me to pass beyond the selfness of myself. What must I do?"

The order came down: "Your release from your you-ness is in following our beloved, Mohammad the Arab—the blessings of the Compassionate be upon him. Treat your eyes with the dust from his footsteps and persevere in following him."

I am amazed at folk who say things that run contrary to this about someone who so esteemed prophecy and who do not understand this point. Such is the case when they said to Bāyazid, "On the morrow of resurrection, God's creatures will be beneath the banner of Mohammad (peace be upon him)."

Bāyazid replied, "By the lordship of the Lord, my banner is greater than Mohammad's, for God's creatures and the prophets will be beneath it." In other words, "They won't find the likes of me in heaven and will not recognize this attribute on earth. My attributes are hidden in the unknown." To speak of anyone who abides in the unknown is mere ignorance and pure backbiting. When someone is this way, how can this person be this person? The tongue of such a person is the Real, and the speaker too is the Real.

The one who spoke is the One who said, *"He speaks through me, he hears through me, he sees through me."*[14] Thus the Real speaks through Bāyazid's tongue, and it was he who said, *"My banner is greater than Mohammad's."* Indeed, the banner of the Real is greater than Mohammad's. Since you hold it proper that *"Verily I am God"* [28:30] is heard from a bush, then hold it proper that *"My banner is greater than Mohammad's"* and *"Glory be to me, great is my majesty"* grow from the bush of Bāyazid's nature.

The Private Devotions of Sheikh Bāyazid

"O Lord, how long will there be a me and a you between me and you? Take out the me, so my me will be in you, so I will be nothing."

"My God, as long as I am with you, I am greater than everything, and as long as I am with myself, I am less than everything."

"My God, provide me with poverty and neediness in you and do not lessen them through your grace."

"O Lord, I don't need to be an ascetic, I don't need to be a Qur'an reader, I don't need to be a scholar. If you want to make me a member of some group, make me one of those who has caught a whiff of your secrets and raise me to the rank of your friends."

"I curry your favor, and I arrive to you through you. My God, how good the inspiration you give to hearts' thoughts! How sweet the way that you make them understand the path through hidden realms! How magnificent the state that your creatures cannot reveal and that the tongue does not know how to describe—this story has no end."

"It is not strange that I love you: I am a weak and powerless and needy servant. What is strange is that you love me: you are the Lord, you are the king, and you need nothing."

"My God, now that I am fearful and still so happy in you, how can I not be delighted if I feel secure?"

❧ ❧ ❧

It is related that Bāyazid was admitted into the presence of majesty seventy times. Every time he returned, he would tie on the sash that the infidels wear and take it off again. When his life was nearing its end, he entered the prayer niche and tied on the sash. He put his fur cloak on inside out and put his hat on upside down.

"My God," he said, "I'm not going to sell you an entire lifetime of austerities or put my night-long prayers on exhibit. I won't speak of fasting throughout my life, and I won't count off all the times I've read the Qur'an from beginning to end. I won't even talk about my rapturous devotions and my nearness to you. You know that I don't look back on anything and that when I give these explanations, it's not because of pride or because I rely on them. Rather, I explain them because I am ashamed of everything I have done. You have given me this robe of honor because this is the way I see myself. All this is nothing—think of it this way: it never happened. I am a seventy-year-old Turkoman whose hair has turned white in paganism. Now I'm coming from the desert and calling to my idol Tangari. Now I'm learning to say God. Now I'm taking off my sash. Now I'm setting foot inside the circle of Islam, and now my tongue utters the profession of faith. What you do has no cause. You do not accept a person on account of devotion nor reject him on account of sinfulness. I think of everything I have done as mere dust. With the pen of forgiveness, cross out whatever you have seen from me that has not been pleasing to your presence. Wash off the dust of sin from me, just as I have washed off the dust of my high opinion of my devotion."

It is related that in the beginning Bāyazid used to say, "God, God" a great deal. At the moment of death, too, he was saying, "God, God." Then he said, "O Lord, only carelessly have I ever mentioned your name. Even now that my soul is departing, I am careless in my devotion to you. I do not know when my soul will be fully present." Then he died, repeating God's name in total presence.

Abu Musā was away the night that Bāyazid died. Abu Musā said, "I dreamt that I had placed the heavenly throne upon my head and was carrying it. I was astonished. At dawn, I hurried to tell Bāyazid. The sheikh had died, and an immeasurable crowd had come from all around. When they picked up his bier, I tried to push my way in so they would give me a corner of it to carry. I didn't succeed, of course, and I was frustrated. I went under the bier and supported it with my head and went along that way, having forgotten my dream. I saw Bāyazid, who said, 'Abu Musā, here's the interpretation of that dream you had last night: that throne that you had lifted up on your head is Bāyazid's bier.'"

It is related that a disciple saw Bāyazid in a dream and asked, "How did you escape from Monker and Nakir?"

Bāyazid said, "When those dear boys questioned me, I said, 'You won't get what you're looking for from these questions, because if I say, "He is my Lord," these words will amount to nothing coming from me. But go back and ask him who I am to him. Whatever he says is how it is. If I say, "He is my Lord" a hundred times, it is no use until he recognizes me as his servant.'"

An eminent person saw Bāyazid in a dream and said to him, "What did the mighty and glorious Lord do with you?"

Bāyazid said, "He asked me, 'Bāyazid, what have you brought?'

"I said, 'O Lord, I have brought nothing that is worthy of your presence, but nevertheless, I have not brought polytheism either.'

"The Real most high said, 'Wasn't that milk at night polytheism?'"

Bāyazid said, "One night I had some milk to drink. My stomach started to ache. My tongue let slip the words 'I drank some milk, and my stomach started to ache.' The Real most high punished me to this extent. This was his way of saying, 'Does anyone act but me?'"

It is related that when they buried Bāyazid, 'Ali's mother—who was Ahmad-e Khezruya's wife—came to pay her respects to the sheikh. When she finished, she asked, "Do you know who Sheikh Bāyazid was?"

"You know best," they said.

"I was circumambulating the Ka'ba one night. I sat down for a while and fell asleep. I dreamt that they carried me up to heaven and I could see as far as the heavenly throne. There beneath the throne, I saw a desert whose length and breadth disappeared into the distance. There were flowers and herbs all over the desert. On each petal was written: 'Abu Yazid is the friend of God.'"

It is related that an eminent person said, "I saw the sheikh in a dream. I said, 'Give me a final testament.'

"He said, 'Human beings are in an endless sea. At a distance from them, there is a ship. Strive to sit in this ship and to rescue your poor body from the sea.'"

It is related that they saw the sheikh in a dream. They asked, "What is Sufism?"

He said, "Closing the door of ease in front of yourselves and sitting clasping the knees of hardship."

When Sheikh Abu Sa'id ebn Abi'l-Kheyr (God's mercy be upon him) came to pay his respects at Bāyazid's grave, he stayed for a while, and when he came back, he said, "Whoever has lost anything in the world will recover it here in this place.

∽ 12 ∽
'Abdollāh ebn al-Mobārak

Time's ornament, faith's fundament, leader in the law and on the path, true warrior against the self and unbelief, commanding pen and sword in the attack, 'Abdollāh ebn al-Mobārak—God's mercy be upon him. They used to call him the potentate of the learned. In learning and valor he had no peer and was among the dignitaries on the path and the respected masters of religious law. He had an admired standing in various fields of learning. He met the great sheikhs and was accepted by all. He composed well-known works and performed celebrated wonders.

One day, as 'Abdollāh was coming toward him, Sofyān-e Sowri said, *"Come forward, O man of the East!"* Fozeyl was present and said, *"And of the West and of everything in between!"* How can one begin to praise a person whom Fozeyl honors?

This was the beginning of his repentance: 'Abdollāh was so enamored by a young maiden that he could find no peace. One winter night he stood beneath the walls of his beloved's house, waiting for her until dawn. It snowed all night. When the call to prayer was given, he thought it was for the night prayer. When day broke, he realized that he had spent the whole night drowned and intoxicated in the beloved. He said to himself, "Shame on you, son of Mobārak! On such a blessed night you stayed on your feet until dawn to satisfy your carnal lust, but if the imam reads a long chapter of the Qur'an during prayer, you go crazy."

All at once, a pain sank into his heart. He repented and devoted himself to worship, until he attained this rank: His mother went into the garden one day. She saw him sleeping in the shade of a rosebush. A snake was holding a stalk of narcissus in its mouth and shooing the flies away from him.

'Abdollāh then set off from Merv and spent some time in Baghdad studying with the sheikhs. He then went to Mecca and dwelt there for a while. He returned to Merv. The people of Merv took him as their leader. Half of them were legalists and half were traditionalists. He conformed with each group, so they call him "Approved of the Two Sects," because of his agreement with each of them. Both sects used to claim him. He built two hospices there, one for those who adhere to hadith and one for those who employ legal opinion. He then went to the Hejaz and dwelt there.

It is related that he would spend one year on pilgrimage, one year fighting in the sacred struggle, and one year as a businessman, dividing his profits among his followers. He used to give dates to the poor and count up the pits. He would give a dirham for every pit to whoever had eaten the most.

It is related that once he traveled with an ill-humored man. When they went their separate ways, 'Abdollāh wept. "Why are you crying?" they asked.

"That helpless fellow left, but his ill humor went right along with him."

It is related that one time 'Abdollāh was traveling through the desert on a camel. He came upon a poor man and said, "Poor man, we are the wealthy. We have been called. Where are you going? You are a parasite."

The poor man answered, "Since the host is generous, he takes care of parasites all the better. If he has called you to his house, then he has called us to himself."

"He asked us wealthy people for a loan."[1]

"If he asked you for a loan, then he did it for us."

'Abdollāh was ashamed and said, "You are right."

It is related that 'Abdollāh was so mindful that once when he owned a valuable horse and alighted at a way station, he was absorbed in prayer, and the horse went into a sown field. He abandoned the horse right there and went on by foot. "It has eaten the crops belonging to the sultan's attendants," he explained. Once he went from Merv to Syria to return a pen that he had borrowed and not given back.

It is related that one day 'Abdollāh was passing by. They told a blind man, "'Abdollāh ebn al-Mobārak is coming. Ask him for whatever you need."

The blind man said, "'Abdollāh, wait!" 'Abdollāh stopped. "Pray for the Real most high to return my eyes to me." 'Abdollāh bowed his head and prayed. Immediately, the man could see.

It is related that one day during the first ten days of the month of the pilgrimage, 'Abdollāh went into the desert, burning with desire to perform the hajj. "I am not there in Mecca," he thought, "but at least let me perform the pilgrims' actions, because whoever follows them in acts such as not combing the hair or cutting the nails will share in their spiritual reward."

In the meantime, an old woman came up, her back bent double and walking with a cane. She said, "'Abdollāh, you really want to go on the pilgrimage, don't you?"

"Yes, I do."

Then she said, "I have been sent for you, 'Abdollāh. Come along with me, so I can take you to 'Arafāt."

'Abdollāh related:

I thought to myself, "There are only three days left. How will you get me to 'Arafāt?"

The old woman said, "One might get there with someone who has performed the traditional pre-dawn prayer in Sanjāb,[2] carried out religious duties at the Amu Darya, and arrived in Merv by sunrise."

"In the name of God," I said, "let's go." I stepped forward and crossed several great bodies of water that would be hard to cross in a boat. Whenever we reached water, she would say to me, "Blink your eyes."

As I blinked my eyes, I would see that I was halfway across the water, and it went on like this until she delivered me to 'Arafāt. After we performed the pilgrimage rites and finished circling the Ka'ba and the running and the lesser pilgrimage[3] and carried out the farewell circumambulation, the old woman said, "Come, I have a son who has lived in a cave in austerity for some time."

I went there to see him. I saw a young man, sallow, weak, and luminous. When he saw his mother, he fell at her feet and rubbed his face against them. He said, "I know you haven't come on your own—the Lord sent you. I am about to depart; you have come to prepare me."

The old woman said, "'Abdollāh, stay here to bury him." Then and there, the young man died. We buried him. Afterward, the old woman said, "I have nothing to do. I will spend the rest of my life at his grave. 'Abdollāh, you go. When you come back next year, you won't see me. Remember me in your prayers."

It is related that 'Abdollāh was in the sacred precincts for a year. He completed the pilgrimage rites and fell asleep for a while. He dreamt that two angels came down from heaven. One of them asked the other, "How many people have come on the pilgrimage this year?"

"Six hundred thousand," the other replied.

"How many of their pilgrimages were accepted?"

"None of them was accepted."

'Abdollāh related:

When I heard this, I felt an uneasiness within me. I thought, "All these people have come *through every deep mountain pass* [22:27], have come by distant roads, and have crossed deserts from every corner of the world with such great pain and hardship—will all this be in vain?"

The angel said, "In Damascus, there is a cobbler named 'Ali ebn al-Movaffaq.[4] He did not come on the pilgrimage, but his pilgrimage has been accepted. Everyone has been forgiven for his sake."

When I heard this, I woke up. I said, "I must go to Damascus and pay this person a visit." When I went to Damascus and searched out his house and called for him, a person came to the door, and I asked, "What is your name?"

"'Ali ebn al-Movaffaq," he said.

I said, "I have a few words to say to you."

"Speak."

"What's your job?" I asked.

"I patch shoes," he said. Then I told him what happened.

He asked, "What is your name?"

I said, "'Abdollāh ebn al-Mobārak." He cried out, collapsed, and lost consciousness. When he came to, I said, "Tell me about what you did."

"For thirty years," he said, "I longed to go on the pilgrimage. I saved three hundred dirhams from patching shoes, and this year I made plans to go. Then one day a pregnant woman in my household happened to catch a whiff of some food coming from a neighbor's. She told me, 'Go and get a bit of that food.' I went to get it, but the neighbor said, 'Realize that my children have had nothing to eat for seven days. Today I saw a dead donkey. I removed a piece of it and prepared a meal. This food is not lawful for you.' When I heard this, my soul caught fire. I took the three hundred dirhams and gave them to her and said, 'Spend these for your children's food. This is my pilgrimage.'"

I said, *"The King speaks truly in dreams, and the King's decision and judgment are sound."*

It is related that he had an indentured servant. Someone told 'Abdollāh, "This servant is robbing graves and turning the money over to you." 'Abdollāh was grief-stricken. One night he followed the servant until he reached a graveyard and opened the lid on one of the tombs. There was a prayer niche inside, and the servant stopped there to pray. 'Abdollāh was watching from afar. Slowly, he drew nearer. He saw his servant wearing sackcloth with shackles around his neck and his face pressed to the earth. He was moaning and weeping.

When 'Abdollāh saw this, he slowly withdrew and sat in an out-of-the-way place and wept. The servant remained in the tomb until morning. Then he came back out, closed the lid, entered the mosque, and performed the dawn prayer. "My God," he said, "my figurative lord will ask me for a dirham. You are the capital of the poor. Give it to me from the place you know best." Immediately, a light appeared in the air, and a dirham sat in the servant's hand.

'Abdollāh could bear it no longer. He rose up and embraced his servant's head and kissed it. He kept saying, "May a thousand lives be

247

sacrificed to such a servant! Would that you were the master of the house, and I the servant."

When the servant saw what was happening, he said, "My God, since my veil is rent and my secret revealed, no comfort is left me in this world. By your might, do not make me the cause of such an uproar. Take my life." His head still in 'Abdollāh's embrace, the servant died. 'Abdollāh buried him in that very tomb, just as he was dressed.

That same night, 'Abdollāh dreamt that the Prophet (peace and blessing be upon him) and Abraham (peace be upon him) were coming toward him, each riding a heavenly steed. "'Abdollāh," they said, "why did you bury our friend in sackcloth?"

It is related that 'Abdollāh had come out of the mosque one day with a splendid retinue and was walking along, when an 'Alavi child[5] said, "Hey, you Hindu! What's all this fuss? How is it that I, a descendant of Mohammad the Messenger of God, ply my awl so much every day just to earn a little food, while you go along with this retinue and pomp?"

'Abdollāh said, "Because I do what your forefather did and commanded, while you do not." (Others say that 'Abdollāh said, "Yes, child of the Prophet, you had a father, and I had a father. Your forefather was Mohammad, and learning remains as his legacy. My forefather belonged to this world, and this world remains as his legacy. I took your forefather's legacy and was honored. You took my forefather's legacy and were abased.")

That night 'Abdollāh saw the Messenger (peace and blessing be upon him) in a dream. He was upset. 'Abdollāh said, "Messenger of God, why are you upset?"

"Do you really find fault with our descendant?"

'Abdollāh woke up and sought out the 'Alavi to apologize. That same night, the young 'Alavi saw the Prophet (peace and blessing be upon him) in a dream. The Prophet said, "If you were as you should be, he could not have said these words to you." When he woke up, the 'Alavi set out to visit 'Abdollāh to apologize. They met one another on the road, talked about what had happened, and repented.

It is related that Sahl ebn 'Abdollāh always came to study with 'Abdollāh ebn al-Mobārak. One day, Sahl left, saying, "I will not come to study with you any longer. Today your maids went up on the roof and called me to them, 'My Sahl! My Sahl!' Why don't you discipline them?"

To his followers, 'Abdollāh said, "Get ready to pray over Sahl's bier."

Sahl soon died, and they prayed over him. Then 'Abdollāh's followers asked, "Sheikh, how was this made known to you?"

"Those were houris from paradise calling him. I don't have a maid."

It is related that 'Abdollāh was asked, "What wonders have you seen?"

"I saw a monk who had grown weak with spiritual striving. I asked him, 'What is the path to the Lord and how long is it?'

"'If you know him,' he replied, 'you know the path to him.' He added, 'How do I worship one whom I do not know, and you rebel against one whom you do? In other words, realization demands fear, but I do not find you fearful. Unbelief demands ignorance, but I find myself to have melted away from fear.' The monk's words were counsel to me and restrained me from many things that are not to be done."

It is related that 'Abdollāh said, "I happened once to be in the city of Byzantium, and I saw a large number of people gathered together. They had strung someone up between two poles, and the people kept urging the flogger, 'If you let up, may you suffer the wrath of the great idol! Beat him hard and fast!'

"The poor man was in great agony, but he did not utter a moan. I asked him, 'In such a grave situation with the hard blows you're taking, why is it you do not moan?'

"'I committed a grave crime,' he said. 'Among our people, it is the custom that until a person is purified of everything he owns, he cannot pronounce the name of the mighty idol. Now you appear to be a Muslim. Know that I mentioned the name of the great idol over the two trays of a scale. This is the punishment for that.'

"I said, 'Among our people, it is the case that anyone who knows him cannot mention him, for *the tongue of one who knows God is mute*.'"[6]

It is related that once 'Abdollāh had gone to join the struggle and was fighting an unbeliever. The time for prayer arrived. He asked the unbeliever for a grace period and prayed. When the time for the unbeliever's prayers arrived, he too asked for a grace period. When he turned toward his idol, 'Abdollāh said, "Now I have gained victory over him!" He went toward the unbeliever with sword drawn to kill him. He heard a voice say, "'Abdollāh, *fulfill every pledge, for someone will be held responsible for every pledge* [17:34]. They will ask about your faithfulness to your promises."

'Abdollāh wept. The unbeliever raised his head. He saw 'Abdollāh with his sword drawn, weeping. "What happened to you?" he asked.

'Abdollāh told what happened, saying, "I have been rebuked like this for your sake."

The unbeliever cried out and said, "It is not chivalrous to resist and rebel against such a lord, who rebukes his friend for his enemy's sake." He converted to Islam and became an honored follower of the path of the faith.

It is related that 'Abdollāh said, "In Mecca I saw a handsome young man who was on his way to enter the Ka'ba. All of a sudden he fell down and lost consciousness. I went up to him, and he immediately recited the profession of faith. I asked him, 'Young man, what happened to you?'

"He said, 'I was a Christian. I was about to slip into the Ka'ba in disguise, so I could see its beauty. A hidden voice called out, *"You are entering the beloved's house, while there is enmity toward him in your heart.* How can you think this proper?"'"

It is related that it was a cold winter, and 'Abdollāh was walking through the marketplace in Nishapur. He saw a slave boy wearing just a smock who was shivering from the cold. 'Abdollāh said, "Why don't you tell your master to buy you an overcoat?"

The slave boy answered, "What should I say when he sees and knows?"

'Abdollāh was overjoyed. He shouted and collapsed. Later he said, "Learn the path from this slave boy."

It is related that a misfortune once struck 'Abdollāh. Some people came to offer him their condolences. A Zoroastrian also went and said, "When misfortune strikes a wise man, he does on the first day what it takes an ignorant man three days to do."

"Write this saying down," 'Abdollāh said. "It is a wise proverb."

It is related that 'Abdollāh was asked, "Which quality in a person is most beneficial?"

"Abundant intellect," 'Abdollāh said.

"If he doesn't have that?"

"Civility"

"If he doesn't have that?"

"A sympathetic brother to consult with."

"If he doesn't have that?"

"A continual silence."

"If he doesn't have that?"

"Instant death."

It is related that 'Abdollāh said, "Whoever thinks civility is simple will be deficient in following the Prophet's example. Whoever thinks following the Prophet's example is simple will be barred from performing religious duties. Whoever thinks performing religious duties is easy will be barred from realization. Whoever is barred from realization, well, you know what he's like."

"These are the poor of this world," they said. "What is the standing of those who are poor in the Real?"

"The hearts of the friends of the Real are never still," 'Abdollāh said. In other words, they are continually seeking. Those who stop reveal their standing.

"We need a little civility more than we need much learning."

"They seek civility now that civil people are gone."

"People have said a lot about it, but to me, civility is knowing the self."

"Being generous toward what other people have is nobler than spending freely of what you have."

"I prefer anyone who gives a dirham back to its owner to someone who gives away a hundred thousand dirhams in alms. Whoever takes a penny illicitly does not trust in God."

"Trust in God is not when you see this trust coming from yourself. Trust in God is when the mighty and glorious Lord knows this trust through you."

"Working for a living is not a hindrance to giving yourself over to God and trusting in him. Both of these forms of worship are in working for a living."

"If someone works for a living, it is fitting that he pay for his own upkeep if he falls sick and for his own shroud if he dies."

"There is no good in a person who has not gone through the humility of working for a living."

"The virtue of contentment is better than the virtue of giving."

"Renunciation is being secure in the Lord most high while loving poverty."

"Anyone who has not tasted servitude will never have any taste."

"If someone has a wife and children and maintains them honestly and wakes up at night and puts covers on his children when he sees them exposed, this act of his is nobler than fighting in the sacred struggle."

"The more important a person is among the people, the more lowly he must consider himself."

They asked, "What is medicine to the heart?"
        "Staying away from people," 'Abdollāh said.

"Meekness is being arrogant toward the rich and meek toward the poor."

"This is meekness: When you are arrogant to those above you in the world and meek to those below you."

"Genuine hope springs from fear. When any hope is not preceded by fear, it does not take long before a person starts to feel safe and becomes sedate."

"What stirs up fear so it settles in the heart is constant watchfulness, both privately and publicly."

✍ ✍ ✍

It is related that backbiting was being discussed before 'Abdollāh. He said, "If I slander anyone, let me slander my parents. They are most deserving of my good deeds."[7]

It is related that one day a young man came and fell at 'Abdollāh's feet and sobbed and said, "I have committed a sin that I cannot speak of out of shame."

"Tell me what you have done."

"I committed adultery."

"I was afraid you might have slandered someone," the sheikh said.

A man asked 'Abdollāh for counsel.

"Keep the Lord," he said.

"What does this mean?"

"Always act as though you see the mighty and glorious Lord."

It is related that during his lifetime, 'Abdollāh gave away all his wealth to the poor. Once a guest came, and 'Abdollāh spent everything he had, saying, "Guests are sent by the mighty and glorious Lord."

His wife came out angrily against him. 'Abdollāh said, "The wife who quarrels with me over this shouldn't be kept in the house." He gave her back her dowry and divorced her.

The Lord most high decreed that a daughter of the nobility came to one of his prayer meetings and liked what he said. She went home and asked her father to give her to 'Abdollāh in marriage. Her father gave her fifty thousand dinars and gave her in marriage to 'Abdollāh.

In a dream it was revealed to him: "You divorced a wife for our sake. Here is your recompense, so you may know that no one loses by us."

253

When he was in his final death throes, 'Abdollāh gave all his wealth to the poor. A disciple was at his bedside and said, "Sheikh, you have three little girls and you are closing your eyes to this world. Leave something for them. What have you done to take care of them?"

'Abdollāh said, "I have spoken of them: *He looks after the pious* [7:196]. Someone whom he looks after is better off than someone who 'Abdollāh does."

At the moment of death, he opened his eyes. He was laughing and saying, *"Those who strive, strive for the likes of this"* [37:61].

Sofyān-e Sowri (God have mercy on him) appeared to people in a dream. "What has the mighty and glorious Lord done with you?" they asked.

"He was merciful."

"How is 'Abdollāh ebn al-Mobārak?"

"He is among those who enter the presence of the Real twice a day."

∾ 13 ∾
Sofyān-e Sowri

The crown of religion and religiosity, the torch of guidance and piety, the sheikh and king of scholars, the court chamberlain of ancient masters, the axis of motions planetary, Sofyān-e Sowri—God's mercy be upon him. He was one of the eminent: they used to call him the Commander of the Faithful and never opposed him. He was a true and acknowledged exemplar. He had no peer in the exoteric and esoteric sciences. He was a founder of one of the five schools of law[1] and achieved the utmost in scrupulousness and fear of God. His meekness and civility were extraordinary. He met many of the great sheikhs and did not backslide a bit in his spiritual work from beginning to end. So it was that Ebrāhim ebn Adham called out to him, "Come, let us listen to hadith." Sofyān came at once. Ebrāhim said, "I had to test his character."

He was born scrupulous. Thus it is related that one day his mother had gone up on the roof. She put a slice of pickle from the neighbors in her mouth. Sofyān squirmed so much in her womb that she realized what she was doing and she went and asked for some lawful food.

This was the beginning of his spiritual life: One day Sofyān carelessly stepped into the mosque with his left foot first. He heard a voice say, "You bull! Don't be a clumsy ox!" That is why they called him *sowri* or "ox-like." When he heard that voice, he fainted. When he came to, he grabbed his own beard and slapped himself across the face. He used to say, "When you don't set foot in the mosque with proper civility, your name is expunged from the rolls of humankind. Watch out how you step."

It is related that he set foot in a farmer's field. The voice said, "Hey, you ox!" *See* what succor comes to someone who cannot take a step contrary to the Prophet's example! When he is outwardly so exacting, who can say anything about his inner state?

For twenty years straight, Sofyān did not sleep at night.

It is related that Sofyān said, "I never heard a saying of the Prophet (peace and blessing be upon him) that I did not put into practice."

"Adherents of hadith!" he used to say, "pay tithe on the Prophet's sayings."

"What is the tithe on the Prophet's sayings?" they asked.

"Do five good deeds for every two hundred hadith."

It is related that the caliph of the time used to pray with Sofyān and as he prayed, he stroked his beard. "Prayer like this," Sofyān said, "is no prayer at all. On the morrow of the resurrection on the plains of judgment, they will throw this prayer back in your face like an old rag."

"Speak more gently!" the caliph said.

"If I disregard such an important matter," Sofyān replied, "my urine will instantly turn to blood."

The caliph was determined to take vengeance. He ordered a gallows erected to hang Sofyān, so no one would ever again be so bold. The day they were building the gallows, Sofyān laid his head in the lap of one of the eminent and rested his feet in the lap of Sofyān-e 'Oyeyna and fell asleep. These two found out what was going on and said to each other, "Let's tell him the news."

Sofyān was awake and asked, "What is it?" They told him and he

255

seemed very depressed. "I have no great attachment to life," Sofyān said, "but the duties of this world must be carried out." Tears filling his eyes, he prayed, "O Lord, seize them and seize them hard!"

At the time, the caliph was on his throne with the pillars of state around him. A tremor shook the palace, and the caliph and his ministers were swallowed into the earth. Those two eminent men said, "We have not seen a prayer answered so exactly and so quickly!"

"Indeed," Sofyān said, "we have not humiliated ourselves at *this* court."

It is related that the next caliph who took the throne believed in Sofyān. It so happened that Sofyān fell sick. The caliph had a very skillful, Christian physician. He sent him to see Sofyān to treat him. When the physician looked at Sofyān's urine sample, he said, "This is a man whose liver has been torn to pieces by fear of the Lord, and his bladder is being excreted bit by bit. No religion that such a man follows can be invalid." The physician converted to Islam then and there.

"I thought the doctor was going to the patient," the caliph said, "but I sent the patient to the doctor."

It is related that when Sofyān was still young, he was already hunchbacked. People said, "Imam of the Muslims, you shouldn't be like this yet." Sofyān did not reply, because meditating on the Real, he did not pay any attention to people.

Then one day they were really insistent on this point. Sofyān said: "I had a mentor, a very eminent man, and I used to study with him. When his life reached its end, and the ship of his life was about to sink into the whirlpool of death, I was sitting at his bedside. He suddenly opened his eyes and said, 'Sofyān, do you see what they're doing to me? For fifty years I have shown people the right path and summoned them to the court of the Real. Now they drive me away and say, "Go! You are not worthy of us."'"

(Others say that Sofyān said, "I attended three teachers and studied with them. When one of them reached the end of his life, he became a Jew and died in that state. Another became a Zoroastrian, and another a Christian.")

Sofyān continued, "A tremor of fear ran up my spine, and my back was broken."

256

It is related that someone sent Sofyān two bags of gold and said, "Take this. My father was your friend, and he worked hard in a legitimate business. I have brought you this from his legacy."

Sofyān handed the money to his son and sent it back, saying, "My friendship with your father was for the sake of the Lord."

Sofyān's son related: "When I came back, I said, 'Father, is your heart made of stone? You see that I have a family and no means of support. Won't you have pity on me?'

"My father said, 'Son, you must eat, but I will not sell the Lord's friendship for the friendship of this world and come up short at the resurrection.'"

It is related that someone brought Sofyān a gift, but he did not accept it. The man said, "I have never studied hadith with you."

"Your brother has," Sofyān said. "I am afraid that because of your money, my heart will be more sympathetic toward him than toward the others. This would be bias." Sofyān never used to take anything from anyone. He would say, "If I knew that I would not come up short in the next world, I would take it."

One day Sofyān coming through the door of an opulent house with someone. His companion was examining the portico. Sofyān stopped him and said, "If you did not look at it, they would not be so extravagant. When you admire it, you share in the cruelty of this extravagance."

Sofyān had a neighbor who died, and Sofyān was present at his funeral prayers. People were speaking well of him, saying, "He was a good man." Sofyān said, "If I had known that people were pleased with him, I never would have come to his funeral, because people are not pleased with a man until he becomes a hypocrite."

Sofyān was in the habit of sitting in the sanctuary of the congregational mosque. When they made an incense burner from funds donated by the sultan, Sofyān fled from there so he would not smell the odor of the incense. He never sat there again.

It is related that one day Sofyān was wearing his clothes inside out. They told him about it, and he was about to put them on right, but he did not. He said, "I wear this shirt for the sake of the mighty and glorious Lord. I do not want to reverse it for the sake of people." He left it the way it was.

It is related that a young man missed the time to go on the pilgrimage. He let out a sigh. Sofyān said, "I have gone on the pilgrimage four times. I give them to you. Do you give me this sigh?"

"I do," the young man said.

That night Sofyān had a dream in which he was told, "You have made such a profit that if you divide it among the people at 'Arafāt, they will all become rich."

It is related that Sofyān came to the bathhouse one day. A handsome, beardless boy came in. "Throw him out," Sofyān said. "For every woman, there is one demon who makes her attractive in men's eyes, and for every beardless boy, eighteen."

It is related that one day Sofyān was eating. There was a dog there, and Sofyān was feeding it. "Why don't you eat with your wife and children?" some people asked.

"If I feed the dog," Sofyān said, "it will keep guard over me until daybreak so I can perform my prayers. If I feed my wife and children, they will keep me from my devotions."

One day Sofyān told his followers, "Good or bad, food is nothing more than what passes through the lips to the gullet. Whether it's good or bad, wait to eat until good and bad are one and the same to you. You can wait for something that passes this quickly." Concerning the honor that Sofyān paid to the poor, they relate that at his prayer meetings the poor were treated like princes.

It is related that Sofyān was once riding in a litter and going to Mecca. Sofyān wept all the way. There was a friend with him who asked, "Do you weep for fear of your sins?"

Sofyān stretched out his hand and picked up a piece of straw. "Although my sins are many," Sofyān said, "they amount to no more than this piece of straw. What I fear is whether this faith that I bring is really faith or not."

ൟ ൟ ൟ

"Others were preoccupied with worship. Their wisdom bore fruit."

"Nine-tenths of weeping is hypocrisy, and one-tenth is for the Lord. If one tear falls from the eyes in a year, that is a great number."

"If a lot of people are sitting somewhere, and someone calls out, 'If anyone knows whether he will live through the day today, let him stand up,' no one will stand up. What's strange is that if they tell all these people, 'If anyone is prepared for death—the mighty affair that awaits us all—let him stand up,' not one person will be able to stand up."

"Refraining from action is harder than acting. Often a person does a good deed, until it is recorded in the register of public esteem. Then he boasts of it so much and recounts it so often that it is recorded in the register of hypocrisy."

"If a dervish hovers around the wealthy, know that he is a hypocrite. If he hovers around the sultan, know that he is a thief."

"A renunciant is the one who acts out his renunciation of the world. A pseudo-renunciant is the one whose renunciation is all talk."

"Renunciation of this world is not in wearing sackcloth or eating coarse barley bread. It is in not attaching your heart to this world and giving up all expectations."

"If you go before the Lord with many sins, the sin that is between you and the Lord is easier than the one that is between you and his servants."

"This is an age when you should keep silent and retire from the world, *the time to be silent and stay at home.*"

Someone asked, "What do you say about sitting in out-of-way places earning merit?"

"Fear the Lord," Sofyān said, "for I never saw a mindful person who needed to earn merit."

"I do not consider a person to be any better than the hole that he runs to and hides in. Our predecessors held it reprehensible to wear clothes that would attract attention, whether they were new or old. Rather, they must be such that people do not talk about them. This is refusing the two notorieties."

"I do not know of anything sounder for the people of this age than sleep."

"The best sultan is one who sits with the learned and learns from them. The worst of the learned is one who sits with sultans."

"First, there is a private devotion, then the quest for knowledge, then its application, and then its dissemination."

"I never stand up out of respect to a person until I have heard a word of wisdom from him."

"Consider this world to be for the body and the next world to be for the heart."

"If sin had a stench about it, no one would escape the smell."

"Anyone who prefers himself to others is arrogant."

"The dearest of God's creatures are of five sorts: a pious scholar, a Sufi lawyer, a humble rich man, a grateful poor man, and a nobleman who follows the Prophet's example."

"If you do not pray humbly, your prayer is not right."

"Someone who pays the tithe and does good works with illicit funds is like the person who washes filthy clothes in blood or urine—they only become filthier."

"Contentment is accepting what is fated with thanks."

"Good humor soothes the wrath of the mighty and glorious Lord."

"Certainty is not suspecting the Lord, no matter what happens to you."

"Praise be to the Lord who kills us and takes our wealth, while we love him all the more."

"He will not loathe someone he loved."

"Breathing is forbidden during contemplation, forbidden during unveiling, and forbidden during vision, but it is permitted during fleeting intuitions."

"If someone says to you, '*You are a good man,*' and it pleases you more than '*You are a bad man,*' then know that you are still a bad man."

They asked him about certainty. He said, "It is an action in the heart. Whenever certainty is sound, realization is secure. Certainty is when you know that whatever happens to you happens to you through the Real. Or it is when you are such that his promise is like something visible to you, even more than visible." In other words, when he is present, or even more than this.

They asked, "Did the Prophet (peace and blessing and salutations be upon him) say, 'The Lord most high hates the house where they eat a lot of meat?'"

"It is said that gossips eat the flesh of Muslims."

It is related that Sofyān told Hātem the Deaf: "Let me tell you four things that arise out of ignorance: First, holding people in reproach—this comes from ignoring fate, and ignoring fate is contrary to the faith. Second, envying your Muslim brothers—this comes from ignoring destiny, and ignoring destiny is contrary to the faith. Third, gathering illicit and questionable wealth—this comes from ignoring the accounting at the resurrection, and ignoring the accounting of the resurrection is contrary to the faith. Fourth, feeling secure from the threats of the Real and despairing of his promises and ignoring his word—all this is contrary to the faith."

✍ ✍ ✍

It is related that when one of his students left on a trip, Sofyān would say, "If you see death somewhere, buy it for me." When the moment of death approached, he said, "I yearned for death, and now death is hard. If only you could get through every trip safely with a walking stick and a canteen. But approaching the mighty and glorious Lord is not easy."[2] Whenever he heard talk about death and its dominion, he would leave himself for several days and to anyone who came he would say, *"Prepare for death before it arrives."*[3] He both feared death and yearned for it.

Then his friends would say, "May paradise please you!"

"What are you saying?" Sofyān said. "Will paradise ever come to me or will it ever be given to someone like me?"

Sofyān fell ill in Basra. The governor of Basra wanted to give Sofyān a post and sought him out: Sofyān was in a stable, suffering from pain in his stomach and not resting for a moment from his devotions. That night, they counted sixty times that he washed his hands, performed his ablutions, and began to pray, but again had to answer the call of nature. They said, "Stop doing your ablutions!"

"I want to be pure when the Angel of Death arrives, not defiled. The filthy cannot approach his presence."

'Abdollāh Mahdi[4] said, "Sofyān said, 'Put my face to the ground, for the moment of my death has drawn near.' I put his face to the ground and came out to inform the people who had gathered. When I came back, his followers were all present. 'Who gave you the news?' I asked.

"They said, 'We were told in a dream to come to Sofyān's funeral.'"

The people came, and his condition had grown critical. He reached a hand under his pillow and pulled out a bag of one thousand dinars and said, "Give this away as alms."

"Praise God," the people said, "Sofyān always used to tell us, 'One must take nothing of this world.' Where did he get so many dinars?!"

Sofyān said, "This was the guardian of my faith. I was able to take care of my body with it, and for this reason, the devil had no hold on me. If the devil had said, 'What will you eat today, what will you wear?' I would have said, 'Look here! Gold!' If he had said, 'You have no shroud,' I would have said, 'Look here! Gold!' I would have warded off his temptations, although I never needed to."

Then he recited the profession of faith and surrendered his soul.

They say that a relative in Bukhara made Sofyān his heir. When he died, the religious officials of Bukhara took care of the money. Sofyān was informed and set off for Bukhara. The people of Bukhara went out to welcome him at the riverbank and escorted him into town with full honors. Sofyān was eighteen years old when they gave him the money. He held onto it so that he would not have to ask anybody for anything. When he was certain that he was about to die, he gave it away as alms.

The night Sofyān died, a voice was heard saying, *"Scrupulousness has died! It has died!"* Then people saw Sofyān in their dreams. They asked, "How were you able to endure the savagery and darkness of the grave?"

"My grave," Sofyān said, "is one of the meadows of paradise."

Someone else dreamt that he saw Sofyān. "What did the Lord most high do with you?" he asked.

Sofyān said, "I took one step on the Narrow Bridge and the next in paradise."

Another person saw Sofyān in a dream. He said, "Sofyān flew from tree to tree in paradise. They asked him, 'How did you achieve this?' He replied, 'Scrupulousness.'"

Concerning the compassion Sofyān had for the Lord's creatures, it is related that one day in the market he saw a little bird in a cage, crying in lament and flapping its wings. Sofyān bought it and set it free. The little bird would come to Sofyān's house every night. Sofyān would pray all night, and the bird would watch and sometimes perch on him. When they bore Sofyān to his grave, the little bird alighted on his bier and cried in lament. The people sobbed and wailed. When they buried the sheikh, the bird beat itself against his grave, until a voice came from the grave: "The Real most high has had mercy on Sofyān because of the compassion that he showed for his creatures." The bird also died and came to Sofyān.

✑ 14 ✑
Dāvud-e Tā'i

The candle of sense and vision, the lantern of creation, worker on the path, knower of the truth, the godly man, Dāvud-e Tā'i—God's mercy be upon him. He was one of the elders of this clan and a chief of this folk. He was the utmost perfection in scrupulousness. He had a full share in various fields of learning, especially jurisprudence, in which he excelled and distinguished himself. He studied with Abu Hanifa for twenty years and met Fozeyl and Ebrāhim ebn Adham; his elder on the path was Habib-e Rā'i. There was, from the first, an overwhelming sorrow within him, and he had always shied away from people.

The reason for his repentance was that he heard this verse from a mourner:

> *On which of your cheeks first appeared decay?*
> *And which of your eyes then melted away?*[1]

This image plunged him into great pain. His composure left him, and he was dismayed. He went to Abu Hanifa's class like this. The imam saw that he was not his usual self. "What has happened to you?" he asked.

Dāvud recounted what had occurred and said, "My heart has turned cold to the world. Something has appeared within me that I do not know how to get at. I don't find the sense of it in any book, and it doesn't enter into any legal case."

"Shun society," the imam said. Dāvud turned his back on people and retired to his house. After some time had passed, the Imam Abu Hanifa went to see him. "This is not an affair," he said, "for hiding yourself away at home. What you must do is sit among the imams and listen to their obscure words. Be patient and say nothing: you'll best learn about these problems from them."

Dāvud realized that it was as the imam said. For one year he went to classes, sat among the imams, and said nothing. He was patient with everything they said, gave no response, and contented himself with listening. When a year had elapsed, he said, "My one year of patience has accomplished thirty year's of work." He then fell in with Habib-e Rā'i, and Dāvud's opening onto this path came through him. Like a true believer, Dāvud set foot on this path: he consigned his books to the water, secluded himself, and gave up all hope in created things.

It is related that Dāvud had inherited twenty gold dinars and spent them over the course of twenty years. As a result, some sheikhs said, "The path is spending freely, not saving."

Dāvud said, "I save as much as will free me from concern. I will make do with this until I die." He never rested from his labors, so much so that he would soak bread in water and drink that. He used to say, "Between the time it takes to do this and the time it takes to eat, one can recite fifty verses of the Qur'an. Why should I waste time?"

Abu Bakr-e 'Eyyāsh[2] relates: "I went to Dāvud's room. I saw him holding a dry piece of bread in his hand and weeping. 'Dāvud,' I said, 'what has happened to you?' He said, 'I want to eat this piece of bread, but I do not know whether it is ritually clean or not.'"

Someone else said: "I went to see Dāvud. I saw a pitcher of water set out in the full sun. I asked, 'Why don't you put it in the shade?' He said, 'When I set it here, it was in the shade. Now I am ashamed before the Lord to take pleasure for the sake of the self.'"

It is related that Dāvud had a large mansion with many rooms. One room would fall into ruins, and he would live in another. "Why don't you repair the room?" they asked.

"I have a pact with the mighty and glorious Lord," Dāvud said, "that I will not repair this world." His entire mansion collapsed, except for the porch. The night he died, the porch too collapsed.

Someone else went to see him and said, "The roof of this room is cracked and is going to fall in."

Dāvud said, "I haven't noticed this roof for twenty years."

It is related that they asked, "Why don't you live with people?"

"With whom should I live?" Dāvud said. "If I live with someone younger than I, he will not enjoin me to work for the faith. If I live with someone older, he will not recount my faults to me and will build me up in my own eyes. So, why should I associate with people?"

They asked, "Why don't you ask a woman to marry you?"

"I cannot deceive a believer," Dāvud said.

"How so?"

"If I propose to her, I have taken on the responsibility of attending to her affairs, both religious and worldly. Since I cannot do this, I will have deceived her."

They said, "At least comb out your beard!"

"What time do I have to spare for this?" Dāvud asked.

It is related that on a moonlit night, Dāvud went up on his roof and gazed at the sky and meditated on the heavens. He wept until he fell unconscious onto his neighbor's roof. The neighbor thought there was a thief on the roof. He went up to the roof with a sword. He saw Dāvud. He took his hand and said, "Who threw you over here?"

Dāvud said, "I don't know. I was unconscious. I have no idea."

It is related that Dāvud was seen running to prayer. "What's the hurry?" they asked.

"There is an army at the city gates, and it is waiting for me," Dāvud said.

"What army?"

"The dead from the graveyard."

When Dāvud completed his prayers, he would hurry off as though he were fleeing from someone until he reached home. He had a great aversion to attending prayers because of his terror of people, so the Real most high absolved him of that hardship. Thus, it is related that one day his mother saw him sitting in the sun with sweat pouring off of him. "My dear child," she said, "it's extremely hot, and you fast all through the day. What difference would it make if you sat in the shade?"

"Mother," Dāvud said, "I am ashamed before the Lord to take a single step for the pleasure of my self. I don't even have the power to move."

"What are you talking about?"

"When I saw the conditions and indecencies in Baghdad, I prayed for the Real most high to take the power of movement away from me, so I would be excused from being present in the congregation and having to see them. For sixteen years now, I have not had the power to move and have not told you."

266

It is related that Dāvud was in constant sorrow. When night came on, he would say to God, "Ah, my sorrow for you overwhelms all other sorrows and robs me of sleep." And he would reply, "How can anyone who suffers continuous hardships escape from sorrow?"

Once a dervish said, "I went to see Dāvud. I found him smiling. I thought this strange. I said, 'Abu Soleymān, where does this happiness come from?' He said, 'This morning I was given a wine that they call the wine of intimacy. Today I celebrated the end of the fast and took up joy.'"

It is related that Dāvud was eating bread, and a Christian passed by. Dāvud gave him a piece to eat. That night the Christian mated with his wife. Ma'ruf of Karkh was conceived.

∽ ∽ ∽

Abu Rabi'-e Vāseti[3] says: "I said to Dāvud, 'Give me counsel.' He said, 'Fast from this world and break the fast on your death and flee from people as they flee from a ferocious lion.'"

Someone else asked him for counsel. He said, "Hold your tongue."
   "Say more."
   "Live alone, away from people, and if you can, sever your heart from them."
   "Say more."
   "Among the things of this world, you should be content with being secure in the faith, just as worldly people are content with being secure in the world."

Someone else asked him for counsel. He said, "Strive in this world to the extent that you will reside in this world and your efforts will be useful to you here. Strive for the next world to the extent that you will reside in the next world and your efforts will be useful to you there."

Someone else asked him for counsel. He said, "The dead are waiting for you."

"The person who puts off repentance and devotion truly resembles someone who hunts while the profit accrues to another."

He said to a disciple, "If you wish for good health, say farewell to this world. If you wish for honor, say 'God is great' as you abandon the next world." In other words, pass beyond both so you may reach the Real.

ꝯ ꝯ ꝯ

It is related that Fozeyl met Dāvud two times in his entire life and took pride in them. Once Fozeyl had ducked under a roof that was caving in. He said, "Get up—this roof is caving in and it's about to collapse." Dāvud said, "As long as I've been sitting on this porch, I haven't noticed the roof. *They detest meddlesome glances as much as they detest meddlesome words.*" The second time was when Fozeyl said, "Give me a piece of advice." Dāvud said, "Flee from people."

Maʿruf of Karkh (God's mercy be upon him) says: "I saw no one who held the world in greater contempt than Dāvud, for in his eyes, all this world and its people were no more than a mote of dust. When he saw one of them, he would complain of the darkness it caused. He was so far from the normal way of things that he said, 'Whenever I wash my shirt, I find that my heart is disturbed.' However, he had a great belief in the poor and regarded them with respect and chivalry."

Joneyd said, "A phlebotomist gave Dāvud a bloodletting. Dāvud gave him a gold dinar. They said, 'This is extravagant.' Dāvud said, '*One who has no chivalry has no faith.*'"

It is related that someone was in Dāvud's presence and stared at him a long time. Dāvud said, "Don't you know that a long look is just as abhorrent as long-windedness?"

It is related that when a disagreement broke out between Mohammad ebn Hasan[4] and Abu Yusof,[5] Dāvud was the arbiter. When they came to see him, Dāvud would turn his face to Mohammad and chat with him but turn his back to Abu Yusof and not say a word to him. If Mohammad said something, Dāvud would say, "This is what Mohammad says." If Abu Yusof said something, Dāvud would say, "This is what is said," without mentioning his name. People asked,

"Both men are greatly learned. Why do you regard one as a dear friend and not allow the other before you?"

Dāvud said, "Because Mohammad ebn Hasan has come to learning from a life of great affluence, his learning has its source in his respect for religion and his contempt for the world. Abu Yusof has come from poverty and mean circumstances and has made learning into the source of his own respect and honor. So, Mohammad will never be like him. They whipped our teacher Abu Hanifa (God's mercy be upon him), but he did not accept the judgeship. Abu Yusof, however, did. I will not speak to anyone who opposes the way of his teacher."

It is related that Hārun ar-Rashid asked Abu Yusof, "Take me to see Dāvud so I may pay my respects." Abu Yusof came to the door of Dāvud's house. He was not allowed in. He asked Dāvud's mother to intercede. "Let him come in," she said to Dāvud.

He refused and said, "What business do I have with tyrants and worldly folk?"

"By your mother's milk," she said, "let him come in."

"I will not see this tyrant." Then Dāvud prayed, "My God, you have commanded us: 'Respect your mother, for her pleasure is my pleasure.' If not for that, what would I have to do with them?"

Dāvud let them in. They entered and sat down. Dāvud began to preach. Hārun often wept. When Hārun left, he set down a gold signet ring and said, "It is legally gotten."

"Take it away," Dāvud said. "I have no need of this. I have sold a house from my legal holdings. I use the money for my daily expenses. I have asked the Lord most high to take my life when these funds run out, so I will have no need of anyone. I hope that he has answered my prayer."

Hārun and Abu Yusof both left. Abu Yusof asked Dāvud's account keeper, "How much of his funds remain?"

"Ten dirhams."

Dāvud used to spend one small silver coin each day. Abu Yusof made some calculations and on the last day he sat with his back to the prayer niche. "Dāvud has died today," he said. They looked into it, and it was so.

"How did you know?" they asked.

"I calculated that nothing would remain of his funds today and I knew that his prayer would be answered."

They asked Dāvud's mother about the circumstances of his death. "He was praying all night," she said. "At the end of the night, he lowered his head in prostration and did not raise it. I was very anxious. I said, 'My son, it is time for prayer.' When I looked closely, he had died."

A great person said, "When he was ill, he was sleeping on the porch of that rundown house. It was extremely hot, and he had placed a brick under his head. He was in his death throes and was reciting the Qur'an. I said, 'Do you want me to carry you out to this field?'

"He said, 'I am ashamed to ask for anything for the sake of the self. The self has never had any hold on me. It is more proper this way.' He died that very night."

Dāvud had left final instructions: "Bury me behind a wall, so that no one can pass in front of my face." They did as he asked, and even today, his grave is like this.

On the night that death came to him, a voice came from heaven: "O people of the earth! Dāvud-e Tā'i has reached the Real, and the Real most high is pleased with him."

Later, he was seen in a dream flying through the air and saying, "This hour, I have been released from prison." The dreamer came to tell Dāvud—he had died.

After his death, a voice came from heaven: "Dāvud attained the goal."

◈ 15 ◈
Ma'ruf of Karkh

Companion of the breeze of loving unity, intimate of the sanctuary of sublimity, leader at the head of the path, guide on the way of truth, aware of the mysteries befitting a sheikh, the axis of the age, Ma'ruf of Karkh—God's mercy be upon him. He was a forerunner on the path and a leader of the clans and distinguished by various graces. He was the chief of the lovers of his time and the epitome of the realized knowers of his age. Indeed, had he not been a knower—a realized *'āref*—he would not have been called *ma'ruf*—the well-known. His wonders and austerities were many, and he was a symbol of gallantry and the fear of God. He possessed a mighty grace and proximity to the Lord and reached the ultimate station of intimacy and yearning.

His parents were Christians. When they sent him to school, his teacher told him to say, "I profess the Trinity." Ma'ruf said, "No, indeed, he is God the Unique." Although the teacher kept telling him to say, "The Lord is three," Ma'ruf kept saying, "He is one." However much the teacher beat him, it did no good.

Once his teacher beat him hard. Ma'ruf fled and could not be found. His parents said, "If only he would come back, we would conform to whatever religion he wished." Ma'ruf went and became a Muslim at the hands of 'Ali ebn Musā ar-Rezā.[1] Some time after that, he came back and knocked on the door of his father's house. "Who is it?" they asked.

"It is Ma'ruf," he replied.

"Which religion do you follow?"

"The religion of Mohammad, the Messenger of God."

His parents converted to Islam then and there.

Ma'ruf then fell in with Dāvud-e Tā'i and endured many austerities and worshiped with utter devotion. He walked so fully in the way of truthfulness that he became an exemplar.

Mohammad ebn Mansur of Tus[2] (God's mercy be upon him) reported: "I was with Ma'ruf in Baghdad. I saw a mark on his face. 'I was with you last night,' I said, 'and this mark wasn't there. What is it?'

"He replied, 'Don't ask about something that will do you no good. Ask about something that will be of some use to you.'

"'For God's sake, tell me,' I said.

"'Last night, I was praying,' he said. 'I asked to go to Mecca and circumambulate the Ka'ba. I went over to the Well of Zamzam to drink some water. My foot slipped, and I fell into it face first. This is the mark it left.'"

It is related that Ma'ruf went to the Tigris to perform his ablutions, leaving his Qur'an and prayer rug in the mosque. An old woman came into the mosque and picked them up. She was leaving, but Ma'ruf tracked her down to say a few words to her. She lowered her eyes so she would not have to look him in the face. Ma'ruf asked, "Do you have a little boy who is studying the Qur'an?"

"No," she replied.

"Give me the Qur'an, and the prayer rug is yours."

The woman was amazed at Ma'ruf's forbearance and put both of them back. Ma'ruf said, "The prayer rug is legally yours. Take it." The woman hurried away in shame and embarrassment.

It is related that one day Ma'ruf was walking along with a group of followers. A group of young men were carrying on wickedly. Reaching the banks of the Tigris, his followers said, "Sheikh, pray for the Real most high to drown all of them, so their disgraceful behavior will come to an end."

Ma'ruf said, "Lift up your hands." Then he prayed, "My God, just as you are pleased with their merriment in this world, give them sweet merriment in the next."

His companions were dumbfounded. "Sheikh," they said, "we do not grasp the secret behind this prayer."

"Wait a bit. It will become apparent."

When the group of young men saw the sheikh, they broke their lutes, poured out their wine, and were overcome with weeping. They laid hold of his hands and feet and repented. "You see," the sheikh said, "everyone's wishes have been met, without drowning and without any harm coming to anyone."

Sari-ye Saqati reported:

On the Feast of the End of the Fast, I saw Ma'ruf gathering date pits. "Why are you doing this?" I asked.

Ma'ruf answered, "I saw this child who was crying. I asked him why he was crying. He said, 'I am an orphan. I have no mother or father. Other children have new clothes, but I have none. They have walnuts, but I have none.' I am collecting these date pits to sell and buy some walnuts for him, so he will stop crying and play."

I told Ma'ruf, "Let me take care of this business and put your heart at ease." I took the child and dressed him in new clothes and bought him some walnuts and made him happy at heart. At once a light appeared in my heart, and I was transformed.

It is related that one day a traveler arrived at Ma'ruf's hospice. He did not know the direction of Mecca and faced the wrong way when he prayed. Afterward, when he found out what he had done, he was embarrassed. "Why in the world didn't you tell me?" the traveler asked Ma'ruf.

Ma'ruf said, "I am a dervish. What business does a dervish have changing things to his liking?" and he treated the traveler with boundless respect.

It is related that Ma'ruf had an uncle who was governor of the city. One day he was passing by some ruined buildings. He saw Ma'ruf sitting there eating and sharing his bowl with a dog. He would put a morsel in his mouth and then one in the dog's. His uncle said, "Aren't you ashamed to be eating with a dog?"

Ma'ruf answered, "It is out of shame that I am feeding the dog." Then he raised his head and called a bird from the sky. The bird came down and perched on his hand and covered its eyes and face with its wings. "Everything," Ma'ruf said, "is ashamed before one who is ashamed before the mighty and glorious Lord." His uncle was embarrassed.

It is related that one day Ma'ruf sullied his state of ritual purity. He immediately performed ablutions with dust. "The Tigris is right there," someone said. "Why are you performing ablutions with dust instead of water?"

"It is possible," Ma'ruf said, "that I won't make it that far."

It is related that Ma'ruf was once overwhelmed by yearning. There was a pillar nearby. He got up and embraced the pillar and squeezed it so tightly that it nearly crumbled.

ༀ ༀ ༀ

Ma'ruf has some lofty sayings:

"Chivalry consists of three things—first, loyalty without dispute; second, praise without the expectation of generosity; and third, giving without being asked."

"The mark of the Lord's displeasure toward someone is that he distracts him with the affairs of the self, with something that is of no use to him."

"The mark of the friends of the mighty and glorious Lord is that their thought is concern for the Lord, their repose is with the Lord, and their occupation is in the Lord."

"When the Real most high wishes to do something good for his servant, he opens the door of good works before him and closes the door of speech. If a man talks about something that is of no use, it is a mark of being deserted. When he wishes to do something evil to his servant, it is the opposite of this."

"The reality of faithfulness is being roused from the sleep of negligence and freeing the mind of meddlesome misfortune."

"When the Lord most high wishes to do something good for his servant, he opens the door of action before him and closes the door of indolence."

"*See*king paradise without good works is sin. Expecting the Prophet's intercession without following his tradition is a kind of pride. Hoping for God's compassion without obeying him is ignorance and foolishness."

"Sufism is grasping the realities and speaking of the subtleties and giving up all hope in what is in his creatures' hands."

"Whoever is in love with political power will never obtain salvation."

"I know a path to the mighty and glorious Lord: Don't ask anyone for anything and have nothing that anyone can ask you for."

"Close your eyes to whether anything is male or female."

"Guard your tongue from praise just as you stop it from censure."

They asked Ma'ruf, "How can we achieve devout worship?"
    "By expelling this world from your heart, because if the least thing from this world enters your heart, you will prostrate yourself before it with every prayer you perform."

They asked him about love. "Love is not something humans can teach. It is among the gifts of the Real and his grace."

"If the realized are not at all affluent, still they live in complete affluence."

It is related that one day Ma'ruf was eating some delicious food. They asked him, "What are you eating?"
    "I am a guest," Ma'ruf replied. "I eat whatever they give. Nevertheless, one day I was telling my self, 'Release me, self, so I may release you too.'"

One day Ebrāhim asked him for counsel. Ma'ruf said, "Trust in the Lord, so the Lord may be with you as an intimate friend and you may turn to him to complain to him about anything, for the entire human race cannot profit you nor ward off any loss." And Ma'ruf said, "When you make a supplication, make it to the one in whom all remedies reside. Know that whatever comes down to you, be it pain or hardship or want, know for certain that relief is in concealment."

Someone else said, "Give me counsel."
    Ma'ruf said, "Beware lest the Lord sees you when you are not in the ranks of the poor."

Sari said, "Ma'ruf told me, 'When you need something of the Lord most high, swear an oath to him. Say, "By Ma'ruf of Karkh, may you fulfill my need." Your prayer will be answered immediately.'"

⁓ ⁓ ⁓

It is related that for thirty-one days people crowded around the door of the Imam Rezā[3] (May God be pleased with him), and Ma'ruf's ribs were broken. He fell ill. Sari said to him, "Give me your final testament."

"When I die," Ma'ruf said, "give away my shirt as alms. I want to leave the world naked just as I came from my mother naked."

Truly he had no peer in detachment, and the power of his detachment was such that after his death, they called him the Proven Antidote, because the Real most high satisfies the needs of anyone who goes to his grave in want. The extent of his humility and meekness was such that after he died, people of all faiths prayed for him, Jews, Christians, and Muslims.

His servant reported: "This was the sheikh's final testament: 'I belong to the group that can pick my bier up from the ground.' Christians and Jews were unable to pick it up. The Muslims came, picked it up, prayed, and buried him there."

It is related that one day Ma'ruf was fasting. The hour had arrived for the evening prayer, and Ma'ruf was walking through the marketplace. A water carrier was crying out, "May God have mercy on anyone who takes a drink of this water!" Ma'ruf took some water and drank it.

"Weren't you fasting?" they asked him.

"Yes, but I got a craving for some water when I heard his prayer."

When Ma'ruf died, people saw him in their dreams. "What did the mighty and glorious Lord do with you?" they asked.

"He accepted the intercession of that water carrier and forgave me."

Mohammad ebn al-Hoseyn[4] (God have mercy on him) said:

I saw Ma'ruf in a dream. I asked, "What did the Mighty and Glorious Lord do with you?"

"He forgave me."

"Because of your renunciation and scrupulousness?"

"No, because I accepted some words that Ebn Sammāk[5] said to me in Kufa. He said, 'The mighty and glorious Lord will turn in compassion toward anyone who turns entirely to him and who turns all the people to him.' His words sank into my heart, and I turned to the Lord and gave up all other occupations except my service to 'Ali ebn Musā ar-Rezā. I told him these words, and he said, 'If you accept this, it will be enough for you.'"

Sari said, "I saw Ma'ruf in a dream, standing at the foot of the heavenly throne like a bewildered madman. The call of the Real most high came to the angels: 'Who is this?' The angels replied, 'O Lord, you know best.' Then the decree came down: 'It is Ma'ruf, who has gone mad because of his love for us. He will not recover unless he sees us and he will know nothing of himself unless he meets us face to face.'"

∽ 16 ∽
Sari-ye Saqati

His self slain by discipline, his heart alive in contemplation, pilgrim in the dominion of the empyrean, witness of the majesty of omnipotence, center of the circle of boundlessness, the sheikh of the age, Sari-ye Saqati—God's mercy be upon him. He was the imam of the Sufis and perfectly accomplished in various fields of learning. He was the sea of sorrow and pain, the mountain of forbearance and stability, and the treasure house of gallantry and compassion. He was a marvel of cryptic and allusive teaching and was the first person in Baghdad to speak of spiritual realities and unity. Most of the sheikhs of Iraq were his disciples. He was Joneyd's uncle and Ma'ruf's disciple, and he met Habib-e Rā'i—God have mercy on them all.

In the beginning, Sari lived in Baghdad and ran a shop. He used to hang a curtain across the door and pray. Every day he would perform several rak'ats of prayer. Someone came from Mount Lokām to visit him. The man raised the curtain over the door, made his greetings, and said to Sari, "The elder So-and-so sends you his greetings from Mount Lokām."

"He's living on a mountain?" Sari replied. "He's really not doing much. The true believer ought to be able to work busily in the middle of the market in such a way that he is not absent for an instant from the Real most high."

It is related that Sari never asked for more than 5 percent profit in his business dealings. Once he purchased almonds for sixty dinars. The price of almonds went up. The almond broker came to see him, and Sari told him to sell. "For how much?" the broker asked.

"Sixty-three dinars."

"But the price of almonds is ninety dinars today."

"It is my policy," Sari said, "to take no more than a half-dinar profit on every ten dinars. I will not annul this resolution."

"But I don't think it's right for me to sell your goods at a loss either," the broker replied. Neither Sari nor the broker sold.

At first, he was a retail grocer, a *saqat-forush*. One day the Baghdad market burned down. They told Sari about the fire, and he said, "Then I have been fired, too." When they looked into it later, it was found that his shop had not burned down. When Sari saw this, he gave away everything he owned to the poor and embarked on the Sufi path.

Sari was asked, "How was the beginning of your spiritual state?"

"One day," Sari answered, "Habib-e Rā'i passed by my shop. I gave him something and told him to give it to the poor. He said, '*May God reward you well.*' From the day he made this prayer, the world turned cold in my heart.

"Then, the following day, Ma'ruf of Karkh came by, accompanied by a child. He said, 'Give this child clothes to wear.' I gave the child clothes to wear. Ma'ruf said, 'May the Lord most high make this world seem an enemy to your heart and may he relieve you of this job.' I was released entirely from this world by the blessings of Ma'ruf's prayer."

No one went to the extremes that Sari did in his austerities, to such an extent that Joneyd said, "I have seen no one more perfect in his devotion than Sari. He lived for ninety-eight years without ever lying down except in his mortal illness."

And Sari himself reported, "For forty years, my self kept after me for carrots soaked in honey, and I did not give them to it." And he said, "Every day I look in the mirror several times fearing that my face has turned black from the evil of sin." And he said, "I wish that every sorrow that weighs on people's hearts would weigh on my heart, so they would be released from sorrow." And he said, "If a brother comes to see me and I stroke my beard, I fear that my name will be registered in the rolls of the hypocrites."

Beshr the Barefoot said, "I did not ask anyone questions except Sari, because I had recognized that his renunciation was such that he was happy whenever he gave something away."

Joneyd reported:

One day I went to see Sari. He was weeping. "What is it?" I asked.

"It occurred to me," he said, "to hang out a jug of water tonight to cool. I fell asleep. I saw an angel. I said, 'Whom do you watch over?' She replied, 'I watch over the person who does not hang out jugs of water to cool.' She smashed the jug on the ground. Look at it there."

I saw broken pottery, and those shards lay there for a long time.

Joneyd reported:

One night I was sleeping. When I awoke, my innermost self demanded that I go to the mosque at Shuniziya. I went, and at the door of the mosque I saw a terrifying figure. I was afraid. He asked, "Joneyd, are you afraid of me?"

"Yes," I said.

"If you have recognized the Lord," he replied, "why would you fear anything besides him?"

"Who are you?" I asked.

"I am Satan."

"I've been wanting to see you," I told him.

"The moment you thought of me," he said, "you neglected the mighty and glorious Lord without realizing it. What did you hope to get out of seeing me?"

"I wanted to ask you if you have any power over dervishes."

"No."

"Why?"

"When I want to seize them with this world, they escape to the other world. When I want to seize them with the other world, they escape to the Lord, and I have no way to get there."

"If you cannot get your hands on them," I asked, "do you ever see them?"

"I see them. When they are listening to music and fall into a trance, I see them and know why they lament."

He said this and vanished. When I entered the mosque, I saw Sari, his head bent to his knees. He raised his head and said, "That enemy of the Lord, he's lying. Dervishes are too dear for him to reveal them even to Gabriel. So, how would he reveal them to his enemy?"

Joneyd reported:

I was with Sari when we passed by a group of homosexuals. In my heart, I thought, "How are *they* going to end up?"

Sari said, "It has never entered my heart to think myself superior to any creature in the entire world."

"But sheikh," I said, "not even queers!"

"Never, no."

And Joneyd reported:

I went to see Sari. I saw that he was upset. "What happened?" I asked him.

"One of the fairy spirits came to visit me and asked, 'What is shame?' I gave him the answer. That sprite melted away into water, just as you see there."

It is related that Sari had a sister. She asked his permission to sweep his house. Sari did not permit it: "My life isn't worth this," he said. Then, one day, she came into his house. She saw an old woman sweeping the house. "Brother," she said, "you wouldn't give me permission to serve you, and now you've brought in an outsider!?"

"Sister," Sari replied, "don't be concerned. This old woman is the world, who was burning with love for me and whom I rejected. Now she has asked the Real most high for permission to have some share in my life. They've given her a broom to sweep up my cell."

One of the eminent said, "I met many sheikhs. I never met one with as much kindness for the creatures of the world as Sari."

It is related that whenever anyone said hello to him, Sari would answer and make a sour face. They asked him about the secret behind this. Sari replied, "The Prophet (peace and blessing be upon him) has said, 'A hundred mercies descend on anyone who says hello to a Muslim, and ninety on anyone who smiles.' I have made a sour face so those ninety mercies will belong to the other person as well."

Someone may object, "This is giving preference to others. This altruism has a higher status than what the other person did. So, how can it be that Sari desired better for the other than for himself?" We reply, *"We judge by the exterior.*[1] We can judge his making a sour face by appearances; however, we cannot judge whether his preference for others over himself was truthful or not or whether it was sincere or not. In appearance, therefore, he did what was in his power to do.

It is related that he once saw Jacob (peace be upon him) in a dream. "Messenger of the Lord," Sari said, "what is this ruckus you've raised in the world for the sake of Joseph? Since you have the perfect love of his Majesty, stop babbling about Joseph!"

A voice came to his innermost self: "Sari, watch your heart!" and they revealed Joseph to him. Sari cried out and fainted. He lay senseless for thirteen whole days, and when he returned to his senses, they said, "This is the punishment for one who demeans the lovers of our court."

It is related that someone brought some food to Sari (God have mercy on him). He asked, "How many days has it been since you've eaten anything?"

"Five days."

"Your hunger was the hunger of avarice, not the hunger of poverty."

It is related that Sari wished to see one of the friends of God. Then, by chance, he saw someone at the end of the street. "Hello," Sari said, "who are you?"

"He."

"What are you doing?"

"He."

"What are you eating?"

"He."

"By this 'he' you keep saying, do you mean the Lord?"

On hearing this word, the man cried out and died.

Joneyd reported:

One day Sari asked me about love. I said, "One group says it is concord, and another group says it is a wordless sign, and other things have been said as well."

Sari pinched the skin on the back of his hand and pulled. The skin could not be lifted away from the hand. "By his might," Sari said, "if I say that this skin has been withered by his love, it is true." He lost consciousness, and his face became as pale and beautiful as the moon.

It is related that Sari said, "Through love, I reach the point that I am unaware if you strike me with an arrow or a sword. If there is some awareness of it in my heart, it lasts only until it becomes clear what has happened." And Sari said, "When I find out that people are coming to study with me, I pray, 'O Lord, you bestow knowledge on them and distract them, so that I will be of no use to them, for I don't like their coming in my direction.'"

It is related that a man persevered in his striving for thirty years. "How did you achieve this?" they asked.

He replied, "Through Sari's prayer."

"How so?"

"One day I went to his house and knocked on the door. He was in private meditation. He called out, 'Who is it?' I answered, 'It's a friend.' 'If you were a friend,' he replied, 'you would be concerned with him and have no concern for us.' Then he prayed, 'O Lord, so distract him with yourself that he is distracted by no one else.' As soon as he made this prayer, something came down into my breast, and now the affair has reached this point."

It is related that one day Sari was preaching. One of the caliph's boon companions was passing by, Ahmad-e Yazid the Scribe[2] by name. He entered the hall with all possible pomp, surrounded by servants and slaves. "Come on," he said, "let's go to this man's prayer meeting. How long will we go places where one shouldn't go? My heart is taken with this place."

As they entered the meeting hall, Sari said, "In the eighteen thousand worlds, nothing is weaker than man, and none of the Lord's various creatures is more disobedient to his command than man. If he becomes good, he becomes so good that the angels envy his condition, and if he becomes bad, he becomes so bad that demons are ashamed to keep him company. How strange that man so weak should disobey a lord so great!"

These words were an arrow that left Sari's bow and struck Ahmad's soul. He wept so much he fainted. Still weeping, he stood up and returned home. That night, he ate nothing and did not say a word. The next day he walked to the meeting hall, pale and grief-stricken. When the meeting ended, he returned home. The third day he came again, alone and on foot. When the meeting ended, he came up to Sari and said, "Teacher, those words that you have spoken have taken hold of me, and this world has turned cold in my heart. I want to seclude myself from people and leave this world behind. Explain the path of the wayfarers to me."

Sari answered, "Do you want the path of the way or the path of the law? Do you want the path of the masses or the path of the elite?"

"Explain them both."

"The path of the masses is that you observe the five prayers behind the imam and pay the tithe if you have the money. The path of the elite is that you crush all of this world under foot, concern yourself with none of its adornments, and accept nothing that is given to you. These are the two paths."

Ahmad then left the hall and set off for the desert. After a few days passed, an old woman came to see Sari; she had torn out her hair and clawed her face. She said, "Imam of the Muslims, I had a young and lovely little boy. He came to your prayer meeting laughing and strutting and returned weeping and wasting away. It's been several days now since he disappeared, and I don't know where he is. My heart burns in his absence. Tell me what to do!"

She wept and moaned so much that Sari had pity on her. He said, "Don't be downcast. Nothing but good can come from it. When he comes back, I will inform you. He has abandoned this world and left it to its inhabitants and has become a true penitent."

When some time had passed, Ahmad returned one night. Sari told a servant, "Go inform the old woman." Then Sari saw how pale Ahmad had become—he was lean and emaciated, and his cypress-like body was bent double. "Kind teacher," he said, "you have given me comfort and freed me from the darkness. May the Lord bestow ease on you in both worlds!"

They were talking this way when Ahmad's mother and his family arrived, bringing his little boy along with them. When his mother's eyes fell on Ahmad, she saw him as she had never seen him before, his clothes worn out and his hair all disheveled. She threw herself into his arms. His family, too, was standing to one side sobbing, and his little boy was crying. A clamor rose from all of them. Sari started to cry. Ahmad's wife threw the child down at his father's feet. However much they tried to take him back home, it was no use. "Imam of the Muslims," Ahmad cried out, "why did you inform them? They will destroy my work."

"Your mother," Sari answered, "cried and sobbed, and I agreed to her request."

Ahmad was about to leave when his wife said, "You have made me a widow and your child an orphan while you still live. If the child asks for you, what shall I do?"

Ahmad was forced to take the boy in his arms. He said, "Here's what I'll do for the child." He took off the child's fine clothes and wrapped him in a scrap of coarse wool and put a basket in his hands and said, "Go!"

When the boy's mother saw this, she said, "I can't stand this!" and snatched the child away from him.

Ahmad said, "I will release you too, if you wish." He then turned away and set off for the desert.

Several years passed. One night at the hour of the evening prayer, someone came into the hospice and said, "Ahmad has sent me. He says to you, 'My affairs are in dire straits. Help me.'"

The sheikh went with the man. He saw Ahmad in a sepulcher lying on the ground, breathing his last. He was moving his lips. Sari held his ear close to him: Ahmad was saying, *"Let those who work, work for the likes of this"* [37:61]. Sari raised Ahmad's head, brushed away the dirt, and held him in his arms. Ahmad opened his eyes and looked at the sheikh. "Teacher," he said, "you have come in time. My affairs are in dire straits." And he ceased breathing.

Weeping, Sari set off for the city to set Ahmad's affairs in order. He saw a group of people coming out of the city. "Where are you going?" he asked.

"Haven't you heard? Last night, a voice came from the heavens, saying, 'Tell anyone who wishes to pray over the Lord's special friend to go to the Shuniziya Cemetery.'"

Sari's inspiring breath was such that he raised many such disciples, and even if Joneyd alone had been raised by serving him, it is enough.

❧ ❧ ❧

"Young people, work with youthful vigor before you reach old age and grow weak and are left with your shortcomings, as I have been." When Sari spoke these words, no youth had the capacity to perform the acts of devotion that he did.

"For thirty years, I have been asking forgiveness for one time I gave thanks."

"How is that?" they asked.

"The marketplace in Baghdad burned down, but my shop was spared. When they told me about it, I said, 'Praise be to God.' Ashamed that I wished to be better off than my brethren and praised God for the sake of this world, I have been asking forgiveness ever since."

"If one word slips in my daily prayers, there is no making up for it."

"Keep your distance from wealthy neighbors and Qur'an readers working the marketplace and from scholars and princes."

"If anyone wants his faith to remain sound, his heart and body to attain repose, and his sorrow to lessen, tell him to forsake people, for now is the time for seclusion and the age of solitude."

"The entire world is useless bother, except for five things: the bread that staves off death, the water that slakes thirst, the clothing that covers nakedness, the house in which one can live, and the knowledge that one can put into action."

"There is hope for the absolution of any sin that results from lust, but there is no hope for the absolution of any sin that results from pride, because Satan's sin comes from pride, while Adam's lapse comes from lust."

"If someone goes into a heavily wooded garden, and there is a bird perched on every tree, and each bird eloquently sings, "Greetings, O friend of God," you must fear for him, if he does not fear that this is God's deception and a false miracle."

"The sign of a false miracle is blindness to the faults of the self."

"God's deception is talk without action."

"Civility is the translator of the heart."

"The mightiest of strengths is overcoming your self. Anyone who is incapable of disciplining himself will be a thousand times more incapable of disciplining another."

"There are many whose words do not agree with their action, but there are few whose actions agree with their speech."

"A person's blessings will dissipate if he does not recognize their value."

"Anyone who obeys those above him will be obeyed by those below him."

"Your tongue is the translator of your heart, and your face is its mirror: whatever you keep hidden in your heart will appear on your face."

"There are three kinds of hearts. There is the heart that is like a mountain, which nothing can shake from its place. There is the heart that is like a tree, whose roots are strong, but which the wind can sometimes set into motion. And there is the heart that is like a feather, which turns whichever way the wind blows."

"The hearts of the pious hang on the conclusion, and the hearts of the intimates hang on the precedent." In other words, the good deeds of the pious are the evil deeds of the intimates. A good deed becomes an evil because they settle into it; whatever action you settle into becomes a conclusion for you. The pious are those who settle—"*Verily the pious are in bliss*" [82:13]. The pious settle for their blessing, and therefore their hearts hang on the conclusion. As for those who hang on the precedent, the intimates, their eyes are fixed on eternity without beginning. Therefore, they never settle down, since they can never attain eternity without beginning. Since they do not settle for anything, they have to be dragged into paradise in chains.

"Shame and intimacy come to the door of the heart. If there is renunciation and scrupulousness in a heart, they alight. If not, they turn back."

"There are five things that do not dwell in the heart if there is anything else there: fear of the mighty and glorious Lord, hope in the Lord, love of the Lord, shame before the Lord, and intimacy with the Lord."

"The extent of any man's understanding depends on the extent of his heart's nearness to the Lord."

"The most understanding person is one who understands the secrets of the Qur'an and manages his life according to those secrets."

"The most patient person is one who can be patient with the Real."

"On the morrow, communities of believers will be called to their prophets, but the friends will be called to the Lord."

"Longing is the highest station of the realized."

"The realized are those who eat like the sick, who sleep like the snake-bitten, and whose delight is the delight of the drowned."

"In some of the revealed books, it is written that the mighty and glorious Lord has said, 'My servant, when you are overpowered by remembrance of me, I will become your lover.'" And here "love" is used in the sense of affection.

"The realized have the quality of the sun, for they shine over the entire world, and the form of the earth, for they carry the weight of all existing things. They are constituted like water, for hearts live through them, and colored like fire, for the world is illuminated by them."

"Sufism is a word with three senses. The first is that the Sufi's realization does not extinguish the light of scrupulousness. Further, the Sufi does not say anything about the inner realm that violates the outer meaning of the Book. And finally, the Sufi performs his wonders so that he can keep people from committing unlawful acts."

287

"These are the signs of renunciation: There is the self resting from its search for what it desires. There is contentment with anything that drives away hunger. There is satisfaction with whatever covers the private parts. There is the self shunning useless bother and banishing malice from the heart."

"The capital of devout worship is the renunciation of this world, and the capital of gallantry is longing for the next world."

"The delight of renunciants is not sweet because they are preoccupied with themselves. The delight of the realized is sweet because they are distracted from themselves."

"I seized all my acts of renunciation by force. Except for renunciation, I obtained everything else I wanted from him."

"Anyone who adorns himself in people's eyes with what is not within him falls from the remembrance of the Real."

"Mixing often with people comes from a lack of truthfulness."

"Good character is not injuring others and suffering the injuries of others without rancor or retaliation."

"Do not be cut off from any brother on the basis of suspicion and doubt and do not stop associating with him without openly rebuking him."

"The most powerful person is one who overcomes his anger."

"Bidding farewell to sin has three aspects. One is the fear of hell, one is the desire for paradise, and one is shame before the mighty and glorious Lord."

"God's servant is not perfected until he prefers his faith to his lusts."

One day Sari was speaking about patience. A scorpion stung him several times. At last, his listeners asked, "Why didn't you defend yourself?"

"I was ashamed to do so when I was speaking about patience."

In his private devotions, Sari prayed: "My God, your grandeur sundered me from my private devotions, but my recognition of you made me intimate with you." And he prayed: "Had you not commanded, 'Remember me with your tongue,' I would not remember you this way." In other words, "You cannot be contained by my tongue and how can I loose a tongue that is polluted by error in remembrance of you?"

✿ ✿ ✿

Joneyd reported:

Sari said, "I do not want to die in Baghdad because I fear that the earth will not accept me and that I will be disgraced. People have entertained a good opinion of me, and evil may befall them."

When Sari fell ill, I went to visit him. I picked up a fan and was fanning him. He said, "Joneyd, put it down. The fire burns hotter when it is fanned."

"What is happening to you?" I asked.

He replied, *"A slave possessed has no power over anything"* [16:75].

I asked him for a final testament.

He said, "Do not be distracted by the company of people from the company of the Real most high."

"If you had said this earlier," I replied, "I would not have kept company with you either."

With that, Sari attained the refuge of the Real.

✿ 17 ✿
Ahmad-e Khezruya of Balkh

On the mystic way a young gallant, in God's court a pure supplicant, holding sway over the path, trusting in God in truth, guide and magistrate of this folk, Ahmad-e Khezruya of Balkh—God have mercy upon him. He was one of the esteemed sheikhs of Khorasan, perfected on the path and renowned for gallantry. He was a sultan in alliance with God and respected by all the sects. He was famous for his austerities, and his lofty sayings were often quoted. He composed books and had a thousand disciples, every one of whom could walk on the water and fly through the air. In the beginning he was a disciple of Hātem the Deaf, and he studied with Abu Torāb and met Abu Hafs. They asked Abu Hafs, "Whom have you met from this clan?"

"I have met no one," he replied, "whose aspiration was higher or whose spiritual states were truer than Ahmad-e Khezruya's." And Abu Hafs also said, "If it were not for Ahmad, gallantry and chivalry would not be found."

Ahmad used to dress in the fashion of soldiers. Fātema, his wife, was an exemplar on the path. She was one of the daughters of the governor of Balkh. She repented and sent someone to Ahmad, saying, "Ask my father for my hand in marriage."

He did not respond to her proposal. Again she sent someone to him: "Ahmad, I thought you too much of a gentleman to waylay travelers on the path to the Real. Be a leader, not a raider!"

Ahmad then sent someone to ask her father for her hand in marriage. To obtain a blessing, he gave her to Ahmad. Fātema bid farewell to worldly occupations and found comfort in seclusion with Ahmad.

Ahmad then decided to visit Bāyazid. Fātema went with him. When they came before Bāyazid, Fātema removed her veil and spoke with Bāyazid openly and frankly. Ahmad was stunned by what she had done, and jealousy overwhelmed his heart. "Fātema," he said, "how can you behave so boldly with Bāyazid?"

"Because you are intimate with my nature," she answered, "but Bāyazid is intimate with my path. Through you I fulfill my passion, but through him I attain the Lord. The proof of these words is that he does not require my company, but you need me."

Bāyazid was always open and frank with Fātema, until one day his eyes fell upon her hands. She had painted them with henna. "Fātema," Bāyazid asked, "why have you applied henna to your hands?"

"Ah, Bāyazid," she said, "up until now, you haven't noticed my hands or the henna. I could sit unveiled before you. Now that your eyes have fallen on them, it is forbidden for me to remain in your company." And if anyone has doubts on this point, remember that earlier we reported that Bāyazid said, "I asked the mighty and glorious Lord to make women and walls look the same in my eyes." When someone is like this, how can he see a woman?

Ahmad and Fātema then left there for Nishapur. The people of Nishapur were on good terms with Ahmad. When Yahyā ebn Mo'āz of Rey came to Nishapur—he was on his way to Balkh—Ahmad wanted to hold a reception for him. He consulted with Fātema: "What do we need to hold this reception for Yahyā?"

Fātema answered, "Several cows and sheep with all the trimmings and some candles and perfumes. Along with all this, we'll need to slaughter twenty donkeys."

"But why do we need to slaughter donkeys?" Ahmad asked.

"When a noble man comes to a party," she said, "the neighborhood dogs should also share in it." This is how chivalrous Fātema was.

Thus, Bāyazid said, "If anyone who wants to see a man disguised in woman's clothing, tell him to look at Fātema."

It is reported that Ahmad said:

For a long while, I was hostile toward my self. One day a group of men left to fight in the sacred struggle. I felt a great desire to join them, and my self presented me with hadiths that have come down explaining the spiritual rewards of fighting in the struggle. I was amazed. I thought, "The self takes no pleasure in divine service. This is some sort of deceit. It comes from me keeping my self fasting constantly. It can't stand the hunger. It wants to travel so it can break its fast."

To my self, I said, "I won't break the fast on the journey."

"That's fine with me," it replied.

I was amazed. "Perhaps it says that," I thought, "because I make it pray at night. It wants to travel so it can sleep at night and rest." I told my self, "I will keep you awake until daybreak."

"That's fine with me," it replied.

I was amazed and considered the matter: "Perhaps it says that because it is tired of being alone and wants to socialize with people." I told it, "Wherever I alight, I will take you aside and won't sit with other people."

"That's fine with me," it replied.

I was baffled, completely at a loss. I turned in earnest supplication to the Real most high so he would guard me from the self's deception and make me understand. The Real made it acknowledge the truth: "You have been killing me a hundred times every day by opposing my desires, and people are unaware of it. This way, at least I will be killed in the battle once and for all. I will escape, and throughout the world it will be proclaimed: 'Hurrah for Ahmad-e Khezruya! He was killed and attained the rank of martyrdom!'"

"Praise the Lord," I said, "who creates a self who is hypocritical in life and still hypocritical after death! It will accept Islam neither in this world nor in the next. I fancied that it was seeking to serve. I didn't realize that it had tied on the infidel's sash." And I increased my opposition to it.

Ahmad related:

Once I entered the desert on the road to the pilgrimage, putting my trust in God. I had traveled some distance when a camel thorn broke off in my foot. I did not pull it out. "This would invalidate my trust in God," I told myself. I continued on. My foot swelled up, but still I did not pull the thorn out. Limping along, I arrived at Mecca and performed the pilgrimage. I returned from Mecca in the same condition. The whole way, something kept oozing from the wound, and I was in utter agony. Some people saw me like that and extracted the thorn from my foot.

I set out toward Bestām on my injured foot and went to visit Bāyazid. When his eyes fell on me, he smiled and said, "What did you do about that problem inflicted on your foot?"

"I placed my will under his will," I replied.

"You polytheist!" Bāyazid said. "Do you speak of 'my will'? So, in other words, you still exist and have a will? Isn't that polytheism?"

Ahmad said, "Hide the nobility of your poverty." Then he related: "During the month of the fast, a poor man brought a rich man to his house. There was nothing in his house but a dry crust of bread. When the rich man returned home, he sent the poor man a purse of gold. The poor man sent the gold back, saying, 'This is exactly what someone deserves who reveals his innermost self to the likes of you. We won't sell this poverty for the price of both worlds.'"

It is related that a thief went to Ahmad's house. He searched all around but found nothing to steal. He was about to turn away in despair when Ahmad said, "Young man, take a bucket and draw some water. Do your ablutions and busy yourself with prayer until something arrives for me to give you so you won't leave my house empty handed."

The young man did as he was told. At daybreak, a gentleman brought a hundred and fifty dinars as a donation to the sheikh. "Take it," the sheikh said. "It is the recompense for your one night of prayer."

Something came over the thief. His limbs began to tremble, and he started to weep. "I had taken the wrong path," the thief said. "I worked for the mighty and glorious Lord for one night, and he honors me like this!" He repented and turned to the Lord most high. He did not accept the gold and became one of the sheikh's disciples.

It is related that one of the eminent said: "I saw Ahmad-e Khezruya seated in a cart. Angels were pulling the cart through the air by golden chains. 'Sheikh,' I asked, 'where are you going in such a state?'

"'To visit a friend,' he replied.

"'Must you go visiting with such pomp?' I asked.

"'If I don't go and he comes to me, then he is in the position of a visitor, not me,' the sheikh answered."

It is related that Ahmad once entered a Sufi hospice wearing ordinary street clothes, indifferent to Sufi practice. He set about performing the duties of those in pursuit of spiritual reality. Inwardly, the members of the hospice were skeptical of him and said to their sheikh, "He does not belong in a hospice."

Then one day Ahmad came to the wellhead. His bucket fell into the well. The steward berated him. Ahmad approached the sheikh of the hospice and said, "Recite the opening verses of the Qur'an, so the bucket will rise from the well."

The sheikh hesitated: "What sort of request is this?"

"If you won't recite them," Ahmad said, "let me." The sheikh gave his permission. Ahmad recited the verses, and the bucket came up to the top of the well.

When the sheikh saw this, he placed his hat on Ahmad's head and said, "Who are you, young man? The harvest of my reputation turned to straw compared to your seed."

Ahmad said, "Tell your friends not to look on travelers with contempt. As for me, I'm leaving."

It is related that a man came up to Ahmad and said, "I am poor and afflicted. Teach me a way to escape this hardship."

Ahmad said, "Write the name of every possible profession on a piece of paper and put them in a feedbag and bring it to me."

The man wrote down all the professions and brought them to the sheikh. Ahmad put his hand in the feedbag and pulled out a piece of paper. The word "robbery" was written on it. "You must be a robber," Ahmad said.

The man was astonished. "The elder of the age orders me to commit robbery. What choice do I have?" He went and approached some men who waylaid travelers on the road. "I have a taste for this sort of work," he said. "What should I do?"

"This job has one requirement: you do what we say," they replied.

"I will do exactly as you say."

He was with them for several days when one day a caravan came along. They attacked. One of the travelers had a great deal of money. They brought him forward and told their apprentice, "Strike off his head!"

The man hesitated. "This bandit has shed so much blood unjustly," he said to himself. "It would be better to kill him instead of this merchant."

The bandit said to him, "If you've come for a job, this is what you have to do. If not, go find yourself another line of work."

"Since orders must be carried out, then I will carry out the orders of the Real, not those of a thief," the man said. He picked up a sword and separated the chief bandit's head from his body. When the robbers saw what he had done, they fled. The caravan's cargo was left intact, and the merchant was released. He gave the man enough gold and silver to become independently wealthy.

It is related that a dervish was once Ahmad's guest. The sheikh lit seventy candles. "I don't like this at all," the dervish said. "Such formalities have nothing to do with Sufism."

Ahmad said, "Go and extinguish any that have not been lighted for the sake of the Lord."

All night until dawn, the dervish kept pouring water and dirt on the candles. He could not extinguish a single one. The next day Ahmad said to the dervish, "Why are you so surprised? Get up, if you want to see something surprising."

They went to the door of a large church. Christians were sitting inside. When they saw Ahmad, the priest told them to come in. They went inside. A table was set, and the priest told Ahmad, "Eat."

"Friends don't eat with enemies," Ahmad replied.

The priest said, "Tell us about Islam." He accepted Islam, and seventy members of the congregation converted. That night Ahmad saw the Real most high in a dream. "Ahmad," he said, "you lighted seventy candles for our sake. For your sake, we lighted seventy hearts with the radiant light of faith."

∽ ∽ ∽

It is related that Ahmad said, "I saw all creation eating from a single manger like cattle and asses."

Someone asked, "Where were you, sir?"

"I was with them, too. But the difference was that they were eating and laughing and jostling together and did not know. I was eating, too, but I was weeping and downcast—I knew."

"Whoever serves the poor is honored by three things: meekness, civility, and generosity."

"If anyone wants the Lord most high to be with him, tell him to adhere to truthfulness, for *verily God is with the truthful.*"

"Whoever is patient in his patience is truly patient, not someone who is patient and complains. Patience is provision for the afflicted, and acceptance is the rank of the realized."

"This is the reality of realization: you love him with your heart, you remember him with your tongue, and you sever your aspiration from everything besides him."

"Those with the finest character are closest to the Lord."

"The Real does not demand favors from anyone except from the person who demands his blessings."

Ahmad was asked, "What is the mark of love?"
    "Nothing in either of the two worlds seems significant to your heart because your heart is filled with the remembrance of the Real most high. You have no desire but to serve him because you see no grandeur in this world or the next but in serving him. You consider yourself a stranger even in the midst of your family because no one conforms with what you have entered into by serving him."

"Hearts journey to circle around the heavenly throne or around purity."[1]

"Living hearts are houses. Whenever they fill with the Real, the abundance of their light shows in the limbs of the body, and whenever they fill with vanities, the sea of their darkness appears in the limbs of the body."

"There is no sleep heavier than the sleep of negligence, and there is no king more powerful than lust, but if it weren't for the heavy sleep of negligence, lust would never prevail."

"The fullness of servitude is in freedom, and freedom is fulfilled in the fulfillment of servitude."

"You must live in between two contraries, between this world and faith."

"The path is manifest, the truth is clear, and the one who calls you is listening. That is enough. After this, there is no cause for bewilderment but blindness."

Ahmad was asked, "What is the noblest act?"
    "To keep one's innermost self from attending to anything but God."

One day, this verse of the Qur'an was recited in Ahmad's presence: *So flee to God!* [51:50]. He said, "This teaches that the best refuge in our affairs is the mighty and glorious Lord."

Someone said to Ahmad, "Counsel me."

"Slay the self," he said, "so you can make it live."

◌ ◌ ◌

When the hour of his death approached, Ahmad had a debt of seven hundred dinars, all of which he had spent on travelers and the poor. As he slipped into his death throes, his creditors all gathered at his bedside. In these circumstances Ahmad began to speak privately with God: "My God, you are carrying me off, but my life is pledged to them and I am their security. Since you are annulling their contract, appoint someone to stand up for their rights. Then take my life."

As he was saying these words, someone knocked at the door. He said, "Let the sheikh's creditors come outside." They all went outside and received the money they were owed. When the debt was paid off, Ahmad's soul departed—God have mercy upon him.

◌ 18 ◌
Abu Torāb of Nakhshab

Warrior in the ranks of adversity, combatant in the arena of loyalty, realized in honesty and purity, standing alone in the portico of piety, affirming God and the Prophet, the axis of the age, Abu Torāb of Nakhshab—God's mercy be upon him. He was among the gallant sentinels of the way and the detached wayfarers of affliction, a traveler in the desert of poverty and a chieftain of this clan. He was one of the eminent sheikhs of Khorasan; he had a firm step in striving and mindfulness and a sublime breath in allusions and adages.

He stood forty times in the plain of 'Arafāt and for many years had never laid his head on a pillow, except once when he fell asleep one morning in the sacred precincts of Mecca. A group of angels wished to present themselves before him. Abu Torāb said, "I care so much for the forgiving that I do not care for angels."

"Great one," the angels said, "even though this is so, our friends will gloat over our disappointment when they hear that we were not admitted into your presence."

Rezvān[1] then intervened: "It is not possible for this dear man to care for you. Go till the morrow when he takes his place in paradise and sits upon the throne of dominion. Then come and make up the shortcomings in your service to him."

"O Rezvān," Abu Torāb said, "if I should alight in paradise, tell *me* to serve."

Ebn Jallā reports: "I studied with three hundred elders. Four were the greatest among them, and the first of these was Abu Torāb." Ebn Jallā further reports: "Abu Torāb entered Mecca. He was refreshed and smiling. 'Where did you eat?' I asked. He said, 'In Basra, again in Baghdad, and once more here.'"

It is related that when Abu Torāb saw something in his followers that was repugnant to him, he would repent for it himself. He would redouble his striving and say, "This poor man has fallen into affliction due to my ill fortune."

He used to tell his followers, "Each one of you who donned the patched frock was looking for a handout. Each one of you who took up residence in the hospice was looking for a handout. Each one of you who read from the Qur'an was looking for a handout."

One day one of his followers stretched out his hand toward a melon rind, not having eaten anything for three days. Abu Torāb said, "Go! You aren't fit for Sufism. You ought to go to the marketplace!"

Abu Torāb said, "There is a pact between the Real most high and me: whenever I stretch out my hand toward something forbidden, he holds me back from it."

Abu Torāb reported: "No desire has ever laid hold on my heart, except once when I was coming through the desert, and the desire for warm bread and eggs passed over my heart. I happened to lose my way. I came upon a tribe. A group of men were standing up, arguing with one another. When they saw me, they grabbed hold of me and said, 'You have stolen our goods.'"

Someone had come by and stolen their goods. The tribesmen seized the sheikh and pummeled him with two hundred blows. As they beat him, an elder passed by. He saw them beating someone. He approached and recognized Abu Torāb. The elder ripped off his patched frock, began to shout, and said, "This is the greatest sheikh of the path! What is this rudeness, this disrespect that you are inflicting on the chieftain of all the elders of the path?"

The men cried out, regretting what they had done, and asked for Abu Torāb's forgiveness. "Brothers," Abu Torāb said, "by my faith in Islam, no moment has ever passed sweeter than this to me. For years I have wanted to see this self get what it deserves. Now I have achieved this desire."

Then the Sufi elder took Abu Torāb's hand, led him to his hospice, and ordered someone to bring some food. The servant left and brought warm bread and eggs and set them before the sheikh. The sheikh was about to stretch out his hand when he heard a voice say, "Abu Torāb, after all these blows, eat! No desire will pass through your heart without being accompanied by two hundred blows."

It is related that Abu Torāb had several sons, and in his time, a man-eating wolf was prowling out in the open. It tore several of his sons to pieces. One day, Abu Torāb was seated on his prayer rug. The wolf stalked him. He was warned of this but remained just as he was. The wolf saw him. It turned away and left.

It is related that once Abu Torāb was going through the desert with his disciples. His followers grew thirsty and wished to perform their ablutions. They appealed to the sheikh. He drew a line, and water bubbled up. They drank and performed their ablutions.

Abu'l-'Abbās[2] used to say: "I was with Abu Torāb in the desert. One of our friends said to me, 'I'm thirsty.' Abu Torāb stamped his foot against the earth: a spring of water appeared. 'But I long to drink from a glass,' the disciple said. Abu Torāb struck his hand against the earth: a goblet made of the finest clear crystal rose from the earth. The disciple drank from it and gave water to our friends. The goblet was with us as far as Mecca."

Abu Torāb asked Abu'l-'Abbās, "What do your companions say about the actions that the Real most high performs through his friends as wonders?"

Abu'l-'Abbās answered, "I have met only a few who have faith in them."

299

Abu Torāb said, "Anyone who does not have faith in them is an unbeliever."

Once in the desert his disciples said, "There's no substitute for food."

The sheikh said, "There's no substitute for the One who has no substitute."

Abu Torāb related:

One night I was going through the desert alone, a night as dark as it could be. All of a sudden, a black man came up to me, as tall as a minaret. I was afraid. "Are you a spirit or a man?" I asked.

He asked, "Are you a Muslim or an infidel?"

"A Muslim," I said.

"Is a Muslim afraid of anything besides the mighty and glorious Lord?"

My heart opened up to me, and I realized that he had been sent from the unseen. I submitted, and fear left my heart.

He further related:

I saw a young man in the desert without provisions or mount. I thought, "If certainty does not go with him, he will perish." Then I said, "Young man, do you travel through a place like this without provisions?"

"Old man," he replied, "raise your head and tell me if you see anyone but the Lord."

"Go now wherever you wish," I replied.

∽ ∽ ∽

"For twenty years," Abu Torāb said, "I did not take anything from anyone and I did not give anything to anyone."

"How so?"

"If I took anything, I took it from him, and if I did not take it, I did not take it from him."

"One day, I was presented with some food. I refused it. As a result of that ill-omened refusal, I was left hungry for fourteen days."

"I do not know of anything more harmful to a disciple than traveling in obedience to the self. If not for the depravity of vain travels, no depravity finds its way into a disciple."

"The Real most high has decreed that you should refrain from mortal sins, and there are no mortal sins except depraved pretensions and vain allusions. This has been taken to include meaningless expressions and hollow words without reality." Then, he said, *"God most high says: 'Devils inspire their allies'"* [6:121].

"No one ever attains satisfaction in the mighty and glorious Lord if this world amounts to even a mote of dust in his heart."

"When God's servant is honest, he finds a sweetness in good works even before he does them, and if he is sincere in performing them, he finds a sweetness in them even as he acts."

"You love three things, and these three things do not belong to you. You love the self, and the self belongs to mighty and glorious Lord. You love the spirit, and the spirit belongs to the Lord. You love riches, and riches belong to the Lord. You seek two things and do not obtain them: happiness and ease. Both these will be found in paradise."

"There are seventeen stages that bring about union with the Real. The lowest of these is having one's prayers answered, and the highest of them is truly trusting in the Lord."

"Trust in God is throwing yourself into the sea of servitude and binding your heart to the Lord: If he gives, you give thanks, and if he withholds, you bear it patiently."

"Nothing darkens the realized, and all darknesses become luminous to them."

"Contentment is taking nutriment from the Lord most high."

"No form of devotion is more profitable than rectifying one's intuitions."

"The true heart among hearts is the one that lives in the light of under-standing through the Lord most high."

"Watch over your thoughts because this is the first step in everything. When someone makes his thoughts right, everything that comes to him later, whether actions or states, will turn out right."

"In every age, the Real most high makes the learned speak in accor-dance with the actions of the people of the age."

"The reality of freedom from want is that you can do without anyone like you, and the reality of destitution is that you need someone like you."

It is related that Abu Torāb was asked, "Do you need us?"

The sheikh answered, "How should I need you or anyone like you when I don't even need the mighty and glorious Lord?" In other words, "I am at the stage of acceptance. What use is need to the accepting?"

"The dervish is one whose food is what he receives, whose clothing is what covers his nakedness, and whose dwelling is where he is."

⁂ ⁂ ⁂

It is related that Abu Torāb died in the desert near Basra. After several years a group of people came upon him. They found him standing up, facing Mecca. His body was desiccated; there was a small water bag set before him, and he was grasping his staff. No wild beast had come near him.

✺ 19 ✺
Shāh-e Shojā' of Kerman

The sharp-eyed seer, the royal falcon of form and behavior, a knower honest and resolute, pure and without attribute, the light of the spiritual lamp, Shāh-e Shojā' of Kerman—God's mercy be upon him. He was the eminent man of the age and honored in his time. He was one of the noble vagabonds on the path and a traveler on the way of truth. He had clairvoyance, a clairvoyance that, of course, did not err. He was the descendant of kings and an author; he composed a book entitled *The Mirror of Sages*. He met many sheikhs, such as Abu Torāb, Yahyā ebn Mo'āz, and others. He used to wear a full-length, formal robe. When Shāh-e Shojā' came to Nishapur and Abu Hafs the Blacksmith saw him, Abu Hafs arose in all his grandeur and came up to him and said, "I have found in a robe what I was looking for in a woolen cloak."

It is related that Shāh-e Shojā' did not sleep for forty years. He used to rub salt in his eyes, and they had become like two goblets of blood. After forty years, one night he fell asleep. He saw the most glorious Lord in a dream and said, "O Lord, I sought you in wakefulness, but I found you in sleep."

"Shāh, you found us in sleep because of your wakefulness. If not for those years of wakefulness, you would have not had such a dream."

After that, everywhere he went, when people saw him, Shāh-e Shojā' would set down a pillow and go to sleep. He used to say, "I may have such a dream once again." He had fallen in love with his dream and would say, "I would not give one iota of this dream for all the wakefulness in the world."

It is related that Shāh-e Shojā' had a son on whose chest the word "Allāh" had been written in fine, delicate hair. Succumbing to his youthfulness, he gave himself over to amusement and learned to play the lute. He had a fine voice. He used to play the lute and sing and weep.

One night he came outside, strumming his lute and singing. He wandered down to a certain neighborhood. A newly wed wife got up from her husband's side and came to gaze at him. The man woke up and did not see his wife. He got up and saw what was going on. He called out, "Boy, hasn't the time come yet to repent?"

These words hit home, and the boy cried, "It has come! It has come!" He tore his clothes, broke his lute, performed ablutions, and retired to his house. The word that he had on his chest became what it named and settled into his heart. For forty days he did not leave the house and ate nothing. Then he came out and departed.

His father said, "What we were given in forty years, he was given in forty days."

It is related that Shāh-e Shojā' had a daughter, and the royal family of Kerman asked for her hand in marriage. He asked for three days to consider the matter, and during those three days, he wandered through the mosques, until he saw a poor man performing his prayers. Shāh-e Shojā' waited for him to finish his prayers and asked, "Do you have a wife?"

"No," the poor man replied.

"Would you like one who knows how to read the Qur'an?"

"Who would give me such a wife? I have only three dirhams."

"I will give you my own daughter for the three dirhams that you have," Shāh-e Shojā' said. "Spend one on bread, one on sweets, one on perfume, and tie the marriage knot."

The dervish did as he was told, and that very night Shāh-e Shojā' sent his daughter to the poor man's house. When the girl entered the house, she saw a dry crust of bread on top of a water jug. "What is this bread?" she asked.

"It was left over from last night," he said, "and I put it aside for tonight." The girl prepared to leave. "I knew the daughter of Shāh-e Shojā' could not live with me."

"Young man," the girl said, "I am not going because of your poverty. I am going because of the weakness of your faith and certainty. You set aside a piece of bread from last night—you have no trust in the Provider. But I am surprised at my father. For twenty years, he kept me at home and said, 'I will give you to a pious man,' and now he gives me to someone who has no trust in the mighty and glorious Lord."

"Is there any way I can apologize for this sin?" the poor man asked.

"There is one apology—either I stay in this house or the crust of bread does."

It is related that Abu Hafs wrote a letter to Shāh-e Shojā'. It read: "I examined my self and my works and my faults. Then I gave up hope. Yours truly."

Shāh-e Shojā' wrote back: "I made your letter into a mirror for my heart. If I can sincerely give up hope in my self, my hope in the Lord will be purified. And if my hope in the Lord is purified, my fear of the Lord will be purified. Thus, let me give up hope in my self. If I give up hope in my self, then I can remember the mighty and glorious Lord. If I remember the Lord, the Lord will remember me. If the Lord remembers me, I will be saved from creatures and joined to all that is beloved."

It is related that there was friendship between Shāh-e Shojāʿ and Yahyā ebn Moʿāz. They both came to live in the same city, but Shāh did not attend Yahyā's prayer meetings. "Why don't you come?" they asked.

"This is a pious act."

They insisted until one day Shāh-e Shojāʿ attended Yahyā's prayer meeting. He sat in a corner, so Yahyā did not know he was there. The words just would not come to Yahyā. "Someone is present here," he said, "who is beyond our preaching."

"I told you that it wasn't advisable for me to come," Shāh said.

✥ ✥ ✥

"Superior people have superiority over everyone until they notice their own superiority. When they notice it, they are no longer superior. Friends of God have their special relationship until they notice it. When they notice it, they are no longer his friends."

"Poverty is a secret that the Real shares with his servant. When the servant keeps his poverty hidden, he is safe. When he reveals it, he loses even the name of poverty."

"There are three signs of poverty. The first is that the values of this world leave your heart, so that silver and gold are like dirt to you, and whenever silver and gold fall into your hands, you brush off your hands to be rid of them, just as you would with dirt. The second is that people's perceptions fall from your heart, so that praise and blame are one and the same to you, and you are neither enlarged by praise nor diminished by blame. The third is that desire's hold on your heart falls away, so that you are as happy with hunger, thirst, and abstinence as the lustful are with eating their fill and satisfying their desires. So, if you are this way, pursue the disciples' path. If you are not, why bother with these words?"

"Fearfulness is constant sorrow."

"Fear is necessary for recognizing that you have come up short in doing right by the Lord most high."

"The sign of good character is that you refrain from harming others and suffer the harm that others cause you."

"The mark of mindfulness is scrupulousness. The sign of scrupulousness is standing back from anything questionable."

"Lovers dropped dead in love. This is because when they achieved a moment of union, they claimed lordship on a whim."

"The sign of salvation is beauty in the externals."

"There are three signs of patience: forsaking complaint, holding true to acceptance, and submitting to fate with a happy heart."

"If anyone keeps his eyes from forbidden things and his body from lustful desires, if he cultivates his inner being with constant contemplation, if he adorns his outer being by following prophetic custom and accustoms himself to eating what is ritually pure, his clairvoyance will not err."

It is related that one day Shāh-e Shojā' said to his friends, "Stay away from lying, treachery, and backbiting. Do anything else you wish."

"Abandon this world, and you have repented. Abandon the passions of the self—you have attained what you desire."

They asked him, "How are you at night?"
    "There's no need to ask a bird skewered on a spit turning over a fire, 'How are you?'"

∽ ∽ ∽

It is related that Khwāja 'Ali Sirgāni,[1] who was giving away food at Shāh-e Shojā's tomb, set out some food one day and said, "O Lord, send me a guest." Out of nowhere, a dog came along. Khwāja 'Ali yelled at it until it went away. From the top of the Shāh's tomb, a voice called out: "You ask for a guest. When I send one, do you turn it away?"

Khwāja 'Ali immediately got up and ran out and wandered through the neighborhoods of town. He did not see the dog. He went into the desert and saw it sleeping off by itself. He set the food that he had before the dog. It paid no attention, and Khwāja 'Ali was ashamed. He stood up to ask forgiveness, removed his turban, and said, "I repent."

The dog spoke up, "Good for you, Khwāja 'Ali! You ask for a guest, and when it comes, you drive it away! You need eyes. If not for Shāh-e Shojā', you would have really seen something!"

∽ 20 ∽
Yusof ebn al-Hoseyn

Secluded in the constant Presence, proof of the power of *"they do not fear the reproach of fault finders"* [5:57], the hidden sun, the water of life in the darkness, the royal falcon of the two worlds, the axis of his time, Yusof ebn al-Hoseyn—God's mercy be upon him. He was among the ancient sheikhs and friends of God, learned in the various external and inner sciences. He had a language to explain spiritual knowledge and secrets and was accepted in the company of the great sheikhs: an associate of Abu Torāb, a companion of Abu Sa'id the Bootmaker, and the disciple of Zu'n-Nun of Egypt. He lived a long life and constantly exerted all earnestness in this affair. He had a firm step in diligent service and a lofty aspiration.

This was the beginning of his spiritual states: When the daughter of an Arab emir caught sight of him, she fell madly in love, for he was extremely handsome. The girl sought an opportune moment and threw herself at him. Yusof trembled and fled from her, moving to a more distant tribe. He did not go to bed that night. He sat with his head bent to his knees all night and dozed off. He saw a place the likes of which he

307

had not seen before and a group of people gathered together dressed in green. Someone was sitting on a throne like a king. Yusof yearned to know who they were. He rushed into their midst. They made way for him and honored him. "Who are you?" Yusof asked.

"We are angels," they answered, "and the person sitting on the throne is the Prophet Joseph (peace and blessing be upon him). He has come to pay a visit on his namesake Yusof ebn al-Hoseyn—Joseph the son of Hoseyn."

Yusof related:

I was overcome with tears as I thought, "Who am I that the Prophet of the Lord should come to ask after me?" As I was thinking this, Joseph (peace be upon him) stepped down from the throne. He embraced me and set me on the throne. "O Prophet of God," I said, "who am I that you should show me this kindness?"

He said, "The moment that that beautiful girl threw herself at you, and you entrusted yourself to the Real most high and sought refuge in him, the Real most high put you on display and showed you to the angels and me. 'Look, Joseph,' he said, 'you are the Yusof who had intentions toward Zoleykhā until you fended her off.[1] He is the Yusof who had no intentions toward the daughter of the Arab king and fled.' He sent me to visit you with these angels and gave good tidings that you are among the elect of the Real." Joseph continued, "In each age there is a sign, and in this age, the sign is Zu'n-Nun of Egypt. He knows the greatest name of God. Go to see him."

When Yusof awoke, his whole being was inflamed. Yearning overwhelmed him, and he set out for Egypt. He was burning with desire for the great name of the Real most high. When he reached Zu'n-Nun's mosque, Yusof greeted him and sat down. "Peace be upon you," Zu'n-Nun said. For one year Yusof sat in a corner of the mosque; he did not have the nerve to ask Zu'n-Nun anything. After a year, Zu'n-Nun asked, "Where does this young man come from?"

"From Rey," Yusof answered.

For another year, Zu'n-Nun said nothing to him, and Yusof still stayed in the corner of the mosque. When another year had passed, Zu'n-Nun said, "What business has brought this young man here?"

"Visiting you," Yusof said.

Zu'n-Nun then asked, "Is there anything you need?"

"I have come so you may teach me the greatest name."

For another year, Zu'n-Nun said nothing. Then he gave Yusof a wooden bowl covered with a lid and said, "Cross the Nile. There is a sheikh in a certain place. Give this cup to him and memorize whatever he tells you."

Yusof picked up the cup and set out. When he had gone part of the way, he felt a temptation: "What's in this cup? It's moving!" He took the lid off the cup. A mouse jumped out and ran away. Yusof was stunned. "Where should I go now? Should I go to the sheikh or back to Zu'n-Nun?"

In the end, he went to see the sheikh with the empty cup. When the sheikh saw him, he smiled and asked, "Have you asked Zu'n-Nun for the great name of the Lord most high?"

"Yes," Yusof replied.

"Zu'n-Nun saw your impatience. He gave you a mouse. Good God, you can't hold onto a mouse. How are you going to hold onto the greatest name?"

Yusof was ashamed and came to Zu'n-Nun's mosque. "Seven times last night," Zu'n-Nun said, "I asked the Real most high to let me teach you the greatest name. He would not allow it. That is to say, it is not yet time. Then the Real most high said, 'Test him with a mouse.' When I tested you, this is how it turned out. Now return to your city until the time comes."

Yusof said, "Give me a parting word of advice."

"Here's my parting advice: I counsel you on three matters, one major, one minor, and one middling. The major one is to forget everything you have read and blot out everything you have written, so the veil will be lifted."

"I cannot do this."

"The middling one is to forget me and not speak my name to anyone, by saying, for example, 'My elder has spoken thus and my sheikh has ordered such.' This is all self-praise."

"I cannot do this either."

"My minor piece of advice is that you preach to the people and call them to God."

"This I can do, God willing . . ."

"But only on the condition that you do not think that you play any part in it."

"I will do so," Yusof said.

Yusof then returned to Rey. He was one of the nobles of the city, and the populace turned out to welcome him. When he began to preach, he expounded the spiritual realities. The externalists rose against him in hostility, for at that time formal learning was the only sort of religious science there was. He also invited public blame by his way of life. Finally, it reached the point that no one came to his prayer meetings. One day he came in to preach and saw no one present. He was about to leave when an old woman called out, "Didn't you swear to Zu'n-Nun that when you preach, you would speak for the sake of the Lord and would not think that creatures play any part in it?"

When he heard this, Yusof was stunned and began to preach. He spent fifty years doing this, whether anyone was present or not.

Ebrāhim-e Khavvās was his disciple, and his spiritual state grew strong. Blessed by following Yusof, Ebrāhim reached the point that he would cross the desert without mount or provisions.

Ebrāhim related:

One night, I heard a voice say, "Go and tell Yusof ebn al-Hoseyn, 'You are among the exiles.'" These words hit me hard—it would have been easier for me to be crushed by a mountain than to say this to him. The next night I heard the same voice. It went on like this for three nights. I would hear the same voice say, "Tell him, 'You are among the exiles.' If you don't tell him, you will be struck by such a blow that you won't be able to get up."

I got up and went to the mosque in deep sorrow. I saw Yusof sitting in the prayer niche. When he saw me, he asked, "Do you know any verses of poetry by heart?" I told him I did. I recalled an Arabic verse and recited it. He was enraptured. He got up and stood there a long while. Tears flowed from his eyes until they were mixed with blood. Then he turned to me and said, "They have been reciting the Qur'an before me since dawn, and not a single teardrop came to my eyes. You recite one verse, and such a state comes over me that a flood flows from my eyes. Truly people say, 'He is an atheist,' and truly the words 'He is among the exiles' come from God's presence. Anyone who is moved by a verse of poetry and remains unmoved by the Qur'an has been exiled."

Ebrāhim continued:

I was stunned by his affair, and my faith was weakened. I was afraid. I got up and set out for the desert. By chance, I fell in with

Khezr. He said, "Yusof ebn al-Hoseyn has been wounded by the Real, but his place is on the summit of the highest heaven. You must walk so firmly in the path of the Real that your place is still on the summit of the highest heaven even if the hand of rejection is placed upon your forehead. On this path, if someone falls from the kingship, he need not fall from the vizierate."

It is related that 'Abd al-Vāhed ebn Zeyd[2] was a thoroughly unruly reprobate. His parents were constantly running after him because he was so very wicked. He happened to pass by Yusof ebn al-Hoseyn's prayer meeting. Yusof was speaking these words: "The Real most high calls his disobedient servant through his grace, like a person who needs someone." 'Abd al-Vāhed cried out and collapsed. He got up and went to the graveyard and stayed there for three whole days. On the first night, Yusof ebn al-Hoseyn dreamt he heard someone say, "Help this repentant youth." Yusof roamed around until he found 'Abd al-Vāhed in the graveyard. He rested his head in his lap. 'Abd al-Vāhed opened his eyes and said, "It's been three whole days since they sent you, and you come only now?"

It is related that a merchant in Nishapur had a Turkish slave girl whom he had purchased for a thousand dinars. There was someone who owed him money in another city. The merchant was about to hurry off and collect his money, but there was no one in Nishapur whom he trusted enough to leave her with. He came to see Abu 'Osmān of Hira and told him the story. Abu 'Osmān said, "I will not take her."

The merchant pleaded with him at length and said, "Allow her into your harem, and I will return as soon as possible." In short, Abu 'Osmān agreed, and the merchant departed.

Unwittingly, Abu 'Osmān glanced at the slave girl and fell so deeply in love with her that he could not stand it. He did not know what to do. He got up and went to see his sheikh, Abu Hafs the Blacksmith. Abu Hafs told him, "You must go to Rey to see Yusof ebn al-Hoseyn."

Abu 'Osmān set out immediately for western Iran. When he reached Rey, he asked for the residence of Yusof ebn al-Hoseyn. The people asked, "What do you want with that atheist anarchist? You seem to be a pious man. Talking to him can only bring you harm." They said many things of this sort. Abu 'Osmān regretted coming and turned back.

When he reached Nishapur, Abu Hafs asked, "Did you see Yusof ebn al-Hoseyn?"

"No."

"Why not?"

Abu 'Osmān told him what happened and said, "I heard that he was like this and that. I did not go to see him and returned here."

Abu Hafs said, "Go back and see him!"

Abu 'Osmān turned around and came back to Rey and asked for Yusof's house. They said a hundred times worse than they had said before. Abu 'Osmān kept saying "It's urgent for me to see him" until they showed him the way. When he reached the door of Yusof's house, he saw an old man sitting there with light pouring from his face. Before him stood a handsome, beardless boy and a cup and decanter. Abu 'Osmān entered, said hello, and sat down. Sheikh Yusof began to speak and spoke such lofty words that Abu 'Osmān was stunned. He said, "For God's sake, sir, with such words and such contemplation, how is it that you have wine and a beardless servant boy?"

Yusof replied, "This beardless boy is my son, and I am teaching him the Qur'an. A decanter had fallen into this trash heap. I picked it up and washed it out well and filled it with water so that anyone who wants a drink can have one. I don't own a water jug."

"For God's sake, why do you do things to make people talk the way they do?"

"I do them so no one will trust me enough to send a Turkish slave girl to my house," Yusof replied.

When Abu 'Osmān heard this, he fell at the sheikh's feet and realized that whoever is most famous for piety has a streak of the blameworthy in his affairs.

It is related that there was a visible redness and weakness in Yusof's eyes due to his long periods of sleeplessness. They asked Ebrāhim-e Khavvās, "How does he worship?"

"When he completes the night prayer," Ebrāhim said, "he stands on his feet until daybreak. He neither bows down nor prostrates himself."

Then they asked Yusof, "Is standing up until daybreak any way to worship?"

"I can easily perform the obligatory prayers," he answered, "but when I want to perform the night prayer and I'm standing up like this, it is not possible for me to bow down and say, 'God is Great,' because of his majesty. All of a sudden, something comes over me and keeps me like this until dawn. When dawn breaks, I perform the obligatory prayer."

It is related that he once wrote a letter to Joneyd: "May the Lord most high not make you taste the food of your self, for if he makes you taste it, you will see nothing afterward."

✑ ✑ ✑

"Each people has its choicest members, given in trust by the mighty and glorious Lord, whom he keeps hidden from men. If they exist among this people, they are the Sufis."

"For Sufis, disaster lies in talking to children, socializing with opponents, and being friends with women."

"The people who are aware that the mighty and glorious Lord is watching them are ashamed before the gaze of the Real, fearing lest they should revere anything beside that which he has commanded. Anyone who truly remembers the mighty and glorious Lord forgets the remembrance of anything else in recalling him. And if anyone forgets the remembrance of things in the remembrance of the Real, everything watches over him, because for him the Lord most high takes the place of everything."

"The allusive teaching of creation is equal to one's perception of creation, and one's perception of creation is equal to one's knowledge of creation, and one's knowledge of creation is equal to one's love of creation, and there is no state dearer to the Lord most high than a servant's love for the Lord."

They asked about love. He said, "If anyone loves the Lord, his humility and lowliness will be stronger, and his compassion and counsel for the Lord's people will be greater."

313

"There are two signs of the honest man: he loves solitude and conceals his devotion."

"This is the unification of the elite: In their innermost self and heart, in their conscience, they imagine that they are standing in his presence. In his firmness and power and in the seas of his unity, he manages their affairs. They pass away from themselves and are not aware of it. Now that they exist, they are just as they were before in carrying out his decree."

"Whoever falls into the sea of detachment is thirstier every day and is never sated because he thirsts for the truth, and it dwells nowhere but in the Real."

"The dearest thing in this world is sincerity, and however much I strive to eliminate hypocrisy from my heart, it grows from my heart in another guise."

"If I see the Lord most high with all my sins, I prefer that to seeing an iota of affectation in myself."

"Among the signs of renunciation is that it does not stop striving until it does away with its own existence."

"The acme of worship is when you are his servant in all things."

"Whoever knows him in his mind worships him in his heart."

"The most contemptible of people are the covetous, just as the noblest of them are the honest poor."

∾   ∾   ∾

When his death drew near, Yusof ebn al-Hoseyn said, "O Lord, you know that I have counseled people in word and have counseled my self in deed. Forgive the treachery of my self in return for my counsel to your creatures."

After his death, Yusof was seen in a dream. "What did the mighty and glorious Lord do with you?" they asked.

"He forgave," Yusof answered.

"Why?"

"As a blessing, for I never mixed jest and earnestness."

∞ 21 ∞
Abu Hafs-e Haddād, the Blacksmith

The exemplar of true believers, perfection's center, the honest wor-shiper, the renunciant lover, the sultan of the four pillars,[1] the axis of the world, Abu Hafs-e Haddād the Blacksmith—God's mercy be upon him. He was the absolute king of the sheikhs and the deserving caliph of the Real. He was among the dignitaries of this clan, and no one was as eminent as he. In his time he was unmatched in austerities, wonder working, humanity, and gallantry. He was without peer in unveiling and exposition, and the mighty and glorious Lord was his teacher and inspiration without intermediary. He was the guide of Abu 'Osmān of Hira. Shāh-e Shojā' came from Kerman to visit him and accompanied him to Baghdad to visit the sheikhs.

This is how Abu Hafs began: He fell so deeply in love with a serving girl that he could find no rest. He was told that there was a Jewish sor-cerer in Nishapur who would arrange this affair for him. Abu Hafs went to see him and told him his story. The sorcerer said, "For forty days, you must not pray or worship or do any good deed or utter the name of the Lord, so that I can conjure and help you reach your goal by magic."

For forty days Abu Hafs did as instructed. Then the sorcerer made a talisman, but it did not have the desired effect. "There's no doubt—you must have done something," the Jew said. "Otherwise, I'm sure that it would have had the intended result."

Abu Hafs said, "I didn't do anything but kick aside a stone that was on the road that I was coming down, so no one would trip over it."

The sorcerer said, "Do not vex the Lord whose commandments you neglected for forty days, but who, in his generosity, did not fail to take such trouble for you!"

At these words, a fire blazed up in Abu Hafs's heart, a fire so strong that he repented at the hands of the Jew. He continued to work as a blacksmith and kept his revelation hidden. He earned one dinar a day and gave it to the poor: at night, he would put the dinar in the key-hole of a widow's door, so no one would know about it. At the hour of the night prayer, he would go begging and break fast with what he earned this way. For a time, he gathered scraps at a pool where people cleaned leeks and made a meal of them. He lived this way for a while.

One day a blind man was passing through the marketplace and reciting this verse: *In the name of God the merciful and compassionate: and something will appear to them from God that they did not reckon with* [39:47]. Abu Hafs's heart was absorbed in this verse, and something came over him. He was no longer aware of himself and instead of the tongs, he stuck his hand in the forge and pulled out a piece of molten iron. He set it on the anvil, and his apprentices were striking it with their hammers. They looked closely and saw that he was turning the iron with his hand. "Master," they shouted, "what are you doing?"

Abu Hafs yelled back at the apprentices, "Strike!"

"Master, where shall we strike? The iron is beaten clean."

Abu Hafs then came to his senses. He saw the red-hot iron in his hand and heard these words: "When it's beaten clean, where shall we strike?" He cried out and threw the iron from his hand. He gave the shop over to looters. "For some time," he said, "we wanted to escape this job by effort and could not. Then these words attacked and stole us from ourselves. Although I had given up the job, it did no good until the job gave up me." Then he began to perform austerities and took up a life of seclusion and contemplation.

Thus it is related that in his neighborhood, people were listening to lectures on hadith. They asked Abu Hafs, "Why don't you come to listen to hadiths?"

He replied, "For thirty years I have tried to do justice to just one hadith, but I haven't been able to. How can I listen to another?"

"Which hadith is that?"

"This one: The Prophet (peace and blessing be upon him) said, 'Part of the soundness of a person's faith in Islam is that he gives up that which is of no use to him.'"

It is related that Abu Hafs had gone to the desert with his friends and preached to them until they were enraptured. A gazelle came down from the mountains and laid its head in Abu Hafs's lap. Abu Hafs slapped himself in the face and cried out. The gazelle ran off. The sheikh came to his senses. His companions asked, "What was that?"

"When we were enraptured," he said, "it occurred to me how nice it would be if there were a sheep, so we could prepare roast lamb and my friends would not disperse tonight. When this occurred to me, the gazelle came."

His disciples said, "Sheikh, when a person is on such terms with the Real, what sense does it make for him to cry out and slap himself?"

"Don't you know that having your desire laid in your lap is the same as being thrown out the door? If the Lord most high had wanted to do good by Pharaoh, he would not have made the River Nile flow at his command."

It is related that whenever Abu Hafs would get angry, he would preach about good character until his anger settled down. Then he would move on to another topic.

It is related that one day Abu Hafs was walking along. He saw someone weeping and perplexed and asked, "What has happened to you?"

The man said, "I had a donkey, and it has gone astray. I owned nothing else."

The sheikh stopped and said, "By your might, I shall not take another step until his donkey comes back to him."

The donkey immediately came into view.

Abu 'Osmān of Hira relates:

One day I was going to see Abu Hafs. I saw several raisins laid out in front of him. I picked one up and put it in my mouth. Abu Hafs grabbed my throat and said, "You traitor! What reason did you have for eating my raisin?"

"I know your heart and I trust you," I said. "I also know that you give freely of whatever you have."

He said, "You ignoramus! I do not trust my own heart. How can you trust it? By the purity of the Real, according to whose wishes I have lived a lifetime, I do not know what will come from me. How can another know what's inside of someone who doesn't know what's inside of himself?"

Abu 'Osmān of Hira also relates:

I was with Abu Hafs at the home of Abu Bakr-e Hanafiya,[2] and a group of our companions were there, reminiscing about a certain dervish. "Would that he were here!" I said.

The sheikh said, "If there were a piece of paper, I would write a note for him to come."

"Here's a piece of paper," I said.

"The owner of the house has gone to the market," Abu Hafs objected. "If he has died on the way and this piece of paper has become part of this legacy, it is not proper to write anything on it."

Abu 'Osmān of Hira relates:

I told Abu Hafs, "It has become clear that I should lecture publicly."

"What has brought you to this conclusion?" he asked.

"Compassion for the people," I replied.

"How far does your compassion for people go?"

"It goes as far as this: If the Lord most high sends me to hell and torments me in place of all the sinners, I consider it just."

"If that is so," Abu Hafs said, "then in the name of God, go ahead. But when you preach, first give counsel to your own heart and body. Moreover, do not let the gathering of people delude you. They observe your outward appearance, while the Lord most high sees your inner being."

I then stepped up on the dais. Abu Hafs sat hidden in a corner. When the meeting concluded, a beggar stood up and asked for a shirt. I immediately gave my shirt to him. "Come down from the pulpit, you liar!" Abu Hafs shouted.

"What lie have I told?" I asked.

"You claimed that you have more compassion for the people than for yourself. You took precedence in giving alms so that you would have the honor that belongs to those who come first. You wanted the best for yourself. If your claim were true, you would have paused a little to let another have the honor of being first. You are thus a liar, and the pulpit is no place for liars."

It is related that one day Abu Hafs was walking through the marketplace. A Jew came up to him. The sheikh collapsed unconscious on the spot. When he came to, people asked him what happened. He said, "I saw a man wearing the clothes of justice and saw myself wearing the clothes of kindness. I feared lest he be dressed in the clothes of kindness that have been stripped from me and I be dressed in the clothes of justice that have been stripped from him."

Abu Hafs said, "This is how I was for thirty years: I perceived that the Lord most high was angry whenever he looked at me." Glory be to God! What burning fear he must have had in that state!

It is related that Abu Hafs decided to go on the pilgrimage. He was a common man and did not know any Arabic. When he reached Baghdad, his disciples said to one another, "It would be a great disgrace if the chief sheikh of Khorasan had to use a translator to understand their language."

Joneyd sent his disciples to welcome Abu Hafs. Abu Hafs knew what his followers were thinking. He immediately began to speak Arabic with such fluency that the people of Baghdad were left amazed at his eloquence. A group of elders gathered before him and asked him about gallantry. Abu Hafs said, "You have the words. You speak."

Joneyd said, "To me, gallantry is not seeing gallantry in yourself or the things you have done. You do not attribute it to yourself, saying, 'Look at what I've done!'"

"That's good," Abu Hafs said, "but to me gallantry is doing justice and not seeking justice."

"Act on this, my followers!" Joneyd said.

Abu Hafs said, "Words won't make it come out right."

When Joneyd heard this, he said, "Get up, friends, for Abu Hafs has exceeded Adam and all his descendants in gallantry." In other words, if gallantry is what he says, then Abu Hafs has run circles around all of Adam's offspring.

Abu Hafs held his followers to high standards of respect and civility. No disciple had the nerve to sit in front of him and did not dare to look him in the face or to sit down without his permission. Abu Hafs used to sit there like a sultan. "He has taught his followers the manner of kings," Joneyd remarked.

"You see no more than the title of a book," Abu Hafs said. "Still, from the title, one can judge the soundness of what the book contains." Then he said, "Order them to prepare a pot of cumin stew and halwa."

Joneyd ordered a disciple to prepare them. When they brought them, Abu Hafs said, "Set them on the head of a porter so he can carry them until he is exhausted. There, he will reach the door of a house. Have him call out and give them to whoever comes outside."

The porter did as he was told and walked until he was exhausted. He set the food in front of the door of a house and called out. The owner of the house said, "If you have brought cumin stew and halwa, come in."

The porter reported, "I was amazed. I asked him, 'What is going on here? How did you know that I had brought cumin stew and halwa?' He said, 'During my private devotions last night, it occurred to me that my children had been asking me for these dishes for some time. I know that my prayer has not fallen on deaf ears.'"

It is related that there was a disciple in Abu Hafs's service who was very well mannered. His civility so pleased Joneyd that he often looked on him favorably. Joneyd asked Abu Hafs, "How long has he been in your service?"

"Ten years," Abu Hafs answered.

"He has great civility and a marvelous aura. He is a deserving youth."

"Yes," said Abu Hafs, "he has lost seventeen thousand dinars on our path and has gone another seventeen thousand into debt and he still doesn't have the nerve to ask us a single question."

Abu Hafs then set out for the desert. He related, "I saw Abu Torāb in the desert. I hadn't eaten anything for sixteen days. I went to the edge of a pond to drink some water. I sank into thought. Abu Torāb asked, 'What has made you pause like this?'

"I said, 'I am wavering between knowledge and certainty to see which will be victorious, so I can ally myself with the victor. That is to say, if knowledge gains the upper hand, I will drink, and if it is certainty, I will leave the water behind.'

"Abu Torāb said, 'Your destiny is growing great.'"

Then when Abu Hafs reached Mecca, he saw a group of poor people, in desperately hard straits. He wanted to do them some kindness. The weather grew hot, and an inspiration came to him. He stretched down his hand and picked up a stone and said, "By your might, if you do not give them something, I will smash all the lanterns in the mosque!" Saying this, he began to circumambulate the Ka'ba. Just then, someone came bringing a purse of gold and gave it to Abu Hafs so he could spend it on the poor.

When Abu Hafs had performed the pilgrimage and returned to Baghdad, Joneyd's followers came out to welcome him. "Sheikh," Joneyd said, "what have you brought us as a souvenir?"

Abu Hafs said, "It seems that one of our companions has not been able to live as he should. Let this be my boon to you when I say: If you see a lapse of civility in a brother, think up an excuse for it yourself and apologize to yourself without bothering him. If the fog of ill-will does not lift with that excuse, and you are in the right, think up a better excuse and apologize to yourself again. If the fog still does not lift, and you are in the right, think up a better excuse and apologize to yourself once again, as many as forty times. After that, if the fog does not lift, and you are in the right, and these forty excuses do not make up for that one sin, sit down and say to yourself, 'Bravo for the bullheaded self, so heavy and dark! Bravo you egotistical boor, how uncivil you are! A brother apologizes to you forty times for a single sin, and you won't accept one of them and you go on just as you are. I wash my hands of you! You know what you want; do as you like.'"

When Joneyd heard this, he was stunned, as though to say, "How can you have such strength?"

It is related that Abu Hafs was Shebli's guest for four months. Every day Shebli would serve several kinds of foods and sweets. Finally, when Abu Hafs was saying goodbye, he remarked, "Shebli, if you come to Nishapur sometime, I will teach you how to be a truly courteous host."

"Abu Hafs, what have I done?" Shebli asked.

"You have been overly formal," Abu Hafs explained, "and formalities and courtesy are not the same thing. You must treat a guest as you treat yourself. You should not feel burdened when a guest comes or be happy when he leaves. When you stand on formalities, it is a burden when a guest comes and a relief when he leaves. Whoever feels this way about a guest is not being courteous."

When Shebli came to Nishapur, he went to stay with Abu Hafs, making forty guests all told. At night, Abu Hafs lit forty-one lamps. Shebli said, "Didn't you say that one should not stand on formalities?"

"What formalities?" Abu Hafs asked.

"You lit forty-one lamps."

"Get up and extinguish them."

Shebli got up, but no matter how hard he tried, he could only extinguish one of the lamps. "What is the meaning of this, sheikh?" Shebli asked.

"You are forty people sent by the Real, for guests are the messengers of the Real. Therefore, I lit a lamp in the name of each one of you for the sake of the Lord most high and one for myself. You could not extinguish the forty that were for the Lord most high, but you extinguished the one that was for me. What you did in Baghdad was for my sake. What I have done, I have done for the sake of the Real. Thus, that was formality, and this is not."

❧ ❧ ❧

Abu 'Ali-ye Saqafi[3] reports that Abu Hafs said, "Do not reckon anyone a true believer who does not suspect his own motivations and fails to weigh his feelings and actions against the Qur'an and prophetic custom every moment."

They asked Abu Hafs, "Is silence or speech better for the friend of God?"

"If a speaker considers speech a hardship, he should remain silent as long as he can, even if he lives as long as Noah. But if a quiet man finds silence a comfort, he should ask the Lord most high to give him a life twice as long as Noah's until he speaks."

They asked, "Why are you hostile toward this world?"

"Because it is an abode that leads God's servant into another sin each moment."

"If this world is evil, repentance is good, and repentance also results from living in this world."

"This is so, but we are certain of the sin that is committed in this world. It is when it comes to being certain that our repentance is accepted that we are in doubt and at risk."

They asked, "What is devotion?"

"It is saying farewell to everything that belongs to you and being diligent in what is commanded of you."

"What is poverty?"

"Displaying your infirmity in the presence of the Lord most high."

"What is the sign of friendship?"

"Your friends are happy the day you die." In other words, one should leave this world so detached that nothing remains of one, for anything would be a contradiction of the claim that one lived in detachment.

"Who is a friend of God?"

"One to whom they have given the power to work wonders and have concealed it from him."

"Who is rational?"

"One who seeks to be delivered from the self."

"Who is a miser?"

"The one who gives up altruism when he needs something."

"Altruism is putting your brethren's lot before your own in matters of this world and the next."

"Generosity is throwing this world away for the sake of someone who needs it and turning to the Lord most high because of the need that you have for him."

"The best means for his servant to draw near to him are constant poverty in all circumstances, adhering to prophetic custom in all acts, and seeking out ritually pure food."

"Anyone who does not suspect himself at all times and does not oppose himself under all circumstances is deluded. Anyone who looks upon himself with a satisfied eye perishes."

"Fear is the lamp of the heart, and with it one can see the good and the evil that dwell in the heart."

"Poverty does not come out right for anyone until he prefers giving to taking."

"No one ought to claim insight into others. Rather, he must fear the insights that others have into him."

"Whoever gives and takes is a true believer. Whoever gives but does not take is half a believer. Whoever neither gives nor takes is a fly, not a person, and there is nothing good in him." They asked Abu 'Osmān of Hira about the meaning of these words. He said, "Whoever takes from the mighty and glorious Lord and gives to the Lord is a true believer because he does not see himself involved in the matter. Whoever gives and does not take is half a man, because what is he doing in this case? He considers himself noble for not taking. Whoever neither gives nor takes is no person because he imagines that he, not the Lord, is the giver and the taker."

"If anyone sees the Lord's grace upon him under all circumstances, I can only hope that he is not doomed to perdition."

"Do not rely on your worship of the mighty and glorious Lord, so that you worship what should be worshiped."

"The noblest thing for people of good works is to watch over themselves alongside the Lord most high."

"How good is freedom from want in the Lord most high, and how ugly it is in sordid men."

"Whoever tastes a sip of the wine of divine intuition will faint so utterly away that he will not recover except when he meets God and sees him directly."

"One does not enjoy separation from the world, unless one separates through acceptance."

"People tell me about union and intimacy and the lofty spiritual stations, but all I want is for them to guide me to the path that leads to the Real, if only for just an instant."

"In appearance, acts of worship are joy, but in reality, they are self-delusion, because that which one is capable of has been predestined, and it comes down to this: one is not happy with one's actions except in self-delusion."

"Sins are the messengers of unbelief, just as bile is the messenger of death."

"If anyone knows that he will be raised up and called to account and does not shun sin or turn away from disobedience, it is certain that he tells us this about himself: I do not believe in the resurrection or the reckoning."

"Tell anyone who likes his heart to be meek, 'Follow the pious and be assiduous in serving them.'"

"Bodies are illuminated by service and souls by steadfastness."

"Salvation is in the unalloyed fear of God."

"Sufism is all civility."

"God's servant has nothing to do with repentance, because repentance is something that comes to him, not something that comes from him."

"If a good deed is worthy, it is carried off, and you are made to forget it."

"A person is blind who sees the mighty and glorious Lord through things but does not see things through the Lord. A person who can see is one who knows that his glance falls on created things through the mighty and glorious Lord."

It is related that someone asked Abu Hafs for counsel. He said, "My brother, attend at one door so all doors open before you and attend one master so all masters bow down before you."

✑ ✑ ✑

Mahmash[4] said, "I followed Abu Hafs for twenty-two years. I never saw him remember the Lord most high with carelessness or gaiety. Indeed, whenever he used to remember the Lord most high, it was with composure, honor, and respect. He would be so transformed that those present would notice it."

In his death throes, Abu Hafs said, "In all circumstances, one must be broken hearted over one's shortcomings."

They asked him, "How have you faced the Lord?"

"How does a poor man face a rich one except in poverty and destitution?" Abu Hafs answered.

Abu 'Abd ar-Rahman Solami's[5] final testament was, "When I die, place my head at the feet of Abu Hafs."

✑ 22 ✑
Joneyd of Baghdad

The unconditional master, the worthy axis, the source of secrets, the meadow of lights, foremost in teaching, the sultan of the path, Joneyd of Baghdad—God's mercy be upon him. He was the sheikh of the elders of the world, the imam of the imams on earth. He was perfect in the varieties of knowledge and the judge of its principles and branches; he had precedence over everyone in proper behavior and ascetic discipline, in wonder-working, subtle words, and lofty allusions. He was esteemed and acknowledged from his earliest days until the end of his life. He was beloved by all the sects, and everyone agreed on his leadership. His words are a proof on the path and praised by every tongue. No one could point to anything within him or without contrary to the tradition of the Prophet, and only the blind could criticize him. He was the model for the Sufis—they called him the Chief of the Clan and the Tongue of the Folk and referred to him as the Most Pious of the Masters, the Peacock of the Scholars, and the Sultan of Initiates.

He reached the utmost extreme in religious law and inner truth. He was without peer in renunciation and love and was the highest authority on the path. Most of the sheikhs of Baghdad, in his age and afterward, held his teachings. His way was the way of sobriety, in contrast to the Tayfurians, who are the followers of Bāyazid. The best-known way on the path and the most famous school of thought are Joneyd's. In his time he was the reference point of the sheikhs; he has many lofty writings on spiritual signs, truths, and meanings. He was the first person to disseminate the lore of allusive teaching. In spite of such a life, enemies and enviers bore witness to his unbelief and atheism many times.

He studied with Mohāsebi[1] and was Sari's nephew and disciple. One day Sari was asked, "Does any disciple have a higher rank than his master's?"

"Yes," Sari said, "and the proof is clear: Joneyd's rank is higher than mine."

Joneyd was all pain and yearning and had an exalted standing in the way of realization and the revelation of unity. He was a divine sign of striving, contemplation, and poverty, to such an extent that, in spite of all the grandeur that Sahl of Tostar possessed, it is related that Joneyd said, "Sahl had the divine signs and forged far ahead, but he had no heart; he had the quality of an angel, but not of a king like Adam (peace be upon him), who was all pain and devotion." In other words, true suffering is another matter.

They know what they are saying. Our business is relating these things, and it is not up to us to prefer one of them to another.

This was the beginning of his spiritual state: From childhood on Joneyd was afflicted with pain, diligent and well-behaved, pensive and clairvoyant. He was wonderfully sharp witted. One day he was coming home from school. He saw his father weeping. "What's happened?" he asked.

His father said, "Today, I took some money from the alms to your uncle Sari, and he didn't accept it. I am weeping because I spent my life for this handful of coins, and they're not fit for any of the Lord's friends."

Joneyd said, "Give them to me, so I can take them. He'll accept them." He took the coins and set out and knocked on his uncle's door. "Who is it?" Sari asked.

"It's I, Joneyd." His door did not open. "Take these bits of gold."

"I won't take them."

"By the Lord who has been so generous to you and so just with my father, take them."

"Joneyd, how has he been generous with me and just with him?"

"He was generous with you by giving you poverty and just with my father by busying him with this world. You will accept them or reject them, as you will, while he must send alms to someone deserving, whether he will or no."

Sari was pleased with these words. He said, "Son, before I accept these alms, I accept you." He opened the door, took the gold, and gave Joneyd a special place in his heart.

Joneyd was seven years old when Sari took him on the hajj. In the Mosque of the Sanctuary there was a discussion going on among four hundred elders about the question of thankfulness. Each of them had something to say, giving four hundred opinions on explicating and explaining thankfulness. Sari told Joneyd, "You say something too."

Joneyd said, "Thankfulness means that you should not disobey the mighty and glorious Lord by means of the blessings that he has bestowed upon you, nor should you make his favor the capital of sin."

When Joneyd said this, each of the four hundred responded, *"Bravo! You're the apple of all honest men's eyes!"* And they all agreed that nothing better could be said on the subject.

Sari said, "Boy, your tongue will soon prove to be God's gift to you."

Joneyd related, "I was considering what Sari said, when he asked, 'Where did you get this?'

"'From your prayer meetings,' I answered."

He went back to Baghdad then and became a glass seller. Every day he used to go to the shop, let down the curtain, and perform four hundred rak'ats of prayer. Some time passed this way. Then he abandoned the shop. There was a room in the vestibule of Sari's house. There he sat and devoted himself to keeping guard over his heart. He unrolled his prayer rug under the watchful eye of the Real, until nothing else passed through his mind.

He lived like this for forty years. Indeed, for thirty years, he would perform the night prayer, stand up and recite "God" until dawn, and perform the morning prayer without having to repeat his ablutions. He said, "When forty years had passed, I had the idea that I had reached the goal. That instant, a voice called out, 'Joneyd! The time has come for us to reveal to you the end of your infidel sash.'

"When I heard this, I said, 'O Lord, what sin has Joneyd committed that it should be this way?'

"I heard a voice say, 'You exist—do you want a greater sin than this?'"

Joneyd lowered his head and sighed. He recited:

Whoever is not worthy of union,
every one of his good works is sin.

So, Joneyd stayed in that room and repeated "God, God" all night. Tongues started wagging about what he was doing, and his story reached the caliph. The caliph said, "He cannot be banned without proof."

"The people are being incited by his words," they said.

The caliph had a slave girl, purchased at a cost of three thousand dinars. There was no one as beautiful as she, and the caliph was in love with her. He ordered that she be arrayed in precious clothes and costly jewels. "Go to Joneyd," she was told. "Reveal your face and offer yourself, your clothes, and your jewels to him. Say to him, 'I have a great deal of money, but my heart has grown weary of the affairs of the world. I have come so you will ask for my hand in marriage. In your company I will devote myself to serving God. My heart will not be at peace with anyone else.' Display yourself to him. Take off your veil. Make every possible effort in this matter."

He then sent her off with a servant. The slave girl and the servant came to see Joneyd, and they did everything they had agreed upon and double that. Joneyd's glance fell on her involuntarily. He was silent and gave no reply. His head was downcast, and the slave girl was repeating her story, when suddenly Joneyd looked up and sighed, "Ahhh." He breathed on the girl, and she toppled over and died on the spot.

The servant went and told the caliph what had happened. The caliph's soul burned with regret. He said, "Whoever does to people what should not be done will see what should not be seen." He arose and went to see Joneyd, remarking, "One must go pay homage to such a person." Then he said to Joneyd, "Sheikh, how could you find it in your heart to destroy such an image of beauty?"

"Commander of the Faithful," Joneyd replied, "was it your kindness for the faithful that made you want to ruin my forty years of discipline, sleeplessness, and suffering? Who am I in all of this? But do not unto others, lest they do unto you!"

After that, Joneyd's affairs prospered, and his fame spread throughout the world. However he was put to the test, he came out a thousand times better. He began to speak publicly. As he once said, "I did not speak to the people until thirty of the Substitutes hinted, 'You are worthy to call the people to the Lord.'"

❧ ❧ ❧

And Joneyd spoke these words:

"I attended two hundred elders, no more than seven of whom deserved to be imitated."

"We did not grasp this Sufism by bickering or acquire it through war and combat; rather, we achieved it through hunger and sleeplessness, through giving up this world and cutting ourselves off from whatever we loved and considered an adornment."

"The person who travels this path has taken up the book of the mighty and glorious Lord in his right hand and the customs of God's chosen Prophet (peace be upon him) in his left; he travels by the light of these two torches, so he will not fall into the ditch of uncertainty or the darkness of heresy."

"In the foundations and branches of the law, in enduring hardship, our master is the Commander of the Faithful 'Ali (peace be upon him). He was a commander whom the Lord most high endowed with such knowledge and wisdom that no one can bear to hear the stories they have told about his conduct in the wars."

"If 'Ali had not magnanimously said a few words, what would the followers of the path have done?" Those words were these: They asked 'Ali, "How did you come to know the mighty and glorious Lord?" He said, "In the way that he made me to know him, for he is the Lord who has no likeness, who cannot be perceived in any way, who cannot be compared to any creature. He is near in his distance and distant in his nearness. He is above all things, yet one cannot say anything is under him. He is not from anything, not like anything, not in anything, not by anything. Praise to the Lord who is like this and like this is nothing else besides." If he were to explain these words, it would amount to volumes—*Whoever understands, understands.*

"Ten thousand honest disciples were led to the path of truth with Joneyd, and through realization, all were carried deep into the sea of wrath, so that Abu'l-Qāsem Joneyd could be raised up and made the sun in the heaven of discipleship."

"If I live a thousand years, I will not lessen my works one iota, unless they hold me back."

"I am in the grips of the sin of the first and last, for Abu'l-Qāsem must bear the responsibility for every last detail." This is a sign of becoming the totality. When a person sees himself to be the whole and sees that all created things are like his limbs and when he reaches the station of *The believers are a single person,*[2] then his words are these: *"No prophet suffered the likes of what I suffered."*[3]

"I passed my life in such a way that the inhabitants of heaven and earth wept for me. Then I became such that I wept for their failing. Now I have become such that I know nothing of them or myself."

"For ten years I sat at the threshold of my heart and kept guard over it. Then for ten years it kept guard over me. Now it's been twenty years since I have had any news of my heart or my heart any news of me."

"For thirty years the Lord most high spoke to his creatures with Joneyd's tongue, and Joneyd had nothing to do with it, and his creatures were unaware of it."

"For twenty years I talked around the edges of this knowledge but said nothing about what lies in its depths, for tongues are prohibited from speaking it and hearts forbidden from perceiving it."

"Fear contracts me, and hope expands me. Thus, wherever I contract in fear, there I am extinguished, and wherever I expand in hope, I am given back to myself."

"On the morrow when the Lord most high says to me, 'Look at me,' I will not look. I will say, 'The eye is in love with the other and the stranger, and jealousy keeps me from looking. In the lower world, I used to see without the intermediary of the eye.'"

"When I learned that *Truly the word is in the heart*,[4] I had to make up thirty years of missed prayers."

"For twenty years, I never finished the first 'God is great' in my prayers, for if any thought of this world occurred to me during prayer, I would make up the prayer, and if any thought of paradise or the afterworld occurred to me, I would make up that prostration."

૭૦ ૭૦ ૭૦

And one day Joneyd said to his followers, "If I knew that supererogatory prayers were more virtuous than sitting with you, I would never sit with you."

It is related that Joneyd fasted continuously. When friends came, he would break the fast with them and say, "The virtue of helping brothers is no less than the virtue of fasting."

It is related that Joneyd and Abu Bakr-e Kattāni[5] corresponded concerning a thousand issues. When Kattāni died, he ordered, "Do not turn these controversies over to anyone. Bury them in the ground with me."

Joneyd said, "I appreciated that those controversies did not fall into anyone's hands."

It is related that Joneyd dressed in the manner of religious scholars. His followers asked, "Elder of the path, how about dressing in a patched frock just to put your followers' minds at ease?"

He said, "If I knew wearing a patched frock would accomplish anything, I'd make a suit of molten iron and wear it. But every moment a voice calls out within me, *'Depend on the fire, not the attire.'*"

When the word rose up within Joneyd, Sari-ye Saqati said, "You must preach."

Joneyd vacillated. He was not fond of the idea and said, "It's not polite to preach in the presence of the sheikh." Then one night he saw the Prophet (peace and blessing be upon him) in a dream. "Preach!" he told Joneyd.

At dawn Joneyd got up to talk to Sari. He saw Sari standing at the door. Sari said, "Were you waiting for others to tell you to preach? Now you must—your words have been made the salvation of the world's people. You did not preach at the urging of your disciples. You did not preach at the pleading of Baghdad's religious leaders. You did not preach when I told you to. Now that the Prophet (peace and blessing be upon him) has commanded it, you must preach."

Joneyd consented, and apologizing, he asked Sari, "How did you know that I saw the Prophet (peace be upon him) in a dream?"

"I saw the mighty and glorious Lord in a dream," Sari replied. "He said, 'I sent my Messenger to Joneyd to tell him to speak from the pulpit.'"

"I will preach only if no more than forty people are present." One day he spoke at a prayer meeting. Forty people were present—eighteen died, and twenty-two fainted away. They were heaved up and carried bodily back to their homes.

One day Joneyd spoke at a meeting in the Friday mosque. A young man entered; he was a Christian, although no one was aware of it. He said, "Sheikh! In the words of the Prophet: 'Beware of the believer's clairvoyance, for he sees by the light of God.'"

Joneyd said, "These words mean that you should become a Muslim and cut your Christian sash, for it is the time of Islam." The young man became a Muslim on the spot.

The response of the people exceeded all bounds. After Joneyd had been preaching for some time, he gave it up and retired to his house. Although they asked him to come back, he refused. "I am happy," he said. "I cannot destroy myself."

Sometime later he returned to the pulpit without anyone saying a thing and began to preach again. "What's the wisdom in this?" they asked him.

"In a tradition," Joneyd replied, "I found that the Prophet (peace and blessing be upon him) has said, 'At the end of time, the leader of the people will be the worst person among them, and he will preach to them.' I know myself to be the worst of creatures. I speak for the sake of the Prophet's words, lest I should contradict them."

They asked him, "How did you attain this rank?"

"For forty years," Joneyd said, "I stood at his doorstep on the feet of striving," meaning Sari's doorstep.

It is related that Joneyd said, "One day my heart was lost. I said, 'My God, return my heart.' I heard a voice say, 'Joneyd, we have stolen your heart so you may abide with us. Do you ask for it back, so you may abide with someone besides us?'"

It is related that when Hoseyn ebn Mansur-e Hallāj (God have mercy upon him) was overwhelmed by his ecstasies and alienated from 'Amr ebn 'Osmān of Mecca, he came to see Joneyd. Joneyd said, "Why have you come? One should not do what you have done to Sahl of Tostar and 'Amr ebn 'Osmān."

Hoseyn said, "Sobriety and intoxication are two attributes of God's servant, and the servant is veiled from his Lord until his attributes are extinguished."

"Ebn Mansur, you've erred," Joneyd said. "There is nothing contrary to this in sobriety and intoxication, because sobriety consists of the soundness of one's standing with the Real. It does not come under the heading of a creature's 'attribute' or 'acquisition.' Son of Mansur, I see much foolishness and meaningless phraseology in your words."

It is related that Joneyd said:

I saw a young man in the desert beneath a thorny acacia tree. "What made you sit here?" I asked.

He said, "I had a spiritual state, and it was lost here. I am going to persevere here until I get it back."

I went on the pilgrimage. When I returned, he was still sitting there the same way. I asked, "Why do you continue to persevere?"

"I found what I was searching for here," he said, "so I must persevere."

I do not know which is nobler: his perseverance in the search or his perseverance in the attainment.

It is related that Shebli said, "At the resurrection, if the Real most high gives me my choice between heaven and hell, I will choose hell, because heaven is my desire, and hell the Beloved's. It is the sign of love not to pick one's choice over the beloved's."

Joneyd was informed of what Shebli had said. He replied, "Shebli is acting childishly. If I'm given my choice, I will not choose. I'll say, 'What business does a servant have choosing? Wherever you send me, I will go; wherever you keep me, I will stay. My choice is what you desire.'"

It is related that one day someone came to visit Joneyd and said, "Remain here a moment, so I can say a few words."

"My dear," Joneyd said, "you are asking for something that I myself have been asking for for some time. I want to remain for a moment with the Real most high, but I haven't succeeded. How can I remain a moment with you?"

It is related that Roveym said, "I went into the desert. I saw an old woman standing at the ready with a cane in hand. She said, 'When you get to Baghdad, tell Joneyd, "Aren't you ashamed to speak of him in front of commoners?"'

"When I delivered the message, Joneyd said, 'God forbid that I should speak of him. No one can speak of him.'"

It is related that one of the eminent dreamt that he saw the Prophet seated with Joneyd in attendance. Someone brought in a legal decision. The Prophet (peace and blessing be upon him) said, "Give it to Joneyd, so he can respond."

The eminent man asked, "Messenger of God, how can anyone respond to a legal decision in your presence?"

"I take as much pride in Joneyd as all the prophets take in all their peoples," the Prophet said.

Ja'far ebn Noseyr[6] said, "Joneyd gave me a dirham and said, 'Get some vizier figs and olive oil.' I bought them. After the evening prayer, when

335

he broke his fast, he put a fig in his mouth. Then he spit it out and wept and said to me, 'Take them away.'

"'What happened?' I asked.

"Joneyd said, 'A voice called out to me, "Aren't you ashamed to return to something that you had forbidden to yourself for our sake?"' And he recited this verse:

> 'Craved' and 'depraved' sound much the same;
> Yield to desire, yield to shame."

It is related that once Joneyd was in pain and said, "God, heal me!"

A voice called out, "Joneyd, why do you meddle between the servant and his Lord? Don't interfere—busy yourself with what he has commanded for you. Be patient with what he has inflicted. What business do you have choosing?"

It is related that once he went to pay a sick call on a dervish. The dervish was complaining. Joneyd asked, "Who are you complaining about?" The dervish fell silent. Joneyd asked, "Who are you suffering in silence?"

The dervish said, "No means to complain, no strength to suffer in silence!"

It is related that once Joneyd had a sore foot. He recited the opening of the Qur'an and blew on his foot. A voice called out, "Aren't you ashamed to spend our words on yourself?"

It is related that once Joneyd's eye was sore. The doctor said, "Don't put any water near that eye if it means anything to you."

When the doctor left, Joneyd performed his ablutions, prayed, and went to sleep. When he awoke, his eye was fine. He heard a voice saying, "Joneyd, you abandoned your eye to please us. If you had asked us for the denizens of hell with this resolve, your wish would have been granted."

When the doctor returned, he saw that Joneyd's eye was fine. "What did you do?" the doctor asked.

Joneyd said, "Ablutions and prayer."

The doctor was a Christian and professed Islam then and there.

He said, "This is the Creator's cure, not the creature's. It was my eye that was sore, not yours. You were the doctor, not I."

It is related that an eminent man was coming to visit Joneyd and saw the devil running away from him. When the eminent man came before Joneyd, he saw that Joneyd was fuming—his anger was clearly evident, and he was berating someone. He said, "Sheikh, I have heard that the devil has the greatest power over the children of Adam when they are angry. You are angry now, but I saw the devil running away from you."

Joneyd said, "Haven't you heard, don't you know, that we are not angry for ourselves? Rather, we are angry on behalf of the Real. So, of course, the devil never flees from us as he does when we get angry. The anger of others is over the fate of their own selves. If not for the fact that the Real most high commanded us to say, *'I seek refuge with God from the cursed devil,'* I would never seek refuge."

It is related that Joneyd said:

I wanted to see Satan. I was standing in the mosque and saw an old man coming from the distance. When I saw him, a feeling of desolation came over me. I said, "Who are you?"

"I am the one you desire," he said.

I asked, "Cursed one, what kept you from bowing down to Adam?"[7]

"Joneyd," he said, "how can you imagine that I would bow down to any but him?"

I was stunned by his words. In my mind, a voice said, "Say to him, 'You lie! If you had been God's servant, you would have obeyed his decree. You would not have taken leave of his command and paid homage to disobedience.'"

When Satan heard this, he cried out and said, "By God, you burned me!" and he vanished.

It is related that one day Shebli said, *"There is neither fear nor power but in God."*

Joneyd said, "This is the way the despondent talk, and despondency comes from no longer accepting one's fate."

Someone came to visit Joneyd and said, "Indicate someone among your disciples who is worthy company."

Joneyd said, "If you're looking for someone to bear your burden, he'll be hard to find. If you want to bear someone else's burden, there are plenty of brethren of that sort around me."

It is related that he was walking along with a disciple one night. A dog barked. Joneyd said, *"I am at your service!"*[8]

"What's come over you?" the disciple asked.

"I saw that the dog's capacity to make such an uproar came from the wrath of the Real most high, and I heard the power of the Real most high in his barking. I didn't see where the dog entered into it. Thus, I responded with *'I am at your service.'"*

One day Joneyd was sobbing. They asked him, "What reason is there for weeping?"

"If hardship turns into a dragon," he said, "I will be the first person to serve myself up as a snack. Although I have spent my entire life in search of hardship, still they tell me, 'You have not been servant enough to deserve the hardship we impose.'"

They said, "Abu Sa'id the Bootmaker experienced great rapture in his death throes."

"There's nothing strange in this," Joneyd said, "if his soul took wing in delight."

"What spiritual station is this?"

"Utter love. This is a dear station that drowns all intellects and effaces all souls. It is a most lofty station in realization. Learning and realization have no standing at this moment—the servant has arrived at the place where he knows that the Lord most high loves him. Thus, this servant says, 'Here's to my reality by you! Here's to my place near you!' So too, he says, 'Here's to your love for me!'

"These are the folk," Joneyd added, "who glory in the mighty and glorious Lord, who are on intimate terms with him. There's no bashfulness between them and the mighty and glorious Lord. They say things that are hideous to the common people."

Joneyd said, "One night, I dreamt that I was standing in the presence of the mighty and glorious Lord. He said to me, 'Why do you speak such words?'

"I said, 'Whatever I say, I speak what is real.'

"He said, 'You have told the truth.'"

It is related that Ebn Soreyj[9] dropped by Joneyd's prayer meeting. He was asked, "Does what Joneyd says correspond to religious learning?"

"That I don't know," he replied, "but I do know that his words are so awesome that the Real seems to utter them with Joneyd's tongue."

In this regard, it is related that when Joneyd spoke of divine unity, he would begin each time with a different expression that no one could understand. One day at Joneyd's prayer meeting, Shebli said, "God."

"If God is absent," Joneyd said, "to mention the absent is absence itself, and this is forbidden. If he is present, to utter his name in full view of his presence is disrespectful."

One day, Joneyd was speaking. Someone stood up and said, "I can't understand that."

"Crush your seventy years of devotion under foot," Joneyd said.

"I have crushed it and still don't understand."

"Crush your head under foot. If you don't understand then, consider it my fault."

Someone sang Joneyd's praises loudly at a prayer meeting. Joneyd said, "What you say has nothing to do with me. You are remembering the Lord and singing his praises."

It is related that someone stood up at Joneyd's prayer meeting and asked, "When is the heart happy?"

"When he is the heart," Joneyd replied.

Someone brought Joneyd five hundred dinars. Joneyd said, "Do you have anything besides this?"

"A great deal."

"Do you need the rest of it?"

"I do."

"Take this away. You're more entitled to it. I have nothing and don't need it."

It is related that Joneyd was leaving the mosque after prayer and saw a great crowd of people. He turned to his companions and said, "All these are mere stuffing for paradise. It's another folk who'll sit together with the Real."

It is related that a man stood up at Joneyd's meeting and began to beg. Joneyd thought, "This man is healthy and he can earn a living. Why does he beg? Why does he humiliate himself like this?"

That night, he had a dream: a covered platter was placed before him, and he was told to eat. When he lifted the lid, he saw the beggar dead and laid out on the platter. He said, "I won't eat carrion!"

"Well, why did you eat it at the mosque yesterday?"

Joneyd knew that he was being taken to task for the backbiting in his heart. He said, "I awoke awestruck and purified myself. I performed two rak'ats of prayer and went in search of the poor man. I saw him on the banks of the Tigris; from the water, he was plucking scraps of leeks that had been cleaned in the river and eating them. He looked up and saw me coming over to him.

"'Joneyd,' he said, 'haven't you repented of what you thought about me?'

"'I have.'

"'Go now. *He is the One who accepts the repentance of his servants* [42:25]. And keep this contrition in mind.'"

It is related that Joneyd said:

I learned sincerity from a barber when I went to Mecca. A barber was trimming a gentleman's hair. "For God's sake," I said, "can you shave my head?"

He said, "I can." He was on the verge of tears and left the gentleman's hair half trimmed. "Get up," the barber told him. "When God is mentioned, everything else must wait." He seated me and kept kissing my head and shaved it. Then he gave me a folded bit of paper with a few gold coins inside. "Spend this on whatever you need."

I resolved to myself to bestow upon him the first donation that came my way. It was not long before a purse of gold reached me from Basra. I took it to him. He said, "What is this?"

I said, "I had resolved to give you the first donation that came my way. This has come."

"Man, have you no shame before the Lord? You said to me, 'For God's sake, shave my head.' And then you pay me!? Who have you ever seen do something for God's sake and then take payment for it?"

Joneyd related:

At night once I was busy praying, but no matter how much I tried, my self resisted my every prostration, and I could not meditate at all. I got depressed and was about to go outside. When I opened the door, I saw a young man wrapped in a blanket and stretched out on the doorstep. When he saw me, he said, "I've been waiting for you until now."

"So it was you who was making me so restless," I said.

"Yes," he said. "Answer this question for me. What do you say about the self: Will it ever be cured by its own pain?"

"It will," I replied, "when it opposes its own desires."

When I said this, he looked down the collar of his robe and said, "Self, how many times have you heard this same answer from me? Now hear it from Joneyd!" He got up and left. I didn't know where he came from or where he went.

Joneyd said, "Jonah wept so much he went blind and performed so many prayers his back was bent double." And he said, "By your might, if a sea of fire lies between you and me, and my path crosses it, I will dive in, so great is the yearning I have for you."

'Ali-ye Sahl (God have mercy upon him) wrote a letter to Joneyd: "Sleep is negligence and indolence. Thus, the lover should have neither sleep nor repose. If he sleeps, he falls short of his goal and neglects both himself and his spiritual moment. In this regard, the Real most high sent this revelation to David (peace be upon him): 'Whoever claimed to love me has lied if he slept when night fell and stopped loving me.'"

Joneyd wrote back this response: "Our wakefulness is our proper behavior on the path of the Real, and our sleep is the action of the Real upon us. So, what we do not choose, what comes to us from the Real, is better than what we choose, than what comes to the Real from us. Sleep is a gift from God to his friends."

What is surprising about this letter is that Joneyd was a partisan of sobriety and here gives the teaching of the school of intoxication. It could be that he wants to convey the meaning of the hadith *"The sleep of the scholar is worship"* or *"My eyes sleep, but my heart does not."*

It is related that a thief had been hanged in Baghdad. Joneyd went and kissed his feet. When asked about it, he said, "A thousand mercies upon him: he was a true believer in what he did. He carried out his job so perfectly that he gave his head for it."

It is related that one night a thief went to Joneyd's house. He found nothing there but a shirt. He picked it up and left. The next day Joneyd was passing through the market and saw his shirt in the hands of a fence who was selling it. The prospective buyer wanted to be sure that the shirt belonged to the fence before he bought it and was looking for someone who knew the fence and could certify that the shirt was his. Joneyd approached and said, "I certify that it belongs to him," and the deal was completed.

It is related that an old woman came to Joneyd and said, "My son is missing. Say a prayer for his return."

Joneyd said, "Be patient."

The old woman left and waited several days. The sheikh said, "Be patient."

After this had happened several times, the old woman came one day and said, "My patience is exhausted. Pray to the Lord."

"If you're telling the truth," Joneyd said, "your son has already returned, for the Real most high calls himself *"the One who answers the distressed when they call on him"* [27:62]. Then he prayed.

The old woman said, "When I returned home, my son had come back."

It is related that someone complained to Joneyd of hunger and nakedness. "Go and have faith," Joneyd said. "He does not give a person

342

hunger and nakedness so he will slander him and fill the world with complaint. He gives them to the righteous and his friends. Don't complain."

It is related that Joneyd was sitting with his followers. A man rich in the things of this world came in and called for a poor man and took him away with him. After a while they returned, the poor man carrying a basket full of food on his head.

Joneyd was enraged when he saw this. He ordered the others to smash the basket over the rich man's head. "Must a poor man serve as your porter?" Then he said, "If the poor do not have prosperity, they have aspiration. If they do not possess this world, they do the next."

It is related that a certain wealthy man gave his alms only to the Sufis. He would say, "They are a folk who aspire to nothing but the Lord most high. When they are in need, their aspiration is dispersed and falls short of the Real. I prefer to deliver one such heart to the presence of the mighty and glorious Lord than a thousand others that aspire to nothing but the things of this world."

Joneyd was told of these words. He said, "These are the words of one of the Lord's friends."

It later happened that this man was reduced to poverty because he took no payment for what the dervishes bought from him. Joneyd gave him some money and said, "For a man like you, no business is a loss."

It is related that a disciple had a lot of money. He lost it all following Joneyd's path and was left with nothing but a house. "Sheikh, what will I do?" he asked.

"Sell it," Joneyd said, "and bring the gold, so you can finish up your business." The disciple went and sold the house. Joneyd said, "Throw the gold in the Tigris." The disciple took the gold, threw it in the Tigris, and entered the sheikh's service.

Joneyd drove him off. "Leave me," Joneyd said and treated the disciple like a complete stranger. No matter how often he came, Joneyd drove him off, as if to say, "Don't be so conceited that you've lost so much gold." It went on like this until the disciple's spiritual progress was complete.

It is related that rapture was manifested in a young man at one of Joneyd's meetings. He repented his former life and ransacked everything he owned. He gave most of it away to others but saved a thousand dinars to bring to Joneyd as a donation. They told him, "Joneyd's presence is not of this world; it cannot be blemished."

The young man sat on the banks of the Tigris and tossed the coins into the water one by one until none remained. Then he got up and went to the Sufi hospice. When Joneyd saw him, he said, "Have you taken the same step a thousand times that you only needed to take once? Go, you are not worthy of us. Didn't your heart tell you that it would be better to throw them all in at once? If you're going to make the same sort of calculations on this path, go. You'll never get anywhere. Go back, return to the market. Accounting and economizing go over well there."

It is related that a disciple imagined that he had reached the stage of perfection and that it would be better for him to be alone. He went to an out-of-the-way place and stayed there a while, until it came about that a camel was brought to him every night. "We'll take you to paradise," they told him. He would mount the camel and ride along until he reached a pleasant and refreshing place where there were handsome folks, proper food, and flowing streams. He would stay there until dawn. Then he would fall asleep and find himself in his meditation cell. It went on this way until he began to put on airs and entertain a high opinion of himself. "They take me to paradise every night," he boasted pretentiously.

Word of this reached Joneyd. He got up and went to the disciple's meditation cell. Joneyd found the disciple utterly full of himself. The sheikh asked how things were, and the disciple revealed everything to him. "When they take you there tonight," Joneyd said, "declare three times: *There is no strength or power but in God the high and almighty!*"

When night fell and they carried the disciple off, deep down he doubted the sheikh. When he reached that place, he said, *"There is no strength"* as a test. Those folks all howled and fled. He found himself on a pile of garbage covered with the bones of carcasses. He realized his error and repented. He joined the sheikh's followers and understood that solitude is poison to a disciple.

It is related that Joneyd was preaching. A disciple let out a shout. Joneyd forbade him from doing that and said, "If you shout again, I'll expel you." The sheikh continued his sermon. The disciple restrained himself, until it reached the point that he could stand it no longer and perished. Everyone went over and found that he had turned to ashes inside his robes.

It is related that a disciple happened to suffer a lapse in civility. He moved away and took up residence in the Shuniziya Mosque. One day Joneyd happened to pass by there and looked at the disciple. He immediately collapsed in awe of the sheikh and cracked open his head. Blood began to flow, and every drop took the form of God's name. Joneyd said, "Are you showing off, telling everyone you've reached the stage of remembrance? Every child is your equal in this. The true believer must attain the One remembered."

These words overcame the disciple's spirit, and he died on the spot. After some time he was seen in a dream and asked, "How did you find yourself?"

"For many long years I have been going forward," he said. "Now I have reached my unbelief and have seen both my unbelief and my faith. It is a long, long ways. All that was deception."

It is related that Joneyd had a disciple in Basra. One day he happened to have a sinful thought in private. He looked in the mirror and saw that his face had turned black. He was stunned. No matter what trick he tried, it did no good. Ashamed, he showed his face to no one until three days had passed. The blackness lessened bit by bit. Suddenly, there was a knock at the door. "Who is it?" he asked.

"I have brought you a letter from Joneyd."

He read the letter. In it was written "Why don't you behave yourself in the presence of his grandeur? For three whole days I've had to work at bleaching and whitening the blackness of your face."

It is related that Joneyd had a disciple. It happened one day that an objection was raised against him. Disgraced, he left and did not return to the hospice. Then, one day Joneyd was passing through the market with his followers. The sheikh caught sight of the disciple. He fled for shame. Joneyd sent his followers back and said, "A bird has flown from our net."

He pursued the disciple. The disciple looked back to see the sheikh coming. He picked up his pace and kept going until he reached a dead end. He put his face against the wall, ashamed to face the sheikh. Just then, Joneyd caught up with him. The disciple said, "Where are you going?"

Joneyd said, "Where the disciple runs face first into the wall, the master has work to do." Then he brought him back to the hospice. The disciple fell at Joneyd's feet and asked for forgiveness. When the people saw what had happened, a graciousness was revealed to them, and many repented.

It is related that Joneyd went into the desert with a disciple. An edge of the disciple's collar was torn. The sun blazed down on him, until the exposed skin was burned, and blood began to flow. "It's a hot day today" slipped from the disciple's tongue.

Joneyd gave him an awesome look and said, "Go, you do not belong among our followers" and sent him away.

It is related that Joneyd had a disciple who was dearest to him of all. The others grew jealous. The sheikh knew this clairvoyantly and said, "His civility and understanding are superior to everyone else's. That's what we're looking for. Let's make a test, so it will be clear to you."

He ordered twenty birds to be brought out and said, "Each disciple should take one of them and go someplace where no one will see him. Kill it and bring it back." Everyone left, killed his bird, and returned, except for that one disciple, who brought his bird back alive.

"Why didn't you kill it?" Joneyd asked.

"Because the sheikh had ordered that we go someplace where no one will see. Everywhere I went, I saw the Real most high."

Joneyd said, "Did you see how his understanding was compared to the others'?" After that, they asked for forgiveness.

It is related that Joneyd had eight disciples who were his elite. A mere thought was sufficient for them. They got the idea that they should go fight in the sacred struggle, and the next day Joneyd ordered his servant, "Make preparations for the war."

346

The sheikh and all eight of these disciples then went to Byzantium to fight in the struggle. When they drew up in a rank, an infidel warrior came forward and martyred all eight of them.

Joneyd looked: "I saw nine litters standing in midair," he said. "The spirits of each one of those martyred disciples were being placed in a litter. Only one was left empty. 'Perhaps that one is for me,' I thought. I entered the ranks of battle. The warrior who had killed my companions came forward and said, 'Abu'l-Qāsem, that ninth litter is mine. You go back to Baghdad and be the guide of the folk. Show me the faith.' He then became a Muslim. Using the very sword with which he had killed the disciples, he slew eight infidels. Then he was martyred. His soul was placed in the ninth litter, and they all disappeared."

It is related that Joneyd was told, "For thirty years, a certain person has not lifted his head from his knees, nor has he tasted food or drink. Lice infested him, and he was unaware of it. What do you say about such a person? Is he in the perfect union of union, or not?"

"It's possible," Joneyd said, "if God wills."

It is related that there was a descendant of the Prophet called Nāseri. He set off on the pilgrimage. When he arrived in Baghdad, he went to visit Joneyd and offered his greetings. Joneyd asked, "Where are you from?"

"From Gilan," he said.

"From whom are you descended?"

"From the Commander of the Faithful 'Ali."

"Your forefather wielded two swords, one against the unbelievers and one against the self. As his descendant, which do you use?"

On hearing this, the descendant of the Prophet wept profusely and groveled before Joneyd. "Sheikh," he said, "my pilgrimage is here. Show me the way to God."

"Your breast," Joneyd said, "is God's special sanctuary. As far as you are able, allow no stranger into that sanctuary."

"It shall be done."

৵৹ ৵৹ ৵৹

Joneyd has these lofty sayings:

"Gallantry is in Syria, eloquence in Iraq, and honesty in Khorasan."

"There are many robbers on this path, and they set three kinds of snares: the snare of deceit and false miracles, the snare of wrath, and the snare of grace. There is no end of them. Now discipleship is necessary to distinguish among these snares."

"When the divine breath appears from the innermost self, it puts the breath of the heart and the body to death. It passes over nothing without burning it up, even if it be the entire empyrean itself."

"When someone beholds God's power, he is loathe to draw a breath. When someone beholds his grandeur, he is prevented from breathing. When someone beholds his awesomeness, he is an unbeliever if he breathes then."

"The breath that comes from a true believer in dire straits burns up all the veils and sins that stand between the servant and the Lord most high."

"Anyone who exalts the Lord can breathe. Breathing is not a sin for him, and he cannot stop himself. Anyone awed by the Lord is given to praising him, but for him, this is a sin, and there he cannot breathe."[10]

"Happy is the person who is truly present for an hour in the course of his entire life."

"The quick glance is ingratitude. Passing intuition is faith. The allusive sign is pardon." In other words, the glance is voluntary.

"Servants are of two sorts: servants of the Real and servants of the Reality. Servants of the Real are there saying, *'I seek refuge in your pleasure from your wrath.'* Servants of the Reality are there saying, *'I seek refuge in you from you.'*"

"The mighty and glorious Lord wants two sorts of knowledge from his servants. The first is the knowledge of servitude; the second, the recognition of lordship. Anything besides this is self-indulgence."

"Meditating in the arena of unity is the noblest of assemblies and the highest form of attendance."

"All paths are closed to creatures unless they follow the path of Mohammad (peace and blessing be upon him). Do not emulate anyone who has not memorized the Qur'an or written down the hadith of the Prophet, for knowledge goes back to the Book and prophetic custom."

"Four oceans stand between the Real most high and his servant; until the servant crosses them, he does not reach the Real. One is this world, and its ship is renunciation. One is people, and its ship is keeping one's distance from them. One is Satan, and its ship is loathing. And one is desire, and its ship is opposition."

"The difference between the urgings of the self and temptations of the devil is that when the self begs for something and you forbid it, it will keep after you until it gets what it wants, even if it takes a while. When the devil calls you and you oppose him, he'll give up."

"This self commands evil, calls us to perdition, abets the enemy, obeys desire, and stands accused of all evils."

"For all his devotion, Satan did not succeed in contemplating the divine. For all his sin, Adam often did."

"Devotion is not the reason for what transpired in pre-eternity, but it gives good tidings that what transpired in that primordial act transpired for the good of the devoted."

"Humans are human because of their good conduct, not because of their form."

"The place of the Lord's secret is in the hearts of his friends, and the mighty and glorious Lord does not place his secret in a heart that loves this world."

"The basic thing is not attending to the desires of the self."

349

"Being negligent of the mighty and glorious Lord is harder than entering into the fire."

"You will not attain the reality of freedom until your servitude lacks nothing."

"The self never becomes familiar with the Real most high."

"Devotion will be easy for anyone who can recognize the self."

"Constant is the friendship of the truly respectful."

"Anyone whose conduct conflicts with his teaching is an impostor and a fraud."

"Anyone who says, 'God' without contemplating him is a liar."

"Anyone who does not know the Lord is never happy."

"Tell anyone who wants a sound faith, a rested body, and a vital heart: Keep away from people, for this is an age of savagery, and anyone who chooses solitude is wise."

"Anyone whom knowledge does not lead to certainty, and certainty to fear, and fear to good works, and good works to scrupulousness, and scrupulousness to sincerity, and sincerity to contemplation is doomed to perish."

"There have been true believers who with certainty walked across water, but the certainty of those who were dying of thirst was superior."

"Respecting rights comes only from protecting hearts."

"If a single person owns the entire world, this will not harm him, but if his innermost self hungers after a single date pit, that will."

"If you can, let all the dishes in your house be made only of earthenware."

"God's servant complains to no one and allows no oversights in his service. Oversight is in deliberation."

"Whenever brethren and friends are present, supererogatory acts of worship occur."

"The honest disciple has no need for the learning of worldly people."

"Truly, the Real most high will treat his servants in the end as they have treated him in the beginning."

"Truly, the Lord most high draws near his servant's heart to the extent that he sees that the servant is close to him."

"If you are known for searching out the truth, the way will be made easy for you. If you face your first afflictions resolutely, many wonders and subtleties will become clear to you. *Before obstacles, patience is best.*"

"Exertion of effort is the guide in everything. The person who seeks the Lord by giving generously of his efforts is not like the one who seeks him by giving his money."

"All the learning of the scholars can be summed up in two phrases: reforming the people and disinterested service."

"Anyone who lives by the strength of his self dies when his spirit departs. But anyone who lives by the strength of the Lord is transported from the life of nature to the life of the essence. In reality, this is life. Any eye that is not busy heeding the warning signs of the Real most high is better off blind. Any tongue that is not absorbed in recalling his name is better off mute. Any ear that is not vigilant in listening to the Real is better off deaf. And any body that is not engaged in the service of the mighty and glorious Lord is better off dead."

"Whoever applies himself to his own works will go astray. Whoever applies himself to wealth will quickly fall. Whoever applies himself to the Lord will become great and glorious."

"When the Real most high wishes a disciple well, he throws him in among the Sufis and keeps him from Qur'an readers."

"It is not fitting that disciples learn anything except what they need for prayer and the first chapter of the Qur'an and the statement *Declare he is the one God.* Nothing comes of any disciple who takes a wife and writes learnedly."

"No one will ever find pleasure in his private devotions when he has placed a full feedbag between himself and the presence of the Lord."

"In disciples' hearts, this world is more bitter than the colocynth of patience. When realization comes to their hearts, this patience becomes sweeter than honey."

"They recognize you dervishes by the Lord and honor you for his sake. Take care how you stand with him in private."

"The earth shines because of the devout just as the heavens shine because of the stars."

"The noblest of works is learning the science of the moments, and this science consists of watching over your self, your heart, and your faith."

"Passing intuitions are of four kinds: There is the intuition from the Real, which calls the servant to the Real. There is the intuition from the angels, which calls the servant to devoted service. There is the intuition from the self, which calls the servant to pamper the self and take delight in this world. And there is the intuition from the devil, which calls the servant to rancor, envy, and enmity."

"Misfortune is the lamp of the realized, the awakener of the disciple, and the destroyer of the ignorant."

"Aspiration is the beckoning of the Lord; discipleship, the beckoning of the angels; and intuition, the beckoning of realization. Adorning the body is the beckoning of Satan; lusts, the beckoning of the self; and sensual pleasure, the beckoning of unbelief."

"The Lord most high never punishes those who aspire, even if sin befalls them."

"Whoever aspires can see. Whoever wills is blind."

"No person takes precedence over another, and no good work has priority over another. Rather, priority exists when one aspirant's aspiration outruns another's, and his aspirations outstrip another's works."

"By the consensus of four thousand elders of the path, this is the end of renunciation: wherever you seek your heart, you find it attending the Real."

"Anyone who has attained reality through concord fears that his good fortune will lapse, slipping away from the mighty and glorious Lord toward something else."

"The spiritual stages are in the inner visions. Whoever contemplates the mystical states is a companion, but whoever contemplates God's attributes is an emir. The torment reaches the point that one must die a thousand times in a single day and night as long as self-ness remains. When one has been extinguished, and the vision of the Real most high has been obtained, one has become an emir."

"The words of the prophets are news of presence. The speech of the righteous is an indication of contemplation."

"The first thing that becomes apparent about the state of those worthy of the mystical states is the sincerity of their actions. No one's actions can be sincere unless his innermost self is pure."

"The Sufi is like the earth: all filth is thrown in, and all goodness comes out."

"Sufism is a chanting in the meetings; it is a rapture in the dances; and it is an action in obedience."

"Sufism is derived from the idea of 'selection': Whoever is chosen from among created things is a Sufi."

"This is the Sufi: His heart is immune to the love of this world, like Abraham's, and he carries out the Lord's commands. His submission to God's will is like Ishmael's. His grief is like David's. His poverty is like Jesus'. His patience is like Job's. His yearning in his private devotions is like Moses'. And his sincerity is like Mohammad's—peace and blessing be upon them."

"Sufism is a quality in which God's servant resides," Joneyd said.
"Is it a quality of the Real or of the created world?"
"Its reality is a quality of the Real, and its name is a quality of the created world."

"This is Sufism: the mighty and glorious Lord makes you die to yourself and makes you live in him."

"This is Sufism: you are with the mighty and glorious Lord without any attachment."

"Sufism is a remembrance, then a rapture, then neither this nor that, until it seems that it does not exist."

They asked him about the essence of Sufism. He said, "May you grasp its outward form. Do not ask about its reality, for that is doing it an injustice."

"Sufis are those who abide with the Lord, for they know nothing but him." So it was that a young man fell in with Joneyd's followers. For several days he did not raise his head except in prayer and then left. Joneyd sent a disciple after him, saying, "Ask him this: 'How does the Sufi who is characterized by his purity perceive something that has no characteristics?'"
The disciple went and asked the dervish. He replied, "Be without characteristics so you may perceive what is without characteristics."
When Joneyd heard this, he pondered the majesty of these words for several days and said, "Alas, he was a mighty bird, and I did not appreciate his worth."

"The realized have to pass through seventy stages. One is not obtaining what they desire from this world."

"One mystical state does not keep the realized from another. One stage of the path does not keep them from another."

"The realized are those whom the Real most high brings to the stage where he speaks through their innermost self, while they remain silent."

"The realized are those who roam through the spiritual ranks in such a way that nothing veils them or holds them back."

"There are two sorts of realization: the realization of becoming known and the realization of making known. The realization of becoming known is when he makes himself familiar with them. The realization of making known is when he recognizes them."

"Realization is a preoccupation with the Lord most high."

"Realization is the deception of the Lord most high." In other words, whoever fancies that he has attained realization is deceived.

"Realization is finding ignorance when you acquire knowledge."
     "Expand on that," they said.
     "He is the knower and the known."

"Knowledge is something all-encompassing, and realization is something all-encompassing. So, where is the mighty and glorious Lord, and where is the servant?" In other words, knowledge belongs to the Lord and realization to his servant. Both are all-encompassing oceans, and one comes from the other as its reflection. When this ocean sinks into that, no duality remains. As long as you say "Lord" and "servant," duality persists. Indeed, the knower and the known are one. Thus, they say, "In reality, it is he." There, where is the Lord and the servant? In other words, all is the Lord.

"First there is knowledge. Then there is the realization of the affair, then a repudiation in denial. Then there is negation, then drowning, then perdition. And when the curtain lifts, all are lords of the veil."

"Knowledge is recognizing your own value."

"Affirmation is deceit, and affirmative knowledge is deceit. Motions are fraud, and everything that exists within is fraud and deceit."

"Knowledge is unity with the Lord through his existence, and his existence is the dispersion of knowledge in him."

"For twenty years the knowledge of unity has been rolled up and put aside, and people have been talking around the edges."

"The unity of the Lord is recognizing his timelessness in the temporal." In other words, you know that if there is a surge in the sea, it is not the sea.

"The farthest extent of unity is the denial of unity." In other words, you deny every unity you know, saying, "This is not unity."

"Love is the Lord's trust."

"Any love given in exchange is over once the exchange is complete."

"Love does not come out right unless it is between two people who call one another I."

"When love comes out right, the rules of etiquette fall away."

"The Real most high has forbidden love to anyone who is already attached."

"Love is an excess of inclination without inclination."

"You cannot attain the Lord by love of the Lord until you give of your life generously on his path."

"To find intimacy in promises and to rely on them is a defect in generosity."

"The folk of intimacy say things in private and in their personal devotions that seem blasphemy to the commoners. If the public hears such things, they condemn this folk as unbelievers. Their mystical states are increased thereby, and they endure whatever is said about them. This is worthy of them."

"Contemplation is drowning. Ecstasy is perdition."

"Ecstasy brings everything to life. Contemplation causes everything to die."

"Contemplation establishes lordship and eliminates servitude, but only if you see no intermediary."

"Viewing something without attaining its essence is contemplation."

"Ecstasy is the perdition of ecstasy."

"Ecstasy is joyfully severing attributes in the advent of the essence." In other words, whatever is an attribute of the you-ness of you is cut away, and whatever is his essence within the unknown reveals itself.[11]

"Proximity to him in ecstasy is union. His absence in being human is division."

"Watchfulness is fearing what has lapsed."
        They asked, "What is the difference between watchfulness and shame?"
        "Watchfulness is expectation of the absent, while shame is embarrassment before the present in contemplation."

"When the moment lapses, it can never be obtained again. There is nothing dearer than the moment."

"If an honest person faces the Real for a thousand years, then turns away from the Real for an instant, what he loses in that instant is greater than what was gained in those thousand years." In other words, in that one instant one could have gained what one gained in those thousand years. Another sense of it is mourning the damage done by wasting the presence of that one instant when one turned away from the mighty and glorious Lord. One cannot make up for such rudeness with a thousand years of worship and dutiful attention.

"Nothing is more difficult for the friends of God than guarding their breaths in moments of rapture."

"Servitude has two qualities: genuine need for the mighty and glorious Lord, both privately and publicly; and sound imitation of the Prophet of the Lord most high."

"Servitude is giving up one's business and busying oneself with that which is the origin of ease."

"Servitude is giving up these two affinities: first, stillness in pleasure, and second, reliance on motion. When these two diminish for you, then servitude has been fulfilled."

"Thankfulness is not counting your self among the prosperous."

"Thankfulness has a defect, and it is that the disciple searches it out for the self's sake and stands by the mighty and glorious Lord for self-gratification."

"The limit of renunciation is being empty and unoccupied by it."

"The reality of honesty is speaking the truth in the gravest situation when only lying will save you."

"There is no one who seeks honesty that does not find it. If not every-one finds it, some do."

"The honest person changes forty times a day, while the hypocrite remains the same for forty years."

"The sign of the honest poor is that they do not question or quarrel, and if someone picks a quarrel with them, they are silent."

"If believing becomes excessive, there's no harm done. If declaring it with the tongue does *not* become excessive, there's no harm done. But performing the rituals of the faith can be both excessive and harmful."

"Patience is self-restraint before the Lord most high without anxiety."

"The utmost patience is trust in God. God most high said: '*Those who are patient trust their Lord*'" [16:42].

"Patience is drinking down bitterness without making a sour face."

"Trust in God is eating without food." In other words, food has nothing to do with it.

"Trust in God is belonging to the Lord as you belonged to him before you existed."

"Before this, trust in God was the reality. Today, learning is."

"Trust in God is not in earning a living or not earning a living, but is the heart's repose in the promise of the Real most high."

"Certainty is a knowledge settling in the heart that never abandons it or changes."

"Certainty is when you do not worry about your daily sustenance and do not struggle for it, and this is enough for you. Occupy yourself with whatever task is imposed upon you, for he will certainly provide for your daily needs."

"Gallantry is not fighting with the poor and not quarreling with the wealthy."

"Gallantry is carrying the burden of the people and giving generously of what you have."

"This is meekness: you do not act arrogantly toward the people of this world or the next, and you are free of want in the Real most high."

"Moral character lies in four things: generosity, friendship, counsel, and kindliness."

"I prefer the company of agreeable degenerates to that of disagreeable Qur'an readers."

"Shame is seeing his favors and your shortcomings. Then, a condition is born from these two that they call shame."

"His solicitude existed before water and clay."

"The mystical state is something that comes down to the heart but is not constant."

"Acceptance is to eliminate choice."

"Acceptance is counting misfortune a blessing."

"Poverty is the sea of hardship."

"Poverty is emptying the heart of forms."

"Fear is expelling what is illicit from within and giving up the use of 'perhaps' and 'shall.'"

"Fasting is half the way."

"Repentance has three meanings—first, regret; second, being resolute in breaking old habits; and third, purifying the self of cruelties and enmity."

"The reality of remembrance is the extinction of the rememberer in remembrance and of remembrance in the contemplation of the remembered."

"Deception is when someone walks on water or flies through the air. Mere fancy makes him believe in this and confirms the signs given to him. This is all a deception for someone who knows."

"For a disciple to feel secure from deception is a mortal sin; for an adept to feel secure from deception is unbelief."

They asked, "What happens when a person is calm, but feels restless when he hears music?"
    "The Real most high made a compact with the descendants of Adam: *'Am I not your Lord?'* [7:172]. All the spirits were drowned in

the delight of those words. When they hear music in this world, they begin to move and feel restless."

"Sufism is purifying the heart of recourse to its created form—it is separation from the characteristics of the natural world, putting to death the attributes of humanness, and keeping distant from the claims of the self. Sufism is the immersion in spiritual attributes and the ascension to true forms of knowledge. It is putting to use what is worthiest for eternity. It is giving counsel to all peoples, acting in good faith toward the truth, and following the Prophet (peace and blessing be upon him) in religious law."

Joneyd was again asked about Sufism. He said, "May you stay far from the word 'Sufism'! Take hold of its outer form and don't ask about its essence." When Roveym insisted, Joneyd said, "The Sufis are a folk who abide with the Lord, in such a way that only the Lord most high recognizes them."

They asked, "What is the ugliest characteristic a Sufi can have?"
"Avarice," Joneyd replied.

They asked Joneyd about unity. He said, "It means this: in it, customs are reduced to nothing, and learning vanishes. It is the Lord most high as he has always been and will be, not subject to extinction or defect."

Again they asked him, "What is unity?"
"The characteristics of servitude are all lowliness, impotence, weakness, and humility, and the characteristics of the Lord are all power and might. Anyone who can separate these, although he is lost, shall experience unity."

Another time when they asked him about unity, he said, "It is certainty."
"How so?"
"You recognize that the motion and quiescence of the created world are the action of the mighty and glorious Lord, and no one shares in this with him. When you put this into effect, you satisfy the condition of unity."

They asked about extinction and subsistence.
"Subsistence belongs to the Real, extinction to what is not him."

They asked, "What is detachment?"
"An outer being detached from accidentals and an inner being detached from self-interests."

They asked Joneyd about love. He said, "It is that which replaces the qualities of the lover with the qualities of the beloved. The Prophet (may God bless him and his family and give them peace) said, *'If you love him, you will hear through him and see through him.'*"

They asked Joneyd about intimacy. He said, "It is when bashfulness disappears."

They asked about meditation. Joneyd said, "It has several aspects. There is meditation on the divine signs, and its mark is that it gives birth to realization. There is meditation on the favors and blessings of the Lord most high, which gives birth to love. There is meditation on the Lord's promises and threats, and this gives birth to awe. And there is meditation on the qualities of the self and the good that the mighty and glorious Lord has done for it, and this gives birth to shame before the Lord most high." If someone asks, "Why does thinking about his promises of reward give birth to awe?" we reply, "By relying on the generosity of the mighty and glorious Lord, one takes flight from the Lord and gets entangled in sin."

They asked about the servant's fulfillment of his servitude. Joneyd said, "When the servant sees all things as the property of the mighty and glorious Lord, sees everything as the manifestation of the Lord, sees the continuance of everything in the Lord, and sees everything returning to the Lord—as the Lord most high has said: *'And glory to him in whose hand is the dominion of all things and to whom you shall be returned'* [36:83]—when all this is fulfilled in the servant, he has attained the purest servitude."

They asked about the reality of watchfulness. He said, "It is a condition in which the watchful expect what they fear will happen. Thus, it is like the characteristic of a person who does not sleep because he fears an attack by night. God most high said: *'So watch out'* [44:10], meaning, expect."

They asked about the honest man, the righteous man, and honesty. Joneyd said, "Honesty is the attribute of the honest man, and when you see him, you see him to be just as you heard he is. Reports about him are like seeing him face to face. In fact, if a report about him reaches you once, you will find his entire life is exactly that way. The righteous man is anyone whose honesty is constant in all his acts, words, and moods."

They asked about sincerity. Joneyd said, *"It is an obligation within an obligation, a supererogation within a supererogation."* He continued, "Sincerity is an obligation within every obligatory act, such as prayer and the like. Since prayer is an obligatory act, it is obligatory according to the traditions to be sincere. Being sincere is the pith of prayer, and prayer is the pith of the traditions."

They asked again about sincerity. Joneyd said, "It is passing away from your acts, eliminating your action and forethought."

"Sincerity is when you remove people from the interaction between the Lord and the self." In other words, the self makes claims of lordship.

They questioned him about fear. Joneyd said, "It is awaiting the final punishment with every breath."

They said, "What does the hardship that he imposes do?"
He said, "It is your crucible, which purifies the true believer. Hardship does not appear to anyone who is purified in this crucible."

They questioned Joneyd about kindliness toward God's creatures. He said, "Kindliness toward God's creatures is willingly giving them what they seek, placing no burden upon them that they cannot bear, and not saying a word to them that they cannot understand."

They said, "When does being alone turn out well?"
He said, "When you are secluded from your self and when your lesson for today is what was written out for you yesterday."

They said, "Who is the dearest of God's creatures?"
He said, "The contented poor."

They said, "Whom shall we follow?"
He said, "Someone who forgets any good that he has done you and fulfills his responsibilities."

They said, "Isn't there anything nobler than weeping?"
He said, "Weeping upon weeping."

They said, "Who is God's servant?"
He said, "One who is free from servitude to other people."

They said, "Who is the disciple and who the guide?"
He said, "The disciple is governed by learning and good works, while the guide is in the keeping of the Real, because the disciple runs, while the guide flies. How can the runner catch up with the flyer?"

They said, "How is the path to the Lord most high?"
He said, "Abandon this world, and you have attained it. Oppose passion so you are joined to the Real."

They said, "What is meekness?"
He said, "Bowing the head and prostrating the body."

They said, "You say that there are three veils: the self, the people, and this world."
He said, "These are the veils of the commoners. The veils of the elite are these: looking to acts of worship, looking to heavenly reward, and looking to miracle working."

"Scholars err in slipping from the licit to the forbidden. Renunciants err in slipping from subsistence to extinction. The realized err in slipping from the Miraculous to miracle-working."

They said, "What is the difference between the heart of the believer and the heart of the hypocrite?"
He said, "The believer's heart changes seventy times an hour, while the hypocrite's remains the same for seventy years."

"O Lord, rouse me blind from the earth on the morrow of the resurrection!"

"What sort of prayer is this?" they asked.

"When he sees you, you should see no one else."

∽ ∽ ∽

As his death approached, Joneyd said, "Have them set the table and lay out the food, so I may die listening to the murmur of my followers while they eat."

When his condition grew desperate, he said, "Perform my ablutions for me." They happened to forget to let the water run through his fingers and beard. He told them to make good the omission. Then he fell to his knees and wept.

"Master of the path," they said, "with all the worship and devotion that you have sent on ahead, is now any time to kneel and bow down?"

He said, "Never has Joneyd been in greater need than he is now."

He then began to recite the Qur'an. As he was reciting, a disciple exclaimed, "You're reciting the Qur'an?!"

"At this hour, what could be more appropriate for me to do?" Joneyd said. "Within the hour, they will roll up the scroll of my life, and I will see my seventy years of worship and devotion suspended in midair by a single hair. A wind will rise up and toss it to and fro. I do not know whether it will be the wind of separation or the wind of union. On one side will be the Narrow Bridge and on the other the angel of death. The Judge who is known for his justice will show no favoritism. The road has already been laid out before me. I do not know which road they will lead me down."

Then Joneyd recited seventy verses of surat *al-Baqara*,[12] and his condition worsened. They said, "Say 'God.'"

"I have not forgotten," he said. He then knotted his fingers around his prayer beads, so that four fingers were gripped around them and the index finger hung down. With a perfect grandeur he said, *"In the name of God the merciful and compassionate."* He closed his eyes and died.

When it was time to wash his body for burial, the washer was about to clean his eyes out with water. A voice called out, "Remove your hand from the eyes of our friend. His eyes were closed upon our name and will not open until he meets us." The washer was then about to pry open the fingers that were knotted around the prayer beads. The voice came: "The finger that was knotted around our name will not be released except by our command."

When they lifted up his bier, a white dove landed on the corner of it. It would not fly off no matter how much they tried to shoo it away. Then the dove spoke: "Don't trouble yourselves or me. My claws are fastened to the corner of his bier with the nail of love. I have landed here because his material form is today the portion of the cherubim. If it weren't for your ruckus, his body would have soared into the air like a white falcon."

Someone saw Joneyd in a dream and asked, "How did you reply to Monker and Nakir?"

"When those two intimates of the court of glory came toward me so dreadfully and asked, 'Who is your Lord?' I looked at them and laughed. I said, 'On the day when he asked, "Am I not your Lord?" I replied, "Yes." Now you've come to ask me, "Who's your Lord?" When someone has given an answer to the sultan, why should he worry about the slave boy? Even today I speak with his tongue: "The One who created me and guides me"' [26:78].

"The two departed from me respectfully and said, 'He is still drunk with love.'"

Someone else saw Joneyd in a dream. He said, "How did you see your situation?"

"The situation was other than what I thought it would be. Some hundred thousand loci of prophecy have bowed their heads and are silent. We, too, have fallen silent to see how the situation will turn out."

Joreyri said, "I saw Joneyd in a dream. I asked, 'What did the mighty and glorious Lord do with you?'

"He said, 'He was merciful. All those signs and warnings of mine were hot air, except for two or three rak'ats of prayer that I performed at midnight.'"

It is related that Shebli was standing one day at Joneyd's grave. Someone asked him about a problem. He gave no answer but said, "For the great ones, it is the same whether they are dead or alive. I am ashamed to give an answer to your problem here before his grave, just as I was ashamed to do so when he was alive."

∞ 23 ∞
Abu'l-Hoseyn Nuri

Enraptured by unity, seized by majesty, the lodestar of lights, the fertile droplet of spiritual secrets, self-slain by separation's agony, the subtle scholar, Abu'l-Hoseyn Nuri—God's mercy be upon him. He was unique in his age and the exemplar of his time, the gentleman of the Sufis and the nobleman of love's partisans. He possessed a venerable austerity and pleasing conduct, lofty epigrams and marvelous enigmas, true vision and honest clairvoyance, perfect love and endless yearning. The sheikhs agreed on his precedence and called him the Emir of Hearts and the Moon of Sufism. He was the disciple of Sari-ye Saqati, studied with Ahmad-e Havāri,[1] and was among Joneyd's contemporaries. He was a precedent-setting judge on the path and had his own school of thought. He was an authority among the sheikhs and the learned and had decisive proofs and luminous arguments concerning the path. The principle of his doctrine is to place Sufism above poverty. In matters of conduct he is in agreement with Joneyd. Among the peculiarities of his path is that he considers companionship without altruism to be unlawful, and in companionship, he enjoins giving preference to a companion's rights over one's own. He states, "Keeping company with dervishes is an obligatory duty, and seclusion is not approved," and he deems the altruism of one companion toward another obligatory.

He is called Nuri, or the Luminous, because light would come from his mouth when he preached on dark nights, illuminating the room. They also called him Nuri because the light of his clairvoyance informed him of hidden secrets. It is also said that he had a meditation cell in the desert where he would worship all night long. People would go there to watch. At night, they would see a light shining and rising up from his meditation cell. Abu Mohammad-e Maghāzeli said, "I never saw anyone with Nuri's devotion."

In the beginning, he used to leave his house early every morning, saying, "I'm going to the shop." He would pick up a couple of loaves of bread and give them away as alms along the road and enter the mosque and pray until the midday prayers. Then, he would go to the shop. The people at home thought that he had eaten something at the shop, while the people at the shop assumed that he had eaten something at home. He conducted himself in this way for twenty years, so that no one was aware of his spiritual states.

It is related that Nuri said:

I struggled and imprisoned myself for years. I turned my back on people and performed austerities. The way did not open before me. I said to myself, "Something must be done to remedy this situation; either that or let me die and escape this self." Then I said to my body, "For years, you have been eating at your whim and desire. You spoke and saw and heard. You went and took and slept. You enjoyed yourself and gratified your lusts. All this has taken a toll on you. Now, go home, so I can fetter you and shackle your neck with what is due the Real. If you keep to it, you will gain good fortune, but if not, at least you will die on the path of the Real."

I lived like this for forty years. I had heard that the hearts of this clan were extremely sensitive and knew the secrets of everything they saw or heard. I could not see this within myself. I thought, "The promises of the prophets and friends of God are real. It seems that I have been striving hypocritically, and the shortcoming is mine, because there no room for conflict there. Now, let me circle around myself to see what it is."

I looked deep into myself. My bane was that the self had become one with the heart. When the self becomes one with the heart, it is a disaster: the self takes its share of everything that shines upon the heart. When I saw how things were, I realized that I was stuck like this because the self was taking its share of everything that came to the heart from God's court. After that, I stopped pursuing anything that made the self feel at ease, and I would seize on something else. For example, if the self was pleased with prayer or fasting or was amenable to seclusion or society, I would do the opposite until I cast it out completely and its gratifications were curtailed. Then the secrets appeared within me. So, I asked my self, "Who are you?"

It said, "I am the jewel from the mine of dissatisfaction. Now go tell the disciples, 'My business is dissatisfaction, and my jewel is the jewel of disappointment.'"

Then I went to the Tigris and stood between two boats and said, "I will not leave until a fish lands on my hook." Finally, one landed. As I pulled it in, I said, "Praise God that my affair has turned out well!" I went and told Joneyd, "Such a revelation has opened up within me!"

Joneyd replied, "Abu'l-Hoseyn, you landed a fish. If you had landed a snake, that would have been your miracle. But since you were still involved, it was a deception, not a miracle. A miracle is something in which you are not involved."

Glory to God! What liberated people these true believers were!

It is related that when Gholām Khalil rose up in enmity against this clan, he said to the caliph, "A group has appeared that dance and sing and utter blasphemies. Its members busy themselves with amusements all day and wander secretly through the catacombs and preach. They are a heretical people. If the Commander of the Faithful orders them killed, this sect of heretics will be wiped out, because they are the head of the entire group. If the authority of the Commander of the Faithful accomplishes this good deed, I guarantee him an abundant spiritual reward."

The caliph immediately ordered Abu Hamza,[2] Raqqām,[3] Shebli, Nuri, and Joneyd (God have mercy on them) to present themselves at court. When the caliph ordered them to be put to death, the executioner made ready to kill Raqqām. Nuri leapt up, threw himself forward in all sincerity, and took Raqqām's place. Laughing and rejoicing, he said, "Execute me first."

"It's not your time yet," the executioner said. "The sword isn't something people rush to meet."

"The foundation of our path rests on altruism, and the most precious of things is life," Nuri said. "For these few moments, I want to work for these brethren, until I have given generously even of my life, although for me, one moment in this world is dearer than a thousand years in the next. This world is the domain of service, and the next, the domain of proximity. Proximity, however, is in service."

When they heard what Nuri said, they reported it to the caliph. The caliph was amazed at his sense of justice and worthy stand. He ordered them to put the execution on hold and referred the matter to the judge so he could look into their case. The judge said, "They cannot be proscribed without good reason." The judge had heard Nuri preach and knew that Joneyd was a perfect master in religious sciences. He thought, "I will ask this madman," meaning Shebli, "something about religious law that he cannot answer."

The judge asked, "Out of twenty dinars, how much must be given as alms?"

Shebli answered, "Twenty and one half dinars."

"Who has done this?"

"The Greatest of the Righteous, Abu Bakr (may God be pleased with him) who gave forty thousand dinars and took nothing in return."

"What is this half dinar for?"

"For the fine," Shebli said. "Why did he hold on to these twenty dinars? He must pay another half dinar."

The judge then asked Nuri a question of religious law. Nuri replied immediately. The judge was ashamed of himself. Nuri said, "Your Honor, you have asked all these questions but haven't asked anything at all. The mighty and glorious Lord has men who stand entirely through him, who move and rest entirely through him, who live through him, and who abide through the contemplation of him. If they stop contemplating the Real for even one moment, their souls fly from them. They sleep through him, they eat through him, they take through him, they walk through him, they see through him, they hear through him, they exist through him. This is learning, not the things you asked about."

The judge was dumbstruck. He sent someone to report to the caliph: "If these men are atheists and heretics, I decree that there is not one person on the face of the earth who believes in God's unity."

The caliph summoned them and asked, "What do you need?"

"What we need," they said, "is for you to forget us, to neither honor us with your acceptance nor banish us with your rejection. For us, your rejection is like acceptance, and your acceptance is like rejection."

The caliph sobbed and sent them on their way with all due respect.

It is related that one day Nuri saw a disciple playing with his mustache while he prayed. Nuri said, "Remove your hand from the mustache of the Real!"

These words were reported to the caliph. The experts on religious law agreed that with these words, Nuri had uttered a blasphemy. He was brought before the caliph. The caliph asked, "Did you say these words?"

"Yes," Nuri said.

"Why did you say them?"

"Who does God's servant belong to?"

"He belongs to the Real."

"Who does his mustache belong to?"

"To the same One to whom the servant belongs," the caliph said and exclaimed, "Praise God that the Lord most high kept me from executing you."

Nuri said, "For forty years, my heart and I have been separated. In these forty years I have had no desire and have not lusted after anything. In my heart nothing seemed good. This has been the case since the time I recognized the Real most high." He said, "I saw a light shining in the unknown. I gazed on it continually until I became entirely that light." And he said, "I once asked the Lord most high to give me a constancy. An unseen voice called out, 'Abu'l-Hoseyn, no one can endure the constant except the Constant.'"

It is related that one day Joneyd came to see Nuri. He fell to the ground before Joneyd, crying for justice: "The battle is hard, and I am exhausted. For thirty years, when he has appeared, I have been lost, and when I have appeared, he has been absent. His presence is in my absence. No matter how much I cry out, He says, 'Either I am, or you.'"

To his followers, Joneyd said, "Behold a person who is tested, bewildered, and left helpless by the Real most high." Then Joneyd said to Nuri, "So it must be. If he comes alive in you, if he appears in you, you do not exist. It is all he."

It is related that a group of people came to see Joneyd and said, "For several days and nights Nuri has been spinning around on a brick and shouting, 'God! God!' He hasn't had anything to eat or drink and hasn't slept, but he performs his prayers on time and carries out the proper rituals."

Joneyd's followers said, "He is conscious, not self-annihilated—he observes the times of prayer and knows to perform the proper rituals. So, this is a show of extravagance, not self-extinction; anyone who passes away from the self is not aware of anything."

"It is not as you say," Joneyd replied. "Those who are in rapture are protected. The Lord most high guards them, lest they are prevented from serving him at the proper time." Then Joneyd went to see Nuri and said, "Abu'l-Hoseyn, if you know that shouting will do you any good with him, then let me start shouting too. But if you know that acceptance is better, then resign yourself, so your heart will be at ease."

At once, Nuri stopped shouting and said, "What a good teacher you are for us!"

It is related that Shebli was preaching. Nuri came, stood off to one side, and said, "Peace be upon you, Abu Bakr."

"And peace be upon you, Emir of Hearts," replied Shebli.

"The Real most high is not pleased with a learned man who speaks of knowledge that he does not put into practice," Nuri said. "If you are acting on what you say, stay where you are. If not, come down."

Shebli looked closely and did not find himself in the right. He came down, and for four months he sat in his house without coming out. The people gathered together and brought him out and placed him on the pulpit. Nuri was informed. He came and said, "Abu Bakr, you kept things hidden from them, so of course, they put you in the pulpit. When I counseled them, they drove me away with stones and threw me into the garbage dumps."

"Emir of Hearts, what was your counsel and what was my concealment?"

Nuri said, "My counsel was that I released the Lord's people to return to the Lord. Your concealment was that you became a veil between the Lord and his people. Who are you to be an intermediary between the Lord and his people? I consider you nothing but a meddler."

It is related that a young man set out barefoot from Isfahan to pay a visit on Nuri. As he approached, Nuri ordered a disciple to sweep the road with a broom for a distance of two miles and said, "A youth is coming upon whom this tradition has shined." When he arrived, Nuri asked, "Where are you from?"

"From Isfahan," he replied. Had he not gone to see Nuri, the ruler of Isfahan would have given him a palace, a thousand dinars' worth of furnishings, and a Turkish slave girl worth a thousand more.

So, Nuri said, "If the ruler of Isfahan would have given you a palace, a beautiful slave girl, and a thousand dinars' worth of furnishings not to leave, did you compare those things to this quest?"

On the spot, the young man cried out, "Slap me!"

"If the Real most high," Nuri said, "places the eighteen thousand worlds on a platter, brings them before a disciple, and the disciple looks at them, then it is not safe for him to speak of the Lord."

It is related that Nuri was sitting with someone, and they were both weeping. When the person left, Nuri turned to his friends and said, "Did you recognize who this was?"

"No," they replied.

"He was Satan. He was recounting his services and telling the story of his life. He was bewailing the pain of separation and weeping, as you saw. I was weeping too."

Ja'far-e Kholdi[4] related: "Nuri was by himself praying privately. I was listening in to hear what he would say. 'O Lord,' he said, 'You are punishing the people in hell. They are all your creatures through your knowledge, power, and pre-eternal will. If you will fill hell with people no matter what, you are able to fill hell with me and take them to heaven.'

"I was stunned. Then I dreamt that someone came to me and said, 'The mighty and glorious Lord has said, "Tell Abu'l-Hoseyn that we have forgiven him because of his kindness and esteem for us."'"

It is related that Nuri said: "One night I found the area around the Ka'ba empty and was circumambulating it. Whenever I reached the black stone, I would pray, 'O Lord, endow me with a state and quality that I will not change for even one day.' From the center of the Ka'ba I heard a voice say, 'Abu'l-Hoseyn, do you wish to be equal to us? We are the One who does not change his quality. However, we keep our servants changing to distinguish lordship from servitude. We are the One whose quality remains the same. Human qualities change.'"

Shebli relates: "I went to see Nuri. I saw him sitting in watchfulness, so that not a hair on his body moved. I asked, 'From whom did you learn such fine watchfulness?'

"'From a cat crouching over a mouse hole,' he said. 'It was much stiller than I.'"

It is related that one night the people of Qādesiyah heard, "One of the friends of the Lord has withdrawn to the Valley of Lions. Help him." The people all came out and went to the Valley of Lions. They saw that Nuri had hollowed out a grave and was sitting in it. They intervened and brought him to Qādesiyah.

Then they asked him what he was doing out there. He said, "It had been some time since I had eaten anything. I was in the desert. When I saw a date tree, I longed for some dates. I thought, 'There is still room for longing within me!' I descended into this valley so the lions would tear me apart and there would be no longing for dates."

It is related that Nuri said: "One day I was washing in a pool. A thief made off with my clothes. No sooner had I come out of the water than he brought them back. His hand was withered and paralyzed. I said, 'My God, since he has brought my clothes back, give him back his hand.' At once, his hand was cured."

Nuri was asked, "How does the Lord most high treat you?"

"When I go to the baths," Nuri said, "he watches over my clothes. One day I went to the baths, and someone made off with my clothes. I said, 'O Lord, give me back my clothes.' At once, the man brought back my clothes and apologized."

It is related that the slave market in Baghdad had caught fire, and many people were burned. In one stall, there were two very handsome Greek slave boys. The fire had surrounded them, and their owner cried out, "I will give a thousand Maghrebi dinars to anyone who brings them out." No one had the nerve to go near them.

Out of nowhere, Nuri arrived. He saw the two slave boys shouting for help. He said, "In the name of God the merciful and compassionate," stepped into the fire, and brought them both out to safety. The slave owner placed the thousand Maghrebi dinars before Nuri. "Take them away," Nuri said, "and give thanks to the Lord most high. The rank given me has been given because I do not take anything. I have exchanged this world for the next."

It is related that Nuri had a maid named Zeytuna. She reported:

One day I brought Nuri some bread and milk. He had been stirring the fire with his hands, and his fingers were blackened with soot. He ate the bread just like that, without washing his hands. "What an uncouth man," I said to myself.

All at once, a woman came and grabbed me, saying, "You have stolen a bundle of my clothes." They took me before the emir.

Nuri came and said to the emir, "Don't torture her. Here, look, they're bringing the clothes." The emir looked and a slave girl came in, bringing the bundle of clothes. Then I was released. The sheikh said to me, "Will you ever say, 'What an uncouth man' again?" I repented.

It is related that Nuri was passing through the city and saw someone collapsed on the ground. His donkey had died, and he was sobbing. Nuri kicked the donkey and said, "Is this any place to sleep? Get up!" It got up immediately. The man put his load on the donkey and went on his way.

It is related that Nuri fell ill. Joneyd came to visit him on his sickbed and brought flowers and fruit. After a while, Joneyd fell ill. Nuri and his followers came to visit him on his sickbed. Nuri said to his friends, "Each one of you take something of Joneyd's illness, so he will recover."

"We have taken it," they said.

Joneyd immediately got out of bed. "From this time forward," Nuri said to Joneyd, "when you visit someone on his sickbed, do it like this. Don't bring flowers and fruit."

Nuri related:

I saw a weak old man sapped of his strength. They were whipping him, and he withstood it patiently. Then they carried him off to prison. I went to see him and said, "You are so weak and powerless, and there they were whipping you. How did you withstand the whip with such patience?"

"My son," he said, "one can endure hardship only with fortitude, not with the body."

"In your opinion," I asked, "what is patience?"

He said, "Being the same way when suffering hardship as when escaping it."

✍ ✍ ✍

It is related that Nuri was asked, "How is the path to realization?"

"There are seven seas of fire and light," he said. "When you have crossed those seven seas, then you will become a morsel, so you can swallow the first and the last in a single bite."

It is related that Abu Hamza had made an allusion to proximity. To one of his followers, Nuri said, "Tell him that Nuri sends his greetings and says, 'When we are involved, the closest proximity is the remotest distance.'"

They asked Nuri about servitude. He said, "It is the contemplation of lordship."

They asked, "When is it proper for a person to preach to the people?"

"When he understands something about the mighty and glorious Lord. If he understands nothing of the Lord, his affliction will be universal throughout the lands of God and among his believers."

They asked about allusive intimation. "Intimation," he said, "has no need of expression, and comprehending it is due to being immersed in the secrets through sincerity."

They asked about rapture. Nuri said, "By the Lord who prohibits the tongue from describing his reality and the description of whose essence renders the eloquence of the cultured mute, the matter of rapture is the greatest of undertakings, and no torment is more painful than curing rapture."

"Rapture is a tongue of flame that the innermost self cannot contain, and it emerges from yearning, so the limbs of the body move, whether with joy or sorrow."

"What is the guide to the Lord?" they asked.

"The Lord," he answered.

"So, what is the role of reason?"

"Reason is weak, and a weak man cannot guide you to anyone except another person as weak as himself."

"The path of being a Muslim has been closed to people. Until they bow down to the writ of the Messenger (peace and blessing be upon him), it shall not be opened."

"The Sufis are a folk whose souls are freed from the pollution of being human, purified of the bane of the self, and delivered from desire so that in the first rank and highest degree, they are at rest with the Real and shy away from everything but him. They neither possess nor are possessed."

"Nothing is bound to the Sufi, and he is bound to nothing."

"Sufism is neither knowledge nor custom. Rather, it is character." In other words, if it were a custom, it could be acquired through striving. If it were knowledge, it could be gained through learning. Indeed, it is character for *they are molded by the character of God*.[5] Emerging in the character of the Lord is not acquired by custom or knowledge.

"Sufism is freedom, gallantry, abandoning formality, and munificence."

"Abstaining is abandoning all shares of the self for a share in the Real."

"Sufism is enmity toward this world and friendship with the Lord."

ॐ ॐ ॐ

It is related that one day a blind man was crying, "God! God!" Nuri went up to him and said, "How can you know him? If you know him, you won't remain alive." He said this and swooned and out of yearning stumbled into the desert into a newly cut cane field. He was spinning around, and the cane pierced his feet and sides. The blood was flowing, and the words "God, God" could be seen in every drop.

Abu Nasr Sarrāj[6] (God have mercy on him) relates that when they brought Nuri from the cane field back to his house, they told him, "Say, 'There is no god, but God.'"

Nuri said, "At long last, I'm on my way there," and with that, he died.

Joneyd (God have mercy on him) said, "After Nuri died, no one spoke about the real nature of sincerity, for he was the truly righteous man of the time."

∽ 24 ∽
Abu 'Abdollāh ebn al-Jallā

The ship on the sea of religion, the repose of people of firm resolution, the guide to the spiritual stations, the mirror of prodigies, the sun in the sky of acceptance, Abu 'Abdollāh ebn al-Jallā—God's mercy be upon him. He was one of the great sheikhs of Syria, accepted and praised by this clan. He was distinguished by his elevated sayings and innovative intimations. He was without peer in spiritual realities and realizations and in the fine points of their subtleties. He met Abu Torāb and Zu'n-Nun and studied with Joneyd and Nuri.

Abu 'Amr of Damascus[1] said, "I heard that Abu 'Abdollāh said, 'In the beginning, I told my parents to put me to work in the Lord's business. They said, "We do so." I then left them for a time. When I returned, I went up to the door of the house and knocked. My father asked, "Who's there?" I answered, "Your son." He said, "We had a son and gave him to the Lord. We won't take back what we've given away." He did not open the door to me.'"

Abu 'Abdollāh reported:

One day I saw a handsome Christian youth. Gazing at him, I was stunned and stopped short in front of him. Sheikh Joneyd was passing by. "Teacher," I asked, "will such a beautiful face burn in the fires of hell?"

"This is the self's little marketplace," Joneyd said, "and the snare of Satan that will catch you. You are not looking at him to gain awareness. If you were, you would see that a marvel exists in every mote of the eighteen thousand worlds. However, it won't be long before you are punished for looking at him with this disrespect."

When Joneyd left, I forgot the Qur'an. For years I sought the aid of the Real most high and wept and repented, until the Real in his grace and munificence bestowed the Qur'an on me once again. For some time now, I haven't had the gall to pay heed to any being, so I won't waste my time looking at mere objects.

It is related that they asked Abu 'Abdollāh about poverty. He fell silent. Then, he went out and came back. "What was that about?" they asked.

"I had four thin silver coins," he answered. "I was ashamed to speak about poverty until I gave them away as alms."

Abu 'Abdollāh said, "Having endured want and hardship, I reached Medina. As I came upon the tomb of Mohammad (peace and blessing be upon him) I said, 'O Messenger of God, I have come as your guest.' Then I fell asleep. I saw the Prophet (peace be upon him) give me a loaf of bread. I ate half of it. When I awoke, the other half was in my hand."

✍ ✍ ✍

Abu 'Abdollāh was asked, "When does a person become worthy of the name of poverty?"

He said, "When nothing remains of him."

"How is it confirmed?"

"When the angel at God's left hand[2] has written down nothing against him for twenty years."

"Anyone who sees praise and blame as one and the same is a renunciant. Anyone who attends to the ritual obligations as soon as possible is a devotee. Anyone who sees all his actions coming from the Lord is united."

"The realized aspire to the Real and do not turn from the Real toward anything else."

"The renunciant looks on the world with the eyes of extinction, until it becomes contemptible in his eyes, so he can remove his heart from it easily."

"If mindfulness does not keep company with someone in his poverty, he will eat the manifestly forbidden."

"The Sufi is a poor man detached from things."

"If it were not for the nobility of meekness, it would be the rule of the poor to swagger proudly."

"Mindfulness is being thankful for realization. Meekness is being thankful for might. Patience is being thankful for hardship."

"One who feels dread before the Lord is kept safe from sorrows."

"Anyone who reaches a certain level through his self will soon fall from there. Anyone who has been brought to a certain level can remain in that position permanently."

"Any truth with which a falseness can associate leaves the category of the true for the category of the false, for the real truth is jealous."

"Pursuing your livelihood drives you away from the Real and makes you dependent on people."

∽ ∽ ∽

It is related that when his death approached, Abu 'Abdollāh was smiling and when he died, he was still smiling. The doctor asked, "He's not alive, is he?" but when they looked he was dead.

∽ 25 ∽

Samnun-e Mohebb, the Lover

All love without temerity, all consciousness without rationality, the moth of the candle of majesty, enamored of the morning of unity, restlessly calm, the beloved of the Real, Samnun-e Mohebb, the Lover[1]—God's mercy be upon him. He was unique in his dignity, accepted by the people of the time, and the most subtle of the sheikhs. He had strange intimations and wonderful enigmas. He was a paragon in love, and all of the elders acknowledged his greatness. He was called Samnun the Lover because of his gallantry and love, but he used to call himself Samnun the Liar. He was a follower of Sari and one of Joneyd's contemporaries.

He had a special doctrine concerning love. He gave love precedence over realization, while most of the sheikhs have given realization precedence over love. Samnun says, "Love is the principle and rule of the path of the Lord. The states and the stations are all games compared to love. Every one of the seeker's recognized way stations is subject to decay, but the way station of love is not subject to decay under any circumstances, as long as his essence exists."

It is related that when Samnun went to the Hejaz, the people of Feyd said to him, "Preach to us."

He climbed the pulpit. He was preaching, but found that no one was listening. He turned to the lamps and said, "I will preach to you of love." The lamps immediately began to smash into one another and shattered into pieces.

It is related that one day Samnun was preaching about love. A bird came down from the sky and alighted on his head. Then it alighted on his hand, then on his breast. It then stuck its beak so hard against the ground that blood began to flow from it. Then it fell over and died.

It is related that toward the end of his life, Samnun took a wife, according to the example of the Prophet. A daughter was born. When she turned three, Samnun began to feel an attachment to her. That very night he dreamt of the resurrection. Banners were being erected for every people. They erected one banner whose light enveloped the entire plain of the resurrection. Samnun asked, "To which people does this banner belong?"

They answered, "It belongs to that people of whom it is said, '*He loves them, and they love him*'" [5:54]. Samnun threw himself into their midst, but someone came and expelled him.

Samnun cried, "Why do you expel me?"

"Because this is the banner of lovers, and you are not among them."

"But they call me Samnun the Lover, and the Real most high knows my heart."

381

An unseen voice called out, "Samnun, you were one of the lovers, but when your heart inclined to that child, we crossed your name off the roll of lovers."

Even in his sleep, Samnun began to sob, "O Lord, if this child is going to waylay me, remove her from the path!"

When he awoke, a cry went up: "The girl has fallen from the roof and died."

It is related that in his private prayers Samnun once said, "My God, however you test me, you will find me true. I will submit and not breathe a word." At that instant, such a pain overwhelmed him that his life seemed about to end. He did not breathe a word.

At dawn, his neighbors said, "Sheikh, what happened to you last night? We couldn't fall asleep with all your crying." Samnun had not breathed a word, but his inner thought had taken form and reached the listeners' ears, so the Real most high could show him that silence is inner silence; if he had really been silent, his neighbors would have known nothing about it. In other words, do not say anything you cannot do.

Once Samnun was reciting this verse:

I have no joy in anything but you,
Put me to the test any way you wish.

Exactly then his urinary tract was blocked. He went around to the grammar schools and told the children, "Pray for your lying uncle, so the Real most high will cure him."

Abu Mohammad-e Maghāzeli relates: "I was with Samnun in Baghdad. They gave the poor forty thousand dirhams as living expenses but gave us nothing. Afterward, Samnun said, 'Let's go someplace and perform a rak'at of prayer for every dirham they gave.' So, we went to Madāyen and performed forty thousand rak'ats of prayer."

It is related that Gholām Khalil had made himself known to the caliph for his Sufism, selling his faith for this world. He was always slandering the sheikhs before the caliph. His aim was that they all be banished and lose all respect, so that his place would be secure and he would not be disgraced. When Samnun gained eminence and his fame began to spread, Gholām Khalil gave him a great deal of trouble and searched for an opportunity to disgrace him. At that point a wealthy woman offered herself to Samnun in marriage. Samnun refused. She went to see Joneyd so he would intercede with Samnun and he would ask for her hand in marriage. Joneyd chided her and drove her off.

She went to see Gholām Khalil and made an allegation about Samnun. Gholām Khalil was overjoyed and turned the caliph against Samnun. The caliph ordered Samnun's execution. When the executioner came forward, the caliph was about to say a few words, but he could not. His tongue was stuck in his throat. At night in a dream he was told, "The downfall of your kingdom is tied to Samnun's death." At dawn, he summoned Samnun, treated him with kindness, and sent him away with all due honor.

Gholām Khalil's hostility grew, until at the end of his life, he was stricken with leprosy. Someone told the story of how Gholām Khalil was stricken with leprosy to an eminent sheikh. "Apparently," he said, "an immature Sufi has not acted well and taken aim at him. He was an opponent of the sheikhs and from time to time obstructed their path by his actions. May the Lord cure him."

They reported these words to Gholām Khalil. He repented of all he had done and sent all the goods he possessed to the Sufis. They accepted nothing. Look at what sort of people they are, who in the end, bring their critic to repent! How will it be with someone who acknowledges them? So, of course, it is said that no one can harm them.

∽ ∽ ∽

They asked Samnun about love. He said, "It is purity of friendship with continual remembrance, just as the Real most high said, '*Remember God and remember him often*' [33:41]. The lovers of the mighty and glorious Lord carried off the honor of this world and the next. As the Prophet (peace and blessing be upon him) said, 'A person is with the one he loves,' so they are with the Lord in this world and the next."

"A thing can only be explained by something that is finer and more subtle than itself, and there is nothing more subtle than love. Thus, how can one explain love?" In other words, love cannot be explained.

They asked, "Why are love and affliction linked?"

Samnun replied, "So that not every vulgar boor will make pretenses to love. When he sees the affliction, he takes to his heels."

They asked him about poverty. Samnun said, "The poor are as intimate with poverty as fools are with money, and the poor are as terrified by money as fools are by poverty."

"Sufism is when nothing belongs to you and you belong to nothing."

∽ 26 ∾
'Ali-ye Sahl of Isfahan

The poor man of wealth, present without self, the knower of realms invisible, the seer of human foible, the treasury of subtleties and ideas, Sheikh 'Ali-ye Sahl of Isfahan—God's mercy be upon him. He was very eminent and well respected. He was one of the great sheikhs, and Joneyd maintained a subtle correspondence with him. He was a companion of Abu Torāb, and his sayings regarding spiritual realities are very lofty. His conduct and austerities were perfect, and he had a proper exposition of the path. 'Amr ebn 'Osmān of Mecca came to visit him in Isfahan; he had a debt of thirty thousand dirhams, and 'Ali-ye Sahl paid it all off.

∽ ∽ ∽

These are 'Ali-ye Sahl's words.

"Rushing to devotions is one of the signs of success. Refraining from transgressions is one of the signs of God's protection. Watching over the innermost self is one of the signs of wakefulness. Coming out with our pretense is part of human pride. Anyone who has not made his intention right in the beginning will not attain prosperity and well-being in the end."

They asked 'Ali-ye Sahl, "Say a few words about the idea of perception."

"Whoever fancies that he is closer is in reality further away. When the sunlight falls through the window, children want to grab a hold of the dust motes. They close their hands. They fancy they have something in their grasp. When they open their hands, they see nothing."

"Being present in the Real is preferable to being certain of the Real, because presence is in the heart and negligence is not admissible there. Certainty is a passing intuition that comes and goes. Those who are present sit at the head of the table, while those who are certain wait at the threshold."

"The negligent live according to the decree of the Lord most high. Those who remember him live in the compassion of the Lord. The realized live in the proximity of the Lord."

"It is forbidden for a person to call on him and know him and to take comfort in anything else."

"May you take heed to avoid pride in the beauty of your good works, leading to the hidden corruption of the innermost self." In other words, Satan was like this.

"I asked for wealth; I found it in learning. I asked for glory; I found it in poverty. I asked for well-being; I found it in renunciation. I asked for a light reckoning; I found it in silence. I asked for ease; I found it in despair."

"From the time of Adam (peace be upon him) forward, until the hour of the resurrection, people have been talking about the heart and still are. I want someone who will counsel me on what the heart is or how it is, but I have not found him."

They asked 'Ali-ye Sahl about the truth of unity. "It is near to where there are speculations, but it is distant in realities."

ço ço ço

It is related that he said, "Do you imagine that my death will be like your death when you fall ill and people visit you on your sickbed? Let them summon me, and I will answer." One day, he was walking along when he said, *"I am at your service"* and lay down his head.

Sheikh Abu'l-Hasan-e Mozayyen[1] related, "At that moment, I said to him, 'Say, *"There is no god but God."'* He smiled and said, 'Are you telling me to say something? By his majesty, there is nothing between me and him but the veil of his majesty!' and he died."

After that, Abu'l-Hasan-e Mozayyen would take hold of his mustache and say, "How can a phlebotomist like me instruct the friends of God in how to die? What a disgrace!" and he would weep.

∞ 27 ∞
Abu 'Abdollāh Mohammad ebn Khafif

Confidant of the Indivisible, sanctified by the Eternal, drawn to his court, chosen by the Lord, the subtle inquirer, the axis of the time, Abu 'Abdollāh Mohammad ebn Khafif—God's mercy be upon him. He was the sheikh of the elders of his age, unique in the world and imitated in the exoteric and esoteric sciences. He was the reference point of the people of the path during that era. He had a mighty vision and a pure mind. He held a particular doctrine concerning the path, and a group of Sufis still follow him. Every forty days he used to compose something concerning the obscurities of spiritual realities, and he has many precious writings about the external aspects of religious learning, all of them well known and accepted. The struggles that he undertook are not within the capacity of humankind. No one during his era had his insight into spiritual realities and secrets. After him, no successor arose in the province of Fars who could rightly claim affiliation with him. He was of princely stock. He often traveled in solitary detachment. He met Roveym, Joreyri, Ebn 'Atā, and Mansur-e Hallāj, as well as Joneyd.

In the beginning, the pain of faith tugged at his heart so much that he used to recite *"Say he is God the One"* ten thousand times during each rak'at of prayer. For twenty years he wore a sackcloth shirt and performed four forty-day fasts each year.[1] Even the year he was dying, he performed four forty-day fasts and died during the last of them and would not take off his sackcloth shirt.

In his time, there was an old man, a seeker of the truth, but not one of the learned men of the path. His name was Mohammad-e Zakiri,[2] and he resided in Fars and never wore a patched frock. Abu 'Abdollāh ebn Khafif was asked, "What are the conditions for wearing the patched frock, and who is permitted to do so?"

"The conditions for wearing the patched frock," Ebn Khafif answered, "are fulfilled by Mohammad-e Zakiri in wearing a white shirt, and he is permitted to do so, while I in my sackcloth don't know whether I fulfill them or not."

They called him Khafif—the Slight—because each night when he broke his fast, his meal consisted of seven hard, dried raisins, and no more. He was lightly burdened, light of spirit, and faces a light reckoning. One night his servant gave him eight raisins. The sheikh did not realize it and ate them. He did not find the sweetness in his devotions that he usually did each night. He summoned his servant and asked him about it. The servant said, "I gave you eight raisins tonight."

"Then you are not my friend," said Ebn Khafif. "Instead, you have been my enemy. If you had been a friend, you would have given me six, not eight." The sheikh then dismissed him from service and appointed another servant.

Ebn Khafif said, "For forty years I have been accepted among the commoners and elite, and they have rained so many riches on me that there is no limit to them. But during this period, I have lived in such a way that I was never required to pay alms."

Ebn Khafif related:
In the beginning, I wanted to go on the pilgrimage. When I reached Baghdad, so many fancies filled my head that I did not go to see Joneyd. When I went down into the desert, I had a bucket and a rope. I got thirsty. I saw a well from which a gazelle was drinking water. When I reached the wellhead, the water sank down into the well. I said, "O Lord, is Abu 'Abdollāh worth less than this gazelle?"

I heard a voice say, "This gazelle does not have a bucket or rope. It relies on us." I was overjoyed. I threw aside the bucket and rope and moved on. I heard a voice say, "Abu 'Abdollāh, we were testing you to see how patient you would be. Go back and drink." I turned back; the water had risen to the top of the well. I made my ablutions, drank, and departed. I needed no water until I reached Medina.

On my way back, when I reached Baghdad, on Friday I went to the congregational mosque. Joneyd caught sight of me. "If you had been patient," he said, "water would have bubbled up beneath your feet."

Ebn Khafif related:

When I was young, a dervish came to see me and saw the effects of hunger on me. He invited me to his house. He had cooked some rancid meat. I was too disgusted to eat and felt sick to my stomach. He was tearing off pieces of the meat and placing them in my mouth, but I was unable to eat. The dervish noticed the disdain in me. He was embarrassed, and I too was ashamed. I got up and set out on a journey with a group of people.

When we reached Qādesiyah, we lost our way and had no provisions. We waited patiently for several days until we were on the verge of perishing. Things got so bad that we bought a dog at a high price and roasted it. They gave me a piece of it. I was about to eat when I remembered that dervish and his meal. I said to myself, "This is the punishment for the day that dervish was shamed by me." I repented on the spot and went back and apologized to him.

Ebn Khafif related:

Once I heard that a youth and an old man were dwelling in Egypt in watchful meditation. I went there and greeted them three times, but they did not answer me. "God save you," I said, "answer my greeting!"

The youth raised his head and said, "Ebn Khafif, this world is a little thing, and of this little only a little is left. Of this little, take an ample share. Ebn Khafif, do you really have the leisure to banter greetings?" He said this and lowered his head.

I was hungry and thirsty. I forgot my hunger and thirst—the two men enveloped my entire being. I halted and performed the noon prayer with them and then the afternoon prayer. "Ebn Khafif," the youth said, "we are people of affliction and have no tongue to give advice. Affliction's followers need someone to advise them."

I remained there three days without eating or sleeping. I said to myself, "What oath must I give for him to advise me?"

The youth raised his head and said, "*Seek* the company of someone whose sight will make you recall the Lord most high, whose awesomeness will strike your heart, and who will advise you with the
tongue of action, not the tongue of speech."

Ebn Khafif related:

One year I went to Byzantium. I went into the desert one day.
They brought out a monk who looked like a ghost. They set fire to him.
They applied his ashes to the eyes of the blind; by the power of the
Lord most high, they could see. The ill ate his ashes and were cured. I
was amazed. They lived in error—how could this be?

I saw Mohammad (peace and blessing be upon him) in a dream.
"Messenger of God," I asked, "what is happening here?"

He said, "This is the effect of honesty and austerity, even on those
who live in error. How would it be, if they lived in the right?"

It is related that Ebn Khafif said, "One night, I dreamt that I saw the
Prophet (peace and blessing be upon him). He came and nudged me
with his foot to wake me up. I stared at him, and he said, 'If someone
knows a road and starts down it, but then stops along the way, the Real
most high will torment him as he torments no other creature on earth.'"

It is related that the Prophet (peace and blessing be upon him) prayed
while standing on the tips of two toes. Abu 'Abdollāh was such that he
would not let any prophetic custom lapse. He wanted to perform two
rak'ats of prayer like this. After he had performed one rak'at, he was
unable to perform the second. He saw the Prophet (peace and blessing
be upon him) in a dream; he emerged from the prayer niche and said,
"This is my special way of praying. Don't you do it."

It is related that one midnight Ebn Khafif said to his servant, "Get me
a wife!"

"Where am I supposed to go in the middle of the night?" the servant asked. "I do, however, have a daughter myself. If the sheikh permits, let me bring her."

"Bring her," the sheikh said.

So, the servant brought his daughter. The sheikh married her at
once. After seven months she gave birth to a child, but it died. The

sheikh told his servant, "Tell your daughter to get a divorce, or if she wishes, to remain as she is."

The servant asked, "Sheikh, what is the secret behind this?"

"The night when I married," Ebn Khafif said, "I saw the Prophet (peace and blessing be upon him) in a dream. There were many people, bewildered and drowning in their own sweat. All of a sudden, a child came and took his father's hand and led him over the Narrow Bridge as quick as the wind. I also wanted to have a child. Since this child has now come and gone, my aim has been achieved." Afterward, they relate, Ebn Khafif married four hundred times. After he repented and his spiritual affairs attained perfection, women used to approach him because he was of princely stock. He would marry them two and three at a time. One of them was married to him for forty years; she was the daughter of the vizier.

It is related that they asked his wives, "How does the sheikh treat you in private?"

They replied, "We have no idea of what his company is like. If anyone knows, it is the vizier's daughter."

They asked her, and she said, "When I heard that the sheikh was coming to my room at night, I would prepare fine food and get all dressed up. When he came and saw that, he would call me and gaze at me a while and look at the food for a time. Then one night, he took my hand, pulled it inside his cloak, and rubbed it against his belly. I felt fifteen knots running from his chest to his navel. He said, 'Girl, ask me what these knots are.' I asked him, and he said, 'These are all the flames and afflictions of patience that I have knotted together when you display such a face and such food before me.' He said this and got up. There was never such boldness between us again, so extreme was his austerity."

It is related that Ebn Khafif had two disciples—Ahmad the Younger and Ahmad the Elder. The sheikh was closer to Ahmad the Younger. His followers grew jealous over this situation; after all, Ahmad the Elder had performed many tasks and undergone many austerities. The sheikh found out about this. He wanted to show them that Ahmad the Younger was the better of the two. There was a camel sleeping at the door of the hospice. The sheikh called for Ahmad the Elder. "At your service," he said.

"Carry this camel to the roof of the hospice," the sheikh said.

"Sheikh, how is it possible to carry a camel to the roof?"

"You are free to go now," the sheikh said.

Then he called for Ahmad the Younger. "At your service," he said.

"Carry this camel to the roof," the sheikh said.

Ahmad the Younger at once tightened his belt, rolled up his sleeves, and ran outside. He put both his hands under the camel and exerted all his effort, but he could not lift the camel. "That's enough, Ahmad," the sheikh said. "Now it's clear."

To his followers, the sheikh said, "Ahmad the Younger did what he could. He obeyed my order and did not object. He looked to our order, not to whether he could do the task or not. Ahmad the Elder went on at length with his excuses and started to argue. One can examine what's going on inside from outside appearances."

It is related that a traveler arrived to see Ebn Khafif. He was wearing a black frock with a black hood over his head. A feeling of jealousy arose within the sheikh. After the traveler performed two rak'ats of prayer and offered his greetings, the sheikh asked, "My brother, why are you dressed in black?"

"Because my gods are dead," he said, meaning his self and his desire. *"And have you seen one who takes desire as his god?"* [45:23].

"Throw him out," the sheikh said. They threw him out contemptuously. Then the sheikh commanded, "Bring him back," and they brought him back. They did this forty times. Afterward, the sheikh got up, kissed the man on the head, and apologized. "It is proper for you to wear black," the sheikh said. "Although you were humiliated forty times, you didn't get angry."

It is related that two Sufis came from a distant place to visit Ebn Khafif. They did not find the sheikh in the hospice and asked, "Where is he?"

"He is at the palace of 'Azod ad-Dowla,"[3] they answered.

"What business does a sheikh have at sultans' palaces? It's too bad—our opinion of him was higher than this." Then they said, "Let's take a walk around town." They entered the marketplace, going to a tailor's shop to mend the pocket on one of their frocks. The tailor's scissors went missing. The two Sufis were accused of stealing it. They

were sent to the palace of 'Azod ad-Dowla in the custody of the consta-
bles. 'Azod ad-Dowla ordered their hands cut off.

Sheikh Abu 'Abdollāh was there. "Wait a moment," he said. "This
isn't their doing." Once he had them released, he said to the two Sufis,
"My gallant young men, your opinion was correct. However, we come
to the sultan's palace for just such affairs." Both of the Sufis became his
disciples. Know that anyone who appeals to true believers will not lose
or throw in his hand.

It is related that a traveler suffering from dysentery arrived to see Ebn
Khafif. That night the sheikh set out the chamber pot and removed it
with his own hands and did not get an hour's sleep. Finally, just before
dawn, the sheikh closed his eyes for a second. "Damn you," the traveler cried out, "where are you?"

The sheikh leapt up at once fearful and trembling and brought the
chamber pot into his room. In the morning the sheikh's disciples said,
"What sort of traveler talks like this anyway? We just didn't have the
strength to put up with it anymore. How did you manage to be so
patient?"

The sheikh replied, "I heard him say, 'Bless you.'"

⤳ ⤳ ⤳

"The Real most high created the angels, the jinn, and humankind. He
created innocence, trickery, and capability. Then the angels were told
to choose. They chose innocence. The jinn, too, were told to choose.
They wanted to choose innocence but were told, 'The angels have
beaten you to it.' They asked for capability. Then humankind was told
to choose. The humans asked for innocence. They were told, 'The
angels have beaten you to it.' They chose capability but were told, 'The
jinn have beaten you to it.' So, humankind chose trickery and practices
it with diligence."

Abu Ahmad-e Saghir[4] said to Ebn Khafif, "Temptation torments me."

The sheikh said, "The Sufis that I have met used to ridicule the
devil. Does the devil now ridicule Sufis?"

"The Sufi wears wool in purity, makes desire taste the food of oppression, and tosses this world away over his shoulder."

"To be unsullied by this world is the source of ease when it is time to leave this world."

"Sufism is persevering under the currents of predestined events, finding repose at the hand of the majestic King, and crossing deserts and mountains."

"There are two sorts of acceptance—acceptance through him and acceptance of him. Acceptance through him lies in good planning, and acceptance of him lies in whatever he decrees."

"Faith is affirming in the heart that which is revealed through him of the unseen."

"Discipleship is continual torment and forsaking ease."

"Union is when a link with the beloved is created through all things and there is absence from all things except the Real most high."

"Expansion is the removal of bashfulness at the time of questioning."

"Mindfulness is being remote from everything that makes you remote from the Lord most high."

"Austerity is breaking the self through service and preventing its laxity in service."

"Contentment is seeking nothing that you do not hold in your hands and needing nothing that you do."

"Renunciation is to find comfort in leaving possessions behind."

"Sorrow is restraining the body from pleasure."

"Hope is rejoicing in the existence of union with him."

"Poverty is the elimination of possessions and leaving one's attributes behind."

"Certainty is the reality of the secrets and decrees of the unseen."

They asked Ebn Khafif, "When does worship come out right?"
    "When one turns over all one's actions to the Lord most high and is patient with hardships."

They asked, "What do they call a dervish who is hungry for three days and then comes out and asks for an amount of food that will suffice?"
    "They call him a liar." And he added, "Eat something and be silent, for if a real dervish comes through the door, he will expose everyone."

☙ ☙ ☙

It is related that when his death approached, Ebn Khafif said to his servant, "I was a disobedient servant. Put a yoke on my neck and fetters on my feet and turn me to face Mecca like that. Perhaps he will accept me."
    After Ebn Khafif died, the servant began to carry out the sheikh's testament. A voice called out, "Hey, you ignoramus, don't do that! Do you want to humiliate one whom we hold dear?"

☙ 28 ☙
Hoseyn ebn Mansur Hallāj

Slain by God on the path of God, the lion in the thicket of confirmation, the valiant and veracious warrior, drowned in the surging sea, Hoseyn ebn Mansur Hallāj—God's mercy be upon him. His undertaking was an astonishing affair; wondrous revelations were his specialty, for he burned with both passionate yearning and the harsh flames of separation. Hoseyn was intoxicated, the restless and frenzied man of the age. He was a pure and honest lover. He struggled and strove mightily with marvelous austerities and wonders. He had high aspiration and great capability. He wrote many compositions containing difficult expressions about spiritual realities, secrets, ideas, and insights. He had a way of speaking, an eloquence and a fluency that no one else had. He had a rapture, a vision, and clairvoyance that no one else had.

Most of the sheikhs condemned his actions and said, "He has no standing in Sufism." But Abu 'Abdollāh ebn Khafif, Shebli, and Abu'l-Qāsem Qosheyri[1] (God have mercy upon them) accepted him, as did all of the later Sufis, except as God willed. Abu Sa'id ebn Abi'l-Kheyr, Sheikh Abu'l-Qāsem of Korakān, Sheikh Abu 'Ali of Fārmad, and Imam Yusof of Hamadan (God have mercy upon them) have traveled in his way and some have halted there. Thus it is that Abu'l-Qāsem Qosheyri said about Hallāj, "If he is accepted by God, he will not be cursed because of the disapproval of the people; and if he is cursed, he will not be accepted because of the approval of the people."

Still others charged Hallāj with magic, and some of the external-ists charged him with irreligion. Some say, "He was an adherent of incarnationism," and some say, "He had an attachment to pantheism." But whoever has received a whiff of unity can never succumb to the fancy of incarnation or pantheism, and whoever says such things has no personal, inner knowledge of unity. Explaining this takes some time, and this book is not the place for it. Nevertheless, there was a group of heretics in Baghdad who, whether through the fancy of incarnation or the error of pantheism, have called themselves Hallājians and have claimed affinity with him, without understanding what he said. They have taken pride in his execution and immolation through blind imita-tion, so that the same thing happened to two of them in Balkh as hap-pened to Hoseyn. But imitation is not what is required in this case.

It seems strange to me that someone should consider it proper for the voice of *"Verily, I am God"* [28:30] to come from a bush, without the bush intervening—Why then isn't it proper for *"I am the Real"* to come from Hoseyn, without Hoseyn intervening? Just as the Real most high spoke with 'Omar's tongue—for *"Indeed, the Real speaks with 'Omar's tongue"*[2]—so did he speak with Hoseyn's tongue. Incarnation and pantheism have nothing to do with it.

Some say, "Hoseyn ebn Mansur Hallāj is one person, and Hoseyn ebn Mansur the Atheist is another. He was the teacher of Mohammad ebn Zakariyā[3] and the companion of Abu Sa'id the Qarmati,[4] and this Hoseyn was a magician. As for Hoseyn ebn Mansur, he was from Bayzā'-e Fars and was raised in Wasit."[5] Sheikh Abu 'Abdollāh ebn

Khafif has said, "Hoseyn ebn Mansur was a theologian." Shebli has said, "Hallāj and I are of one school. But they imputed insanity to me, and I was released. The soundness of Hoseyn's mind destroyed him." If Hoseyn were damned, these two great men would not have said this about him. Two witnesses are enough for us.

Hallāj was constantly performing austerities and devotions and expounding realization and unity. When these words were first revealed through him, he wore the garb of the pious, the legalists, and the traditionalists. But for the sake of the religion and faith, some of the sheikhs rejected him. Thus it was that the sheikhs' displeasure with his intoxication had these results: First he came to Tostar[6] to serve Sahl ebn 'Abdollāh and spent two years with him. Then he set off for Baghdad, being eighteen years old at the time of his first journey. He then went to Basra and fell in with 'Amr ebn 'Osmān of Mecca and studied with him for eighteen months. Abu Ya'qub al-Aqta[7] gave Hoseyn his daughter in marriage. 'Amr ebn 'Osmān then got angry with Hoseyn, and Hoseyn left there for Baghdad to see Joneyd. Joneyd ordered him to remain silent and go into seclusion. Hoseyn remained patiently in Joneyd's company for some time. Hoseyn set off for the Hejaz and lived in the holy cities for one year. He came back to Baghdad. He went before Joneyd with a group of Sufis and asked him about some controversial issues. Joneyd did not reply, but said, "It won't be long before you turn the gallows red."

"The day I turn the gallows red," Hoseyn said, "you will don the clothes of the formalists."

Thus it is related that the day that the imams issued the decision that Hoseyn was to be executed, Joneyd was wearing his Sufi clothes and did not endorse the decision. The caliph had ordered that Joneyd's signature was necessary, so Joneyd put on his turban and long robe and went to the seminary. In response to the decision, he wrote: "*We judge on the externals.*" In other words, Hallāj deserves to be killed based on external circumstances—the decision concerns the surface, but only God knows what is within.

When Hoseyn heard no reply from Joneyd about these controversies, he was indignant. He went to Tostar without Joneyd's permission and stayed there for a year. He was met with great approval. He gave no weight to what the people of the time said, so they envied him. 'Amr ebn 'Osmān of Mecca wrote letters about him to Khuzistan and made his way of life appear repulsive in the eyes of the populace. He also grew tired of the place. He took off his Sufi clothes and put on a coat and began to associate with the people of this world. But it made no difference to him.

He disappeared for five years. For some of this time he was in Khorasan and Transoxiana and for some of it in Sistan. He returned to Ahvaz and preached to the people there. He was accepted by the commoners and elite alike. He preached to the people about the secrets, so they called him *Hallāj al-asrār*, the Cotton-Carder of the Secrets.

Then he donned the patched frock and set out for Mecca. On this journey there were many dervishes with him. When he reached Mecca, Abu Ya'qub of Nahrajur[8] accused him of magic. So, he left there for Basra and returned to Ahvaz. Then he announced, "I will go to the land of the polytheists and call the people to God." He went to India and then came to Transoxiana. Then he ended up in China and Mongolia and called the people to God and prepared writings for them.

When he came back, people wrote to him from the most distant parts of the world. The people of India wrote to him as Father Helper; the people of China as Father Clarifier; the people of Khorasan as Father Love; the people of Fars as Abu 'Abdollāh the Pious; and the people of Khuzistan as Cotton-Carder of the Secrets. In Baghdad, they called him the Uprooted, and in Basra, the Herald. Many things were said about him then.

After that, he set off for Mecca and lived for two years in the sacred precincts. When he returned, his spiritual states were transformed, and the situation took on an entirely different color, for he called people to the inner meaning. No one could comprehend it, so they reported, "They have expelled him from fifty cities, and nothing is stranger than the fate that has befallen him."

They called him Hallāj—the Cotton-Carder—because he once passed by a cotton warehouse. He made a sign, and the seeds immediately separated from the cotton. The people were stunned.

It is related that he used to perform four hundred rak'ats of prayer in a single day and required it of himself. "With the rank you hold," they asked, "why take such pains?"

"Neither pain nor comfort," he said, "have any effect on the affairs of friends. Friends are characterized by extinction, so pain has no effect on them, nor does comfort."

It is related that at fifty years of age, Hoseyn said, "Until now, I have not followed any school of religious law, but have chosen for my self whatever is most difficult from each school. Up to today, when I am fifty years old, I have prayed, and I have performed ablutions for every prayer."

It is related that in the beginning, when he was undergoing his austerities, he had an old cloak that he had not removed for twenty years. One day they removed it from him by force. Many fleas and lice had gotten into it. They weighed one of them; it weighed as much as half a copper coin.

It is related that a scorpion was seen circling around Hoseyn. As they were making ready to kill it, he said, "Don't touch it! For twelve years, it has been our boon companion and keeping us company."

They say that Rashid-e Khard of Samarqand⁹ started off to visit the Ka'ba. On the way he was speaking at a prayer meeting. He told this story: Hallāj set out into the desert with four hundred Sufis. Several days passed, and they had not found a thing to eat. They said to Hoseyn, "We need roast lamb's head."
"Sit down," he said.
Then he pulled his hand out from behind his back and gave each one a roast lamb's head with two loaves of bread, four hundred lamb's heads and eight hundred loaves of bread in all. After that, they said, "We need fresh dates."
He got up and said, "Toss me up in the air."
They threw him up in the air, and fresh dates rained down from him until they ate their fill. The rest of the way, wherever he leaned back against a thorn bush, it would bear fresh dates.

It is related that in the desert a clan of Sufis said to Hoseyn, "We need some figs." He put his hand into the air and set a platter of fresh, moist figs before them. Another time they asked for halva. Hoseyn set a plate of warm, sugared halva before them. They said, "This is halva from the Arched Gate in Baghdad!"

"The desert and Baghdad are one and the same to me," Hoseyn replied.

It is related that there were once four thousand people with Hoseyn in the desert. He went to the Ka'ba and stood bare-chested in front of it for one year in the hot sun, until his skin split open and the fat from his limbs ran over the black stone. He did not budge. Every day they brought him a loaf of bread and a jug of water. He would break his fast with the crusts and set the rest of the loaf on top of the jug of water. They say that a scorpion had made its nest in his trousers.

Then at 'Arafāt he said, "O Guide of the Perplexed!" and when he saw that everyone was praying, he too placed his head on a heap of sand. He looked about and when everyone left, he sighed and said, "O God, O dear King! I know you are pure and I call you the Pure, by the prayer beads of all those who count them, by the praises of all those who praise you, by the fancies of all those who imagine you. O my God, you know that I am incapable of thanking you. You thank yourself in my place, for that alone is thanks."

It is related that one day in the desert Hallāj asked Ebrāhim-e Khavvās, "What are you doing?"

Ebrāhim said, "I am walking forthright in the trust of the Lord."

"You've spent your life in the palace of the belly," Hallāj replied. "When will you pass away into unity?" In other words, the essence of trust in God is in not eating. Will you spend your whole life in the belly's trust in God? When will there be passing away into unity?

⌘ ⌘ ⌘

They asked Hallāj, "Do the realized have moments of rapture?"

"No," he said, "because the moment of rapture is an attribute of the one who has it, and whoever is content with his attributes is not realized." What he meant is this: *I have a moment with God.*

They asked him, "What is the path to the Lord like?"

"There are two steps and an arrival: Take one step from the world and one step from the afterworld and, behold, you have arrived at the Master."

They asked him about poverty. "The poor man," he said, "is one who looks to God and needs nothing but God."

"Realization consists of seeing things and destroying them all in the spirit."

"When God's servant arrives at the station of realization, he is sent an intuition and his innermost self is made mute, until no thought comes to him but the thought of the Real."

"*An exalted character* [68:4] is one that is not affected by the injustice of people; then it has recognized the Lord most high."

"This is trust in God: As long as you know someone in the city who deserves to eat more than you do, you do not eat."

"Sincerity is purifying actions of the blemishes of resentment."

"The speaking tongue is the destruction of silent hearts."

"Speech is bound up with causes, and actions with polytheism. The Real is void and independent of all. God most high said, '*And most of them do not believe in God without associating others with him*'" [12:106].

"The visions of the seers, the knowledge of the realized, the light of the theologians, and the path of the foremost are all the deliverance from eternity without beginning and from eternity without end, from what comes between, and from transitory occurrence. But how do they know this? *It is for anyone who has a heart and lends an ear, bearing witness*" [50:37].

"In the world of acceptance, there is a dragon that they call certainty; in its maw, the actions of the eighteen thousand worlds are like a mote in the desert."

"All year we search for his affliction like a sultan who constantly searches for dominion."

"The intuition of the Real is that which brooks no opposition."

"The disciple lives in the shadow of his repentance; the master, in the shadow of his purity."

"The disciple's efforts run ahead of his revelations, while the master's revelations outstrip his efforts."

"The moment of a true believer is a shell in the ocean of his breast. On the morrow these shells will be smashed open on the plain of the resurrection."

"Passing beyond this world is the renunciation of the self; passing beyond the afterworld is the renunciation of the heart. Bidding yourself farewell is the renunciation of the soul."

They asked Hoseyn about patience. He said, "It is when they cut off your hands and feet and hang you on the gallows." What's amazing is that they did all of this to him.

ص ص ص

It is related that one day Hoseyn said to Shebli, "Abu Bakr, give me your hand, for we have undertaken a mighty task, and we are bewildered by this task, such a task that we are near to killing ourselves."

Since people were confused by his actions, innumerable skeptics and countless supporters appeared and saw him do wondrous things. They started wagging their tongues and conveyed his words to the caliph. They all agreed on his execution because he would say, *"I am the Real."*

They said, "Say: *'He is the Real.'"*

"Yes, he is all," said Hoseyn. "You ask, 'Is he lost?' Yes, Hoseyn is lost, but the all-encompassing sea will not be lost and will not diminish."

They asked Joneyd, "Is there an interpretation for the words that Hoseyn ebn Mansur utters?"

"Let them kill him," Joneyd replied. "It is not the day for interpretations."

A group of scholars then came out against Hoseyn and condemned his words before Moʿtasem[10] and his vizier ʿAli ebn ʿIsā, turning them against him. The caliph ordered Hoseyn to be taken to prison for one year. The people, however, would go to see him and ask him about controversial issues. Later, the people were also forbidden from coming. For a period of five months no one went to see him, except once when Ebn ʿAtā went and once when Abu ʿAbdollāh ebn Khafif did (God have mercy upon them). And one other time Ebn ʿAtā sent someone to say, "Sheikh, ask forgiveness for what you said so you will be released."

Hallāj said, "Tell the one who said it to ask for forgiveness."

When Ebn ʿAtā heard this, he wept and said, "Do all of us equal even one Hoseyn ebn Mansur?"

It is related that the first night after they imprisoned Hoseyn, they came and did not find him in his cell—they went through the cell from top to bottom and could not see anyone. The second night they found neither him nor his cell. The third night they found him in his cell. "Where were you the first night?" they asked, "and where were you and your cell the second night?"

"The first night," Hoseyn answered, "I was in his presence, so I wasn't here. The second night his presence was here, so both the cell and I were absent. The third night I was sent back in order to preserve religious law. Come and do your job."

It is related that each day in prison he would perform a thousand rakʿats of prayer. They asked, "Since you say, 'I am the Real,' to whom do you pray to?"

"We esteem ourselves," Hoseyn answered.

It is related that there were three hundred people in the prison. When night fell, Hoseyn said, "Prisoners, I release you!"

They said, "Why don't you release yourself?"

"We are the Lord's prisoner and keep the peace. If we wish, we can undo all these fetters with a single sign."

Then he made a sign with his finger; all the fetters fell away. "Where should we go now?" they asked. "The prison door is locked."

Hoseyn made a sign, and cracks appeared in the door. "Now go your way."

"Aren't you coming?"

"We share a secret with him that can only be spoken on the gallows."

The next day they asked, "Where did all the prisoners go?"

"I freed them."

"Why didn't you go?"

"The Real has a reason to rebuke us. I did not go."

This news reached the caliph. He said, "Hoseyn will cause a riot. Either kill him or beat him until he renounces these words." They beat him with three hundred blows. Each time they struck him, an eloquent voice was heard to say, *"Fear not, Ebn Mansur!"*

Sheikh 'Abd al-Jalil the Coppersmith[11] says, "My belief in the man delivering the blows is greater than my belief with regard to Hoseyn. How strong that man's belief in religious law must have been to hear such a clear voice and not to let his hand tremble and to continue to strike!"

Then they carried Hoseyn off again to kill him. A hundred thousand people gathered, and he looked around at all of them and kept saying, *"The Real, the Real, the Real, I am the Real."*

It is related that a dervish in the midst of the crowd asked him, "What is love?"

Hoseyn said, "You will see it today and tomorrow and the day after."

They killed him on that day and burned him on the second day and threw his ashes to the wind on the third. In other words, this is love.

While this was going on, his servant asked him for a final testament. Hoseyn said, "Busy the self with something worth doing. If not, it will busy you with something not to be done."

His son said, "Give me a final testament."

Hoseyn said, "While the worldly grapple with their affairs, you grapple with one thing, a mote of which is better than the myriad affairs of men and jinn, and that is nothing other than knowledge of the reality."

403

Hoseyn strutted as he went along the road, throwing his hands up in the air and prancing like a dandy in spite of the thirteen heavy chains around him. "What's this swagger?" people asked.

"Because I'm going to the sacrifice," he replied. He let out a shout and recited:

> *Without a hint of injustice, my friend*
> *gave me the same thing to drink that he drank,*
> *just as a guest acts with his one-time guest.*
> *And when the cup came around, he called for*
> *the sword and executioner's mat. Here's how*
> *to drink wine with the Dragon in summer.*

When they brought Hallāj under the archway at the Arched Gate, he placed his foot on the ladder. "How are you doing?" they asked.

"For true believers, the heavenly ascension goes to the top of the gallows," he said.

He wore a loincloth around his waist and a mantle over his shoulders. He raised his hands and prayed privately facing Mecca and asked for what he asked. Then he climbed the gallows. A group of his disciples asked, "What words do you have for us, your disciples, and what words for those who deny you and would pelt you with stones?"

Hallāj said, "They have two heavenly rewards, and you have one, because you have no more than a good opinion of me, while they move with the strength of unity in the firmness of the law. Unity in the law is the root, and good opinion is the branch."

It is related that in his youth, Hallāj had glanced at a woman. To his servant he now said, "Whoever glances up like that gazes down like this."

Shebli then stopped before him and cried out, *"And did we not restrain you before the world's creatures?"* [15:70]. And he asked, *"Hallāj, what is Sufism?"*

Hallāj replied, "The least of it is what you see before you."

"And what is higher?"

"You have no access to it."

Then everyone threw a stone at him. For conformity's sake, Shebli threw a rose. Hoseyn ebn Mansur sighed. They asked, "Why didn't you sigh over all these stones? What's the secret behind sighing over a rose?"

"Because they don't know, they are forgiven. What Shebli did is hard for me to take; he knows that one shouldn't throw anything."

When they cut off his hands, he burst out laughing. "What's there to laugh about?" they asked.

"It's easy to cut off the hand of a person who's chained up. The true believer is one who cuts off the hand of attributes, swindling aspiration from the highest throne of heaven."

When they chopped off his feet, he smiled and said, "With these feet I used to travel the earth. I have other feet that are traversing both worlds at this very moment. Cut off those feet, if you can."

Hallāj rubbed his two bloody, severed hands against his face and smeared his face and forearms with blood. "Why did you do that?"

"I have lost a lot of blood. I knew that my face had grown pale. You might imagine that the pallor of my face comes from fear. I rubbed blood on my face so my face would look red to you. True believers wear the rouge of their own blood."

"If you painted your face red with blood, well, why did you smear your forearms?"

"I am performing ablutions."

"What ablutions?"

"Only the ablution of blood is adequate for two rak'ats of love."

Then they pulled out his eyes. A tumult rose from among the people; some wept, and some threw stones. Then they asked for his tongue to be cut out.

"Wait while I say a few words," Hallāj said. He raised his face to heaven and said, "My God, do not condemn them for all the trouble that they are taking for your sake. Do not deprive them of this good fortune of theirs. Praise be to God that they cut off my hands and feet on your path! If they remove my head from my body, they will place it upon the gallows, contemplating your glory."

Then they cut off his ears and nose, and the stones began to fly. An old woman came by carrying a piece of linen. "Wrap this handsome little cotton-carder up tight. What business does he have speaking the secrets?"

405

Hoseyn's final words were these: *"It is enough for the joyous lover to make the one single."* Then he recited this verse: *"Only those who do not believe in the resurrection rush toward it. Those who believe fear it, knowing it is real"* [42:18]. These were his final words.

Then they cut out his tongue. When they cut off his head, it was the hour of the evening prayer. As his head was being cut off, Hoseyn smiled and died. The people roared. Hoseyn shot the ball of his fate to the final goal of acceptance. From each one of his limbs came the cry of *I am the Real.*

The next day they said, "The uproar over this will turn out to be greater than when he was alive." So, they burned his body—from his ashes came the cry of *I am the Real.* When he was executed, the form of God's name appeared in every drop of blood that dripped from him to the ground.

Hoseyn ebn Mansur had said to his servant, "When they throw my ashes into the Tigris, the water will well up with such strength that Baghdad will fear being drowned. When that happens, take my robe to the banks of the Tigris, so the water will recede."

On the third day, when Hoseyn's ashes were given over to the water, the cry of *I am the Real* came forth, and the water welled up. The servant took the sheikh's robe to the banks of the Tigris. The water receded, and the ashes fell silent. Then his ashes were gathered and buried. None of the people of the path have had a victory like Hoseyn's.

An eminent person said, "Adherents of the inner sense! Behold what they did to Hoseyn ebn Mansur! What will they do with mere pretenders?"

'Abbāsa of Tus said, "On the morrow of the resurrection, they will bring Hoseyn ebn Mansur to the plain of judgment bound securely in chains, for if they were to release him, the entire resurrection would crumble to pieces."

An eminent person said, "That night, I prayed under the gallows until dawn. At daybreak a voice cried out, 'We informed him of one of our secrets, and he revealed it. This is the punishment for anyone who reveals the secrets of kings.'"

It is related that Shebli said, "That night I went to his tomb and prayed until dawn. As morning broke, I spoke privately with God: 'My God, this was your servant, a believer, realized in oneness with you. Why did you afflict him so?' Sleep overpowered me. In a dream I saw the resurrection and heard these words from the Real: 'I did this to him because he exposed our secret to others.'"

It is related that Shebli said, "I saw him in a dream. I asked, 'What did the Lord most high do to these people?'

"He replied, 'He forgave both groups. Those who took pity on me knew me and took pity for the sake of the Real. Those who bore malice toward me did not know me and bore malice for the sake of the Real. He had mercy on both groups, for both were excused.'"

In a dream, an eminent person saw him standing headless with a goblet in his hand and asked, "What is this?"

Hoseyn said, "He hands a goblet to those who have lost their heads."

It is related that when they put him on the gallows, Satan came and said to him, "Once you said 'I' and once I did. How is it that mercy is the result of your 'I' and damnation the result of mine?"

Hoseyn said, "Because you carried your 'I' within you and I distanced myself from mine, mercy came to me and damnation to you. Know that asserting the 'I' is not good, while driving it away is utterly so."

NOTES

Author's Introduction

1. Este'lāmi suggests that these two Arabic phrases are 'Attār's own invention based on Qur'an 12:37.

2. On these works, see "Translator's Introduction."

3. According to Este'lāmi, 'Attār here gives a variant form of the hadith *"I was given all of the words and sent to bring [humankind's] noble qualities to completion."*

4. On Ansāri, see Translator's Introduction; ebn 'Emād is a corruption of ebn 'Ammār, the proper form of the name of Ansāri's mentor.

5. Abu 'Ali Daqqāq (d. 1021) is the spiritual guide and father-in-law of Abu'l-Qāsem Qosheyri, the renowned Sufi master and author of Nishapur.

6. Mahfuz ebn Ahmad-e Kalvazāni (1041–1116) was a Hanbalite legal scholar in Baghdad; see *EI²*, s.v. "al-Kalwadhānī."

7. 'Attār here adds a Persian translation of this verse that greatly extends the meaning of the word "prophets": "O Mohammad, we tell you the stories of those who have passed on, so that your heart will be calmed and strengthened by them."

8. This hadith is frequently cited by Persian Sufi writers: see Bāqer Sadri-Niyā, *Farhang-e ma'surāt-e motun-e 'erfāni: moshtamal bar ahādis, aqvāl va emsāl-e motun-e 'erfāni-ye Fārsi* (Tehran: Sorush, 2001), 512.

9. 'Abd ar-Rahmān Akkāf was a legal scholar and ascetic of Nishapur killed during the Ghozz invasions of 1154.

10. Abu 'Ali Seyāh (d. 1021) was a Sufi sheikh of Merv and a student of Abu 'Ali Daqqāq (see note 5 above).

11. This hadith is popular with Persian Sufis; see Sadri-Niyā, *Farhang*, 484.

12. This Majd ad-Din is traditionally identified with Majd ad-Din al-Baghdādi (1149–1210 or 1220), a disciple of the famous Sufi sheikh Najm ad-Din Kobrā. Modern scholars are skeptical of this identification. Apparently assuming a textual corruption, Este'lāmi suggests that 'Attār here refers to Abu Mohammad Qāsem ebn al-Hoseyn al-Khwārazmi Sadr al-Afāzel (d. 1220), a grammarian and litterateur who wrote commentaries on a number of Arabic

grammars and literary works. Unlike al-Baghdādi, he can at least be placed in Nishapur during 'Attār's lifetime. Based on an unspecified manuscript, Shafi'i Kadkani suggests (*Zabur-e Pārsi,* 71) that this name should read Imām Ahmad Khwāri, a little-known student and follower of Majd ad-Din al-Baghdādi.

13. 'Attār here alludes to the story of the companions of the cave or the seven sleepers told in Qur'an 18:9–22.

14. Este'lāmi identifies Jamāl-e Mowseli (772–849) as a musician from the court of al-Ma'mun in Baghdad. This sounds suspiciously like a description of Eshāq ebn Ebrāhim al-Mowseli, although the story of Eshāq's death in Abu'l-Faraj al-Esbahāni's *Ketāb al-aghāni,* ed. Ibrāhīm al-Abyārī, 31 vols. (Cairo: Dār al-Sha'b, n.d.): 5:2074–79, contains no mention of the details given here for Jamāl. My efforts to identify this Jamāl from other sources have been fruitless.

1. Ja'far as-Sādeq

1. Mohammad ebn 'Ali (676–735) was the fifth Shi'ite imam; he established many of the basic doctrines of Shi'ite law and theology. See *EI²,* s.v. "Muḥammad b. ʿAlī Zayn al-ʿĀbidīn."

2. The point here is that Abu Hanifa mixes figures revered by the Sunnis (Abu Bakr, 'Omar, 'Osmān, and 'Ā'esha) with those revered by the Shi'ites ('Ali and Fātema).

3. Mansur was the second caliph of the 'Abbasid dynasty, reigning from 754 until 775 during a time great political and intellectual ferment. *See EI²,* s.v. "al-Manṣūr Abū D̲j̲aʿfar."

2. Oveys of Qaran

1. A semi-legendary figure who reportedly died in 657; see *EI²,* "Uways al-Ḳaranī."

2. *Tābe'in* ("the second generation of Muslims") refers to those who did not meet Mohammad but were acquainted with his companions and followers. *Arba'in* ("Forty Substitutes") refers to the *abdāl,* the "substitutes," the holy people who "substituted" divine attributes for their human characteristics. Although their identity may not be known to the mass of believers, they will always be forty in number with a new "substitute" appearing whenever one dies. *See* Maryam Sādāt Ranjbar, *Farhang-e Foruzānfar* (Isfahan: Nashr-e Porsesh, 1995), 15–17.

3. This hadith is quoted in Arabic and translated into Persian; it is also alluded to in Rumi's *Masnavi:* see Badi' az-Zamān Foruzānfar, *Aḥādis-e Masnavi,* 4th ed. (Tehran: Amir Kabir, 1987), 73.

4. For another use of this hadith in one of 'Attār's *ghazals,* see "Translator's Introduction" herein. This hadith was cited by Hojviri and Rumi; see Foruzānfar, *Ahādis,* 52.

5. Harem ebn Hayyān was an early Muslim preacher and warrior for the faith from Basra who died in 656–57.

6. Rabi' ebn Kheysam (d. 689–90) was an early Muslim ascetic and transmitter of sayings of the Prophet.

7. This battle for control of the early Islamic state took place on the banks of the Euphrates in 657 between the Omayyad leader Mo'āviya and 'Ali ebn Abi Tāleb; see *EI²,* s.v. "Ṣiffīn."

3. Hasan of Basra

1. Omm Salama (d. 682–83) was one of the wives of the Prophet Mohammad and an early transmitter of his sayings.

2. The battle of Badr (624) was fought between Mohammad and his Meccan opponents near Medina and helped secure the position of the nascent Muslim community.

3. Sa'id-e (ebn) Jobeyr was an early Muslim ascetic executed by Hajjāj in 713–14.

4. Abu 'Amr was a renowned philologist and founder of one of the seven canonical schools of Qur'an reading. He died in the early part of the eighth century in Kufa.

5. 'Attār here inserts this Persian translation of the Qur'anic verse: "I forgive all your sins, but if you incline toward another in a corner of your mind and bring in a partner for the mighty and glorious Lord, I will never forgive you."

4. Mālek-e Dinār

1. This story is based on a pun on the name Mālek-e Dinār, which may mean either Mālek, son of Dinār, or Mālek, owner of the dinar.

2. After serving as the governor of Syria for twenty years and defeating 'Ali ebn Abi Tāleb at the battle of Seffin, Mo'āviya (d. 680) became the first caliph of the Omayyad dynasty.

3. A Persian version of this saying is included among the aphorisms of Hasan of Basra above. A manuscript variant here adds: "It will be just like this on the day of resurrection."

4 . Este'lāmi speculates that this name should be read "Hafs ebn Soleymān," who became vizier under the first 'Abbasid caliph, as-Saffāh, and died in 750–51. However, Ja'far ebn Soleymān az-Zab'i was a contemporary

411

of Mālek and is the subject of a biography in Abu No'eym, *Helyat al-owliyā'*, 10 vols. (reprint ed., Beirut: Dār al-Fekr, 1996): 6:287–96.

5. *Labbayka* (I am at your service) is uttered by pilgrims as they circumambulate the Ka'ba at Mecca.

6. The first of these sentences is quoted in Arabic and translated into Persian. The second appears only in Persian.

7. Mohammad ebn Vāse' (d. 740–41) is recognized as one of the most reliable transmitters of hadith and is the subject of a short biography in the *Memorial* that is not included in this translation.

5. Habib-e 'Ajami

1. Narrow Bridge: the *serāt* is the bridge, a hair's width wide, that extends over the abyss of hell and leads to paradise.

6. Rābe'a-ye 'Adaviya

1. Nicholson's edition (1:60) reads 'Isā Zādān.

2. This image comes from Qur'an 7:143.

3. This is a *hadith-e qodsi,* that is, the words of God as spoken by Mohammad but not included in the text of the Qur'an.

4. 'Attār alludes to Qur'an 27:12, where God instructs Moses to place his hand next to his chest and hold it before Pharaoh "white, without blemish" as a sign of his prophecy.

5. Sāleh-e Morri, a hadith scholar, died in Baghdad in 788–89.

6. This is how Pharaoh orders his men to address him in Qur'an 79:24.

7. I have been unable to identify this person. The name should probably read 'Abd al-Vāhed ebn Zeyd, a follower of Hasan of Basra who died in 793.

8. Each of the four sentences beginning "No one is sincere" is given first in Arabic and then in a Persian translation. I have followed the Persian where the two diverge.

9. Rābe'a here alludes to the story of Joseph and Zoleykhā (Potiphar's wife). When her serving women questioned Zoleykhā's love for Joseph, she had him come into the room while they were holding knives in their hands; stunned by his beauty, each one cut her own hand. *See* Qur'an 12:31.

10. This saying of the Prophet is quoted in Arabic with a Persian translation.

11. Mohammad ebn Aslam, a renowned codifier of hadith, died in 856. He is the subject of a short biography in the *Memorial* not included here.

12. My spelling of the name is tentative, and I have not been able to identify this person from other sources.

7. Fozeyl ebn 'Ayāz

1. Merv (now Mary) and Abivard are located in Khorasan, north of the modern border of Iran in Turkmenistan.

2. A member of the famous clan of high officials under the 'Abbasid dynasty, Fazl-e Barmaki served as grand vizier and governor of Khorasan province. He fell from favor in 803 and died in prison in 808–9; see *EI²*, "Faḍl b. Yaḥyā al-Barmakī."

3. This saying is attributed to the Prophet.

4. An early Islamic scholar and traditionist (d. 724–25).

5. The vizier of the Pharaoh who encouraged his enmity against Moses and the Israelites and thus became a type of the evil royal counselor.

6. *Labbayka* (I am your service) is uttered by pilgrims as they circumambulate the Ka'ba at Mecca. Fozeyl's reply apparently puzzled copyists. Nicholson's edition (1:80) offers a substantially different reading: "I hope that no one who says *I am at your service* will be behind anyone who sees himself this way at that waystation [i.e., the Ka'ba]." In either version the idea seems to be that awestruck reticence will overshadow ritual correctness.

7. I have followed Nicholson's edition (1:81) here. Este'lāmi's version would read: "Whoever speaks through his actions seldom speaks."

8. A contemporary of Hasan of Basra best known as the first Muslim dream interpreter; see *EI²*, s.v. "Ibn Sīrīn."

9. In a variant reading, this statement is attributed to Fozeyl himself.

10. The "Narrow Bridge," a hair's width wide, extends over the abyss of hell and leads to paradise.

8. Ebrāhim ebn Adham

1. This is a spot northeast of Mecca in the Arabian Peninsula near the junction of two major pilgrimage routes.

2. The Yamāni Pillar is located on the southwest corner of the Ka'ba.

3. Este'lāmi does not identify this narrator, and I have not been able to locate his name in other sources.

4. Again Este'lāmi does not identify this narrator, and I have not been able to locate his name in other sources.

5. Zamzam is a well located in the sacred precincts of Mecca.

6. The Substitutes, always forty in number, are holy people who "substituted" divine attributes for their human characteristics.

7. For Ṣuri, Nicholson's edition (1:104) reads Ṣanowbari. Neither name can be identified with any contemporary of Ebrāhim.

9. Beshr al-Hāfi, the Barefoot

1. A recognized collector and transmitter of hadith, d. 872.
2. This is a Persian rendering of Qur'an 78:6.
3. Several of the Prophet's companions bore the name Sa'laba (Tha'laba).
4. This hadith was also alluded to by Rumi; see Foruzānfar, *Ahādis*, 14.
5. Este'lāmi does not identify this narrator; he is the source of a similar tale in Abu No'eym, *Helyat*, 9:187.
6. Este'lāmi does not identify this narrator.
7. Este'lāmi suggests that this name should be read Abu 'Ali Jowzāni, although this identification is unlikely for chronological reasons.

10. Zu'n-Nun of Egypt

1. This is a well-known saying of the Prophet; see Sadri-Niyā, *Farhang*, 350.
2. The Substitutes, always forty in number, are holy people who "substituted" divine attributes for their human characteristics; see Sādāt Ranjbar, *Farhang-e Foruzānfar*, 15–17.
3. This anecdote is also narrated by Abu Ja'far-e A'var in Qosheyri's *Resāla* (*Tarjoma-ye Resāla*, 663), but this narrator cannot be otherwise identified.
4. The 'Abbasid caliph Motavakkel reigned from 847 to 861.
5. Ahmad ebn Mohammad Salmā lived in the second half of the ninth century.
6. 'Attār here alludes to the story of Moses and "one of our servants," commonly identified with Khezr, found in Qur'an 18:65–82. Much to Moses' consternation, Khezr kills an apparently innocent child who was destined to turn from God and lead his parents into perdition.
7. Nicholson's edition (1:131) splits the aphorism into two at this point.

11. Bāyazid of Bestām

1. Bestām is located in the modern province of Semnān in Iran, near the city of Shāhrud.
2. This "fine point" allows travelers to eat during the month of the fast, provided they make up the fast later.
3. Abu Musā 'Isā ebn Ādam was Bāyazid's nephew and disciple.

414

4. This probably refers to Abu'l-Fazl Mohammad ebn 'Ali Sahlaji, who was a prayer leader in Bestām and compiled a collection of Bāyazid's sayings, d. 1084.

5. *See* note 3 above.

6. Bāyazid here alludes the story of Joseph and Zoleykhā (Potiphar's wife); see Chapter 6, note 9.

7. Sufi ascetic of Nishapur, d. 849, the subject of a biography in the *Memorial* not included here.

8. Abu Eshāq Ebrāhim of Herat is known as an associate of Ebrāhim ebn Adham (Abu No'eym, *Helyat:* 10:43–44).

9. Tabaristan is the region south of the Caspian Sea now known as Gilan and Mazandaran.

10. This person has not been identified from other sources.

11. Abu Sa'id the Shepherd (Rā'i) is not mentioned in other sources that I have consulted.

12. The eldest son of Abu'l-Qāsem Qosheyri and a teacher of religious law, d. 1120.

13. These are the words of God as spoken in a hadith, frequently cited by Sufi authors; see Sadri-Niyā, *Farhang,* 95.

14. These are again the words of God as spoken in a hadith; see Sadri-Niyā, *Farhang*, 180.

12. 'Abdollāh ebn al-Mobārak

1. This alludes to Qur'an 5:12, where God instructs the Israelites "to lend God a good loan," referring to spending generously in God's cause.

2. The place name cannot be precisely located but is most likely a village in Khorasan.

3. The ceremonies of the "running" and the "lesser pilgrimage" *('omra),* although not technically part of the hajj, are often included in the annual pilgrimage rituals; see F. E. Peters, *The Hajj: The Muslim Pilgrimage to Mecca and the Holy Places* (Princeton, NJ: Princeton University Press, 1994), 129–132.

4. There is a brief notice on this figure in Abu No'eym, *Helyat,* 10:312.

5. A descendant of 'Ali ebn Abi Tāleb, a Shi'ite.

6. This hadith (used earlier by Bāyazid) is also alluded to by Rumi; see Foruzānfar, *Ahādis,* 67.

7. The idea behind this saying is that the sins of those who have been slandered fall back on the shoulders of the person who has slandered them.

13. Sofyān-e Sowri

1. Although no longer recognized as one of the four "orthodox" schools of legal practice, Sofyān's system of jurisprudence was current for several centuries after his death.
2. 'Attār gives both Arabic and Persian versions of this sentence with a slight difference: the Arabic can be translated, "But the approach to God is hard."
3. Again 'Attār gives slightly different versions of this sentence in Arabic and Persian. Here I have followed the Arabic; the Persian would read, "Be prepared for death before it seizes you unawares."
4. An otherwise unknown servant and disciple of Sofyān.

14. Dāvud-e Tā'i

1. 'Attār's Persian prose rendition of this verse differs somewhat from its Arabic source: "Which cheek, what hair, has not crumbled to dust? Which eye has not tumbled to the ground?"
2. A hadith scholar and Qur'an reader who died in Kufa in 808–9.
3. Another hadith scholar.
4. Abu 'Abdollāh Mohammad ebn Hasan Sheybāni, a celebrated student of Abu Hanifa.
5. A student of Abu Hanifa, Abu Yusof served as chief judge of Baghdad under Hārun ar-Rashid.

15. Ma'ruf of Karkh

1. The eighth of the Shi'ite imams, 765–818. See *EI²*, s.v. "'Alī al-Riḍā."
2. According to Este'lāmi, Abu Ja'far Mohammad ebn Mansur at-Tusi died ca. 966 and thus could not have met Ma'ruf; Este'lāmi also suggests a possible reference to his father, Mansur ebn Dāvud, but this identification also strains chronological possibility.
3. *See* note 1 to this chapter.
4. Abu Ja'far Mohammad ebn Hoseyn Barjalāni was one of Ma'ruf's students, d. 852–53.
5. The subject of a short notice in the *Memorial* (not included here), Ebn Sammāk was a Sufi ascetic contemporary with Hārun ar-Rashid, d. 799.

16. Sari-ye Saqati

1. This is a saying of the Prophet; see Foruzānfar, *Ahādis*, 126.

2. 'Attār here may have in mind Ahmad ebn Abi Khāled, who was a member of the inner circle of the caliph Ma'mun (r. 813–33), but the attribution of this story to him is no doubt apocryphal.

17. Ahmad-e Khezruya of Balkh

1. Nicholson's edition (1:293) reads *bāki* for *pāki*, "around the heavenly throne or a fear."

18. Abu Torāb of Nakhshab

1. Rezvān is the angel that guards the gates of paradise.

2. A number of Sufi sheikhs share this name; the one meant here may be Abu'l-'Abbās ebn 'Atā a close companion of Hallāj. He was executed in 922.

19. Shāh-e Shojā' of Kerman

1. A wandering dervish from Kerman who was active in the eleventh century.

20. Yusof ebn al-Hoseyn

1. Zoleykhā is the Qur'anic counterpart of Potiphar's wife in Genesis 29. The mention of Joseph's intentions toward Zoleykhā alludes specifically to Qur'an 12:24: "She desired him, and he, her."

2. 'Abd al-Vāhed ebn Zeyd, a follower of Hasan of Basra, died in 793, too early to have met Yusof ebn al-Hoseyn. In a textual variant the name reads 'Abdollāh ebn Zeyd.

21. Abu Hafs-e Haddād, the Blacksmith

1. "Pillars" *(owtād)* here refers to the four friends of God who are assigned to support the world in the four cardinal directions and ensure its stability and prosperity.

2. This would seem to refer to Abu Bakr ebn 'Ali, a well-known Hanafi legal scholar, but he lived a century after Abu Hafs.

3. Abu 'Ali-ye Saqafi was a Sufi, legal scholar, and preacher in Nishapur, d. 939–40.

4. Este'lāmi speculates that Mahmash may be a colloquial pronunciation of the name Mamshād-e Dinvari, a Sufi who died in 910–11.

5. The author of one of 'Attār's principal sources, *Tabaqāt al-sufiya*; see "Translator's Introduction" herein.

22. Joneyd of Baghdad

1. Abu 'Abdollāh al-Hāres al-Mohāsebi (d. 857) was a Sufi writer especially known for his work on moral psychology.

2. 'Attār here quotes a saying of the Prophet; see Foruzānfar, *Ahādis*, 43.

3. This is also a saying of the Prophet; see Sadri-Niyā, *Farhang*, 457.

4. According to Este'lāmi, this is an excerpt from a verse by the Arabic poet al-Akhṭal.

5. A leading Sufi sheikh of Baghdad, d. 934, and subject of a short biography in the *Memorial* not included here.

6. Abu Mohammad Ja'far-e Kholdi (d. 959) was a student of Joneyd.

7. On the disobedience of the fallen angel Eblis (Satan), see Qur'an 7:11.

8. *See* note 5 to Mālek-e Dinār, chapter 4.

9. A prolific Shafi'i legal scholar of Baghdad, d. 918–19.

10. This aphorism is textually problematic, and Este'lāmi's suggested emendation does little to clarify the difficulty.

11. I have followed Este'lāmi's suggested emendation in translating the final sentence.

12. *Al-Baqara* is the second and longest chapter of the Qur'an.

23. Abu'l-Hoseyn Nuri

1. Subject of a short biography in the *Memorial* not translated here, Abu'l-Hasan Ahmad ebn Abi al-Havāri was active in Baghdad in the latter part of the ninth century.

2. This is probably Abu Hamza Khorāsāni (d. 921–22), a companion of Joneyd.

3. Apparently a Sufi active in Baghdad in the later ninth century.

4. Abu Mohammad Ja'far-e Kholdi (d. 959) was a student of Joneyd.

5. An oft-quoted saying of the Prophet; see Sadri-Niyā, *Farhang*, 184.

6. The author of one of the earliest treatises on Sufism *(Ketāb al-loma'*

fi'l-tasavvof), which was one 'Attār's sources of the *Memorial*, Sarrāj was active in Khorasan. He died in 988.

24. Abu 'Abdollāh ebn al-Jallā

1. A Sufi associated with Zu'n-Nun and Ebn al-Jallā, d. 932.
2. This is the angel who records our sins.

25. Samnun-e Mohebb, the Lover

1. A contemporary of Joneyd in Baghdad, d. ca. 909–10; see *EI²*, s.v. "Samnūn."

26. 'Ali-ye Sahl of Isfahan

1. A Sufi from the circle of Joneyd in Baghdad, d. 939–40.

27. Abu 'Abdollāh Mohammad ebn Khafif

1. The text reads "forty forty-day fasts": I have amended it based on *Kashf al-mahjub.*
2. This Sufi has not been identified from other sources.
3. 'Azod ad-Dowla here refers to Fanā Khosrow Abu Shojā', the ruler of the Buyid dynasty who ruled Fars province from 949 to 983; see *EI²*, s.v. "'Adud al-Dawla."
4. A companion of Ebn Khafif, Abu Ahmad Hasan ebn 'Ali of Shiraz died in 995, and is probably the Ahmad the Younger mentioned in an earlier anecdote.

28. Hoseyn ebn Mansur Hallāj

1. Great Sufi teacher of Nishapur and the author of *Resāla;* see "Translator's Introduction" herein.
2. This saying of the Prophet refers to 'Omar ebn al-Khattāb.
3. This is the famous physician Abu Bakr Mohammad ebn Zakariyā ar-Rāzi, d. ca. 932; see *EI²*, s.v. "al-Rāzī, Abū Bakr Muhammad b. Zakariyyā'."
4. The founder of the sectarian Qarmati movement, d. 913; see *EI²*, s.v. "al-Djannābī, Abū Sa'īd Hasan" and "Karmatī."

5. Bayzā'-e Fārs is the name of a village located in the district of Shiraz. Wāsit is a medieval city in central Iraq on the banks of the Tigris (see *EI²*, s.v. "Wāsiṭ").

6. Tostar, now called Shushtar, is a regional center in the province of Khuzistan in southwestern Iran.

7. Sufi sheikh of Basra and Mecca, contemporary with Joneyd.

8. Abu Ya'qub Eshāq of Nahrajur was another Sufi resident of Mecca, d. 941–42.

9. This preacher is not identified by Este'lāmi and has not been located in other sources.

10. Hallāj was, in fact, executed during the reign of the caliph al-Moqtader, 908–32; 'Ali ebn 'Isā (known as Ebn Jarrāh, d. 945–46) served as the vizier for several 'Abbasid caliphs, including al-Moqtader; see *EI²*, s.v. "'Alī b. 'Īsā."

11. 'Abd al-Jalil-e Saffār is not identified by Este'lāmi.

GLOSSARY OF PERSONAL NAMES

'Abbāsa of Tus—Abu Moḥammad 'Abbās, Sufi preacher of Nishapur, d. 1153–54; see Shafi'i Kadkani, *Zabur-e Pārsi*, 79.

'Abdollāh ebn Mobārak—see *Ebn Mobārak, 'Abdollāh*.

Abu 'Abdollāh ebn al-Jallā—see *Ebn al-Jallā, Abu 'Abdollāh*.

Abu 'Abdollāh ebn Khafif—see *Ebn Khafif, Abu 'Abdollāh*.

Abu 'Ali of Fārmad—Sufi preacher and scholar active in Nishapur, student of al-Qosheyri, 1011–80; see *El² Supp.*, s.v. "Abū ʿAlī al-Fārmadī."

Abu Bakr—the first caliph and one of the earliest followers of Mohammad, known as aṣ-Ṣaddiq, d. 634; see *El²*, s.v. "Abū Bakr."

Abu Hafs the Blacksmith (al-Ḥaddād)—Sufi ascetic of Nishapur, d. ca. 874; see *EIr*, s.v. "Abū Ḥafṣ Ḥaddād."

Abu Hanifa—founder of one of the four major schools of Islamic law, d. 767; see *El²*, s.v. "Abū Ḥanīfa al-Nuʿmān."

Abu Mohammad-e Maghāzeli—Sufi active in the later ninth century.

Abu 'Osmān of Hira—Sufi sheikh of Nishapur, d. 911, associated with Abu Hafs and Shāh-e Shojāʿ.

Abu'l-Qāsem of Korakān—Sufi active in Nishapur, d. 1076, contemporary with Abu Saʿid ebn Abi'l-Kheyr.

Abu Saʿid ebn Abi'l-Kheyr—renowned Sufi master of Nishapur, d. 1049; see *El²*, s.v. "Abū Saʿīd b. Abī'l-Khayr" and *EIr*, s.v. "Abū Saʿīd Fażlallāh b. Abī'l-Kayr."

Abu Saʿid the Bootmaker (al-Kharrāz)—Aḥmad ebn 'Isā, Sufi master, d. ca. 890, follower of Zu'n-Nun.

Abu Torāb of Nakhshab—widely traveled Sufi ascetic, d. 859; see *EIr*, s.v. "Abū Torāb Nakšabī."

'Ā'esha-ye Sādeqa—the Prophet's third and favorite wife, d. 678; see *El²*, s.v. "ʿĀ'isha bint Abī Bakr."

Ahmad ebn Hanbal—celebrated jurist, founder of one of the four major schools of Sunni religious law, d. 855; see *El²*, s.v. "Aḥmad b. Ḥanbal."

Ahmad-e Khezruya—Abu Ḥāmed al-Balkhī, a mystic active in Balkh and Khorasan, d. 864.

'Ali ebn Abi Tāleb—son-in-law of the Prophet Mohammad, the fourth caliph,

and the first imam of Shi'ite Islam, assassinated in 660; see *EI²*, s.v. "'Alī b. Abī Ṭālib."

'Ali-ye Sahl—ascetic and scholar of Isfahan, d. 893.

'Amr ebn 'Osmān of Mecca—Sufi sheikh, d. 904 or 910, disciple of Joneyd.

Bāyazid of Bestām—Khorasanian Sufi, famous for his ecstatic utterances and founder of the so-called intoxicated school of Sufism, d. ca. 875; see *EI²*, s.v. "Abū Yazīd al-Bisṭāmī" and *EIr*, s.v. "Besṭāmī, Bāyazid."

Beshr al-Hāfi—Sufi ascetic born in Merv and active in Baghdad, d. 840–42; see *EI²*, s.v. "Bishr al-Ḥāfī."

Dāvud-e Tā'i—Legal scholar and ascetic, d. 781–82.

Ebn 'Atā—Sufi sheikh, executed in 922, and close companion of Ḥallāj.

Ebn al-Jallā, Abu 'Abdollāh—Sufi sheikh born in Baghdad and active in Syria, d. 753.

Ebn Khafif, Abu 'Abdollāh—Sufi sheikh and author of Shiraz, d. 982; see *EI²*, s.v. "Ibn Khafīf."

Ebn Mobārak, 'Abdollāh—merchant, scholar, and traditionist, d. 797; see *EI²*, s.v. "Ibn al-Mubārak."

Ebrāhim ebn Adham—Sufi ascetic, d. ca. 777; see *EI²*, s.v. "Ibrāhīm b. Adham."

Ehrāhim-e Khavvās—Sufi active in Baghdad in the circle of Joneyd, d. 904.

Esrāfil—the archangel whose trumpet will herald the day of resurrection.

Fozeyl ebn 'Ayāz—brigand who became an exemplary ascetic, d. 803; see *EI²*, s.v. "Fuḍayl b. 'Iyāḍ."

Gholām Khalil—ascetic preacher of Baghdad, d. 888.

Habib-e 'Ajami—Sufi ascetic, disciple of Ḥasan of Basra, d. 738.

Habib-e Rā'i—pious hermit-shepherd of the early eighth century.

Hajjāj (ebn Yusof)—governor of Iraq under Umayyad dynasty, known for the rigor and authoritarianism of his rule, d. 714; see *EI²*, s.v. "Ḥadjdjādj b. Yūsuf."

Hallāj, Hoseyn ebn Mansur—mystic theologian and martyr of Baghdad, d. 922; see *EI²*, s.v. "Ḥallādj" and *EIr*, s.v. "Ḥallāj."

Hārun ar-Rashid—fifth caliph of the 'Abbasid dynasty, reigned from 786 to 809; see *EI²*, s.v. "Hārūn al-Rashīd."

Hasan of Basra—ascetic preacher, 642–728; see *EI²*, s.v. "Ḥasan al-Baṣrī."

Hātem the Deaf (al-Aṣamm)—Sufi sheikh of Balkh in Khorasan, d. 851–52.

Hoseyn ebn Mansur Hallāj—see *Hallāj, Hoseyn ebn Mansur.*

Ja'far as-Sādeq—700 (or 703)–765, sixth Shi'ite imam and one of the seminal intellectuals of his time; see *EI²*, s.v. "Dja'far al-Ṣādiḳ."

Joneyd of Baghdad—Sufi of Baghdad and founder of the so-called sober school of Sufism, d. 910; see *EI²*, s.v. "Djunayd, Abū'l-Ḳāsim."

GLOSSARY OF PERSONAL NAMES

Joreyri—Abu Moḥammad, Sufi sheikh, d. 924, disciple of Sahl of Tostar and active in the circle of Joneyd.

Khezr—Popular figure of myth and legend, commonly identified with Moses' servant in Qur'an 18:59–81, known as the immortal guide of lost travelers; see *EI²*, s.v. "Khaḍir (al-Khiḍr)."

Mālek-e Dīnār—moralist and preacher of Basra, d. 748–49; see *EI²*, s.v. "Mālik b. Dīnār."

Ma'ruf of Karkh—Sufi ascetic of Baghdad, d. 815–6, sheikh of Sari al-Saqati; see *EI²*, s.v. "Maʿrūf al-Karkhī."

Mohammad ebn Kaʿb of Qaraz—transmitter of the early history of Islam, died middle of eight century in Medina.

Monker and Nakir—the two angels who tear the soul from the body at death.

Moʿtasem—ʿAbbasid caliph, d. 842, son of Hārun ar-Rashid; see *EI²*, s.v. "Muʿtaṣim Bi'llāh."

ʿOmar ebn ʿAbd al-ʿAziz—fifth caliph of Umayyad dynasty, reigned 717–20; see *EI²*, s.v. "ʿUmar (II) b. ʿAbd al-ʿAzīz."

ʿOmar ebn al-Khattāb—second caliph of Islam, assassinated in 644; see *EI²*, s.v. "ʿUmar (I) b. al-Khaṭṭāb."

Rābeʿa-ye ʿAdaviya—early woman Sufi, d. ca. 801; see *EI²*, s.v. "Rābiʿa al-ʿAdawiyya."

Rajā' ebn Heyva—also known as Abū Meqdām Rajā' al-Kendi, a preacher and scholar, d. 730; he supported the caliphate of ʿOmar ebn ʿAbd al-ʿAziz.

Roveym—Abu Moḥammad, Sufi sheikh of Baghdad. d. 915.

Sābet Bonāni—transmitter of early history of Islam, d. ca. 743 in Basra.

Sahl ebn ʿAbdollāh—Sufi sheikh and writer of Tostar in Khuzistan, d. 896; see *EI²*, s.v. "Sahl al-Tustarī."

Sari-ye Saqati—Sufi master of Baghdad, d. 867, uncle and mentor of Joneyd; see *EI²*, s.v. "Sarī al-Saḳaṭī."

Shāfe'i—founder of one of the four major schools of Islamic law, 767–820; see *EI²*, "al-Shāfiʿī."

Shāh-e Shojāʿ—nobleman turned ascetic, d. after 884; associated with Abu Torāb.

Shaqiq of Balkh—Abu ʿAli, Sufi and religious scholar, d. 810, companion of Ebrāhim ebn Adham.

Shebli—a disciple of Joneyd famous for his eccentric behavior and allusive sayings, 861–945; see *EI²*, s.v. "Shiblī."

Sofyān-e ʿOyeyna—traditionist and Qur'an commentator active in Mecca, d. 811; see *EI²*, s.v. "Sufyān b. ʿUyayna."

Sofyān-e Sowri—important figure in the early development of Islamic law, Qur'an commentary, and hadith transmission, d. 778; see *EI²*, s.v. "Sufyān al-Thawrī."

Yahyā ebn Mo'āz of Rey—an early Sufi preacher active in Khorasan, d. 872.

Yusof ebn al-Hoseyn—Sufi sheikh and preacher of Rey, d. 916.

Yusof of Hamadān—ebn Ayyūb, Sufi author and preacher who studied and taught in Baghdad before retiring to Merv, 1049–1141.

Zu'n-Nun of Egypt—early Sufi master, d. ca. 861; see *EI²*, s.v. "Dhu'l-Nūn Miṣrī" and *EIr*, s.v. "Dhu'l-Nūn."

BIBLIOGRAPHY

Abu No'eym, Aḥmad ebn 'Abd Allāh. *Ḥelyat al-owliyā'*. 10 vols. Reprint edition. Beirut: Dār al-Fekr, 1996.

Aḥmadi, Bābak. *Chahār gozāresh az Tazkerat al-owliyā'-e 'Aṭṭār*. Tehran: Nashr-e Markazi, 1997.

Anṣāri, Kwāja 'Abdollāh. *Intimate Conversations*. Translated by Wheeler M. Thackston. With Ibn 'Ata'llah. *The Book of Wisdom*. Translated by Victor Danner. New York: Paulist Press, 1978.

'Aṭṭār, Farid ad-Din. *Conference of the Birds*. Translated by Afkham Darbandi and Dick Davis. New York: Penguin Press, 1984.

———. *Divān*. Edited by Taqi Tafażżoli. 4th ed. Tehran: 'Elmi va Farhangi, 1987.

———. *Elāhi-nāma*. Edited by Hellmut Ritter. Reprint edition. Tehran: Tus, 1989; Istanbul, 1940.

———. *The Ilāhī-nāma, or Book of God*. Translated by John Andrew Boyle. Manchester, UK: Manchester University Press, 1976.

———. *Le Mémorial des Saints*. Translated by A. Paret de Courteille. Paris: Editions de Seuil, 1996.

———. *Mokhtār-nāma*. Edited by Moḥammad Reżā Shafi'i Kadkani. 2nd ed. Tehran: Sokhan, 1996.

———. *Muslim Saints and Mystics: Episodes from the Tadhkirat al-Auliya' ("Memorial of the Saints") by Farid al-Din Attar*. Translated by A. J. Arberry. Chicago: University of Chicago Press, 1966.

———. *Tazkerat al-owliyā'*. Edited by Moḥammad Este'lāmi. 2nd edition. Tehran: Zavvār, 1984.

———. *Tazkerat al-owliyā'*. Edited by Reynold A. Nicholson. 2 vols. Reprint edition. Tehran: Donyā-ye Ketāb, [1984]; London, 1905–07.

Barthold, W. *An Historical Geography of Iran*. Translated by Svat Soucek. Princeton, NJ: Princeton University Press, 1984.

de Bruijn, J. T. P. *Of Piety and Poetry: The Interaction of Religion and Literature in the Life and Works of Ḥakīm Sanā'ī of Ghazna*. Leiden: E. J. Brill, 1983.

———. *Persian Sufi Poetry: An Introduction to the Mystical Use of Classical Poems*. Surrey, UK: Curzon, 1997.

425

Cooperson, Michael. *Classical Arabic Biography: The Heirs of the Prophet in the Age of al-Ma'mūn*. Cambridge, UK: Cambridge University Press, 2000.

Dehkhodā, 'Ali Akbar. *Loghatnāma*. Edited by Moḥammad Mo'in and Ja'far Shahidi. 14 vols. Tehran: University of Tehran Press, 1993.

Dowlatshāh Samarqandi. *Taẕkerat ash-sho'arā*. Edited by Moḥammad Ramażāni. Tehran: Khāvar, 1959.

Early Islamic Mysticism: Sufi, Qur'an, Mi'raj, Poetic and Theological Writings. Translated, edited, and with an introduction by Michael A. Sells. New York: Paulist Press, 1996.

Ebn Monavvar, Moḥammad. *The Secrets of God's Mystical Oneness (Asrār al-Towḥīd)*. Translated by John O'Kane. Costa Mesa, CA: Mazda, 1992.

Encyclopaedia Iranica (EIr). London: Routledge and Kegan Paul, 1982– .

Encyclopedia of Islam. (*EI²*) 2nd ed. 11 vols. Leiden: E. J. Brill, 1960–2002.

Foruzānfar, Badi' az-Zamān. *Aḥādis̱-e Mas̱navi*. 4th ed. Tehran: Amir Kabir, 1987.

———. *Sharḥ-e aḥvāl va naqd va ās̱ār-e Sheykh Farid ad-Din 'Aṭṭār-e Nishāpuri*. Tehran: Anjoman-e Ās̱ār-e Melli, 1961.

The Heritage of Sufism. Vol. 1: *Classical Persian Sufism from Its Origins to Rumi (700–1300)*. Edited by Leonard Lewisohn. Oxford, UK: Oneworld, 1999.

Hojviri, 'Ali ebn 'Os̱mān. *Kashf al-maḥjub*. Edited by V. A. Zhukovskii. Reprint edition. Tehran: Ketābkhāna-ye Ṭahuri, 1997; Leningrad, 1926.

———. *The Kashf al-maḥjub: The Oldest Persian Treatise on ṣūfism*. Translated by Reynold A. Nicholson. Reprint edition. Karachi: Darul-Ishaat, 1990; Leiden, 1911.

Ibn al-Fāriḍ, 'Umar ibn 'Ali. *'Umar Ibn al-Fāriḍ: Sufi Verse, Saintly Life*. Translated and introduced by Th. Emil Homerin. New York: Paulist Press, 2001.

Jāmi, Nur ad-Din 'Abd ar-Raḥman. *Nafaḥāt al-ons men hażarāt al-qods*. Edited by Maḥmud 'Abadi. Tehran: 'Eṭṭelā'āt, 1991.

Lefevere, Andre. *Translation, Rewriting and the Manipulation of Literary Fame*. New York: Routledge, 1992.

Lewis, Franklin D. "Reading, Writing and Recitation: Sanā'i and the Origins of the Persian Ghazal." PhD dissertation, University of Chicago, 1995.

———. *Rumi—Past and Present, East and West: The Life, Teaching and Poetry of Jalāl al-Din Rumi*. Oxford, UK: Oneworld, 2000.

Losensky, Paul. "The Creative Compiler: The Art of Rewriting in 'Aṭṭār's *Taẕkerat al-awliyā*'." In *The Necklace of the Pleiades: Studies in Persian Literature Presented to Heshmat Moayyad on his 80th Birthday*. Edited by Franklin Lewis and Sunil Sharma, 107–19. Amsterdam: Rozenberg Publishers; West Lafayette, IN: Purdue University Press, 2007.

BIBLIOGRAPHY

————. "Words and Deeds: Message and Structure in 'Aṭṭār's *Tadhkirat al-awlīyā'*." In *Farid al-Din Attar and the Persian Sufi Tradition: The Art of Spiritual Flight*. Edited by Leonard Lewisohn and Charles Shackle, 75–92. London: I. B. Tauris, 2006.

Mahdavi Dāmghāni, Aḥmad. "Naẓari be-'adad-e 73 dar ḥadis̲-e 'tafreqa.'" In *Ḥāṣel-e awqāt: majmū'a'i az maqālāt*. Edited by Sayyed 'Ali Moḥammad Sajjādi, 615–622. Tehran: Sorush, 2002.

Nafisi, Safiid. *Jostuju dar aḥvāl va ās̲ār-e Farid ad-Din 'Aṭṭār*. Tehran: Eqbāl, 1941.

Peters, F. E. *The Hajj: The Muslim Pilgrimage to Mecca and the Holy Places*. Princeton, NJ: Princeton University Press, 1994.

Qosheyri, Abu al-Qāsem. *Principles of Sufism*. Translated by B. R. von Schlegell. Berkeley, CA: Mizan Press, 1990.

————. *Tarjoma-ye Resāla-ye Qosheyriya*. Edited by Badi' az-Zamān Foruzānfar. Tehran: 'Elmi va Farhangi, 1961.

Radtke, Bernd. "The Concept of *Wilāya* in Early Sufism." In *Heritage of Sufism*, vol. 1: 483–496.

Reinert, B. "'Aṭṭār, Shaikh Farīd-al-Dīn." In *EIr*.

Ritter, Helmut. *Das Meer der Seele*. Leiden: E. J. Brill, 1978.

————. *The Ocean of the Soul: Man, the World and God in the Stories of Farīd al-Dīn 'Aṭṭār*. Translated by John O'Kane, with editorial assistance of Bernd Radkte. Leiden: E. J. Brill, 2003.

————. "Philologika XIV: Farīduddīn 'Aṭṭār, II." *Oriens* 11 (1958): 61–76.

Sādāt Ranjbar, Maryam. *Farhang-e Foruzānfar*. Isfahan: Nashr-e Porsesh, 1995.

Ṣadri-Niyā, Bāqer. *Farhang-e ma'ṣurāt-e motun-e 'erfāni: moshtamal bar aḥādis̲, aqvāl va ams̲āl-e motun-e 'erfāni-ye Fārsi*. Tehran: Sorush 2001.

Sells, Michael. *Approaching the Qur'ān: The Early Revelations*. Ashland, OR: White Cloud Press, 1999.

Shafi'i Kadkani, Moḥammad. *Zabur-e Pārsi: negāhi be-zendagi va ghazalhā-ye 'Aṭṭār*. Tehran: Āgāh, 1999.

Solami, Abu 'Abd ar-Raḥmān Moḥammad. *Ketāb aṭ-Ṭabaqāt aṣ-ṣufiya*. Edited by Johannes Pedersen. Leiden: E. J. Brill, 1960.

Waley, Muhammad Isa. "Contemplative Disciplines in Early Persian Sufism." In *Heritage of Sufism*, 1:497–548.

INDEX

INDEX

INDEX

Other Volumes in This Series

Other Volumes in This Series

Other Volumes in This Series

Other Volumes in This Series

The Classics of Western Spirituality is a ground-breaking collection of the original writings of more than 100 universally acknowledged teachers within the Catholic, Protestant, Eastern Orthodox, Jewish, Islamic, and Native American Indian traditions.

To order any title, or to request a complete catalog, contact Paulist Press at 800-218-1903 or visit us on the Web at www.paulistpress.com